MW01680610

# Families Crossing Boundaries

## Oedipus and Electra Myths from Antiquity to Modernity

Edited by Mike Lippman
*University of Arizona*

University Readers™
San Diego, CA

First published in the United States of America in 2011 by University Readers, Inc.



15 14 13 12 11 1 2 3 4 5

Printed in the United States of America

ISBN: 978-1-60927-722-2

University Readers™
800.200.3908 | www.universityreaders.com

# Contents

# Poetics

## Aristotle

## I. Introduction

Let us discuss the art of poetry in general and its species—the effect which each species of poetry has and the correct way to construct plots if the composition is to be of high quality, as well as the number and nature of its component parts, and any other questions that arise within the same field of enquiry. We should begin, as is natural, by taking first principles first. 1 47a

## 2. Poetry As A Species Of Imitation

Epic poetry and the composition of tragedy, as well as comedy and the arts of dithyrambic poetry and (for the most part) of music for pipe or lyre, are all (taken together) *imitations*.[1] They can be differentiated from each other in three respects: in respect of their different *media* of imitation, or different *objects*, or a different *mode* (i.e. a different manner).

### 2.1 Medium

Some people use the medium of colour and shape to produce imitations of various objects by making visual images (some through art, some through practice); others do this by means of the voice.[2] Similarly in the case of the arts I have mentioned: in all of them the medium of imitation is rhythm, language and melody, but these may be employed either separately or in combination. For example, music for pipe or lyre (and any other arts which have a similar effect, e.g. music for pan-pipes) uses melody and rhythm only, while dance uses rhythm by itself and without melody (since dancers too imitate character, emotion and action by means of rhythm expressed in movement).

The art which uses language unaccompanied, either in prose or in verse (either combining verse-forms with each other or using a single kind of verse), remains without a name to the present day. We have no general term referring to the mimes of Sophron and Xenarchus and Socratic dialogues,[3] nor to any imitation that one might produce using iambic trimeters, elegiac couplets or any other such verse-form. Admittedly people attach 'poetry' to the name of the verse-form, and thus refer to 'elegiac poets' and 'hexameter poets'; i.e. they do not call people 'poets' because they produce imitations, but indiscriminately on the basis of their use of verse. In fact, even if someone publishes a medical or scientific text in verse, people are in the habit of applying the same term. But Homer and Empedocles have nothing in common except the form of verse they use; so it would be fair to call the former a poet, but the latter a natural scientist rather than a poet.[4] On the same principle, even if someone should produce an imitation by combining all the verse-forms (as Chaeremon composed his Centaur, which is a rhapsody combining all the verse-forms)[5] he should still be termed a poet. So this is the way distinctions are to be drawn in this area. 47b

There are also some arts which use all the media mentioned above (i.e. rhythm, melody and verse), e.g. dithyrambic and nomic poetry,[6] tragedy and comedy; these differ in that the former use them all simultaneously, the latter in distinct parts.

These, then, are what I mean by differences between the arts in the medium of imitation.

### 2.2 Object

Those who imitate, imitate agents; and these must be either admirable or inferior. (Character almost always corresponds to just these two categories, since everyone is differentiated in character by defect or excellence.) Alternatively they must be better people than we are, or worse, or of the same sort (compare painters: Polygnotus portrayed better people, Pauson worse people, Dionysius people similar to us).[7] So it is clear that each of the kinds of imitation mentioned above will exhibit these differences, and will be distinguished by the imitation of distinct objects in this way. These dissimilarities are possible in dance and in music for pipe or lyre, and also in connection with language and unaccompanied verse (for example, Homer imitates better people; Cleophon people similar to us; Hegemon of Thasos, who invented parodies, or Nicochares, the author of the *Deiliad*, worse people);[8] similarly in connection with dithyrambs and nomes (one could imitate as Timotheus and Philoxenus did the Cyclopes).[9] The very same difference distinguishes tragedy and comedy from each other; the latter aims to imitate people worse than our contemporaries, the former better. 2 48a

### 2.3 Mode

A third difference between them is the mode in which one may imitate each of these objects. It is possible to imitate the same objects in the same medium sometimes by narrating (either using a different *persona*, as in Homer's poetry,[10] or as the same person without variation), or else with all the imitators as agents and engaged in activity. 3

So imitation can be differentiated in these three respects, as we said at the outset: medium, object and mode. So in one respect Sophocles would be the same kind of imitator as Homer, since both imitate admirable people, but in another the same as Aristophanes, since both imitate agents and people doing things.[11] This is the reason—some say—for the term 'drama': i.e. that the poets imitate people doing things. It is in consequence of this too that the Dorian lay claim to tragedy and comedy. The Megarians lay claim to comedy—both those on the mainland (who allege that it arose in the period of their democracy), and those in Sicily (that being the birthplace of the poet Epicharmus, who was much earlier than Chionides and Magnes); and some of the Peloponnesian lay claim to tragedy. They use the names as evidence. They say that they call outlying villages *kômai*, while Athenians call them *demoi*, the assumption being that comedians were so-called not from the revel or Winos, but because they toured the villages when expelled from the town in disgrace. And they say that they use the term *dran* for 'do', the Athenians *prattein*. 48b

So much, then, for the number of ways in which imitation is differentiated, and what they are.

## 3.1 Origins

In general, two causes seem likely to have given rise to the art of poetry, both of them natural.[12] 4

Imitation comes naturally to human beings from childhood (and in this they differ from other animals, i.e. in having a strong propensity to imitation and in learning their earliest lessons through imitation); so does the universal pleasure in imitations. What happens in practice is evidence of this: we take delight in viewing the most accurate possible images of objects which in themselves cause distress when we see them (e.g. the shapes of the lowest species of animal, and corpses). The reason for this is that understanding is extremely pleasant, not just for philosophers but for others too in the same way, despite their limited capacity for it. This is the reason why people take delight in seeing images; what happens is that as they view them they come to understand and work out what each thing is (e.g. 'This is so-and-so'). If one happens not to have seen the thing before, it will not give pleasure as an imitation, but because of its execution or colour, or for some other reason.

Given, then, that imitation is natural to us, and also melody and rhythm (it being obvious that verse-forms are segments of rhythm),[13] from the beginning those who had the strongest natural inclination towards these things generated poetry out of improvised activities by a process of gradual innovation.

## 3.2 Early history

Poetry bifurcated in accordance with the corresponding kinds of character: more serious-minded people imitated fine actions, i.e. those of fine persons; more trivial people imitated those of inferior persons (the latter at first composing invectives, while the others composed hymns and encomia). We are not in a position to identify a poem of the latter kind[14] by any of the poets who preceded Homer, although they are likely to have been numerous; but beginning with Homer we can do so (e.g. his *Margites* and similar poems). Because of its suitability, the iambic verse-form developed in these poems; indeed, the reason it is now called 'iambic' is that they wrote lampoons or *iamboi* against each other in that verse-form. And so some of the ancients became composers of heroic poetry, others of lampoons. But just as Homer was the outstanding poet of the serious kind, since he did not just compose well but also made his imitations dramatic,[15] so too he was the first to adumbrate the form of comedy; what he composed was not an invective, but a dramatization of the laughable. His Margites stands in the same relation to comedy as the Iliad and Odyssey do to tragedy. When tragedy and comedy made their appearance those who inclined towards either kind of poetry became, in accordance with their nature, poets of comedy (instead of lampoons) or of tragedy (instead of epic), because these forms were greater and more highly esteemed than the others. 49a

## 3.3 Tragedy

This is not the place for a detailed investigation of whether or not tragedy is now sufficiently developed with respect to its formal constituents ( judged both in its own right and in relation to theatrical performances). But originally it developed from improvisations. (This is true of tragedy, and also of comedy: the former arose from the leaders of the dithyramb, the latter from the leaders of the phallic songs which are still customary even now in many cities.)[16] Then tragedy was gradually enhanced as people developed each new aspect of it that came to light. After undergoing many transformations tragedy came to rest, because it had attained its natural state.

The number of actors was increased from one to two by Aeschylus, who also reduced the choral parts and made the spoken word play the leading role; the third actor and scene-painting were introduced by Sophocles. In addition, the magnitude increased from short plots; and in place of comic diction, as a consequence of a change from the satyric style,[17] tragedy acquired dignity at a late stage, and the iambic verse-form was adopted instead of the trochaic tetrameter. (They used tetrameters at first because the composition was satyric in manner, and more akin to dance. But when speech was introduced nature itself found the appropriate form of verse, iambic being the verse-form closest to speech. There is evidence of this: we speak iambics in conversation with each other very often, but rarely dactylic hexameters—and only when we depart from the normal conversational tone.)[18] As for the number of episodes and other such features, the way each of them is said to have been elaborated may be taken as read; it would probably be a major undertaking to go through them all individually.

### 3.4 Comedy

Comedy is (as we have said) an imitation of inferior people—not, however, with respect to every kind of defect: the laughable is a species of what is disgraceful. The laughable is an error or disgrace that does not involve pain or destruction; for example, a comic mask is ugly and distorted, but does not involve pain.[19]

The transformations which tragedy has undergone, and those responsible for them, have not been forgotten; but, because it was not taken seriously, little attention was paid to comedy at first. Indeed, it was relatively late that the archon first granted a comic chorus;[20] before that the performers were volunteers. So comedy already had some of its features before there is any mention of those identified as comic poets, and it is not known who introduced masks, prologues, the number of actors and so forth. But plot-construction came originally from Sicily; among Athenian poets it was Crates who first abandoned the form of a lampoon and began to construct universalized stories and plots.' 49b

### 3.5 Epic

Epic poetry corresponds to tragedy in so far as it is an imitation in verse of admirable people. But they differ in that epic uses one verse-form alone, and is narrative. They also differ in length, since tragedy tries so far as possible to keep within a single day, or not to exceed it by much, whereas epic is unrestricted in time, and differs in this respect. (At first, however, people used to make no distinction between tragedy and epic in this respect.)

Some of the component parts are common to both, others are peculiar to tragedy. Consequently anyone who understands what is good and bad in tragedy also understands about epic, since anything that epic poetry has is also present in tragedy, but what is present in tragedy is not all in epic poetry.

## 4. Tragedy: Definition And Analysis

### 4.1 Definition

We shall discuss the art of imitation in hexameter verse and comedy later;[22] as for tragedy, let us resume the discussion by stating the definition of its essence on the basis of what has already been said. 6

Tragedy is an imitation of an action that is admirable, complete and possesses magnitude; in language made pleasurable, each of its species separated in different parts; performed by actors, not through narration; effecting through pity and fear the purification[23] of such emotions.

(By 'language made pleasurable' I mean that which possesses rhythm and melody, i.e. song. By the separation of its species I mean that some parts are composed in verse alone; others by contrast make use of song.)

## 4.2 Component parts

Since the imitation is performed by actors, it follows first of all that the management of the *spectacle* must be a component part of tragedy. Then there is *lyric poetry* and *diction*, since these are the medium in which the actors perform the imitation. (By 'diction' I mean the actual composition of the verse; what is meant by 'lyric poetry' is self-evident.)

Now, tragedy is an imitation of an action, and the action is performed by certain agents. These must be people of a certain kind with respect to their character and reasoning. (It is on the basis of people's character and reasoning that we say that their actions are of a certain kind, and in respect of their actions that people enjoy success or failure.) So *plot* is the imitation of the action (by 'plot' here I mean the organization of events); *character* is that in respect of which we say that the agent is of a certain kind; and *reasoning* is the speech which the agents use to argue a case or put forward an opinion. 50a

So tragedy as a whole necessarily has six component parts, which determine the tragedy's quality: i.e. plot, character, diction, reasoning, spectacle and lyric poetry. The medium of imitation comprises two parts, the mode one, and the object three; and there is nothing apart from these.

## 4.3 The primacy of plot

Virtually all tragedians, one might say, use these formal elements; for in fact every drama alike has spectacle, character, plot, diction, song and reasoning.[24] But the most important of them is the structure of the events:

(i) Tragedy is not an imitation of persons, but of actions and of life. Well-being and ill-being reside in action, and the goal of life is an activity, not a quality; people possess certain qualities in accordance with their character, but they achieve well-being or its opposite on the basis of how they fare. So the imitation of character is not the purpose of what the agents do; character is included along with and on account of the actions. So the events, i.e. the plot, are what tragedy is there for, and that is the most important thing of all.

(ii) Furthermore, there could not be a tragedy without action, but there could be one without character. The tragedies of most modern poets lack character, and in general there are many such poets. Compare, among painters, the relation between Zeuxis and Polygnotus: the latter is good at depicting character, but Zeuxis' painting has no character.[25]

(iii) Also, if one were to compose a series of speeches expressive of character, however successful they are in terms of diction and reasoning, it will not achieve the stated function of tragedy; a tragedy which, though it uses these elements less adequately, has a plot and a structure of events will do so much more effectively.

(iv) Additionally, the most important devices by which tragedy sways emotion are parts of the plot, i.e. reversals and recognitions.[26]

(v) A further indication is that those who are trying to write poetry are capable of accuracy in diction and character before they can construct the events; compare too almost all the early poets.

## 4.4 The ranking completed

So the plot is the source and (as it were) the soul of tragedy; character is second. (It is much the same in the case of painting: if someone were to apply exquisitely beautiful colours at random he would give less pleasure than if he had outlined an image in black and white.) Tragedy is an imitation of an action, and on account above all of the action it is an imitation of agents. 50b

Third is reasoning. This is the ability to say what is implicit in a situation and appropriate to it, which in prose is the function of the arts of statesmanship and of rhetoric. Older poets used to make people speak like statesmen; contemporary poets make them speak rhetorically.[27] Character is the kind of thing which discloses the nature of a choice; for this reason speeches in which there is nothing at all which the speaker chooses or avoids do not possess character. Reasoning refers to the means by which people argue that something is or is not the case, or put forward some universal proposition.

Fourth is diction. By 'diction' I mean, as was said before, verbal expression; this has the same effect both in verse and in prose speeches.

Of the remaining parts, song is the most important of the sources of pleasure. Spectacle is attractive, but is very inartistic and is least germane to the art of poetry. For the effect of tragedy is not dependent on performance and actors; also, the art of the property-manager has more relevance to the production of visual effects than does that of the poets.

## 5. Plot: Basic Concepts

Given these definitions, let us discuss next what qualities the structure of the events should have, since this is the first and most important part of tragedy. 7

### 5.1 Completeness

We have laid down that tragedy is an imitation of a complete, i.e. whole, action, possessing a certain magnitude. (There is such a thing as a whole which possesses no magnitude.) A *whole* is that which has a beginning, a middle and an end. A *beginning* is that which itself does not follow necessarily from anything else, but some second thing naturally exists or occurs after it. Conversely, an end is that which does itself naturally follow from something else, either necessarily or in general, but there is nothing else after it. A *middle* is that which itself comes after something else, and some other thing comes after it. Well-constructed plots should therefore not begin or end at any arbitrary point, but should employ the stated forms.

### 5.2 Magnitude

Any beautiful object; whether a living organism or any other entity composed of parts, must not only possess those parts in proper order, but its *magnitude* also should not be arbitrary; beauty consists in magnitude as well as order. For this reason no organism could be beautiful if it is excessively small (since observation becomes confused as it comes close to having no perceptible duration in time) or excessively large (since the observation is then not simultaneous, and the observers find that the sense of unity and wholeness is lost from their observation, e.g. if there were an animal a thousand miles long). So just as in the case of physical objects and living organisms, they should possess a certain magnitude, and this should be such as can readily be taken in at one view, so in the case of plots: they should have a certain length, and this should be such as can readily be held in memory. 51a

The definition of length which is determined by theatrical performances and perception is not relevant to the art of poetry; if it were necessary to perform a hundred tragedies they would time the performances by the clock, as they say used to be done on other occasions.[28] But the definition which agrees with the actual nature of the matter is that invariably the greater the plot is (up to the limits of simultaneous perspicuity) the more beautiful it is with respect to magnitude; or, to state a straightforward definition, 'the magnitude in which a series of events occurring sequentially in accordance with probability or necessity gives rise to a change from good fortune to bad fortune, or from bad fortune to good fortune', is an adequate definition of magnitude.

## 5 .3 Unity

A plot is not (as some think) unified because it is concerned with a single person. An indeterminately large number of things happen to any one person, not all of which constitute a unity; likewise a single individual performs many actions, and they do not make up a single action. So it is clear that a mistake has been made by all those poets who have composed a *Heracleid* or *Theseid*, or poems of that kind, on the assumption that, just because *Heracles* was one person, the plot too is bound to be unified. Just as Homer excels in other respects, he seems to have seen this point clearly as well, whether through art or instinct. When he composed the *Odyssey* he did not include everything which happened to Odysseus (e.g. the wounding on Parnassus and the pretence of madness during the mobilization: the occurrence of either of these events did not make the occurrence of the other necessary or probable);[29] instead, he constructed the *Odyssey* about a single action of the kind we are discussing. The same is true of the *Iliad.* *8*

## 5.4 Determinate structure

Just as in other imitative arts the imitation is unified if it imitates a single object, so too the plot, as the imitation of an action, should imitate a single, unified action—and one that is also a whole. So the structure of the various sections of the events must be such that the transposition or removal of any one section dislocates and changes the whole. If the presence or absence.of something has no discernible effect, it is not a part of the whole.

## 5.5 Universality

It is also clear from what has been said that the function of the poet is not to say what *has* happened, but to say the kind of thing that *would* happen, i.e. what is possible in accordance with probability or necessity. The historian and the poet are not distinguished by their use of verse or prose; it would be possible to turn the works of Herodotus into verse, and it would be a history in verse just as much as in prose. The distinction is this: the one says what has happened, the other the kind of thing that would happen.[30] 9 51b

For this reason poetry is more philosophical and more serious than history. Poetry tends to express universals, and history particulars. The *universal* is the kind of speech or action which is consonant with a person of a given kind in accordance with probability or necessity; this is what poetry aims at, even though it applies individual names. The particular is the actions or experiences of (e.g.) Alcibiades.

In the case of comedy this is in fact clear. The poets construct the plot on the basis of probabilities, and then supply names of their own choosing; they do not write about a particular individual, as the lampoonists do. In the case of tragedy they do keep to actual names. The reason for this is that what is possible is plausible; we are disinclined to believe that what has not happened is possible, but it is obvious that what has happened is possible—because it would not have happened if it were not. To be sure, even in tragedy in some cases only one or two of the names are familiar, while the rest are invented, and in some none at all, e.g. in Agathon's Antheus;[31] in this play both the events and the names are invented, but it gives no less pleasure. So one need not try at all costs to keep to the traditional stories which are the subjects of tragedy;

in fact, it would be absurd to do so, since even what is familiar is familiar only to a few, and yet gives pleasure to everyone.

So it is clear from these points that the poet must be a maker[32] of plots rather than of verses, insofar as he is a poet with respect to imitation, and the object of his imitation is action. Even if in fact he writes about what has happened, he is none the less a poet; there is nothing to prevent some of the things which have happened from being the kind of thing which probably would happen, and it is in that respect that he is concerned with them as a poet.

### 5.6 Defective plots

Of simple plots[33] and actions, the episodic ones are the worst. By an episodic plot I mean one in which the sequence of episodes is neither necessary nor probable. Second-rate poets compose plots of this kind of their own accord; good poets do so on account of the actors—in writing pieces for competitive display[34] they draw out the plot beyond its potential, and are often forced to distort the sequence. 52a

## 6. Plot: Species And Components

### 6.2 Astonishment

The imitation is not just of a complete action, but also of events that evoke fear and pity. These effects occur above all when things come about contrary to expectation but because of one another. This will be more astonishing than if they come about spontaneously or by chance, since even chance events are found most astonishing when they appear to have happened as if for a purpose—as, for example, the statue of Mitys in Argos killed the man who was responsible for Mitys' death by falling on top of him as he was looking at it.[35] Things like that are not thought to occur at random. So inevitably plots of this kind will be better.

### 6.2 Simple and complex plots

Some plots are simple, others complex, since the actions of which the plots are imitations are themselves also of these two kinds. By a *simple* action I mean one which is, in the sense defined, continuous and unified, and in which the change of fortune comes about without reversal or recognition. By *complex*, I mean one in which the change of fortune involves reversal or recognition or both. These must arise from the actual structure of the plot, so that they come about as a result of what has happened before, out of necessity or in accordance with probability. There is an important difference between a set of events happening *because* of certain other events and *after* certain other events. 10

### 6.3 Reversal

A *reversal* is a change to the opposite in the actions being performed, as stated—and this, as we have been saying, in accordance with probability or necessity. For example, in the *Oedipus* someone came to give Oedipus good news and free him from his fear with regard to his mother, but by disclosing Oedipus' identity he brought about the opposite reresult;[36] and in the *Lynceus*, Lynceus himself was being led off to be killed, with Danaus following to kill him, but it came about as a consequence of preceding events that the latter was killed and Lynceus was saved.[37] 11

### 6.4 Recognition

Recognition, as in fact the term indicates, is a change from ignorance to knowledge, disclosing either a close relationship[38] or enmity, on the part of people marked out for good or bad fortune. Recognition is best when it occurs simultaneously with a reversal, like the one in the Oedipus.

There are indeed other kinds of recognition. Recognition can come about in the manner stated with respect to inanimate and chance objects; and it is also possible to recognize whether someone has or has not performed some action. But the one that has most to do with the plot and most to do with the action is the one I have mentioned. For a recognition and reversal of that kind will involve pity or fear, and it is a basic premise that tragedy is an imitation of actions of this kind. Moreover, bad fortune or good fortune will be the outcome in such cases. 52b

Since the recognition is a recognition of some person or persons, some involve the recognition of one person only on the part of the other, when it is clear who the other is; but sometimes there must be a recognition on both sides (e.g. Iphigeneia is recognized by Orestes from the sending of the letter, but the recognition of Orestes by Iphigeneia had to be different).[39]

### 6.5 Suffering

So there are these two parts of the plot—reversal and recognition; a third is suffering. Of these, reversal and recognition have already been discussed; *suffering* is an action that involves destruction or pain (e.g. deaths in full view, extreme agony, woundings and so on).

### 6.6 Quantitative parts of tragedy

We have already mentioned the component parts of tragedy which should be regarded as its formal elements. In quantitative terms, the separate parts into which it is divided are as follows: prologue; episode; finale; choral parts, comprising entry-song and ode—these are common to all tragedies, while songs from the stage and dirges are found only in some. 12

The *prologue* is the whole part of a tragedy before the entry-song of the chorus; an episode is a whole part of a tragedy between whole choral songs; the *finale* is the whole part of a tragedy after which there is no choral song. Of the choral part, the entry-song is the first whole utterance of a chorus; an ode is a choral song without anapaests or trochaics; a *dirge* is a lament shared by the chorus and from the stage.

We have already mentioned the component parts of tragedy which should be regarded as its formal elements. In quantitative terms, the separate parts into which it is divided are these.[40]

## 7. The Best Kinds Of Tragic Plot

### 7.1 First introduction

What, then, should one aim at and what should one avoid in constructing plots? What is the source of the effect at which tragedy aims? These are the topics which would naturally follow on from what has just been said. 13

### 7.2 First deduction

The construction of the best tragedy should be complex rather than simple; and it should also be an imitation of events that evoke fear and pity, since that is the distinctive feature of this kind of imitation. So it is clear first of all that decent men should not be seen undergoing a change from good fortune to bad fortune—this does not evoke fear or pity, but disgust. Nor should depraved people be seen undergoing a change from bad fortune to good fortune—this is the least tragic of all: it has none of the right effects, since it is neither agreeable, nor does it evoke pity or fear. Nor again should a very wicked person fall from good fortune to bad fortune—that kind of structure would be agreeable, but would not excite pity or fear, since the one has to do with someone who is suffering undeservedly, the other with someone who is like ourselves (I mean, pity has to do with the undeserving sufferer, fear with the person like us); so what happens will evoke neither pity nor fear. 53a

We are left, therefore, with the person intermediate between these. This is the sort of person who is not outstanding in moral excellence or justice; on the other hand, the change to bad fortune which he undergoes is not due to any moral defect or depravity but to an error[14] of some kind. He is one of those people who are held in great esteem and enjoy great good fortune, like Oedipus, Thyestes, and distinguished men from that kind of family.

It follows that a well-formed plot will be simple[42] rather than (as some people say) double, and that it must involve a change not to good fortune *from* bad fortune, but (on the contrary) *from* good fortune to bad fortune—and this must be due not to depravity but to a serious error on the part of someone of the kind specified (or better than that, rather than worse). There is evidence of this in practice. At first poets used to pick out stories at random; but nowadays the best tragedies are constructed around a few households, e.g. about Alcmeon, Oedipus, Orestes, Meleager, Thyestes, Telephus and any others whose lot it has been to experience something terrible—or to perform some terrible action.[43]

So the best tragedy, in artistic terms, is based on this structure. This is why those who criticize Euripides for doing this in his tragedies, most of which end in bad fortune, are making the same mistake;[44] for this is, as has been stated, correct. There is very powerful evidence for this. On stage and in performance people recognize that plays of this kind (provided that they are successfully executed) are the most tragic, and Euripides, even if his technique is faulty in other respects, is regarded as the most tragic of poets.

Second-best is the structure which some say comes first—that which has a double structure like the *Odyssey,* and which ends with the opposite outcome for better and worse people.4s It is thought to come first because of the weakness of audiences; the poets follow the audiences' lead and compose whatever is to their taste. But this is not the pleasure which comes from tragedy; it is more characteristic of comedy. In comedy even people who are the bitterest enemies in the story, like Orestes and Aegisthus, go off reconciled in the end, and no one gets killed by anybody.[46]

## 7.3 Second introduction

It is possible for the evocation of fear and pity to result from the spectacle, and also from the structure of the events itself. The latter is preferable and is the mark of a better poet. The plot should be constructed in such a way that, even without seeing it, anyone who hears the events which occur shudders and feels pity at what happens; this is how someone would react on hearing the plot of the *Oedipus*. Producing this effect through spectacle is less artistic, and is dependent on the production. Those who use spectacle to produce an effect which is not evocative of fear, but simply monstrous, have nothing to do with tragedy; one should not seek every pleasure from tragedy, but the one that is characteristic of it. And since the poet should produce the pleasure which comes from pity and fear, and should do so by means of imitation, clearly this must be brought about in the events. 14 53b

## 7.4 Second deduction

Let us therefore take up the question of what classes of events appear terrible or pitiable.

Necessarily, we are concerned with interactions between people who are closely connected[47] with each other, or between enemies, or between neutrals. If enemy acts on enemy, there is nothing pitiable either in the action itself or in its imminence, except in respect of the actual suffering in itself. Likewise with neutrals. What one should look for are situations in which sufferings arise within close relationships, e.g. brother kills brother, son father, mother son, or son mother—or is on the verge of killing them, or does something else of the same kind.

Now one cannot undo traditional stories (I mean, for example, Clytaernnestra's death at Orestes' hands, or Eriphyle's at Alcmeon's);[48] but one has to discover for oneself how to use even the traditional stories well. Let us state more clearly what this involves. It is possible for the action to come about in the way that the old poets used to do it, with people acting in full knowledge and awareness; this is in fact how Euripides portrayed Medea killing her children.[49] It is also possible for the action to be performed, but for the agents to do the terrible deed in ignorance and only then to recognize the close connection, as in Sophocles' *Oedipus*. (This is outside the play: examples in the tragedy itself are Astydamas' Alcmeon or Telegonus in the *Odysseus Wounded*.)[50]A third possibility besides these is for someone to be on the verge of performing some irreparable deed through ignorance, and for the recognition to pre-empt the act. Besides these there is no other possibility: necessarily the agents must either act or not act, either knowingly or in ignorance.[51]

Of these, being on the verge of acting wittingly and not doing so is worst; this is disgusting, and is not tragic since there is no suffering. So no one composes in this way, or only rarely (e.g. Haemon and Creon in the *Antigone*).[52] Performing the action is second; but it is better if the action is performed in ignorance and followed by a recognition—there is nothing disgusting in this, and the recognition has great emotional impact. But the last case is best; I mean, for example, in the Cresphontes Merope is on the verge of killing her son but does not do it, but instead recognizes him;[53] the same happens with sister and brother in the *Iphigeneia;*[54] and in the Helle the son recognizes his mother when on the verge of handing her over.[55] 54a

For this reason, as I said some time ago,[56] tragedies are concerned with a limited number of families. Although their search was guided by chance rather than art, poets discovered how to produce this kind of effect in plots; so they are forced to turn to just those households in which this kind of suffering has come about.

## 8. Other Aspects Of Tragedy

### 8. 1 Character

Enough has been said about the structure of events and what plots is should be like; as for character, there are four things to aim at:

(i) First and foremost, *goodness*. As was said earlier, speech or action will possess character if it discloses the nature of a deliberate choice; the character is good if the choice is good. This is possible in each class of person: there is such a thing as a good woman and a good slave, even though one of these is perhaps deficient and the other generally speaking inferior.[57]

(ii) Secondly, *appropriateness*: it is possible for the character to be courageous, but for this to be an inappropriate way for a woman to display courage or cleverness.[58]

(iii) Thirdly, *likeness*: this is not the same as making character good and appropriate, as has already been stated.[59]

(iv) Fourthly, *consistency*: even if the subject of the imitation is inconsistent, and that is the kind of character that is presupposed, it should nevertheless be consistently inconsistent.

An example of unnecessary badness of character is Menelaus in the Orestes;[60] of impropriety and inappropriateness, Odysseus' lament in the Scylla[61] and Melanippe's speech.[62] An example of inconsistency is the Iphigeneia in Aulis:[63] when she pleads for her life to be spared she is not at all like her later self—but in characterization, just as much as in the structure of events, one ought always to look for what is necessary or probable: it should be necessary or probable that this kind of person says or does this kind of thing, and it should be necessary or probable that this happens after that.

(Clearly, therefore, the resolutions of plots should also come about from the plot itself, and not by means of a theatrical device, as in the Medea, or the events concerned with the launching of the ships in the *Iliad*.[64] A theatrical device may be used for things outside the play—whether prior events which are beyond human knowledge, or subsequent events which need prediction and narration —since we grant that the gods can see everything. But there should be nothing irrational in the events themselves; or, failing that, it should be outside the play, as for example in Sophocles' *Oedipus*.)[65] 54b

Since tragedy is an imitation of people better than we are, one should imitate good portrait-painters. In rendering the individual form, they paint people as they are, but make them better-looking. In the same way the poet who is imitating people who are irascible or lazy or who have other traits of character of that sort should portray them as having these characteristics, but also as decent people. For example, Homer portrayed Achilles as both a good man and a paradigm of obstinacy.[66]

One should observe these points closely, and in addition those corresponding to the perceptions that are necessary concomitants of the art of poetry. It is possible to make many mistakes with respect to these. But they have been discussed in sufficient detail in my published works.[67]

## 8.2 Kinds of recognition

We have already said what recognition is. Its kinds are: 16

(i) First of all, the least artistic kind (and the one which people use most, because of their lack of ingenuity) is that by means of tokens. Some of these are congenital (e.g. 'the spear the earth-born bear',[68] or stars such as Carcinus used in his *Thyestes*),[69] and some are acquired; of the latter, some are physical characteristics (e.g. scars), others are external (e.g. necklaces, or the use of the boat in the *Tyro*).[70] It is possible to make better or worse use of these. For example, Odysseus is recognized by means of the scar both by the nurse and by the swineherds, but in different ways. Recognitions that are used only for confirmation are less artistic (so too all recognitions of that kind); recognitions which arise out of a reversal, as in the bath-scene, are better.[71]

(ii) Second are those which are contrived by the poet; for that reason they are inartistic. For example, Orestes in the *Iphigeneria* revealed his own identity; Iphigeneia's identity is revealed by the letter, but Orestes declares in person what the poet (instead of the plot) requires. This brings it close to the error mentioned above: it would have been possible actually to bring tokens with him.[72] There is also the 'voice of the shuttle' in Sophocles' Tereus.[73]

(iii) The third is by means of memory, when someone grasps the sign nificance 55a of something that he sees. This is how it is in Dicaeogenes' *Cyprlans*, where he sees the painting and bursts into tears, and in the tale told to Alcinous, where Odysseus listens to the lyre-player, is reminded of his past and weeps; recognition results in both cases.[74]

(iv) Fourth is that which arises from inference. For example, in the *Choephorl*: 'someone similar has come; no one is similar except Orestes; so he has come'.[75] There is also the recognition which Polyidus the sophist suggested for Iphigeneia; he said that it was probable for Orestes to infer that his sister had been sacrificed, and so it was now his turn to be sacrificed. Also in *Theodectes' Tydeus*, that he came to find a son, but is perishing himself. And the recognition in the *Sons of Phlneus*; when the women saw the place they inferred that it was their fate to die there, since that was where they had been exposed.[76]

(v) There is also a composite kind arising from a false inference on the part of the audience. For example, in *Odysseus the False Messenger*.[77] the fact that he can bend the bow and nobody else is contrived by the poet as a premise, as is his claim that he will recognize the bow which he has not seen; and although he is going to make himself known by means of the former, he actually does so by means of the latter, which involves a false inference.

(iv) The best recognition of all is that which arises out of the actual course of events, where the emotional impact is achieved through events that are probable, as in Sophocles' *Oedipus and the Iphigenela* (her wish to send a letter is probable). Only this kind does without contrived tokens and necklaces. Second-best are those which arise from inference.

## 8.3 Visualizing the action

When constructing plots and working them out complete with their linguistic expression, one should so far as possible visualize what is happening. By envisaging things very vividly in this way, as if one were actually present at the events themselves, one can find out what is appropriate, and inconsistencies are least likely to be overlooked. The criticism made of Carcinus provides evidence of this: Amphiaraus was coming back from the temple; this would have escaped the notice of anyone who did not see it, but it failed in performance because the audience was dissatisfied with it.[78] 17

One should also, as far as possible, work plots out using gestures. Given the same natural talent, those who are actually experiencing the emotions are the most convincing; someone who is distressed or angry acts out distress and irritation most authentically. (This is why the art of poetry belongs to people who are naturally gifted or mad; of these, the former are adaptable, and the latter are not in their right mind.)[79]

## 8.4 Outlines and episodization

Stories, even ones which have been the subject of a previous poem, should first be set out in universal terms when one is making use of them oneself; on that basis, one should then turn the story into episodes and elaborate it. 55b

As an example of what I mean by considering the universal, take the *Iphigeneia*: 'A girl has been sacrificed and has disappeared without those who performed the sacrifice being aware of it. Set down in another country, where it was the custom to sacrifice foreigners to the goddess, she becomes the priestess of this rite. It subsequently happens that the priestess's brother arrives (the fact that the god ordered him to go there is outside the universal; so too the reason);[80] on his arrival he is captured, but when he is on the verge of being sacrificed he discloses his identity (either as Euripides did it, or as in Polyidus,[81]1 by saying—as was quite probable—that it was his lot, as well as his sister's, to be sacrificed). Escape ensues.' After that, one should supply the names and turn the story into episodes. The episodes must be appropriate—for example, in the case of Orestes the fit of madness which resulted in his capture, and the escape by means of the purification.

In plays the episodes are concise, but in epic poetry they are used to increase the length. The story of the *Odyssey* is not very long: 'A man has been away from home for many years; he is kept under close observation by Poseidon, and is alone; at home affairs are in such a state that his property is being squandered by the suitors, and plots are being laid against his son. Despite being shipwrecked he reaches home, reveals his identity to a number of people and attacks. He survives and destroys his enemies.' That much is integral; the rest is episodes.

## 8.5 Complication and resolution

Every tragedy consists of a complication and a resolution. What is is outside the play, and often some of what is inside, comprises the complication; the resolution is the rest. By *complication* I mean everything from the beginning up to and including the section which immediately precedes the change to good fortune or bad fortune; by resolutlon I mean everything from the beginning of the change of fortune to the end. Thus in Theodectes' *Lynceus* the complication consists of events before the play, the seizure of the child and the disclosure of the parents; the resolution is everything from the capital charge to the end.[82] 18

## 8.6 Kinds of tragedy

There are four kinds of tragedy (since that was also the number of component parts mentioned):[83] complex tragedy, depending entirely on reversal and recognition; tragedy of suffering (e.g. plays about Ajax or Ixion); tragedy of character (e.g. *Women of Phthia* and *Peleus*); and, fourth, simple tragedy (e.g. *Daughters of Phorcys*, Prometheus and plays set in the underworld). 56a

By preference one should try to include all the component parts, or failing that most of them and the most important, especially given the captious criticisms which people make of poets nowadays. Because there have been poets good at each part, people expect individual poets to surpass the particular excellence of every one.[84]

The proper basis for contrasting and comparing tragedies is principally in virtue of the plot, i.e. whether the complication and resolution are the same. Many poets are good at complication but handle the resolution badly;[85] but both should be treated with equal care.

## 8.7 Tragedy and epic

Bearing in mind what I have already said several times, one should not compose a tragedy out of a body of material which would serve for an epic—by which I mean one that contains a multiplicity of stories (for example, if one were to use the whole plot of the *Illad*). In epic, because of its length, every part is given the appropriate magnitude; but in plays the result is quite contrary to one's expectation. There is evidence of this in the fact that everyone who has composed a *Sack of Troy* as a whole, and not piecemeal like Euripides, or a *Niobe* and not like Aeschylus, has either failed or done badly in the competition; even Agathon failed in this one respect.[86]

## 8.8 Astonishment

In reversals and in simple actions poets use astonishment to achieve their chosen aims;[87] this is tragic and agreeable. This happens when someone who is clever but bad (like Sisyphus) is deceived, or someone who is courageous but unjust is defeated. There is no violation of probability in this; as Agathon said, it is probable for many improbable things to happen.[88]

## 8.9 The chorus

One should handle the chorus as one of the actors; it should be part of the whole and should contribute to the performance—not as in Euripides, but as in Sophocles. In the other poets the songs have no more to do with the plot than they do with any other play; this is the reason why they sing interludes. This is a practice which Agathon was the first to start;[89] but what is the difference between singing interludes and transferring a speech or a whole episode from one play into another?

## Notes To The Translation

1. For 'imitation' (mimesis) see Introduction 2. The dithyramb was a kind of lyric poetry performed by a chorus. Pipe (*autos*) and lyre (*kithara*) were the two most common forms of Greek wind and string instrument; the addition of the pan-pipes (*syrinx*) below implies a more general concept of instrumental music.
2. The reference is to the mimicry of, for example, animal noises (cc. Plato, *Republic*, 397a, *Laws*, 669c-d).
3. Sophron and his son Xenarchus worked in Syracuse in the late fifth century; their sketches of everyday life, and the philosophical dialogues of Plato and Xenophon (and others whose works have not survived), are cited as examples of imitation in prose.
4. The fifth-century philosopher Empedocles expounded his theories of nature in hexameter verse. Aristotle greatly admired the artistic quality of his work: fragment 70 (from *On Poets*) comments on his 'Homeric' mastery of poetic language, and especially his use of metaphor; he is cited several times in the Poetics (57b13f, 24, 58ar, 61a24f.). The present point is therefore not evaluative, but intended to define a restricted technical usage for the term 'poetry'.
5. A fourth-century tragic poet; little is known about his *Centaur* (see also 60a2), apparently a piece for recitation ('rhapsody') in a variety of metres.
6. The nome, like the dithyramb (n. I), was a kind of choral lyric.
7. All fifth-century painters. Polygnotus (cf. soa27f. and n. 25) is famous; little is known of the other two, but at *Politics*, 1340a35–8 Pauson's work is described as less suitable for young people to view than that of Polygnotus.
8. Cleophon may be the fourth-century tragic poet of that name; on his style cf. 58a18–21. Hegemon wrote epic burlesques in the late fifth century; *Nicochares Deiliad* (derived from deilos, 'cowardly', by analogy with *Iliad*) also suggests epic burlesque.
9. For dithyramb and nome cf. 47b26 (n. 6). Timotheus (cf. 54a3of. and n. 6 ) was a lyric poet of the late fifth and early fourth centuries noted for musical and stylistic innovations; his poem is presumably mentioned as an example of a serious treatment of the Cyclops Polyphemus, since the portrayal of Polyphemus by Philoxenus of Cythera was said to be a caricature of the tyrant Dionysius I, whose mistress the poet had seduced. But the text here is uncertain, and we cannot be quite sure what point Aristotle is making.
10. For Homer's quasi-dramatic style, making extensive use of direct speech, cc. 48b34–8,60a5—I 1. Aristotle's classification of modes is an adaptation of Plato's (*Republic*, 392d-4c); unlike Aristotle, Plato regarded the dramatic mode with disfavour.
11. The verb for 'do' here is *dran*, whence 'drama'. The Dorian claim to have invented tragedy and comedy assumes (as becomes clear at the end of the following digression) that *drain* implies an origin among speakers of the Doric dialect; Aristotle is rightly sceptical of this assumption, and of the alleged derivation of 'comedy' from home ('village'). The democracy of the city of Megara in mainland Greece is dated to the sixth century BC; the Megarians in Sicily are the colonists at Megara Hyblaea. Epicharmus (from another Sicilian city, Syracuse) worked in the late sixth and early fifth centuries, not really 'much earlier' than the Athenian comic poets Chionides and Magnes (active from the 480s and 47os).
12. The 'two causes' are probably the human instincts for (a) imitation and (b) melody and rhythm (48b2of.). Many interpreters try to identify two distinct causes related to imitation; but this would not explain poetry as imitation *in verse*. The human instinct for rhythm and melody is also recognized by Plato (*Laws*, 6S3d-654a).
13. A rhythm can in principle be continued indefinitely; a verse-form such as the dactylic hexameter is a defined segment of that potentially infinite rhythmic continuum. Cf. *Rhetoric*, 14081)29.
14. That is, one imitating inferior agents. The *Marmites* was not an invective, but a burlesque narrative about a hero of wide-ranging incompetence (he 'knew many things, but knew them all badly'). The attribution of the poem to Homer makes it antedate the earliest extant lampoons (those of the seventh-century poet Archilochus); but Aristotle reasonably infers that there must have been earlier lampoonists whose poems had not been preserved.
15. For Homer's quasi-dramatic style cf. 48a21. (n. 6oa5–11.
16. The assumption is that a chorus-leader singing a solo response to the choral parts was the first step towards an actor wholly separate from the chorus. The number of actors was subsequently increased to two and three (49a16–19); but it remained the custom in Greek theatre for a limited number of actors to play all the roles.

17. Satyr-plays were mythological burlesques with a chorus of satyrs (idle, drunken and lascivious followers of Dionysus, with a mixture of human and animal features), written and produced by tragic dramatists as a regular part of the tragic competition. Aristotle infers that they preserve characteristics of tragedy's pre-dramatic choral antecedents (cf. 49al 0–13 and n. 16) which had disappeared in the evolution of tragedy proper. The text of this whole sentence is extremely uncertain.
18. On the characteristics of iambic verse cf. 59a10–13,59b34–8, *Rhetoric*, 1404a29-33
19. By contrast tragedy evokes fear and pity, emotions which Aristotle defines as responses to painful and destructive harm (*Rhetoric,* 1382a21f. , 1385b13f ; cf. 52bI if. below). A mask like that of the blinded Oedipus, distorted by agonizing wounds, fulfils the function of tragedy, but would be out of place in comedy.
20. The archon chose the poets to compete in an Athenian dramatic festival, and assigned a wealthy citizen to each to finance the production-costs (especially the costume and training of the chorus). The earliest official comic competition in Athens was in 486 BC.
21. By 'universalized' Aristotle means constructed in accordance with necessity or probability; cc. chapter 9 below. Crates was an Athenian comic dramatist active from c. 450 BC.
22. By imitation in hexameter verse Aristotle means epic; his discussion begins in chapter 23. The promised discussion of comedy is not included in the extant P0etics; it was probably contained in a lost second book.
23. *Katharsis*: see Introduction 8.
24. The text and interpretation of this sentence are extremely uncertain.
25. For Polygnotus cf. 48a5f. (n. 7); he is cited as an example of painters good at portraying character at Politics, I 340a37f. Zeuxis, a painter active in the late fifth and early fourth centuries, reappears at 6IbI2f. to illustrate idealization in portraiture.
26. For reversals and recognitions see chapter II.
27. Statesmanship forms judgements on the right conduct of public affairs; statesmen may express these judgements using natural eloquence, or exploiting the systematized persuasive techniques of rhetoric. Speech expressive of character and moral choice (*prohairesis*) is contrasted with speech based on reasoning at Rhetoric, 1417a16–28.
28. Litigants in the Athenian courts were allocated a limited time for their speeches, measured by a water-clock. But the last part of this sentence has never been satisfactorily explained.
29. As a young man Odysseus was wounded by a boar during a hunt; later he tried to avoid joining the Greek expedition against Troy by pretending to be insane. There is no causal relationship between these two events. The wounding is, in fact, recounted in *Odyssey,* 19.393–466, to explain the scar which establishes Odysseus' identity (see 54b26–30 and n. 71); but it is not part of the poem's plot, which is Aristotle's current concern.
30. For Aristotle's view of history cf. 59a21–9.
31. Agathon was a prominent Athenian tragic poet of the late fifth century (Plato's *Symposium* is set at a party celebrating his first victory, in 46 Be); cf. 56a18f., 24f., 29f. His *Anthhes* is otherwise unknown.
32. The same word (poetess) means both 'poet' and 'maker'. Aristotle's point (here as in chapter I) is that writing in verse is not sufficient to identify a poet; the poet is an imitator of action, and therefore a maker of plots.
33. 'Simple' is defined in chapter 10.
34. Greek dramatic festivals were competitive events, and there had been a competition between the leading actors (separate from that between the dramatists) since 449 Be. Aristotle comments on the contemporary dominance of actors over poets at *Rhetoric*, 1403b33.
35. An Argive named Mitys is mentioned in a speech falsely attributed to Demosthenes (59.33); nothing more is known about the incident referred to here.
36. At Sophocles, *Oedipus,* 924ff. a messenger brings the good (934) news that Oedipus has succeeded to the Corinthian throne on the death of his supposed father; when he learns that Oedipus is reluctant to return to Corinth for fear of committing incest with his mother, he is eager to allay that fear too (1002ff.); but in doing so he sets in train the sequence of events which leads to the discovery of Oedipus' parricide and incest.
37. For the *Lynches,* by Aristotle's friend Theodectes, see 55b29–32 (n. 82).
38. *Philip*: see Introduction, 57. As Aristotle goes on to say, this is not the only kind of recognition; but its close bearing on good and bad fortune makes it particularly effective in tragedy.
39. For the recognitions in Euripides' *Iphigeneia in Tauris* see 54a7 54b31–6 (n. 72), 55a18., 55b3–12.
40. For this section see Introduction, n.10.

41. *Hamartia:* see Introduction §7.
42. Referring to the *outcome*; this does not contradict the statement that the *structure* of the plot should be complex rather than (in a different sense) simple (52a12–18, 52b3 if.).
43. Alcmeon, like Orestes, avenged his father's death by killing his mother (cf. 53b24f., 33); Oedipus killed his father and slept with his mother in ignorance of their identity; likewise Meleager and Telephus killed their uncles; Thyestes unwittingly ate his children's flesh (served to him at a feast by his brother Atreus in revenge for the seduction of the latter's wife) and committed incest with his own daughter.
44. That is, Euripides' critics make the same mistake as the advocates of the double outcome mentioned in the previous paragraph.
45. Odysseus triumphs, the wicked suitors are killed (cf. 53b24f.).
46. In tragedy Orestes kills Aegisthus to avenge his father's death. The fourth-century comic poet Alexis wrote an Orestes, but we do not know whether Aristotle is alluding to the plot of that (or some similar) play or suggesting a hypothetical extreme.
47. *Phalli:* cf. n. 38 and Introduction §7.
48. Both cases of matricide (cf. n. 33)
49. In Euripides' *Medep*, Medea punishes the infidelity of her husband Jason by killing their children.
50. Astydamas was a leading tragic dramatist in the mid fourth century; it is not known how he contrived to keep Alcmeon (cf. 53a20 and n. 33, 53b²4) in ignorance of his mother's identity. In Odysshes W0unded, a lost play by Sophocles, Telegonus was Odysseus' son by Circe; having never seen his father, he did not recognize him when they fought.
51. One possibility (knowing and not acting) has been overlooked in the foregoing enumeration, although it is included (somewhat dismissively) in the following ranking. It does appear in the Arabic translation (after the reference to Medea at 53b29); but 'third possibility' at 53b33 suggests that this may be a later addition by a reader who has noticed the omission.
52. Sophocles, *Antigone,* 1231–7: the distraught Haemon tries to stab his father Creon, and then in remorse kills himself.
53. The *Cresphontes* is a lost play by Euripides. When Merope's husband was murdered she managed to smuggle their baby son Cresphontes to safety; many years later she tries to kill the stranger who comes to claim the reward for killing Cresphontes, but discovers before it is too late that the stranger is Cresphontes himself, returning in disguise to avenge his father's death.
54. See the summary of the story at 55b3–12.
55. Nothing is known of this play; and while Helle's family (including Athamas, Phrixus and Info) was fertile in tragic events, none of the attested stories corresponds to the incident Aristotle describes here.
56. In chapter 13 (53a18–22).
57. For Aristotle's views on whether and in what sense slaves and women, can be 'good' cf. especially *Politics*, I.13 (1259b18–60b24).
58. The character should display the right kind of goodness; a good woman should be courageous, but not in the same way as a man (cf. Politics, 1260a20–24, 1277b20–25; 'a man would be regarded as a coward if he were courageous in the same way that a woman is courageous'). 'Cleverness' looks forward to the example of Melanippe below (53231 and n. 62).
59. The reference is obscure; Aristotle probably means 'like us' (the precondition of fear at 53a4–6, and cf. 38a4–14). See Introduction §9.
60. In Euripides' *Orestes* Menelaus' failure to support his nephew Orestes violates the obligations owed to a *philos* (see Introduction §7); the example recurs at 6Ib21.
61. A dithyramb (also mentioned at 6Ib32) by Timotheus (38aI5 and n. 9) which portrayed Odysseus lamenting the loss of his comrades, eaten by the monster Scylla (cf. *Odyssey*, 12.233-59).
62. The reference is to Euripides' lost *Melpnippe* the Wise. Melanippe gave birth to twins by the god Poseidon, and exposed them; when the babies were found being suckled by a cow Melanippe's father, assuming that the cow had given birth to them, decided to have them destroyed as unnatural monsters. Melanippe tried to prevent this by arguing that the cow could not have given birth to human children; her speech included advanced cosmological and theological arguments, thus displaying a cleverness inappropriate in a woman (cf. n. 58).

63. In Euripides' *Iphigeneia in Aulis* Iphigeneia's first reaction on learning that she is to be sacrificed to Artemis to secure the Greek army's passage to Troy is to plead for her life (1211–52); but later she patriotically embraces her fate (1368–1401).
64. 'Resolution' is defined in chapter 18 (55b23–32); cf. 56a9f. for poor technique in resolutions. 'Theatrical device' renders *mekhane;* literally, this was a crane used in the Greek theatre for the appearance of a god who might conclude the play by outlining subsequent events or (less appropriately, in Aristotle's view) by imposing an arbitrary resolution on the plot. The two examples are Euripides' *Medep,* in which Medea's escape from Corinth after the killing of her children (see 53b29 and n. 39) is contrived by means of a supernatural chariot, and llipd, 2.1o9–21o, where Agamemnon proposes abandoning the siege of Troy in an oblique attempt to stimulate the army's fighting spirit; but the army, taking the proposal at face value, accepts it with enthusiasm, and the goddess Athene has to intervene to resolve the crisis which ensues.
65. Referring to Oedipus' ignorance of the circumstances of Laius' death (see 60a30).
66. The text of this sentence is uncertain.
67. No one knows what this paragraph means. By 'published works' Aristotle presumably means his *On Poets.*
68. The 'earth-born' were the men who sprang from the dragon's teeth sown by Cadmus; their descendants had a birth-mark in the shape of a spearhead. In one version of the story, Creon recognized Maeon, son of Haemon and Antigone, by this mark; but we do not know the source of the line which Aristotle quotes.
69. Carcinus was a tragic poet of the early fourth century (cf. ssa26–9). We do not know anything about the plot of this play; for Thyestes see S3a21 (n. 43); the star-shaped birthmark was a characteristic of his family (the descendants of Peoples).
*70.* *Tyro* set her twin sons by Poseidon adrift in a small boat; in Sophocles' (lost) *Tyro* the boat served as a recognition-token.
71. In the bath-scene (Odyssey, ¹9.386–375; cc. 6oa25f. and n.122) the Nurse penetrates Odysseus' disguise when she observes his scar (cf. 5 a26 and n. 29). This is an unplanned consequence of Odysseus' own request (19.333–8) that his feet be washed by one of the older female servants, and is thus linked to a reversal. But in Odyssey, 21.188–223 Odysseus simply declares his identity to the herdsmen Eumaeus and Phioetius, and shows them the scar by way of confirmation.
72. In Euripides' *lphigeneia in Tauris* (see 52b6–8 and n. 39) Iphigeneia's identity is revealed when she asks one of the two strangers to deliver a message addressed to her brother Orestes (769–93); Orestes then declares himself, confirming his identity by displaying knowledge of their home (808–26). Aristotle's point is that he could equally well have brought some physical recognition-token with him.
73. Tereus was married to Procne, and raped her sister Philomela. To keep his crime secret he cut out her tongue, but she wove a tapestry showing what had happened; this picture was the 'voice of the shuttle'.
74. Dicaeogenes was a late fifth-century tragedian; nothing is known of his *Gyprians.* In *Odyssey,* 8.485–586 Odysseus weeps on hearing a song about the fall of Troy; this prompts his host Alcinous to enquire about his identity, and Odysseus's reply (Odyssey, 9–12) is the tale told to Alcinous.
75. In Aeschylus' *Ghoephori*, 66–211 Electra finds a lock of hair and a footprint at her father's tomb, and infers Orestes' presence from their similarity to her own. Despite this example, Aristotle is not thinking primarily of recognition through reasoning from signs, but (as the following examples make clearer) situations in which one character's reasoning discloses his or her identity to another. As with recognition through memory, a character's spontaneous response to the situation provides a clue by means of which their identity can be inferred.
76. Nothing more is known of Polyidus; his suggestion is mentioned again at 55brof. For Theodectes cf. 52a27–9 (n. 37), ssb29–32 (n. 82); nothing more is known about his *Tydhes.* The *Sons of Phinhes* is also unknown.
77. Unknown. Aristotle's account is very cryptic. Presumably Odysseus on his homecoming concealed his identity by bringing a false report of his own death; the audience is led to expect him to establish his identity by stringing the bow (which no one but Odysseus could do), but instead he is accepted simply because he recognizes the bow (which anyone who had seen or heard a report of it might do). For the exploitation of false inference by poets see also 60a18–26.
78. For Carcinus cf. n. 69; we have no further information about the mistake referred to here.
79. To imitate convincingly the poet must be able to project himself into the emotions of the subjects. This is made easier by the versatility of a genius or by the madman's weak grasp on his own identity; more generally, acting

out the part with gestures may help. This was evidently a well-established view of a poet's method of work; Aristophanes has fun with it (Thestnophoria-zusae, 156–8).

80. The universal here seems to be more abstract than in chapter 9. There universality rested on the necessary or probable connection between events; here it designates the barest outline of a story, which only becomes a plot with causally connected events when the outline is turned into episodes. The text of this parenthesis is uncertain.
81. Cf. 55a6–8 (n. 76).
82. Danaus ordered his daughters to kill their husbands; Hypermestra alone disobeyed, sparing her husband Lynceus; she bore his son, presumably keeping him and the child secret. In Theodectes' play the child must have been found and his parentage revealed; Danaus condemned Lynceus to death but somehow (cf. 52a27–9 and n. 3f) this led to a reversal, and it was Danaus who died; Lynceus survived. But the text here is uncertain, and our limited knowledge of the play's plot makes it impossible to reconstruct Aristotle's words with complete confidence.
83. A perplexing statement: there has been no mention of four parts of tragedy before now. To add to the confusion, the name of the fourth kind has been lost in the Greek text; the conjectural text translated here makes the passage consistent with the cross-reference at 5967–9 (another widely accepted conjecture makes the fourth kind the 'tragedy of spectacle'). The examples do little to cast light on Aristotle's meaning.
84. The obscurity of the preceding paragraph casts a shadow over this one as well. Presumably poets with a special talent for the depiction of character were criticized for failing to depict suffering as effectively as poets who specialized in that kind of tragedy, and *vice versa*.
85. For faulty resolutions cf. 54a37-b2.
86. The Spck of Troy was the title of an epic poem and of several lost tragedies; Euripides' *Trojan Wotnen* and *Hecubp* both deal with events drawn from this larger story. The reference to *Niobe* is perplexing, since there was no epic on that subject; Aristotle perhaps wrote something different, but the text cannot be corrected with any confidence. We do not know what failure of Agathon (cf. n. if) Aristotle is referring to.
87. The text and interpretation here are uncertain.
88. For Agathon cf. n. 31; and cf.61b1 5 for the principle stated here.
89. Instead of composing choral lyrics in the traditional way, the poet could simply mark the points at which the chorus should perform and leave it to the producer to choose the songs to be sung in these interludes. In comedy we can observe this being done sporadically by Aristophanes in his later work at the beginning of the fourth century, and consistently by Menander at the end of the fourth century.

# Seven Against Thebes

## Aeschylus

### Introduction To Seven Against Thebes

This strange, archaic play was produced in 467 B.C. It is probably the last play of a trilogy written by Aeschylus on the theme of the Oedipus cycle. It is at once undramatic and yet, in a paradoxical way, very theatrical. Who can take seriously a play with almost no action, in which the main event is the recital of the blazonry on the shields of the Seven Champions? But a careful reading will reveal the tremendous effect that the dancing accompaniments would have made. The effect of the whole is, despite its disadvantages for a modern reader, very powerful.

The play is extremely hard to translate. The style is heroic in the good parts and bombastic in the bad. It is never simple and luminous. Whereas the same quality of diction in the elevated parts of the PROMETHEUS is always suited to a majesty of theme comprehensible to a modern reader, the matter of the SEVEN is remote from the interest of a reader today, and it needs imagination to conceive of it in the Greek theater, let alone on the stage as we now know it.

It is perhaps better understood by a modern reader in the mood in which he would now attend a ritual ceremony, a church service, or a pageant such as the coronation of an English monarch. The recital of the devices on the shields, the matching of the champions, and, in the last part of the play, the antiphonal keening of the sisters over the dead bodies of their brothers are all properly traditional ritual. They were probably filled for the Greek spectator with matter pertinent to his own time. The political relation of Argos, Thebes, and Athens was then much discussed, and Aeschylus has undoubtedly used the popular interest in these matters to render the old story vital for his audience. It may be that the names of the champions had many associations for the mid-fifth-century Greek. Aeschylus has similarly used the general interest in the Areopagus in the years 462-459 B.C. for the pageant drama of the *Oresteia.* Though many of the clues to his employment of this method in the *Seven* are lost to us, we are almost certainly correct in assuming that this is again the course he adopted. The *Seven,* like the *Eumenides,* is the last play of the trilogy, and in both Aeschylus has managed to raise progressively a particular story to the level of a general process of history culminating in a particular historical occurrence known to his contemporaries.

## Characters

Eteocles, son of Oedipus and present ruler of Thebes Antigone)
mis sisters
Ismene
Messenger
Chorus of Theban Women

## Seven Against Thebes

*Scene:* Thebes. The Prince Eteocles confronts a crowd of Thebans.

Eteocles

You citizens of Cadmus, he must speak home
that in the ship's prow watches the event
and guides the rudder, his eye not drooped in sleep.
For if we win success, the God is the cause
but if—-may it not chance so—there is disaster,
throughout the town, voiced by its citizens,
a multitudinous swelling prelude
CRIES on one name "Eteocles" with groans:
which Zeus defender keep from the city of Cadmus
even as his name implies.
You must help her now—you still something short
of your young manhood and you whose time of youth
is gone, your body grown to its full bigness—
each of you to such charge as fits you:
help the city, help the altars of your country's Gods;
save their honors from destruction:
help your children, help Earth your Mother.
She reared you, on her kindly surface, crawling
babies, welcomed all the trouble of your nurture,
REARED you to live in her, to carry a shield
in her defense, loyally, against such needs as this.
Now to this God kindly inclines this day.
For those who have been held in siege so long
the Gods grant commonly a favorable fight.
So says the prophet now, bird shepherding
With skill unlying, ears and mind and fire
tending the oracular birds.
The master of these prophecies declares
enemy's night council framed a plot for the greatest Achaean
assault upon us. All to the battlements, to the gates of the
towers! Haste, in full armor, man the breastworks: stand on the
scaffolding and at the exit gates be firm, abide, your hearts

confident: fear not that mighty mob of foreigners. God will
dispose all well: I have sent scouts and spies upon their host:
they will not—well I know it—make the journey vainly, and by
their information 1 shall be armed against enemy's stratagems.

Messenger
Eteocles, great prince of the Cadmaeans,
I come bringing a clear word from the army
of matters there: 1 myself too
have seen the things I speak of
There were seven men, fierce regiment commanders,
who cut bulls' throats into an iron-rimmed
shield, and with hands touched the bulls' blood,
taking their oaths by Ares and Enyo,
by the bloodthirsty God of Battle Rout
either to lay your city level
with the ground, sacked, or by their death to make a bloody
paste of this same soil of yours. Remembrances of themselves for
parents at home their hands have hung upon Adrastus' chariot:
their tears ran down,
but never a word of pity was in their mouths.
Their spirits were hard as iron and ablaze
breathed courage: war looked through their lion-eyes.
You will not wait long for confirmation
of this my news: I left them casting lots
how each should lead his regiment against your gates.
Wherefore the choicest men within your city set at the entrance gates: set them quickly
for near already the armed host of Argives
comes in a cloud of dust, flecks of white,
panted from horses' lungs, staining the ground.
You, like the skilful captain of a ship
barricade your town before the blast of Ares
strikes it in storm: already bellows
the armed land wave. Take quickest opportunity
for all these things and I for the rest
will keep my eye, a trusty day watcher.
Thanks to my clear reports you shall know whatever
happens within the gates, and come to no harm.

Eteocles
O Zeus and Earth and Gods that guard the city My
father's Curse, mighty evil spirit,
do not root out this city of mine, do not
give her to ruin and destruction, do not
give her to capture nor her homes and hearths.
This is a town that speaks with a Greek tongue.

City and land of the Cadmaeans are free:
do not bind her in slavish yoke; be her protector.
I think I speak for everybody's good, for a city
prosperous honors the Gods.

Chorus

My sorrows are great and fearful: I cry aloud: the
army has left the camp and is gone.
Look at the forward rushing river, the great tide of horsemen! I
see a cloud of dust, sky high, and am convinced; a messenger
clear and unlying, though voiceless.
Treading feet on the earth of my country, trampling hoofs, the
sound of these draws near.

(Shout is heard.)

It floats, it rings
like a resistless mountain waterfall.
O gods, O goddesses, the trouble raised! Turn it aside!

(Shouts.)

Over the walls they spring
the Horse of the White Shield
well equipped, hastening upon our city.
Who will protect us? Who will be our champion
of gods or goddesses?
Shall I kneel at the images of the Gods?
O Blessed Ones, throned in peace, it
is time to cling to your images. We
delay and wail too much.

Do you hear or do you not the rattle of shields?

When, if not now, shall we hang
robes and garlands on your statues, supplicating?

I see the sound!
No one spear rattled so.

What will you do? Will you betray, ancient lord of our land
Ares, your own land?

O spirit of the golden helmet look down upon us, look down
upon a city which once you dearly loved.

City guarding gods of our land, come, come all of you! Look
upon us a band of virgins, suppliants against slavery!
Around our city the wave of warriors, with waving plumes,
roars; blasts of the War God stirred them.

Alas alas Zeus, Father Omnipotent! all fulfilling!
Let us not fall into the hands of the foeman!
For the Argives are around Cadmus' city.
Fear is stronger than arms.
There is murder in the ringing bits between their horses[5] jaws.
Seven proud captains of the host, with harness and spear, having won their place by lot, stand champions at seven gates.
O victory, battle-loving, Zeus begotten, save our city!

O Pallas, and the Horseman, Prince of the Sea, King of the Trident, Poseidon, deliverance from fear, deliverance grant.
You, Ares, protect the city of Cadmus, that bears your name.

Show your care for it, in manifest presence.
And Cypris, who are our ancestress
turn destruction away. We are sprung from your blood
we approach you and cry
with prayers for the ears of the Gods.

And you, Wolf God, be a very Wolf
in the enemy host. And you, daughter of Leto,
make ready your bow.

Ah, ah,
the rattle of chariots round the city: I hear it. O Lady Hera,
the groaning axles of the loaded wheels. Beloved Artemis!
The air is mad with the whirr of spears.
What will happen our city, what will become of it,
whereto shall the Gods bring an end upon us?

There comes a shower of stones on the top of the battlements!
O beloved Apollo!
There is the rattle of bronze-bound shields at our gates!
O Son of Zeus
from whom comes the war's fulfilment,
from whom comes the fight's holy consummation.

O Athene, Blessed Queen, Champion of the city,
deliver her from the assault of the Seven.

O Gods all sufficient,
O Gods and Goddesses, Perfecters,
Protectors of our country's forts,
do not betray this city, spear-won,
to a foreign-tongued enemy.
Hear O hear the prayers, hand outstretched,

of the virgins supplicating in justice.
O beloved Spirits,
that encompass our city to its deliverance, show how much
you love it: Bethink you of the public sacrifices. As we have
thought of you, rescue us. Remember, I pray you, therites
with loving sacrifice offered.

Eteocles

You insupportable creatures, I ask you,
is this the best, is this for the city's safety,
is this enheartening for our beleaguered army,
to have you falling at the images
of the city's gods crying and howling,
an object of hatred for all temperate souls?
Neither in evils nor in fair good luck
may I share a dwelling with the tribe of women!
When she's triumphant, hers a confidence
past converse with another, when afraid
an evil greater both for home and city.
Here now running wild among the citizenry
you have roared them into spiritless cowardice.
So, outside of our gates, gains strength the enemy
while we are by ourselves, within, undone. All this you may have, for
living with women. Now if there is anyone that will not hear my orders,
be he man or woman or in between, sentence of death shall be decreed
against him and public stoning he shall not escape.
What is outside is a man's province: let no
woman debate it: within doors do no mischief! Do you hear me or not?
Or are you deaf?

Chorus

Dear son of Oedipus, the bumping rattle of the chariots, rattle, rattle, I
am afraid when I hear, when the naves of the axles screech in their
running when the fire-forged bits speak ringingly, rudder oars in horses' mouths.

Eteocles

What, shall the sailor, then, leave the stern and run to the prow and find device for safety
when his vessel is foundering in the sea waves?

Chorus

But it was to the images of the Gods the ancient images I ran, trusting in
the Gods, when the stony snowflakes crashed upon our gates: nay, then I
was lifted up with force and betook me to prayer to the Blessed Ones, for
our city, that they may make their strength its protection.

Eteocles

For protection pray that our towers hold off the enemy's spears.

Chorus

And shall not that be as the Gods dispose?

Eteocles

The Gods, they say, of a captured town desert her.

Chorus

Never in my lifetime, never may this assembly of
Gods desert us: never may I live to see this city
overrun, an enemy soldiery putting the torch to it.

Eteocles

Do not call upon the Gods and then be guided
wrongly. Obedience is mother to success, and
success is parent of rescue— so runs the proverb.

Chorus

This is true: but the strength of God is still greater.
Oftentimes when a man is hopelessly sunk in misfortune
He raises him, yes from his greatest sorrow while the
clouds still hang over him, high above our eyes.

Eteocles

But it is man's part, the sacrifice, the consultation of the
Gods, when the enemy assault us; it is yours to be silent
and stay within doors.

Chorus

It is thanks to the Gods that we have our city
unconquered: it is thanks to them that our towers reject
the mob of foemen. What should be resented in these words?

Eteocles

I do not grudge your honoring the Gods.
But lest you make our citizens cowards, be
quiet and not overfearful.

Chorus

It was but now that I heard the noise and the confusion
and trembling in fear came to this citadel, sacred seat.

Eteocles

If you shall learn of men dying or wounded, do not be eager to anticipate it with cries, for murdered men are the War God's nourishment.

Chorus

The snorting of horses! There, I hear it.

Eteocles

Do not listen; do not hear too much.

Chorus

Our city groans from its foundation: we are surrounded.

Eteocles

I shall think of this: that is enough for you.

Chorus

I am afraid: the din at the gates grows louder.

Eteocles

Silence! Do not speak of this throughout the city. CHORUS O Blessed Band, do not betray this fort.

Eteocles

Damnation! Can you not endure in silence?

Chorus

Fellow-citizen Gods, grant me not to be a slave.

Eteocles

It is you who enslave yourselves, and all the city.

Chorus

O Zeus, All Mighty, your bolt upon our foes!

Eteocles

O Zeus, what a tribe you have given us in women!

Chorus

Base is the tribe of men of a captured town.

Eteocles

Words of ill omen, YOUR HANDS on the images[1]

Chorus

Fear captures my tongue, and my spirit is nought.

Eteocles

Grant me, I pray you, the small thing I ask.

Chorus

Speak it quickly, that I may know.

Eteocles

Silence, you wretches, don't frighten your friends.

Chorus

I am silent: with others Ill endure what is fated.

Eteocles

I like this word better than those before. Furthermore,
get you away from the statues, and being so, utter a
better prayer: "May the Gods stand our allies." First
hear my prayer and then offer yours— a holy gracious
paean of thanksgiving, the cry of sacrifice, our Grecian
custom, joy to our friends, dissolving fear of foes.

(He approaches the images himself)

Gods of the city, of this country Gods, Lords of its fields, and its
assembly places, Springs of Dirce, waters of Ismenus— to you my vow:
if all go well with us, if the city is saved, my people shall
dye your hearths with the blood of sacrificed sheep, aye
with the blood of bulls slaughtered to honor the Gods. I
shall myself dedicate trophies, spoils of my enemies, their
garments fixed on spear points, in your sanctuaries. (To the Chorus)
These be your prayers, unlamenting with no vain wild
panting and moaning. For all such you will not escape your doom.
I will take six men, myself to make a seventh and go to
post them at the city's gates, opponents of the enemy,
in gallant style, before quick messengers are on us and
their words of haste burn us with urgency.

Chorus

I heed him but through fear
my spirit knows no sleep:
and neighbors to my heart,
anxieties, kindle terror
of the host that beleaguers us.
As the all-fearing dove
dreads for its nestlings' sake

the snakes that menace them.
For they against our forts
with all their host, with all their people,
come. What will become of me?
Jagged rocks they hurl
upon our citizens, on both sides pelted.
O children of Zeus, ye Gods,
I pray you—protect the city and the army, the Cadmus born.
What country will you take in exchange, than this one
better, if you abandon this deep-soiled land to her enemies,
and Dirce's water, fairest to drink
of all that come from Poseidon
the Earth Upholder, and Tethys' sons?
Therefore, you city-guarding Gods,
upon the men outside our forts
rain slaughtering destruction
and ruin, that will cast away their shields:
and for these citizens here
win glory and of the city be the rescuers.
Then stand fair in your places to receive our shrill prayers.
Pity it were that this city, so ancient,
should be cast to the House of Death,
a spear-booty, a slave,
in crumbling ashes, dishonorably,
sacked by an Achaean, with the Gods' consent;
that its women be haled away,
captives, young and old,
dragged by the hair, as horses by the mane,
and their raiment torn about them.
Emptied the city wails
as the captive spoil, with mingled cries,
is led to its doom.
This heavy fate is what I fear.
It is a woeful thing for maidens unripe,
before the marriage rites, to tread
this bitter journey from their homes.
I would say that the dead
are better off than this.
Alas, unlucky indeed the fate
of a city captured—
murder, fire, and rapine,
all the city polluted by smoke,
and the breath of Ares on it
maddened, desecrating piety, slaying the people.
There is tumult through the town.
Against her comes a towering net.

Man stands against man with the spear and is kil
Young mothers, blood-boltered,
cry bitterly for the babes at their breast.
The roving bands of pillagers are all brothers;
he that has plunder meets with another; he that is empty
calls him that is empty, wishing to have a partner, eager
for a share neither less nor yet equal. From such things
what shall one augur?

All sorts of grain fallen
strewn on the ground vex,
embitter the eye of the housewife.
The great, profuse gifts of the earth
in reckless streams of waste are poured out.
The girls, new servants, new to misery,
must endure a war captive's bed,
bed of a man successful.
Theirs the expectation of night's consummation but for a
triumphant enemy to help their tearful sorrow.

Half-Chorus

Here, I think, friends, your scout comes bringing some
news of the enemy—hastily urging the joints of his legs
to carry him here. HALF-CHORUS And here is the king
himself, the son of Oedipus in the nick of time to hear
the messenger's story. He too is in haste and nimbly steps along.

Messenger

I can declare— I know it
well—the enemy's position: how each at the gates has
won by lot his station. At the Proetid gate Tydeus now
thunders but dares not cross Ismenus' ford; the prophet
forbids. The sacrifices are unfavorable. Tydeus, enraged
and thirsting for the fight, threatens, like serpents' hiss at noonday;
strikes with ABUSE the wise seer, Oecleides, "battle and
death make him cringe through cowardice"—so he shouts
aloud and shakes his threefold shadowing plumes, mane of
his crested helm. Beneath his shield, inside, ring brazen
bells, a peal of terror, and on the shield he bears this
arrogant device—a fashioned sky afire with stars. In the
shield's midst a glorious full moon, night's eye, the eldest
of the stars, stands out. With such mad bragging and with
overweening trappings of war he roars along the banks in
love with battle, like the horse that chafes against the bit,
high mettled, impatient, hearing the trumpet's sound.
Against this champion whom will you set?

When the bolts are shot back at the Proetid gates, who will be champion fit to deserve our trust?

Eteocles

No equipment of a man will make me tremble Devices on a shield deal no one wounds. The plumes and bells bite not without the spear. And for this night you speak of on his shield glistening with all the stars of heaven—someone may find his folly prophetic to himself. For if in death night fall upon his eyes, to him that bears this pompous blazonry it shall be truly and most justly pregnant, and he shall make his insolence prophesy against himself.
I nominate against him as champion of
these gates to challenge Tydeus, the worthy son of
Astacus—right noble, one honoring the throne of
Modesty and hating insolent words.
Laggard in all things base he is wont to be but not a coward. From those sown men whom Ares spared his root springs—very native is Melanippus to this land. His deeds shall Ares with his dice determine; but Justice, blood of his blood, sends him forth, surely, to turn the enemy's spear away from the mother that has borne him.

Chorus

May the Gods grant good luck to
our champion, since justly he comes
forward a fighter for us. But I fear for
our friends to look upon bloodshed of
those we love, dying.

Messenger

Yes, may the Gods grant him good luck. At Electra's gates stands by lot Capaneus, a giant this man, taller than the other, and his threats breathe inhuman arrogance. Our towers he menaces with terrors—Fortune fulfil them not!—for he declares he'll sack our city with the Gods' good will or ill. Not even Zeus's wrath striking the earth before him shall be obstacle to his purpose. The lightnings and the thunderbolts he likened to the sun's warm rays at noontide. His device a naked man that carries fire, in his hands, ablaze, a torch all ready. In gold are letters that declare "I'll burn the city." Against this man send—who will meet him? Who will abide his threats and never tremble?

Eteocles

This man's boasts, too, beget us other gain.

For of the haughtiness of vain men, true
accuser proves their own tongue. Capaneus
threatens to do—and is prepared to do—
disdains the Gods, and giving exercise
to his mouth, in vain joy, up to heaven
mortal though he is, against Zeus sends his words,
shouted in swelling pride. I trust on him
will justly come the bolt that carries fire
in no way like the sun's warm rays at noontide.
Against him, be his lips never so insolent,
a man of fiery spirit shall be stationed,
strong Polyphontes, a guard trustworthy,
by favor of protecting Artemis
and of the other Gods. Tell me another
that has his place by lot at another gate.

Chorus

Destruction on him that against the city vaunts huge threats;
may the thunderbolt's blast restrain him
before he burst into my house,
before he ravish me from my maiden room.

Messenger

Now I shall tell him that by lot won next
station at the gates. The third lot cast
jumped from the upturned brazen helmet
in favor of a third man, Eteoclus,
that he should lead his regiment in a charge
against the gates of Neis. He wheels his mares
snorting in their nose bands, ready to charge the gate.
Pipes on the bridle bands filled with insolent
nostril breath whistle in a foreign note.
His shield, too, has its design—and that no lowly—
a man in armor mounts a ladder's steps to the enemy's
town to sack it. Loud cries also this man in his written
legend "Ares himself shall not cast me from the tower."
Against him send some champion trustworthy to turn
the yoke of slavery from this city. *Eteocles*
This man 111 send and may good luck go with him!
There, he is gone. His boast is in his hands
Megareus, Creon's son, and of the seed
and race of the sown men. He will not blench
at the furious neighing of horses nor yield the gates.
Either by death hell pay his nurture's due
to his own land or he will capture two men
and city as depicted on the shield

and crown his father's house with the spoils of war.
On with another's boasts—don't grudge me the story.

Chorus

Good success to you, I pray,
Champion of my house, and to
the enemy ill success! | as with
wild extravagance they prate
against the city with maddened
heart, so may Zeus the Avenger
look on them in wrath. I

Messenger

Another, the fourth, holds the gate that neighbors Onca
Athena, and takes his station with a shout,
Hippomedon's vast frame and giant form. He whirled a
disc around—I mean the circle of his shield—until I
shuddered. I speak truth. The armorer cannot have
been a poor one that put upon the shield this work of
art— a Typho hurling from his fiery mouth
black smoke, the flickering sister of fire.
The rim that ran around the hollow boss
of the shield is solid wrought with coiling snakes.
The man himself cried out his warcry, he,
inspired by Ares, revels in violence
like a Bacchanal with murder in his glance.
Take good heed how you deal with such a man;
he boasts even now at the gate he will raise panic.

Eteocles

First Onca Pallas, with her place beside
our city, neighbor to our gates, will hate
the fellow's violence and keep him off,
as it were a chill snake from her nestling brood.
And then Hyperbius, the stout son of Oenops,
has been chosen to match him man for man, right willing,
at fortune's need, to put his fate to question—
no man to be reproached either in form
or spirit or in bearing of his arms.
Hermes has matched the two with excellent reason,
for man with man they shall engage as foes
and on their shields shall carry enemy Gods.
The one has Typho breathing fire, the other,
Hyperbius, has father Zeus in station
sitting upon his shield, and in his hand
a burning bolt.

No one has yet seen Zeus defeated anywhere. Such on
each side are the favors of the Gods; we are on the winning
side, they with the vanquished if Zeus than Typho mightier prove in battle.

Chorus

Sure am I that he who hath
Zeus's foe upon his shield
the unloved form of the earth-born God,
the likeness hated by men
and the long-living Gods,
shall lay his head before our gates.

Messenger

So may it prove. Now I shall take the fifth that has his station at the fifth,
the Northern gate, right by Amphion's tomb that sprung from Zeus. By
his lance he swears—and with sure confidence
he holds it more in reverence than a god,
more precious than his eyes—he will sack the town
of Thebes in despite of Zeus. Such the loud vaunt
of this creature sprung of a mountain mother, handsome,
something between man and boy.
The beard is newly sprouting on his cheeks,
the thick, upspringing hair of youth in its bloom.
His spirit unlike his maiden name* is savage,
and with a grim regard he now advances.
He too boasts high as he draws near our gates.
For on his brazen shield, his body's rounded
defense, he swings an insult to our city,
the Sphinx that ate men raw, cunningly wrought, burnished, embossed,
secured with rivets there. A man she bears beneath her, a Cadmaean, so
that at him most of our darts shall fly. When he comes to the battle, so it
seems, he will not play the petty shopkeeper nor shame the course of his
long journey here— Parthenopaeus of Arcadia. He lives among our
enemy presently and pays to Argos a fair wage for his keep, with threats
against our forts—which God fulfil not.

Eteocles

Would that they might obtain what from the Gods
they pray against us—them, and their impious boasts.
* Parthenopaeus: Maiden One.

Then would they perish utterly and ill. We have a
man to encounter your Arcadian,
a man unboasting but his hand looks for the thing that

should be done—Actor, the brother of him I spoke of earlier. He will not suffer a heedless tongue to flow within our gates and to breed mischief, nor to cross our walls, one bearing on an enemy shield the likeness of the most hateful Sphinx—or else the' beast borne outside shall have cause of blame against him that would carry her in, for many a hammering blow she will get beneath the city's walls. With the God's will, I may indeed speak truth.

Chorus

The. words go through my heart; the hair stands upright on my head; as I listen to mighty words of impious boasting men. May the Gods destroy them within our land!

Messenger

A sixth I'll tell you of—a most modest man greatest in might of battle, yet a prophet, strong Amphiaraus, at the Homoloian gates stationed, shouts insults at strong Tydeus: "Murderer, cause of confusion to the city, greatest teacher of evil to Argos; of the Fury a summoning herald; servant of bloodshed; adviser to Adrastus of all these evils." And then again with eyes uplifted calling on your own brother, strong prince Polyneices, he dwells twice on the latter part of his name.* And this is the speech to which his lips give utterance: "Is such a deed as this dear to the Gods,

* The latter half of the Greek word Polyneices means "strife."

and fair to hear and tell of, for posterity, for one to sack his native city, destroy the gods of his country, bringing in an alien enemy host?
What justice shall quench the spring of guilt of another murder?
Your fatherland destroyed by the spear
which your own zeal impelled—shall it be your ally?
But for myself I shall make fat this soil
a prophet buried under enemy ground.
Let us fight. The fate I look for is right honorable."
So spoke the prophet brandishing his round
brazen shield. No device is on its circle.
He is best not at seeming to be such
but being so. Deep indeed is the furrow
of his mind from which he gathers fruit, and good
the counsels that do spring from it. For him
send out, I recommend, wise and good challengers,
for he is dangerous who reveres the gods.

Eteocles

Alas, the luck which among human beings conjoins an honest man with impious wretches! In every enterprise is no greater evil than bad companionship: there is no fruit that can be gathered. The field of doom bears death as its harvest. Indeed, a pious man, going on board as shipmate of a crew of rascal sailors and of some mischief they have perpetrated, has often died with the God-detested breed; or a just man, with fellow citizens themselves inhospitable, forgetful of the Gods, has fallen into the same snare as the unrighteous, and smitten by the common scourge of God has yielded up his life.

Even so this seer, this son of Oecles, wise, just, good, and holy, a prophet mighty, mingling with the impious— against his better reason—with loud-mouthed men who pursue a road long to retrace, with God's will shall be dragged to their general doom. I think he will not even assault the gate— not that he is a coward or faint of spirit— but well he knows how he must die in the battle if Loxias' prophecies shall bear fruit. Loxias either says nothing or speaks seasonably. Yet against him, the strong prince Lasthenes we shall range in combat, an inhospitable sentry, in mind an old man but a young one in his body's vigor, in his swift-swooping charge, in his hand, undelaying to snatch a spear and hurl it against the unprotected shield side. But success—that is for men the gift of God alone.

Chorus

Hear, O ye Gods, our lawful prayers
and bring them to fulfilment that
the city prosper, averting the horrors
of war upon our invaders. May Zeus
strike them and slay them with his
bolt outside of our walls.

Messenger

Lo, now, the seventh at the seventh gate I shall unfold—your own, your very brother. Hear how he curses the city and what fate he invokes upon her. He prays that once his feet are set upon her walls, once he is proclaimed a conqueror of this land, once he has cried paean

of triumph in its overthrow, he then may close
in fight with you and killing may find his death
beside your corpse.
Or if you live, that he may banish you— in the selfsame
way as you dishonored him— to exile. So he shouts and
calls the Gods of his race and of his fatherland to witness
his prayers—a very violent Polyneices. He bears a
new-made, rounded shield and a twofold device
contrived thereon: a woman leading modestly a man
conducts him, pictured as a warrior, wrought all in gold.
She claims she is Justice, and the inscription reads: I will
bring him home and he shall have his city and shall walk
in his ancestral house.
Such are the signs. But you
yourself determine whom to send. You shall not
find a fault in my report: but you determine how
to steer the state.

Eteocles

Our race, our race, the race of Oedipus,
by the Gods maddened, by them greatly hated;
alas, my father's curses are now fulfilled!
But for me no crying and no lamentation
lest even sorer sorrow be begotten.
I tell you, Polyneices, so well named,
soon we shall know the pertinence of your sign,
whether your golden characters on the shield,
babbling, in wild distraction of the mind,
will indeed bring you home. This might have been,
if Justice, Zeus's virgin daughter had stood
by his actions and his mind. But in his flight
out of the darkness of his mother's womb,
in his growth as a child, in his young manhood,
in the first gathering of his chin's hair—no, never
did Justice look upon him nor regard him.
I do not think that now he comes to outrage this fatherland
of his she will stand his ally,
or else she is called falsely Justice, joining
with a man whose mind conceives no limit in villainy.
In this I trust and to the conflict with him
111 go myself. What other has more right?
King against king, and brother against brother,
foe against foe we'll fight.
Bring me my greaves
to shield me from the lances and the stones.

Chorus

O dearest son of Oedipus, do not be like in temper to this
utterer of dreadful sayings. There are enough
Cadmaeans to grapple with the Argives: such blood is
expiable. But for the blood of brothers mutually shed
there is no growing old of the pollution.

Eteocles

If a man suffer ill, let it be without shame; this is the
only gain when we are dead. For deeds both evil and
disgraceful never will you say word of good.

Chorus

What do you long for, child? Let not the frantic lust for
battle, filling the heart carry you away. Expel the evil
passion at its birth.

Eteocles

It is the God that drives this matter on. Since it is
so—on, on with favoring wind this wave of hell that has
engulfed for its share all kin of Laius, whom Phoebus has so hated.

Chorus

Bitter-biting indeed
is the passion that urges you
to accomplish manslaying, bitter in fruit,
where the blood to be shed is unlawful.

Eteocles

Yes, for the hateful black
curse of my father loved
sits on my dry and tearless eyes
and tells me first of gain and then of death.

Chorus

Resist its urging: coward you shall not be called if you rule your life well.
Forth from your house the black-robed Fury
shall go, when from your hands the Gods shall receive a sacrifice.

Eteocles

We are already past the care of Gods. For
them our death is the admirable offering.
Why then delay, fawning upon our doom?

Chorus

Not when the chance is yours— for in the
veering change of spirit though late
perhaps the God may change and come
with kinder breath Mow his blast is full.

Eteocles

The curse of Oedipus has fanned that blast.
Too true the vision of sleepy nightmares
showing division of my father's heritage.

Chorus

Listen to women though you like it not.

Eteocles

Speak then of what may be. Nor should it be long.

Chorus

Go not you, go not, to the seventh gate.

Eteocles

No words of yours will blunt my whetted purpose.

Chorus

Yet even bad victory the Gods hold in honor.

Eteocles

No soldier may endure to hear such words.

Chorus

Do you wish to reap as harvest a brother's blood?

Eteocles

If Gods give ill, no man may shun their giving.

Chorus

I shudder at the Goddess,
unlike all other Gods,
who compasses destruction of the house,
utterly unforgetting, prophet of ill,
the Fury invoked by a father's curse.
I dread that it bring to pass
the furious invocations
of Oedipus astray in his mind.
This strife, death to his sons, spurs it on.

A stranger grants them land-allotment, a Chalyb,
Scythian colonist, a bitter divider of possessions—
iron-hearted Steel.
Yes, he has allotted them land to dwell in as much
as the dead may possess: no share theirs of their broad acres.
When they die with mutual hand mutually
slaughtering and earth's dust shall drink black
clotted murder-blood,
who shall then give purification,
who shall wash away the stain?
O new evils of the house, new mingled with the old.
Old is the tale of sin 1 tell but swift in retribution: to the
third generation it abides. Thrice in Pythian prophecies
given at Navel-of-Earth Apollo had directed King Laius
all issueless to die and save his city so . . .

but he was mastered by loving folly and begot for
himself a doom, father-murdering Oedipus, who sowed
his mother's sacred womb, whence he had sprung
himself, with bloody root, to his heartbreak.
Madness was the coupler of this distracted pair.

Now, as it were, a sea
drives on the wave:
one sinks, another rises,
triple-crested around the prow
of the city, and breaks in foam.
Our defense between is but a little thing
no bigger than a wall in width.
fear that with our princes our city be subdued.
For heavy is the settlement of ancient curses, to
fulfilment brought. That evil when fulfilled passes not away.

Prosperity grown over fat of men, gain seeking,
compels jettisoning of all goods, utterly.

What man has earned such admiration of Gods and men that shared his city and of the general throng of
mortal men, as Oedipus—who ever had such honor as he THAT from his land had banished the Sphinx,
that ate men up?
But when in misery he knew the meaning of his dreadful marriage, in pain distraught, in heart distracted
he brought a double sorrow to fulfilment. With patricidal hand he reft himself of eyes
that dearer to him were than his own children.
And on those children savage
maledictions he launched
for their cruel tendance of him

and wished they might divide
with iron-wielding hand his own possessions.
And now I fear
that nimble-footed Fury bring those wishes to fulfilment.

Messenger

Take heart, you mother's darlings, this your city has escaped the yoke of slavery. Fallen are the vauntings of the monstrous men. Our city is in smooth water and though many the assaults of the waves, has shipped to sea. Our wall still stands protecting us, our gates we barricaded with trustworthy champions. For the most part all is well—at six of the gates. The seventh the Lord Apollo, Captain of Sevens, took to HIMSELF: on Oedipus' race he has fulfilled Laius' ancient follies.

Chorus

What new and evil thing concerns the city?

Messenger

The city is saved, but the twin princes—

Chorus

Who? What do you mean? Through fear of your words I am frantic.

Messenger

Get your wits and hear. Oedipus' two sons—

Chorus

Alas, alas, the ills I prophesied.

Messenger

In very truth, crushed to the ground.

Chorus

They lie there? Bitter though it be, yet speak.

Messenger

The men have fallen, one another's killers.

Chorus

Did brother's hands achieve a mutual murder?

Messenger

The ground has drunk the blood shed each by each.

Chorus

So all too equal was their guiding spirit.

Messenger

Surely he destroys this most unlucky race. Here is store of sorrow and joy at once. The city has good fortune, but its lords, the two generals, have divided the possessions with hammered steel of Scythia. They shall have what land suffices for a grave, swept thither
down the wind of their father's ill-boding curses.

Chorus

O great Zeus and Spirits that guard
the city, you Protectors
that guard our walls:
shall I rejoice, shall I cry aloud
for our city's safety?
or for those wretched ones, luckless and childless,
our generals, shall I lament?
They have earned their name too well
and "men of strife" they have perished
through impious intent.
black curse consummated
on the race, the curse of Oedipus! An evil chill assails my heart.
raise the dirge at the tomb like a Bacchanal, hearing
of their blood-dripping corpses, of their ill-fated death.
Ill-omened indeed is this melody of the Spear.
It has worked to an end, not failed,
the curses called on them by their father of old.
The decisions of Laius, wanting in faith,
have had effect till now.
My heart is troubled for the city;
divine warnings are not blunted.
O FALL of sorrows, this you have done
a deed beyond belief.
Woes worthy of groaning
have come in very truth.
(The bodies of the princes are carried in, escorted by their two sisters, Ismene and Antigone.)
Here is visible evidence of the messenger's tale. Twofold our griefs and double
the ills these two men wrought;
double the fated sorrow
now brought to fulfilment.
What shall I say but that
here sorrows, sorrows' children,
abide at the hearth of the house?
But, my friends, down the wind of groans
with hands that beat the head
ply the speeding stroke
which sends through Death's waters
the dark-sailed ship of mission

to the shore, untrodden by Apollo, and sunless,
the shore unseen, that welcomes all at last.
Here they come to their bitter task,
Ismene and Antigone,
to make the dirge for their brothers.
With true sincerity, I think,
from their deep bosoms,
they shall utter a song of grief that fits the cause.
Us it concerns to sing,
before their song,
the ill-sounding Furies' dirge,
and the hateful Hades paean.
O most luckless of all women
that fasten the girdle about their robes,
I cry, I groan: there is no guile
in my heart to check my true dirge.

Antigone (speaking over the bodies)

O you misguided ones, faithless to friends, unwearied in evil, you who plundered your father's house to your misery, with the spear.

Chorus

Wretched indeed those who wretched death have found to the ruin of their house.

Ismene

O you that tore the roof from our house,
you that glimpsed the bitter sovereignty, at
last you are reconciled—by the sword.

Chorus

Too truly has that dread spirit, the Fury of Oedipus, brought all this to fulfilment.

Antigone

Stricken through the left sides stricken indeed,
through sides born of a common mother. Alas,
strange ones, alas for the curse of death that answered death!

Chorus

A straight thrust to house and body delivered
by unspeakable wrath, by the doom invoked by a
father's curse, which they shared without discord.

Ismene

Through the city the cry of weeping; the walls
groan aloud; the plain that loved them groans
aloud. There abide for their descendants the

possessions for which their bitter fate was
paid, for which their strife arose, for which
they found the end of death.

Chorus

In bitterness of heart they shared their
possessions in equality: no blame from
friends has their arbitrator, Ares, impartial to both sides.

Antigone

By the stroke of the sword they are as they are By the stroke
of the sword there awaits them—what? The share in their
ancestral tomb, says someone.

Chorus

A shrill cry escorts them from their house, a cry heartrending,
a cry for its own griefs, its own woes, in anguish of mind with no thought of joy, weeping tears from a heart that breaks, for these our two princes.

Ismene

One may say over the bodies of this unhappy pair:
much they have done to their fellow citizens, and much to all the ranks of foreigners who died in this destructive war.

Chorus

Unlucky she that bore them above all womankind that are called by a mother's name. She took as husband her own child and bore these who have died their brotherly hands working each other's murder.

Antigone

Brotherly indeed in utter destruction in unkindly severance, in frantic strife, in the ending of their quarrel.

Chorus

Their enmity is ended, in the earth blood-drenched their life is mingled. Very brothers are they now.
Bitter the reconciler of their feud, stranger from over the sea, sped hither by the fire, whetted steel
A bitter and evil divider of possessions, Ares, who made their father's curse a thing of utter truth.

Ismene

They have their share, unhappy ones of Zeus given sorrows: beneath their bodies, earth in fathomless wealth shall lie.

Chorus (speaking over the bodies)

You who have made your race blossom with many woes: over you at last have cried the Curses their shrill lament, and the race is turned to confusion and rout. The trophy of Destruction stands at the gates where they were smitten and conqueror of the two the Spirit at last has come to rest.
*(The dirge proper. The sisters stand each at the head of one of the corpses.)*

Antigone
You smote and were smitten.

Ismene
You killed and were slain.

Antigone
By the spear you killed.

Ismene
By the spear you died.

Antigone
Wretched in acting.

Ismene
Wretched in suffering.

Antigone
Let the groans go forth.

Ismene
Let the tears fall

Antigone
You He in death—

Ismene
*HAVING killed—*

Antigone and Ismene
Woe, woe.

Antigone
My mind is distraught with groans.

Ismene
With groans my heart is full.

Antigone
Alas, alas, creature of tears.

Ismene
Alas, again, all-miserable.

Antigone
By a loving hand you died.

Ismene
And killed one that loved you.

Antigone
A double sorrow to relate.

Ismene
A double sorrow to see.

Antigone
Two sorrows hard by one another.

Ismene
Brother's sorrow close to brother's.

Chorus
O wretched Fate, giver of heaviness, awful shade of Oedipus, black Fury, verily a spirit mighty in strength!

Ismene and Antigone
*Woe, woe.*

Antigone
Evils unfit to look upon—

Ismene
have you shown after banishment.

Antigone
He came not back when he had slain

Ismene
This one saved, lost his own life.

Antigone
This one died—

Ismene
and killed the other.

Antigone
Race unhappy.

Ismene
Deed unhappy

Antigone
Grievous sorrows of kindred.

Ismene
Grievous, thrice grievous sorrow.

Chorus
O wretched Fate, giver of heaviness, awful shade of Oedipus, black Fury, verily a spirit mighty in strength.

Antigone
You have learned the lesson by experience.

Ismene
And you have learned it, no whit later.

Antigone
When you returned to the city—

Ismene
yes, to face him with your spear.

Antigone
Deadly to tell.

Ismene
Deadly to see.

Antigone
Pain—

Ismene
Ill

Antigone
To house and land—

Ismene
and most of all to me.

Antigone
O unhappy king of sorrow!

Ismene
O of all most rich in pain!

Antigone
Where shall we lay them in the earth?

Ismene
Where their honor is greatest,

Antigone
O brothers possessed by evil spirits, in doom—

Ismene
that will sleep by the side of their father to his hurt.

Herald
It is my duty to declare to you,
counselors of the people, the resolves
already taken and the present pleasure
of this Cadmaean city. . . .
Our Lord Eteocles for his loyalty
it is determined to bury in the earth
that he so loved. Fighting its enemies
he found his death here. In the sight
of his ancestral shrines he is pure and blameless
and died where young men die right honorably.
These are my instructions to communicate
with respect to him. His brother Polyneices,
or rather his dead body, you must cast out
unburied, for the dogs to drag and tear
as fits one who would have destroyed our country
had not some God proved obstacle to his spear.
Even in death he shall retain this guilt
against his Gods ancestral whom he dishonored
when he brought his foreign host here for invasion
and would have sacked the city. So it is resolved
that he shall have, as his penalty, a burial
granted dishonorably by the birds of the air
and that no raising of a mound by hand
attend him nor observance of keening dirge.
Unhonored shall his funeral be by friends.
This is the pleasure of the Cadmaean state.

Antigone
So I to the Cadmaean magistrates
declare: if no one else will dare to join me

in burying him, yet will I bury him
and take the danger on my head alone
when that is done. He is my brother. I
am not ashamed of this anarchic act
of disobedience to the city. Strange,
a strange thing is the common blood we spring from—
a mother wretched, a father doomed to evil.
Willingly then with one that would not will it,
live spirit with dead man in sisterhood
I shall bear my share. His flesh
the hollow-bellied wolves shall never taste of.
Let that be no one's "pleasure or decree."
His tomb and burying place I will contrive
though but a woman. In the bosom folds
of my linen robe I shall carry earth to him.
And I shall cover him: let no one determine
the contrary. Be of good cheer (TO HER SISTER)
I shall find means to bring my will to pass.

Herald
I forbid
this act, defiance of the city's pleasure.

Antigone
I forbid you your superfluous proclamations.

Herald
Harsh is the people now that danger's past.

Antigone
Harsh truly. But HE shall not go unburied.

Herald
Him the state hates, will you grace with a tomb?

Antigone
Long since the Gods determined of his honor.

Herald
Not till he cast in peril this land of ours.

Antigone
He suffered ill and gave back what he suffered.

Herald

This deed of his was aimed at all, not one.

Antigone

Last of the Gods Contention ends her tale. But I shall bury him: spare me long speech.

Herald

Have your own way: but I forbid the act.

Chorus

Alas, alas.
O high-vaunting, ruin to the race
fatal Furies, who have destroyed
the race of Oedipus so utterly—
What will happen me? What shall I do?
What shall I plan?
How shall I be so heartless,
not to mourn for you,
not to give escort to your funeral?
But I fear the dreadful authority
of the people: I am turned from my purpose.
(To the body of Eteocles)
Many mourners you shall win:
(To the body of Polyneices)
But this poor wretch unwept
save for his sister's single dirge
shall go his road. Who would yield
so much obedience as this?

(The Chorus divides in two.)

First Half-Chorus

Let the state do or not
what it will to the mourners of Polyneices.
We will go and bury him;
we will go as his escort.
This grief is common to the race
but now one way and now another
the city approves the path of justice.

Second Half Chorus

But we will go with the other, as the city
and Justice jointly approve.
For after the Blessed Ones and the strength of Zeus
he is the one who saved the city

from utter destruction, from being overwhelmed
by the wave of foreign invaders.

# Phoenician Women

## Euripides

### Introduction to the Phoenician Women

This is a translation of the play which came down to later antiquity as Euripides' *Phoenician Women,* a play first produced in one of the years 411–409 B.C. What it actually is, is that play, as added to by fourth-century producers. The play in its original form undoubtedly covered, in its episodic action and in its reminiscences of the past and prophecies for the future, more stages of the Oedipus legend than one would have thought a single play could hold. The producers improved on this situation. Their additions brought in everything really memorable in the dramatic tradition of Oedipus which Euripides had left out, drawing freely on earlier plays from the *Seven against Thebes* to the *Oedipus at Colonus.* (This last, of course, Euripides had been unable to draw on, as he died before it was produced.) They also went in for heightening the melodrama, which took some doing.

This has been recognized ever since Valckenaer's edition of 1755, and there are three long passages which modern critics are pretty well agreed in rejecting as the work of Euripides. The first two are easily recognized. One is the messenger's description of the Argive heroes (11.114–40). The second is the report of Eteocles' challenge, and the arming of the brothers for battle (11.1221–58). The reader of this translation will not be able to judge the linguistic points which furnish much of the evidence for setting them aside. But I think he can see the extent to which the first is extraneous. Euripides did as much as he wanted to with the Seven in lines 119–81. And the second passage is, among other things, a patchwork of bits from the *Children of Heracles.* These two I have bracketed, to warn the reader.

The third long interpolation begins at line 1582 and may include all the rest of the play.

It seems likely enough that besides the lyric lamentations there was some dialogue between Creon, Oedipus, and Antigone, pointing ahead to the next stages of the story. But the Creon-Oedipus-Antigone scene we have is certainly not the one Euripides wrote.

Note, for one thing, that Antigone is apparently planning both to go into exile, at once, with Oedipus and, in defiance of Creon, to bury Polyneices. This is impossible, but the author is simply assimilating his figure to both Sophoclean Antigones.

However, I am not as sure as some critics are that everything from line 1582 on is invented, or even everything in lines 1582–1709. I think what we may well have here is a Euripidean groundwork, once self-consistent, to which have been added references to those portions of the later story which Euripides chose to omit. (And of course this reworker probably had to do some deleting.) I am unable to disentangle the

Euripidean strands in what I suspect to be a collaboration rather than a simple insertion and have therefore bracketed nothing, simply warning the reader here.

Finally, it is obvious that a play which has been so freely handled in gross would probably be tinkered with in detail. This has happened; single lines and short passages have been inserted here and there. For example, line II looks very much as if someone wanted to get Creon into the program notes as soon as possible, even though this interrupts Jocasta's identification of herself. Lines 41–44 clear up the sort of point that might have bothered a prompter, and borrow from lines 95–98 to do it. Line 1225 is one of many lines of which the scholiast says, "In many copies this line does not occur." Line 1346 was originally omitted in four manuscripts.

In these, and all analogous cases, I have not troubled the reader with brackets. Editors disagree. However, I have tried to play fair and not to weave an inorganic line into context. Therefore even a reader confined to this translation can join centuries of scholars in spotting the inconsistencies and redundancies. However, he should remember that many of them may well be Euripides' own. Anyone who wishes to pursue these questions further might start with D. L. Page's *Actors' Interpolations in Extant Greek Tragedy* and the Preface to J. U. Powell's edition of this play.

The translation was made from Murray's Oxford text of 1909. The places where I have departed from his readings are these:

Line 22: †(obelus) βρέφος, manuscripts, Murray; λέχος Schoene, Powell.

Line 1533: ἐπὶ, manuscripts, Murray (who obelizes the passage); ἔπι "anonymus," quoted by Wecklein, Powell.

Line 1606: I read this as a single line, without the lacuna which Murray assumes.

Line 1740: I give this line to Oedipus, with the manuscripts and Powell, rather than to Antigone, with Murray (who had evidence from the scholiast).

## Characters

*Jocasta*
*Pedagogue*
*Antigone*
*Chorus of young women from Phoenicia*
*Polyneices*
*Eteocles*
*Creon*
*Teiresias*
*Menoeceus*
*Two Messengers*
*Oedipus*

## The Phoenician Women

SCENE: *Thebes, before the royal palace. Jocasta enters from its great central door.*

Jocasta

You who cut your way through heaven's stars,
riding the chariot with its welded gold,

Sun, with your swift mares whirling forth our light,
evil the shaft you sent to Thebes that day
when Cadmus came here, leaving Phoenicia's shore,
he who wed Cypris' child, Harmonia,
fathering Polydorus, who in turn
had Labdacus, they say, and he had Laius.
Now I am known as daughter of Menoeceus,
Creon my brother by the selfsame mother,
my name Jocasta, as my father gave it,
Laius my husband. When he still was childless
after long marriage with me in the palace,
he went to Phoebus asking and beseeching
that we might share male children for the house.
But he said, "Lord of Thebes and its famed horses,
sow not that furrow against divine decree.
For if you have a child, him you beget
shall kill you, and your house shall wade through blood."
But Laius, in his lust, and drunk beside,
begot a child on me, yet when he had,
knowing his sex was sin, as God had said it,
he gave the child to shepherds to expose
in Hera's field, high on Cithaeron's rock,
when he had pinned its ankles with sharp iron
(and this is why Greece called it Oedipus).
Then Polybus' herdsman-riders took the child
and brought it home and gave it to their mistress.
She took my labor's fruit to her own breast
and told her husband that it was her own.
When his red beard was growing, my young son,
who had guessed or heard the truth, set off to learn,
at Phoebus' house, his parents. So did Laius,
seeking to learn if the child he had exposed
were still alive. They met in middle journey
at the same spot in the split road of Phocis.
Then Laius' runner ordered him away:
"Stranger, yield place to princes." But he came on,
silent, in pride. So with their sharp-edged hooves
the mares of Laius bloodied up his feet.
And so—why give the detail of disaster?*
son slew his father, and he took the team
to give to Polybus, his foster parent.
When the Sphinx bore down our city with her raids,
my husband gone, Creon proclaimed my marriage:
whoever might guess the clever maiden's riddle,
to him I should be wed. And so it happened.
It was Oedipus, my son, who guessed her song.

So he became the ruler of this land
and got the scepter of this realm as prize.
The wretch, unknowing, wedded with his mother;
nor did she know she bedded with her son.
And to my son I bore two further sons,
Eteocles and mighty Polyneices,
and daughters two. Her father named Ismene
while I before had named Antigone.
When Oedipus learned I was his wife and mother,
he had endured all suffering, and he struck
with terrible gory wounding his own eyes,
bleeding the pupils with a golden brooch.
When his sons' beards had grown, they shut him up
behind the bolts that this fate might be forgotten
which needs too much intelligence to explain it.
There in the house he lives, and struck by fate
he calls unholy curses on his children. They shall divide this house with sharpened steel.
They were afraid that if they lived together
the gods might grant his prayers. So they agreed
that Polyneices should go, a willing exile,
while Eteocles stayed in this land and held the scepter,
to change though, year by year. Yet when Eteocles
sat safe on high, he would not leave the throne,
but keeps his brother exiled from this land.
He went to Argos, married Adrastus' daughter,
and brings the Argive force he has collected
against these very seven-gated walls,
seeking his share of the land, and his father's scepter.
I have persuaded son to come to son
under a truce before they take to arms.
I hope for peace. The messenger says he'll come.
0 Zeus who lives in heaven's shining folds
save me and let my sons be reconciled.
If you are wise you should not leave a mortal
constantly wretched throughout all of life.

*(Jocasta returns to the palace. Enter, from the palace, Antigone and the old Pedagogue.)*

Pedagogue

Antigone, flower of your father's house,
your mother has said you may leave the maiden's room
to climb the very steepest of the roof
and see the Argive army, as you asked.
But wait, that I may track the road before you
in case some citizen is in the way.
Then some slight blame would come on me the slave,
worse on your highness. Since I know, I'll tell
all that I saw and heard among the Argives

when I went there from here to make the truce
with your brother's army, and came back again.

*(The Pedagogue goes up the steps to the house roof)*

No citizen is near the house at all.
Try the old cedar ladder with your feet,
look over the plain and see by Ismenus' stream
and Dirce's spring how great the enemy host.

*(Antigone goes up the stairs and speaks at the top.)*

Antigone
Reach your old hand to my young one. Help me step
up from the stairs.

*Pedagogue (pulling her* up)
Take hold, my girl. You're here, but just in time.
The Argive army is moving, the companies part.

Antigone
Hecate, Leto's child! The lightning-shine
of bronze all over the plain!

Pedagogue
Polyneices comes no trifler to this land.
He brings the clamor of many horse and foot.

Antigone
The gates, and their locks! Are the brazen bolts
holding firm Amphion's wall of stone?

Pedagogue
Take heart, all's well and safe inside the city.
Look at the first man, if you want to mark him.

Antigone
Who is he with the crest of white
who comes at the head of the host and lightly shakes
the brazen shield on his arm?

Pedagogue
A captain, lady.

Antigone
Yes, but who, and whence?
Speak out his name, old man.

Pedagogue
He boasts his birth from Mycenae and he lives

by Lerna's waters, lord Hippomedon.

Antigone
How prideful, how hateful to see!
Like an earth-born giant hurling flame in a picture,
not like the race of day.

Pedagogue
Do you see the one who is crossing Dirce's stream?

Antigone
How strange, how strange his arms! And who is he?

Pedagogue
Tydeus, the warrior from far Aetolia.

Antigone
Is this the one who has married the very sister
of Polymerizes' bride?
How strange his arms, half-barbarous to see! *Pedagogue*
All the Aetolians carry such a shield
and hurl light lances so they hit the mark.

Antigone
Old man, how did you learn all this so well?

Pedagogue
I knew them, for I saw their arms before
when I went from here to there to make the truce
with your brother's army. I know them in their harness.

Antigone
Who comes by Zethus' tomb with falling curls,
a youth, and frightful to see?
Some captain, since an armed crowd follows on.

Pedagogue
Parthenopaeus, Atalanta's son.

Antigone
I hope that Artemis, ranging the hills with his mother,
strikes with her shaft and destroys him
who comes to plunder my town.

Pedagogue
I hope so, child. But the right is on their side.

And I am afraid the gods may see things clear.

Antigone

And where is he whom my selfsame mother bore to a painful fate?
Dear ancient, tell me, where is Polyneices?

Pedagogue

He stands with Adrastus, close by the maidens' tomb,
Niobe's seven daughters. You see him now?

Antigone

Not clearly, but enough to guess his shape.
Oh, could I run on my feet like a wind-swift cloud through the sky
to my own dear brother, and throw my arms round his neck,
poor exile—but how he shines in his golden arms
ablaze with the light of dawn.

Pedagogue

He is coming to this house, you may be glad.
Under a truce.

Antigone

But who comes here, old man?
Who mounts and drives a chariot of white?

Pedagogue

That is the prophet Amphiaraus, lady,
bringing the victims whose blood shall please this land.

Antigone

Seine, daughter of shining-girdled Sun,
you with your round gold light, how calm he comes,
how gently prods his horses!
—Where is the man who insulted us so fiercely?

Pedagogue

Capaneus? There he marks the approaches out,
takes the walls' measures up and down the towers.

Antigone

Nemesis, and you, deep thunder of Zeus,
and shining flare of the lightning, it is for you
to put his boasting to sleep.
He said he would bring the Theban girls
as slaves to Mycenaeans women,
would give them to Lerna's triple fount,

slaves to Poseidon's lover's waters.
Artemis, golden-locked, child of Zeus, may I never
endure that slavery.

Pedagogue

Child, back into the house, and stay inside
your maiden chamber. You have had the joy
of that desired sight you wished to see.
Noise in the city proves a crowd of women
is pressing toward the royal palace now.
The female sex is very quick to blame.
If one of them gets a little launching place,
far, far she drives. There seems to be some pleasure
for women in sick talk of one another.

*(Antigone and the Pedagogue go into the palace. Enter, from the side, the Chorus of Phoenician women.)*

Chorus

I came, I left the wave of Tyre
the island of Phoenicia,
as prize for Loxias, slave to Phoebus' house,
to rest by Parnassus' snowy ridge.
I came on a ship through the Ionians' sea,
over the fruitless plain,
though the west wind rushed from Sicily,
a beautiful blast from heaven.
Chosen most beautiful of my town,
an offering to Apollo,
I came to Cadmus' land, as I am Agent's kin,
sent to Laius' kindred towers.
I might, like the golden statue-girls,
have served Phoebus by now.
But Castalia's water is waiting still
to wet my hair for his service.

O rock that shines in the fire,
double gleam on the heights
where Dionysus dances,
and vine who distils the daily wealth,
the fruitful cluster of grapes,
holy cave of the serpent, mountain rocks
where the gods keep watch, O sacred mountain of snow,
may I, unfearing, dance the Immortal's dance
by Phoebus' central hollow with Dirce left behind.

Now before the walls
savage Ares comes

kindling the frame of death
for this city—may it not happen.
Shared are the griefs of friends,
shared; if she must suffer,
this seven-gated land, then does Phoenicia share it.
Common blood, common children,
through Io who wore the horns.
I also have my part in this.

A cloud about the town,
a close cloud of shields,
kindles the scheme of death.
Soon shall Ares know
that he brings to Oedipus' sons
the curse of the very Furies.
Ancestral Argos, I fear your strength,
and I fear the gods' part too.
For this man at arms
comes against our home with justice.

*(Enter, from the side, Polyneices, with drawn sword.)*

Polyneices

The warders' bolts have let me through the walls
with ease, and so I fear once in the net
I won't get out unbloodied. Thus I look
hither and yonder, watching for a trick.
My hand that holds this sword shall prove my courage.
  Ah, who is there? Or do I fear a noise?
All things seem terrible to those who dare
when they set foot upon the enemy's land.
I trust my mother, and I do not trust her
who brought me here under a pledge of truce.
Defense is close. The sacrificial hearths
are near, nor is the palace desolate.
I'll thrust my sword in the darkness of its case
and ask who are these women by the house.
  Ladies, what land was it you left to come
to our Hellenic halls?

Chorus

It was Phoenicia reared me. Agenor's grandsons
have sent me here a captive, prize for Phoebus.
And while the sons of Oedipus delayed
to send me on to Loxias' oracle
there came the Argives' war against this city.
Give answer in return, you who have come
to the gated fortress of the Theban land.

Polyneices

My father is Oedipus, Laius' son, my mother
Jocasta, daughter of Menoeceus.
The Theban people call me Polyneices.

Chorus

Kin of Agenor's children who are my lords,
who sent me here—.

Master, I fall on my knees,
the humble habit of home.
At last you have come to your father's land.
Queen, queen, come forth,
open the gates!
Mother who bore him, do you hear us now?
Why your delay in leaving the halls
and taking your son in your arms?

*(Enter Jocasta from the palace.)*

Jocasta

I heard your Phoenician cry,
girls, and my poor old feet,
trembling, have brought me out.
My child, my child, at last I see you again.
Embrace your mother's breast with your arms,
stretch forth your face and your dark curly hair,
to shadow my throat. Oh, oh, you have barely come,
unhoped for, unexpected, to your mother's arms.
What shall I say, how phrase the whole
delight in words and actions
that compasses me about.
If I dance in my joy shall I find the old delight?
Child, you went as an exile; your father's house
was left in desolation, your brother's doing.
But your own yearned after you
Thebes itself yearned.
And so I weep, and cut my whitened hair.
No longer, child, do I wear white robes,
I have changed to these dark gloomy rags.
And the old man in the house, the blind old man,
since the pair of you left the house,
clings to his weeping desire. He seeks the sword
for death by his own hand, he casts a noose
over the roof beams mourning his curse on his children.
He is hidden in darkness and steadily wails his woe.
And I hear that you have paired yourself in marriage,
the joy of making children.

In a stranger's house you have taken a stranger bride,
a curse to your mother and Laius who was of old.
Doom brought by your wedding.
I did not light your wedding torch
as a happy mother should.
Ismenus gave no water to the marriage;
your coming to your bride was never sung in Thebes.
May the cause of these sufferings perish, be it the steel
or strife, or your father, or a demon-rout
in Oedipus' house.
For all their grief has fallen upon me.

Chorus

Childbirth is terrible for womankind.
Therefore all women love their children so.

Polyneices

Mother, with reason, unreasoning have I come
among my enemies. But all men must still
love their own country. Who says something else
enjoys his talk while thinking far away.
I was so scared, had gone so far in fear
lest brother's craft might kill me on the way,
that through the town I came with sword in hand,
turning my face about. Just one thing helped,
the truce—and your own pledge which led me on
through the ancestral walls. I came in tears
seeing at last the halls and the gods' altars,
the playing fields that reared me, Dirce's spring,
which I have left unjustly and now live
in a stranger town, blurring my eyes with tears.
I come from grief and find you grief indeed.
Your hair is shorn; your garments are of black.
Alas, alas, my sorrows and myself!
Mother, how frightful is the strife of kindred,
and reconciling hard to bring about!
What does my father do within the house,
he who sees darkness? What of my two sisters,
do they, poor girls, lament my exile now?

Jocasta

Some god is ruining all of Oedipus' children.
The beginning was my bearing outside law.
It was wrong to marry your father and to have you.
But what of this? The god's will must be borne.
Still, I must ask you, fearing it may sting,

one question for whose answer I am yearning.

Polyneices

Ask openly, leave nothing out at all.
Your wish is mine, my mother.

Jocasta

So now I ask what first I wish to know.
What is it to lose your country—a great suffering?

Polyneices

The greatest, even worse than people say.

Jocasta

What is its nature? What so hard on exiles?

Polyneices

One thing is worst, a man cannot speak out.

Jocasta

But this is slavery, not to speak one's thought.

Polyneices

One must endure the unwisdom of one's masters.

Jocasta

This also is painful, to join with fools in folly.

Polyneices

One must be a slave, for gain, against one's nature.

Jocasta

The saying is that exiles feed on hopes.

Polyneices

Lovely to look at, but they do delay.

Jocasta

And doesn't time make clear that they are empty?

Polyneices

They have their charm in troubles.

Jocasta

How were you fed before your marriage fed you?

Polyneices
Sometimes I'd have a day's worth, sometimes not.

Jocasta
Your father's foreign friends, were they no help?

Polyneices
Hope to be rich! If you are not—no friends.

Jocasta
Your high birth brought you to no lordly height.

Polyneices
Want's the bad thing. My breeding did not feed me.

Jocasta
It seems one's country is the dearest thing.

Polyneices
You couldn't say in words how dear it is.

Jocasta
How did you get to Argos, and with what plan?

Polyneices
Apollo gave Adrastus a certain answer.

Jocasta
What sort? Why mention this? I cannot guess.

Polyneices
To marry his daughters to a boar and a lion.

Jocasta
What has my son to do with wild beasts' names?

Polyneices
I do not know. He was calling me to my fate.

Jocasta
For the god is wise. How did you meet your marriage?

Polyneices
It was night; I came upon Adrastus' portal.

Jocasta
A wandering exile, looking for a bed?

Polyneices
*Just* so—and then another exile came.

Jocasta
And who was he? Wretched as you, no doubt.

Polyneices
That Tydeus who is named as Oneness' son.

Jocasta
But why did Adrastus think you were those beasts?

Polyneices
Because we fought over the pallet there.

Jocasta
And then he understood the oracle?

Polyneices
And gave us two his daughters two to wed.

Jocasta
Were you happy or unhappy in these weddings?

Polyneices
Right to this day we have no fault to find.

Focasta
How did you lure the army to follow you here?

Polyneices
Adrastus promised his two sons-in-law,
Tydeus and me—Tydeus is now my kinsman—
that both should be brought home, but I the first.
So many Mycenaean chiefs are here
and many Danaans, doing me a favor
which hurts me, though I need it. My own town
I fight against. I call the gods to witness
against my will I fight my willing kindred.
But—you can possibly undo these troubles—
Mother, you reconcile these kindred-friends,
save you and me and the city from these sorrows.
This has been sung before, but I shall say it:

"Men honor property above all else;
it has the greatest power in human life."
And so I seek it with ten thousand spears.
A beggar is no nobleman at all.

Chorus
Here comes Eteocles to hold his parley.
Jocasta, as their mother, it's for you
to say the words to reconcile your sons.
*(Enter Eteocles.)*

Eteocles
Mother, I'm here. I came to do a favor
for you. Now what's to come? Let someone speak.
I have broken off my ambushing of chariots
about the walls that I might hear from you
that arbitration for which I have admitted
this one within the walls—at your persuasion.

Jocasta
Check for a moment. Swiftness brings not justice.
It is slow speech that brings the greatest wisdom.
Check your dread glare, the seething of your spirit.
It is not Gorgon's severed head you see;
you look upon your brother who has come.
And you, Polyneices, look upon your brother,
for if you look upon his face once more
you will speak better and will hear him better.
I want to give you both some good advice.
When friend falls out with friend and they come together
looking at one another, let them look
at that for which they came, forget old wrongs.
Son Polyneices, you may speak the first.
For you have come, and brought the Argive army,
as one who claims a wrong. Now may some god
be judge and reconciler of these griefs.

Polyneices
The word of truth is single in its nature;
and a just cause needs no interpreting.
It carries its own case. But the unjust argument
since it is sick, needs clever medicine.
I took good foresight for our father's house,
for him, and for myself, hoping to flee
those curses with which once our father cursed us.
So willingly myself I left this land,
leaving the rule to him for a year's circle,

so that I myself might take the rule in turn.
Thus we should not fall into hate and envy
doing and suffering evil—but that has happened.
For he who swore this, and called the gods to witness,
did nothing of what he promised and still holds
the tyranny and his share of my own house.
And now I am ready, if I get my own,
to send away the army from this land,
to take my own house for my proper turn,
and yield it back to him for equal time,
so not to plunder my fatherland nor besiege
her towers with the scaling ladder's steps.
But if I get not justice I shall try
to do just this. I call the gods to witness
I have done all in justice, now most unjustly
I am robbed of my fatherland, an offense to heaven.
The facts I've told you, Mother, without heaping
great twists of argument. The clever and the humble
alike can see that I have spoken right.

Chorus
I think, though I am not a Helen born,
that what you say is argued very well.

Eteocles
If all men saw the fair and wise the same
men would not have debaters' double strife.
But nothing is like or even among men
except the name they give—which is not the fact.
I'll speak to you, Mother, without concealment:
I'd go to the stars beyond the eastern sky
or under earth, if I could do one thing,
seize tyranny, the greatest of the gods.
I will not choose to give this good thing up
to any other, rather than keep it myself.
It's cowardice to let the big thing go
and settle for the smaller. Besides, I should be shamed
that he should come in arms and sack the land,
and so achieve his purpose. This would be for Thebes
real shame, if fearing spearmint from Mycenae
I yielded up my scepter for him to hold.
He should not seek his truce with arms in hand,
for argument can straighten out as much
as enemy steel can do.
If he will live here on some other terms,
he can. But what he asks I will not yield.

When I can rule should I become his slave?
So—on with fire, on with swords of war,
harness the horses, fill the plain with chariots,
knowing that I will never yield my rule.
If one must do a wrong, it's best to do it
pursuing power—otherwise, let's have virtue.

Chorus

It isn't right to speak so well of evil.
This is no good thing, but a bitterness to justice.

Jocasta

My son Eteocles, old age is not
a total misery. Experience helps.
Sometimes we can speak wiser than the young.
Why do you seek after the goddess Ambition?
The worst of all; this goddess is Injustice.
Often she comes to happy homes and cities,
and when she leaves, she has destroyed their owners,
she after whom you rave. It's better, child,
to honor Equality who ties friends to friends,
cities to cities, allies to allies.
For equality is stable among men.
If not, the lesser hates the greater force,
and so begins the day of enmity.
Equality set up men's weights and measures,
gave them their numbers. And night's sightless eye
equal divides with day the circling year.
While neither, yielding place, resents the other.
So sun and night are servants to mankind.
Yet you will not endure to hold your house
in even shares with him? Where's justice then?
Why do you honor so much tyrannical power
and think that unjust happiness is great?
It's fine to be looked up to? But it's empty.
You want to have much wealth within your halls,
much trouble with it?
And what is "much"? It's nothing but the name.
Sufficiency's enough for men of sense.
Men do not really own their private goods;
we simply care for things which are the gods',
and when they will, they take them back again.
Wealth is not steady; it is of a day.
Come, if I question you a double question,
whether you wish to rule, or to save the city,
will you choose to be its tyrant? But if he wins

and the Argive spear beats down the Theban lance,
then you will see this town of Thebes subdued
and many maidens taken off as slaves,
assaulted, ravished, by our enemies.
Truly the wealth which now you seek to have
will mean but grief for Thebes; you're too ambitious.
So much for you.
                    Your turn now, Polyneices:
ignorant favors has Adrastus done you,
and you have come in folly to sack your city.
Come, if you take this land—heaven forbid it—
by the gods, what trophies can you set to Zeus?
How start the sacrifice for your vanquished country,
and how inscribe your spoils at Inches' stream?
"Polyneices set these shields up to the gods
when he had fired Thebes?" Oh, never, Son,
be this, or such as this, your fame in Greece!
If you are worsted and his side has best,
how shall you go to Argos, leaving here
thousands of corpses? Some will surely say:
"Adrastus, what a wedding for your daughter!
For one girl's marriage we have been destroyed."
You are pursuing evils—one of two—
you will lose the Argives or fail in winning here.
Both of you, drop excess. When double folly
attacks one issue, this is worst of all.

Chorus
O gods, in some way yet avert these evils
and make the sons of Oedipus agree!

Eteocles
Mother, it's too late for talking, and this intermission time
has been wasted; your good purpose can accomplish nothing now.
For we cannot come to terms except as I have laid them down:
that I shall hold the scepter of power in this land.
Leave off your long advising, now Mother, let me be.
And *you—outside* these walls now, or surely you shall die.

Polyneices
What invulnerable someone will lay a sword on me
for slaughter and not bring away a murder for himself?

Eteocles
Near enough, he hasn't left you. Do you see these hands of mine?

Polyneices

Oh, I see you. Wealth's a coward and a thing that loves its life.

Eteocles

Then why come you with so many for a battle with a no one?

Polyneices

Oh, a prudent captain's better than a bad one in the war.

Eteocles

You can boast, when we've a truce that saves you from your death.

Polyneices

So can you. Again I'm claiming rule and sharing of this land.

Eteocles

No use to ask. My house shall still be ruled by none but me.

Polyneices

Holding more than is your sharing?

Eteocles

Yes. Now leave this land at once.

Polyneices

Altars of our fathers' worship—

Eteocles

which you come to plunder now

Polyneices

hear me!

Eteocles

Which of them will hear you when you fight your fatherland?

Polyneices

Temples of the gods who ride white horses—

Eteocles

and who hate you.

Polyneices

I am driven from my country—

Eteocles
for you came to ruin it.

Polyneices
wrongfully, O gods.

Eteocles
Don't call on these gods, but Mycenaeans!

Polyneices
Impious by nature!

Eteocles
Never have I been my country's foe.

Polyneices
who drive me off without my portion.

Eteocles
And I'll kill you yet, besides.

Polyneices
Oh, my father, hear my sorrow!

Eteocles
And he hears what you are doing.

Polyneices
and you, Mother!

Eteocles
It's indecent that you speak of her at all.

Polyneices
O my city!

Eteocles
Go to Argos, and call on Lerna's stream.

Polyneices
I'm going, never worry. Thank you, Mother.

Eteocles
Leave the land!

Polyneices
I am going, but our father, let me see him.

Eteocles
You shall not.

Polyneices
Or the girls our sisters.

Eteocles
Never shall you look on them again.

Polyneices (calling)
O my sisters!

Eteodes
Now why call them when you are their enemy?

Polyneices
Fare you very well, my mother.

Jocasta
Well, I suffer very much.

Polyneices
I'm no longer son of yours.

Jocasta
I was born for suffering.

Polyneices
For this man has done me insult.

Eteocles
And I stand insulted back.

Polyneices
Where'll you be before the towers?

Eteocles
And why should you ask that?

Polyneices
I shall stand against, to kill you.

Eteocles

I desire the selfsame thing.

Jocasta

Oh, woe is me, my children, what will you do?

Polyneices

You'll see.

Jocasta

Won't you flee your father's cursings?

Eteocles

Let the whole house fall to ruin.

Polyneices

Soon my bloody sword no longer shall be lazy in its sheath.
By the land herself who bore me and her gods I now do swear
that dishonored, badly treated, I am thrust outside the land
like a slave, as if I were not son of Oedipus, as he is.
0 my city, if you suffer, lay the blame on him, not me:
I attack against my will, I was thrust away unwilling.
Apollo of the roadways and rooftrees, fare you well,
and my friends of youth and statues of the gods we fed with honey.
I don't know if I can ever speak a word to you again.
But I still have hope that somehow if the gods are on my side
I shall kill him and be master of this our Theban land.

Eteocles

Leave this place; your name means "quarrel" and our father named you well.

*(Jocasta returns to the palace and Polyneices leaves.)*

Chorus

Tyrian Cadmus came to this land.
Here the heifer bent her legs and fell,
proved the oracle, told him here to build
his house on the fertile plain,
where comes the moisture of fair-flowing waters,
Dirce's water over the furrows green that take the seed,
where his mother bore Bacchus after her marriage with Zeus.
He was still a child when the twining ivy came,
green tendrils and all, to cover him over,
to be part of the Bacchic dances of Theban girls
and the women who call his name.

And there the bloody dragon was,
savage monster who guarded Ares' spring,

looked with his roving eyes on its running stream.
The beast was slain with a boulder
when Cadmus came seeking water of lustration,
and struck the bloody head with the blows of his monster-slaying arm,
sowing its teeth in the furrows deep, at unmothered Pallas' bidding.
Then earth sent up armed terror over its surface.
Iron-hearted slaughter sent them back again,
and their blood bedewed the land which had briefly showed them to the shining winds of heaven.

On you also I call, IoM's child,
Epaphus, son of our mother, and of Zeus,
—with foreign cry, with foreign prayers—
come, come to this land!
It was your descendants who founded it,
and the two-named goddesses own it, Korea and dear Demeter,
who is ruler of all, nurse of all, the earth.
Epaphus, send us the goddesses of the torch,
defend this land, for the gods all things are easy.

Eteocles (to an attendant)
Go, and bring here Creon, Menoeceus' son,
the brother of Jocasta, my own mother,
saying I would consult him on private matters
and state affairs before I go to war.
But he has saved your trouble; here he is.
For now I see him coming to my house.

*(Enter, from the side, Creon.)*

Creon
I've traveled far, trying to see you, King
Eteocles; round the Cadmean gates
and all their guards I went, to hunt you down.

Eteocles
Creon, be sure I wished to see you too.
I found the terms of peace from Polyneices,
when we discussed them, far from what we need.

Creon
I've heard that he desires more than Thebes,
trusting his new connection and his army.
But this we must leave hanging on the gods.
I've come to tell you what's immediate.

Eteocles
What's this? I do not know what you will tell.

Creon
We have a prisoner from the Argive side.

Eteocles
What does he say that's new from over there?

Creon
He says the Argive host will shortly circle,
armor and all, the old Cadmean town.

Eteocles
Then Cadmus' town must hurry out her arms.

Creon
But where? Are you too young to see what's needed?

Eteocles
Over the trenches, where they are to fight.

Creon
This land is few in numbers, they are many.

Eteocles
And well I know that they are bold—in speech.

Creon
Well, Argos has a swelling fame in Greece.

Eteocles
Fear not. I'll fill the plain up with their blood.

Creon
I hope so. But I see much labor here.

Eteocles
*So* I'll not coop my army within walls.

Creon
To take good counsel—this is victory.

Eteocles
You want that I should turn to other roads?

Creon
All of them, lest our fate depend on one.

Eteocles
Should we lay ambush and attack at night?

Creon
So, if you failed, you would come safe again.

Eteocles
Night holds all even, but favors more the daring.

Crean
It's dread to have ill luck under the darkness.

Eteocles
A spear-attack while they are at their dinner?

Creon
A brief surprise—but we need victory.

Eteocles
But Dirce's stream is deep for their retreat.

Creon
Nothing's as good as holding on to safety.

Eteocles
Suppose we rode against the Argive camp?

Creon
They're well walled in, with chariots around.

Eteocles
What shall I do? Give enemies the town?

Creon
No, but take counsel, though you are so clever.

Eteocles
And what forecounsel's cleverer than mine?

Creon
They say that seven men, as I have heard—

Eteocles
What's their assignment? This is a small force.

Creon
will lead their companies to assault the gates.

Eteocles
What shall we do? Not wait till I am helpless?

Creon
You also choose out seven for the gates.

Eteocles
To take command of troops, or fight alone?

Creon
With troops, when they have chosen out the best.

Eteocles
I see—to ward off scalings of the walls.

Creon
And choose lieutenants; one man can't see all.

Eteocles
Choosing for courage or for prudent minds?

Creon
Both. Neither's any good without the other.

Eteocles
So be it. To the seven-gated town
I'll go, and set the captains as you say
in even numbers against their enemies.
It would take long, long talk to give each name,
now while the enemy camps outside our walls.
But I will go, my arm shall not be idle.
I hope my brother may be my opponent,
that I may fight and take him with my spear
and kill him who came to sack my fatherland.
The marriage of Antigone, my sister,
and your son Daemon, will be your affair
if I should fail. Their earlier betrothal
I ratify, as I move off to war.
You are my mother's brother. I need not tell you
to care for her, for my sake and your own.
My father bears the weight of his own folly,
self-blinded. I won't praise this, and his curse
may kill his sons if it is brought to pass.

One thing we haven't done. We should find out
if seer Teiresias has some word for us.
I'll send your son Menoeceus after him,
the boy who has your father's name, to bring him.
With kindness will he come to speak to you,
but I have blamed his seercraft and he hates me.
I lay one charge on you, and on the city,
if our side wins, let never Polyneices
be buried here in Theban earth. If someone
tries burial, he must die, though he be dear.
So much to you. And now to my own followers:
bring out my arms and armor. To the fight
which lies before me now I go with Justice,
who will bring victory. And I pray to Prudence,
kindest of gods, that she will save this city.

*(Exit Eteocles.)*

Chorus

Ares, who brings us trouble, lover of blood and death,
why do you love them, why stand away from Bromides' feasts?
Never, when dances are fair and the girls are crowned,
do you loosen your locks and sing to the breath of the flute
which the Graces have given for dancing. No, you rouse the host,
the armed host of Argos against our Thebes with blood.
You dance first in the dance that knows no music.
Not when the tarsus whirls and the fawns are there
do you come to Ismenus' stream.
But with sound of chariots, clatter of bits and hooves,
you urge the Argives against our earth-sown race,
a dancing crowd in arms that swells with shields,
decked in bronze to batter our walls of stone.
Strife is a terrible god, she who has planned
these sufferings for our rulers, the Labdacid kings.
0 glade with the holy foliage, loved by the many beasts,
Artemis' own Cithaeron that wears the snow,
would you had never taken Jocasta's child
and brought to rearing Oedipus, child cast out of his house,
marked by the golden pins. And would that the winged maid,
the mountain portent of grief had never sung her songs,
the Sphinx whose music was no music at all,
who climbed over our walls with hoof and claw
and dragged our youth on high
to heaven's height untrodden, she whom Dades sent
against the people of Cadmus. And another evil strife,
the strife of Oedipus' children, comes on the town and its homes.
Evil is never good, nor are these lawless sons,
their mother's travail, their father's shame.

She came to her kinsman's bed .... .
[A few words are missing at the end of this antistrophe.]
Earth, you bore, you bore
—I heard the news in my foreign home, I heard it well—
the race that grew from the teeth of the crimson-crested monster,
Thebes' noblest shame.
And the sons of heaven they came to Harmonia's marriage,
the walls of Thebes they rose to Amphion's lyre,
midway between the streams
which pour their moisture over the rich green plain
from Dirce and Ismenus.
And Io, my horned mother, was also mother to kings of Thebes.
This city has shifted from one rule to another, but ever
has stood on high, decked with the crowns of war.

*(Enter the prophet Teiresias, led by his young daughter, accompanied by Menoeceus.)*

Teiresias

Now lead me on, my daughter. You're the eye
for my blind steps, as star is to a sailor.
Now set my path upon the level plain
and lead me lest I stumble. Your father's weak.
Guard my lot-tablets with your maiden hand
which on my holy seat of prophecy
I drew when I had marked the oracle-birds.
O young Menoeceus, Creon son, now tell me,
how far is still our journey to the town,
and to your father? My knees begin to buckle.
I've come so far I hardly can go on.

Creon

Take courage. You have come to harbor now,
among your friends. Now hold him up, my son.
Mule cars, and old men's feet, they need the help
of someone else's hand.

Teiresias

Ah, we are here. Why did you want me, Creon?

Creon

I've not forgotten. But collect your strength,
and draw your breath; forget your laboring road.

Teiresias

I am fatigued, since only yesterday
I came from labor for Erechtheus' sons.
There they had war against Eumolpus' spear,
and I gave Cecrops' children victory.

So, as you see, I wear a golden crown,
as first fruit of their plunder from the foe.

Creon

I'll take your crown of victory as an omen.
We're in mid-wave of danger, as you know,
Dana's sons against us, strife for Thebes.
Our king is gone, dressed in his warrior-arms,
against Mycenaeans force, Eteocles.
But he enjoined me to find out from you what
we should do in hope to save our city.

Teiresias

As far as he goes, I'd have locked my mouth,
withheld the oracles, but at your asking,
I'll tell you. Creon, the land has long been sick,
since Laius made a child against heaven's will,
and begot poor Oedipus, husband to his mother.
The bloody ruin of his peering eyes
is the gods' clever warning unto Greece.
And Oedipus' sons who tried to cloak this up
with passage of time, as if to escape the gods,
erred in their folly, since they gave their father
neither his rights nor freedom to depart.
And so they stung the wretch to savage anger.
Therefore he cursed them terribly indeed,
since he was ailing and, besides, dishonored.
What did I not do, what did I not say?
All the result was hatred from those sons.
Death by their own hands is upon them, Creon;
and many corpses fallen over corpses,
struck with both Argive and Cadmean shafts,
will give the Theban land a bitter mourning.
You, my poor city, will be buried with them,
if no one is persuaded by my words.
This would be best, that none of Oedipus' house,
live in the land as citizen or lord,
since the gods hound them on to spoil the state.
But since ;-he bad is stronger than the good
there is one other way to save the town.
But even for me it is not safe to say
that which is bitter to the man in power
who yet could save this city. Fare you well.
One among many, I will take what comes.
What else to do?

Creon
Stay here, old man.

Teiresias
Do not lay hands on me.

Creon
Now wait! Why flee?

Teiresias
Luck flees you, not myself.

Creon
Speak the salvation of the town and townsmen.

Teiresias
Now you may wish it; soon you'll wish it not.

Creon
I could not fail to wish my country's safety.

Teiresias
You really want to hear, and you are eager?

Creon
What should I be more earnest for than this?

Teiresias
Soon you will hear about my prophecies.
—But first there's something that I need to know.
Where is Menoeceus, he who brought me here?

Creon
He isn't far away, he's close to you.

Teiresias
Let him withdraw, far from my prophecies.

Creon
He is my son and will not talk at large.

Teiresias
You wish that I should speak while he is here?

Creon
Yes. He'll be glad to hear of what will save us.

Teiresias

Then shall you hear the way of prophecy,
what you must do to save the Theban town.
You must kill Menoeceus for his country's sake,
your child—since you yourself have asked your fate.

Creon

What are you saying? What's your word, old man?

Teiresias

Just what it is, and this you needs must do.

Creon

Oh, you have said much evil in short time.

Teiresias

Evil to you, great safety to your city.

Creon

I wasn't listening, I didn't hear. City, farewell.

Teiresias

This is no more the man he was. He dodges.

Creon

Go, and goodbye. I do not need your seer craft.

Teiresias

Das truth now died because you are unhappy?

Creon

Oh, by your knees and by your old man's beards—

Teiresias

Why fall before me? What you ask is ruin.

Creon

be quiet; don't reveal this to the town.

Teiresias

You tell me to do wrong; I won't keep quiet.

Creon

What will you do? You plan to kill my child?

Teiresias
Others must deal with action. I must speak.

Creon
Why is this curse on me, and on my son?

Teiresias
You are right to ask, and bring me to debate.
He must, in that chamber where the earth-born dragon
was born, the watcher over Dirce's streams,
be slaughtered, and so give libation blood
for Cadmus' crime, appeasing Ares' wrath,
who now takes vengeance for his dragon's death.
Do this, and Ares will be your ally.
If earth gets fruit for fruit, and human blood
for her own offspring, then this land shall be
friendly to you, she who sent up the crop
of golden-helmeted Sown Men. One of their race,
child of the dragon's jaws, must die this death.
You are the one survivor of the Sown,
pure-blooded, on both sides, you and your sons.
Daemons betrothal saves him from the slaughter.
For he is not unheeded, though still virgin.
This boy, who belongs to none but to the city,
if he should die, might save his fatherland,
make harsh homecoming for Adrastus and the Argives,
casting the dark of night upon their eyes,
and make Thebes famous. There you have your choice,
to save your city or to save your son.
Now you have all I know. Child, take me home.
A man's a fool to use the prophet's trade.
For if he happens to bring bitter news
he's hated by the men for whom he works;
and if he pities them and tells them lies
he wrongs the gods. No prophet but Apollo
should sing to men, for he has nought to fear.

*(Exeunt Teiresias and his daughter.)*

Chorus
Creon, why are you silent, holding your tongue?
But I myself am stricken and amazed.

Crean
What can one say? But my response is clear.
I'll never walk into such wretchedness
as to give my city the slaughter of my son.

It's part of human life to love one's children.
No one would give his own son up to death.
Let no one praise me who would kill my sons!
Though I, since I am in the prime of life,
am ready to die to set the country free.
Up, son, before the whole town learns of this,
pay no attention to these wanton boding,
fly quickly, get yourself outside this land.
For he will tell this to the chiefs and captains
making the rounds of the gates and their commanders.
If we anticipate him, you are safe.
If you come second, we're destroyed, you die.

Menoeceus
Where shall I flee, what city and what friend?

Creon
As far away from here as you can get.

Menoeceus
You'd better tell me where, and I will do it.

Creon
Go beyond Delphic—

Menoeceus
and where on beyond?

Creon
into Aetolia.

Menoeceus
And where after that?

Creon
Thesprotia's plain.

Menoeceus
Where holy Dodo stands?

Creon
Yes.

Menoeceus
What protection will that be for me?

Creon

The god will guide you.

Menoeceus

And for my supplies?

Creon

I'll give you gold.

Menoeceus

Thank you for that, my father.
Go get it then. I'll go to see your sister Jocasta, she who nursed me at her breast,
when my mother died and I was lefi an orphan.
I'll go to see her, and I'll save my life.
—Please hurry, Father, *you* don't want to keep me.

*(Exit Creon. Menoeceus addresses the Chorus.)*

Women, how well I've taken away his fear,
cheating with words, to get what I desire.
He'd steal me out, robbing the state of safety,
give me to cowardice. This can be forgiven
an ancient, but not pardoned in myself,
that I should so betray my fatherland.
Know well, I'm going, and I'll save the town,
and give my life to death to save the land.
How shameful if men who are not under omens,
and so constrained by heaven's necessity,
stand at their shields and do not shrink at death,
fighting before the towers for fatherland,
while I, betraying my father and my brother
and my own city, leave the land a coward.
Wherever I'd live, I'd show myself a weakling.
By Zeus, among the stars, and bloody Ares,
who set the sprouting offspring of this land
to be its rulers, I am going now.
I'll take my stand on the high battlements
over that precinct where the dragon lived,
there slay myself above its gloomy depths
that the seer spoke of; so I'll free the land.
I've said my say, and now I go to give
my city no mean gift. I'll cure this ailing land.
If every man would take what good he can
and give it to his city's common good,
cities would suffer less, be happy from now on.

*(Exit Menoeceus.)*

Chorus

You came, you came,

you winged thing, earth's offspring, monster's child,
to seize the sons of Cadmus.
Half a maiden, a fearful beast,
with roving wings and claws that fed on blood.
You who snatched the youths from Dirce's plain,
crying your Fury's shriek,
the song that knows no music,
you brought, you brought sorrows upon our land,
bloody ones—and bloody was the god
who brought these things about.
Mornings of the mothers,
mornings of the maidens,
filled our homes with grief.
Groan and cry ran back and forth
from one to another through the town,
and thunder groaned as they did
each time the winged bird seized one of the city's men.

In time there came
by Scythian sending Oedipus the wretched,
here to this land of Thebes.
Then were we glad, but later we grieved.
He conquered the riddle; poor wretch, he wed his mother.
De stained the town and through slaughter he came to strife,
casting the curse on his sons.
We praise him who goes,
we praise the man who is dying to save his land.
Groaning he leaves to Creon.
But the seven-gated town,
her he makes to conquer.
Pallas, make us mothers
of sons as good as this,
you who checked the dragon-blood,
by the rock you urged Cadmus to throw.
Yet from this saving came
a curse of God on this land, and slaughter with it.

Messenger

You there, whoever's watching at the gate,
open, and bring Jocasta from the house.
Open, I say! You've waited long, but now
come forth and hear, famed wife of Oedipus,
leaving your wailing and your tears of grief

*(Enter Jocasta from the palace.)*

Jocasta

Dear friend, you haven't come to tell disaster,
Eteocles' death, you who march by his shield,
constantly keeping off the enemy shafts.
What is the new word that you bring to me?
Is my son alive or dead? Now tell me true.

Messenger

De lives, so tremble not, that fear is gone.

Jocasta

Dow is the circuit of the seven gates?

Messenger

They stand unbroken,, the city is not plundered.

Jocasta

Were they endangered by the Argive spear?

Messenger

Right on the verge. But our Cadmean Ares
was stronger than the Mycenaean spear.

Jocasta

By the gods, tell one thing more! What do you know
of Polyneices? I care for his life too.

Messenger

Both of your sons are living to this moment.

Jocasta

God bless you! Dow, when you were sore besieged,
did you force back the Argives from the gates?
Tell me, that I may please the blind old man,
sitting inside, with news of the city's saving.

Messenger

When Creon's son, who died to save the city,
on the highest tower standing, had thrust his sword
through his own throat and saved this land of ours,
your son sent seven companies and their captains,
to the seven gates, to keep the Argives off.
Dorses against the horsemen did he set,
foot against infantry, so where the wall
was weak against assault, he guarded it.
From the high citadel we saw the host,

white-shielded men of Argos. They left Teumesus,
they rushed the ditch to set the town on fire.
Then the paean and the trumpet played together,
from there, and from our walls.
[Then first attacked were the Titian gates
by a company bristling with its thick-set shields.
Parthenopaeus led them, the huntress' child,
whose family sign was blazing on his shield,
Atalanta with her distant-ranging arrows
killing Adtolia's boar. Against the gate
of Foetus, came the man of sacrifice,
carrying victims on his car, no signs
of insolence on his shield. Wisely, his arms were blank.
Against the Ogygian gate the lord Dippomedon
came with a sign in middle of his shield,
the All-Seeing one, with eyes all over him,
some eyes that look forth as the stars come up,
others that hide among the setting stars,
and will look later when that man has died.
Against the next gate Tydeus took his stand.
He bore a lion's hide upon his shield
with bristling mane. And there Prometheus held
in his right hand the torch to burn the town.
Your Polyneices by the Gate of Springs
led on the war. Upon his shield the fillies
of Potniae raged and ran in panic-fear,
worked by the pivots near the handle-grip.
They did seem mad indeed.
And he who loves war even as Ares does
Capaneus led against the Electron gate.
The iron markings on his shield were these:
an earth-born giant carried on his shoulders
a whole town wrenched away from its foundations,
this to suggest what our town is to suffer.
Adrastus himself was at the seventh gate.
A hundred snakes were drawn upon his shield.
Yes, on his left arm rode the Argive Dydra.
And from our walls these snakes, with snatching jaws,
were taking Cadmus' children.
Now all these things I very well could see
since it was I who took the password round.]
So first we fought with arrows and throwing-spears
and far-flung slingshots and the crash of stones.
When we had won this fighting, Tydeus cried,
sudden, so did your son, "O Canaan men,
do not delay, before their shafts have stunned you,

Ell on the gates, light-armed, and horse, and chariots."
And when they heard the cry, no man was slow
and many fell, their heads bedaubed with blood.
On our side too you might have seen as many
dive to the plain and breathe their life away.
They dewed the dry earth with their streams of blood.
Then that Arcadian, Atalanta's son,
no Argive, rushed upon the gates a storm,
crying for double-axes and for fire,
meaning to overturn our town, but then
the sea-god's son, Periclymenus, cast a stone,
a wagon's load, from the high cornice-top,
broke up his yellow head, shattered the joining
of bone on bone; straightway his blushing face
blushed with his blood. De'll not return his life
to the queen of archers, his mother, the mountain maid.
When he had seen that this gate was defended,
your son went on, I followed, and I saw
Tydeus, and many shield him beside
dashing Aeolian spears against the front
of our defenses, so that many fled
the outer battlements. But against him too
your son brought on the crowd as a huntsman does
and saved the towers. So to the next gate
we hurried on, having stopped the sickness there.
How can I tell you how Capaneus raged?
For he came with the steps of a long ladder.
This was his boast, that Zeus's awful fire
could not hold him back from overturning the city.
He cried this as they threw the stones against him,
and still climbed up, cowered within his shield,
step after step, the ladder rung by rung.
Just as he reached the cornice of the wall
Zeus struck with lightning, and the earth rang out
so all were frightened. From the ladder he fell,
limbs whirling like a sling. His hair streamed high;
his blood fell down to earth. His arms and legs
went spinning like Ixion on his wheel.
De fell upon the ground a flaming corpse.
When Adrastus saw Zeus wads his enemy,
he drew his army back behind the ditch.
But we, who saw the omen on our side,
horsemen and chariots and foot rushed out.
We crashed our spears into their very center;
ruin was everywhere. They died, they fell
down from the chariot's rim. The wheels rebounded.

Axle on axle, corpse on corpse was heaped.
This land's defenses have been kept from ruin
this day. The gods must see if this our land
shall still be fortunate, for some god has saved her.

Chorus
Dow fair is victory! If the gods have still
a better plan, I'll hope for my own fortune.

Jocasta
The gods and fortune both have served us well.
My sons are alive. The country has escaped.
But Creon, he has reaped a mournful harvest,
who married me to Oedipus. Gone is his son:
good fortune for the town, a grief to him.
Go on and tell me what my son will do.

Messenger
Let be the rest. So far your fortune holds.

Jocasta
Suspicious sayings. This I'll not allow.

Messenger
What more do you want than to know your sons are saved?

Jocasta
To hear if I have happiness in the future.

Messenger
Let me go. Your son's near helper is not with him.

Jocasta
You hide some evil and cover it up in dark. *Messenger*
I would not add your sorrows to your gains.

Jocasta
You must, unless you fly away to heaven.

Messenger
Alas, why not have let me leave good news?
Why force me to die bad?
Your sons intend—Oh shamefulness of daring!—
a single combat, severed from the host.
[And they have said to Argives and Cadmeans
words which should never have been said at all.

Eteocles began. Digh on a tower,
he ordered that the army be called to silence
and said, "0 leaders of the land of Dellas,
lords of the Danaans, you who here have come,
and Cadmus' people, not for Polyneices
nor for myself should you exchange your lives.
For I myself, putting this danger off,
alone will join in battle with my brother.
If I kill him, I'll hold my house alone;
if I am worsted, to him alone I'll yield it.
Give up the fight, Argives, and leave the land;
of the Sown Men there are already dead enough.
So much he said, and your son Polyneices
straightway leapt up and praised what he had said.
And all the Argives shouted their approval,
and Cadmus' people, for they thought it just.
So truce was made. In no man's land the chiefs
took solemn oath they would abide by it.
Then did they cover their bodies with brazen arms,
the two young sons of the old Oedipus.
Their friends were dressing them. The Theban lords
saw to our captain, the Argive chefs the other.
Then they stood shining, and they had not paled.
And from about their friends came up to them,
cheered them with speech and said such words as this:
"Polyneices, now you can set up for Zeus
his triumph-statue and make Argos famed."
To Eteocles: "Now you are fighting for your city,
now if you conquer, you will hold the rule."
Such things they said, exhorting them to battle.
The seers slew sheep and marked the points of flame,
its cleavages, any damp signs of evil,
and that high shining which may have two meanings,
a mark of victory, or of the losing side.]
If you have help or any words of wisdom
or spells of incantation, go, hold back
your children from dread strife. The danger's great.
Your dreadful prize will only be your tears
if you should lose both sons this very day.

*(Exit the messenger.)*

Jocasta

My child Antigone, come outside the house.
No help for you in maidens' works and dances.
The gods have set it so. But those brave men
your brothers, who are rushing on their death,
you and your mother must keep from mutual murder.

*(Enter Antigone from the palace.)*

Antigone
Mother, what new terror for your own
do you cry out before the palace front?

Jocasta
Daughter, your brothers' lives are falling fast.

Antigone
What do you say?

Jocasta
They're set for single fight. *Antigone*
What will you tell me?

Jocasta
Hard words. Follow me.

Antigone
Where, as I leave my chamber?

Jocasta
To the armies.

Antigone
I fear the crowd.

Jocasta
Modesty will not help.

Antigone
What shall I do?

Jocasta
Undo your brothers' strife.

Antigone
But how?

Jocasta
Fostrate, with me, before them.

Antigone
Lead, Mother, to the plain. We can't delay.

Jocasta

Then hurry, hurry, daughter. If I catch them
before they hurl their spears, my life's in light.
But if they die, I'll lie with them in death.

*(Exeunt Jocasta and Antigone.)*

Chorus

Alas, alas, my shuddering heart!
Pity, pity goes through my flesh.
as I think of that wretched mother.
Which of her children will kill her child
—Oh, the sufferings, Zeus, Oh earth—
cutting his brother's throat, spilling his brother's breath?
and I, poor soul, which corpse shall I lament?
Woe, oh woe, twin beasts!
Bloody spirits, shaking the spear,
how soon they will work their murders!
Unhappy that ever they came to this duel.
With foreign failings I'll mourn the dead.
The fortune of death is near, the light will show what comes.
Murder the Furies have wrought is a fate beyond all fates.
But I see Creon coming to the house
with clouded face, and break off this lament.

*(Enter, from the side, Creon, and attendants carrying the body of Menoeceus.)*

Cram

What shall I do? And do my tears lament
myself, or this poor city, held in gloom
as if it traveled over Acheron.
My child has perished, dying for the land.
The name he leaves is noble, but sad for me.
Just now I took him from the dragon-rocks,
took in my arms my son who killed himself.
My whole house mourns. And I, in my old age,
I come for my old sister, Queen Jocasta,
to lay my son out for his funeral.
For to the dead we who are not yet dead
should pay respect, honoring the god below.

Chorus

Gone is your sister, Creon, from the house. And with her went the maid Antigone.

Creon

Where? And what trouble called them? Tell me now.

Chorus

She heard her sons were planning single fight
with spear and shield over the royal house.

Crean
What are you saying? This I had not heard,
since I was caring for my own son's corpse.

Chorus
Your sister left the house some time ago.
I think the mortal combat of those sons,
Oedipus' sons, is at an end by now.

Creon
Alas, indeed I see a sign of that.
The dark and scowling face of one who comes
to bring the news of everything that's happened.

*(Enter a messenger, from the side.)*

Messenger
Woe is me, how tell my story or the groaning that I bring?

Creon
We are ruined, I can tell it from the gloom with which you start.

Messenger
"Woe is me," I cry again, for the trouble I bring is great.

Creon
To be heaped upon the suffering we had suffered. What's your news?

Messenger
Creon, your sister's children are no longer in the light.

Creon
Alas!
Great is the sorrow you bring, for me and for the state.
O house of Oedipus, have you heard the news?
Your sons have perished, both in one disaster.

Chorus
The house might weep, if it could understand.

Creon
Alas, disaster, born of heavy fate!
Ah, for my sorrows, how I suffer now!

Messenger
Then do you know the further misery?

Creon
How could there be a worser fate than this?

Messenger
Your sister died along with her two sons.

Chorus
Lead off the wailing, batter your head in mourning
with your fair white arms!

Creon
Jocasta, what an ending to your life,
and to your marriage which that riddle made.
Tell me about the slaughter of the sons,
the working-out in fight of Oedipus' curse.

Messenger
You know our first good fortune before the towers,
for the girdle walls are not so far away
you couldn't see the things that happened there.
When they were ordered in their shining arms,
the two young sons of Oedipus the old,
they rose and went into the middle plain,
the two commanders, the pair of generals,
for the struggle of the single fight in arms.
Looking toward Argos Polyneices prayed,
"O lady Dera, yours I am, since wed
to Adrastus' child and living in your land.
Grant I may kill my brother, so my hand
show sign of victory, my opponent's blood."
De asked a shameful crown, his brother's death.
Tears came to many at fate's monstrosity.
Men slipped their eyes about among the crowd.
Eteocles prayed, looking toward the house
of golden-shielded Pallas, "Caughter of Zeus,
grant me to cast my spear in victory
against my brother's breast from this my arm,
to kill the one who comes to sack my land."
Then the Tyrrhenian trumpet-blast burst forth,
like fire, as the signal for the fight;
they ran a dreadful race at one another
and like wild boars that sharpen their savage teeth
drew close, both foaming slaver down their beards.
Both shook their spears, but drew within their shields
so that the steel might spend itself in vain.
If either saw the other's eye peer up

above the rim, he darted with his spear,
hoping to catch him quickly with its point.
But both were clever, peering through the shield-slits,
so neither's spear was any use at all.
We who were watching sweated more than they,
all fearful for our friends.
Eteocles slipped a little on a stone
that turned beneath his foot. One leg came out
around the shield; and Polyneices struck,
seeing the mark thus offered to his steel.
The Argive spear went cleanly through his calf
and all the Canaan army cried in joy.
And then Eteocles saw his brother's shoulder
bare in the struggle, and he struck at that.
Thebans rejoiced; the spearhead broke off short.
Dis spear no use, he fell back step by step,
then seized and hurled a rugged rock which broke
his brother's spear, so now on even terms
they stood, since neither had a lance in hand.
Then snatching at the handles of their swords
they came together, and they clashed their shields,
pushed back and forth, and frightful was the noise.
Eteocles, who'd been to Thessalian,
had learned and used a fine Thessalian trick.
De disentangled from their present struggle,
fell with his left foot back, watching his mark
in his foe's belly. Then he jumped ahead
on his right foot and struck him in the navel.
The sword went through and stuck right in the spine.
Stooped over his belly Polyneices falls
with gasps of blood. The victor stuck his sword
into the earth, began to strip his arms.
Not mindful of himself, only of that.
This was his finish. The other had some life left,
had kept his sword all through his painful fall,
scarcely he managed, but he thrust that sword,
he the first-fallen, through his brother's liver.
They bit the dust and lie near one another;
the two did not divide their heritage.

Chorus

O Oedipus, how much I mourn your woes.
It seems a god has now fulfilled your curse.

Messenger

Hear now the woe that followed upon these.

Just as her fallen children left this life
their mother came upon them in her haste,
she in her hurry, with her daughter too.
And when she saw them with their mortal wounds,
she groaned, "0 children, I bring help too late."
Falling upon her children, each in turn,
she wept, she mourned them, all her wasted nursing.
Their sister at her side like a warrior's helper
cried, "0 supporters of our mother's age,
you have betrayed my marriage, dearest brothers."
Eteocles' hard dying breath was coming
out from his chest, and yet he heard his mother,
laid his damp hand on hers. He could not speak.
But tears fell from his eyes in sign of love.
The other had breath, and looking toward his sister
and his old mother, Polyneices said:
"Mother, we're dead. I pity you indeed,
and this my sister and my brother corpse,
my friend turned enemy, but still my friend.
Mother, and you, my sister, bury me
in my own land. Persuade the angry state
to grant me this much of my father's soil,
though I got not our house. Close up my eyes,
Mother," he said, and put her hand upon them.
"Farewell, the darkness now is closing in."
So both together breathed out their sad lives.
But their mother, when she looked on this disaster
snatched a sword off the corpses and she did
a dreadful deed. Straight through her neck she drove
the steel. So now she lies among her own.
In death her arms are cast about them both.
Then did the people rush to strife of words,
we claiming that my master won the day,
and they the other. The captains quarreled too.
Some claimed that Polyneices' spear struck first,
the others that dead men have no victory.
Meanwhile, Antigone had left the armies.
They rushed for weapons, but by prudent forethought
the Theban host had halted under arms.
So we fell on them not yet in their armor,
swooping upon the Argive host in haste.
No one withstood us, they fled, and filled the plain.
Blood flowed from myriad corpses slain by spears.
When we had conquered, some set up for Zeus
his trophy-statue, others stripped the corpses
and sent the shields as spoil within the walls.

And others, with Antigone, bring the dead
so their own friends may give them mourning here.
Of these sad contests, some have ended well
for this our city, others ill indeed.

*(Exit the messenger. Enter Antigone with attendants bearing the bodies of the brothers and Jocasta.)*

Chorus

No longer for hearing alone
is the city's grief You may see
the three dead on their way
move to the palace, they who found
together their darkened end.

Antigone

No veil now covers the curls on my delicate cheek,
nor in maiden shame have I hidden the blush on my face,
I come as a bacchant, celebrating death.
I have thrown the veil from my hair, my saffron robe hangs loose.
I bring on the dead with my groans.
O Polyneices, you followed your quarreling name.
Woe it was for Thebes; and your strife which was more than strife,
but ended as murder on murder has brought the end
of Oedipus' house in blood.
What singer, what singers, O house,
shall I call for this song of grief,
I who bring three kindred bloodily dead,
mother and children, the Fury's delight?
Celight of her who has ruined the house entire,
Oedipus' house; and the ruin began
when he griddled the riddling song
of the singing Sphinx and slew her dead.

O Father, woe for you!
What Greek or foreign man of a noble race
in the course of our brief day's life
has suffered so many griefs so clear to see?

My poor self, how my song rings out!
What bird that sits in the oak or the high twigs of the olive
will join my lamenting, alone, without my mother,
helping the song of my grief.
Woe for the failings with which I mourn,
I who shall live my life alone
among my falling tears.

On which of them first shall I cast my shorn-off hair?
On my mother's breasts where I drew my milk,

or the horrible wounds of my brethren?
Oh, oh, come forth from the house,
with your blinded face,
old father Oedipus, show your wretched age,
you who drag out long life
there in the house after casting the dark on your eyes.

*(Enter, from the palace, Oedipus.)*

Oedipus

Why have you brought me forth to the light,
dragging my blindness along on a stick,
with your pitiful tears, from my bed in the dark,
a gray, invisible ghost of the air, a corpse, a flying dream?

Antigone

You must hear the telling of dreadful news.
Father, your sons are dead.
And so is the wife who tended and guided your stumbling steps,
O Father, woe is me.

Oedipus

Woe for my frightful griefs. One must moan, one must cry aloud.
Three lives gone! My child,
how did they leave the light, what was the fate that fell?

Antigone

Not in reproach do I say it, nor glad at your grief,
but in simple sorrow: the avenging power of your curse,
heavy with swords and fire and wicked fighting, fell,
Father, on your sons.

Oedipus

Alas!

Antigone

Why this lament?

Oedipus

My children!

Antigone

You are in grief
But, Father, if you could see the chariot of the sun
and cast your eyes on these corpses!

Oedipus

It's clear what disaster came on my sons.

But what doom struck down my wife?

Antigone
She showed all men her groaning tears.
She went to her sons as a suppliant, to adjure them by her breast.
Wielding their spears in war with each other,
their mother she found them like lions wild.
There in the flowering meadow, beside Electra's gate,
they were fighting and wounded; already the blood
was running to make them cold.
Hades' libation, which Ares grants.
So taking the bronze-hammered sword from the dead,
she plunged it in flesh, and in grief for her sons,
she fell on her sons.
The god who brought this about
has brought together all of these griefs for our house,
Father, in one short day.

Chorus
This day has started very many sorrows
for Oedipus' house. May later life be better!

Creon
Cease from your mourning. Now it is the time
to think of burial. Oedipus, hear this speech:
Eteocles, your son, gave me the rule
over this land, and made that rule the dowry
for Daemon's marriage with Antigone.
I will not let you live here any more,
for clearly has Teiresias said that never,
while you are here, can the city prosper well.
So, on your way! This proclamation comes
not as an insult, nor am I your enemy.
I simply fear that the Avengers who pursue you
may yet do damage to our fatherland.

Oedipus
O fate, you bred me wretched from the start,
for suffering, if ever mortal was.
Before I came to light from my mother's womb
Apollo prophesied that I, the unborn,
should kill my father—suffering indeed.
Once I was born, the father who begot me,
counting me as his enemy, tried to kill me
since he must die through me, and so he sent me,
still a breast-loving baby, to be food

for the wild beasts.
There was I saved. Cithaeron, you should sink
in the deathless chasms of the underworld,
you who did not destroy me, but your spirit
gave me in servitude to Polybus.
So when, ill-fated, I had killed my father,
I came into my wretched mother's bed
and begot brothers whom I now have killed,
passing on to my children Laius' curse.
For I am not so foolish in my nature
as to do what I did to my eyes, and to their lives,
if it were not some god who had contrived it.
Well, what's to do now with my wretched self?
Who is to guide the blind man? She who's dead?
Full well I know, were she alive, she would.
Or my good pair of sons? They are no more.
Am I still young enough to make my living?
From what? Creon, why kill me utterly?
For you are killing me if you cast me out.
Yet I'll not clutch your knees and prove a coward.
Even in misery, I won't betray my birth.

Creon

It is well thought of not to grasp my knees;
I could not let you live within this land.
Now, of these dead, the one must straight be taken
into the house. The other, he who came
to sack his fatherland with alien help,
that Polyneices do you cast unburied
beyond the boundaries of his fatherland.
And this shall be proclaimed to all the Thebans:
"Whoever lays a wreath upon this corpse
or buries him, shall find reward in death.
Leave him unwept, unburied, food for the birds."
And you, Antigone, leave your triple dirge
and come within the house. For one more day
you shall be maiden, but tomorrow Daemon
and marriage are for you.

Antigone

Father, what wretchedness is on us now!
I mourn for you still more than for the dead.
For yours is not mixed grief heavy and light;
but you are perfect in your misery.
But you, new ruler, I would ask you this:
Why wrong my father, sending him from the land?

Why lay down laws against this pitiful corpse?

Creon
Eteocles' this decision, and not mine.

Antigone
Senseless. And you a fool to follow it.

Creon
Is it not right to do what is commanded?

Antigone
Not when wrong deeds are wickedly laid down.

Creon
Is it not right to give him to the dogs?

Antigone
The punishment you seek is not the law's.

Creon
It is, for a foe who should have been our friend.

Antigone
Therefore he yielded up his life to fortune.

Creon
And therefore let him yield his burial.

Antigone
What wrong, if you should give him his share of earth?

Creon
Be sure, this man is going to lie unburied.

Antigone
Then I shall bury him, though the state forbids.

Creon
Then will you bury yourself close by that corpse.

Antigone
It's glorious that two friends should lie together.

Creon
Lay hold on her and take her to the house.

Antigone
Oh no! I will not loose my hold on him.

Creon
The gods' these judgments, and not yours, my girl.

Antigone
And it is not judged right to assault a corpse.

Creon
No one shall lay the damp dust over him.

Antigone
They must. I pray it for Jocasta's sake.

Creon
You work in vain. You cannot get your wish.

Antigone
At least allow me but to bathe his body.

Creon
This too shall be forbidden by the state.

Antigone
But then to bandage up his savage wounds.

Creon
There is no tendency you may give this corpse.

Antigone
O dearest, but at least I kiss your mouth.

Creon
Con't mar your marriage with these lamentations.

Antigone
Do you think that living I will wed your son?

Creon
You'll be forced to it. What refuge from his bed?

Antigone
That night will make me one with the Canards.

Creon (to Oedipus)
Do you see the daring of her insolence?

Anqone
Let the steel know. My oath is by the sword.

Crean
Why do you wish so to avoid this marriage?

Antigone
I'll go to exile with my wretched father.

Creon
You show nobility, as well as folly.

Antigone
And know you well that I will die with him.

Creon
Go! You'll not kill my son. Now leave the land.

*(Exit Creon into the palace.)*

Oedipus
Caughter, I praise your loving zeal for me.

Antigone
How could I marry and send you alone to exile?

Oedipus
Stay and be happy. I will bear my woes.

Antigone
But you are blind. Who'll care for you, my father?

Oedipus
Where fate decides it I will fall and lie.

Antigone
Ah, where is Oedipus and his famous riddle?

Oedipus
Perished. One day, my fortune and my fall.

Antigone
Should I not have some part in all your troubles?

Oedipus
Exile with a blind father is disgrace.

Antigone
Not for the dutiful. Then it is an honor.

Oedipus
Now lead me forward, that I may touch your mother.

Antigone
There. Lay your hand upon your aged dear.

Oedipus
O Mother, O unhappy wife of mine!

Antigone
She lies there piteous, having suffered all.

Oedipus
Where is Eteocles' corpse, and Polyneices'?

Antigone
Dere lie they, stretched out close to one another.

Oedipus
Put my unseeing hand upon their faces.

Antigone
There. Lay your hand upon your sons in death.

Oedipus
O dear dead sons, unhappy as your father!

Antigone
O Polyneices, dearest name to me.

Oedipus
Now Loxias' doom is working to its end.

Antigone
What is it? Further woes on top of woes?

Oedipus
That, wandering, I shall die on Attic soil.

Antigone
Where? Which of Athens' forts will shelter you?

Oedipus
It will be Colonus, where the horse-god lives.
But come, help your blind father on his way,
since you are eager to be exiled with me.

Antigone
On to our exile. Father, stretch out your hand.
I help your steps as the wind helps on the ship.

Oedipus
I come, I come.
Oh my poor child, now lead me.

Antigone
I do, I do, most wretched I, of all the girls of Thebes.

Oedipus
Where shall I set my old foot?
Daughter, give me my staff.

*Antigone*
This way, this way, with me.
Like this, like this, your feet.
Your strength is like a dream.

Oedipus
Oh you, Oh you, who are driving an ancient man
in exile from his land.
What terrible things I have suffered!

Antigone
Why of your suffering speak? Justice regards not the wicked.
She gives no prizes for folly.

Oedipus
And I am the one who reached the heights of song.
When I found out the maiden's riddle, no fool was I.

Antigone
You go back to the Sphinx, and our shame.
Stop speaking of past good fortune.
There awaits you pitiful suffering
and, somewhere, an exile's death.

And I leave tears for the girls my friends
as I part from my fatherland
to wander, unmaidened.

Oedipus
Alas for your honest heart!

Antigone
It will give me fame as great as my father's sorrows.
I mourn for your wrongs, and for those which are done my brother,
who goes from the house a corpse to lie unburied.
Father, even if I must die,
in secret I'll bury that body.

Oedipus
Return again to your friends!

Antigone
My own laments are enough.

Oedipus
You can pray to the holy altars.

Antigone
They have had enough of my troubles.

Oedipus
Then go to Bacchus' shrine in the hills
where none but the Maenads are!

Antigone
To go where once I went
in Theban fawnskin clad,
and danced in Semite's holy choir!
It would be no grace I should do the gods.

Oedipus
You that live in my ancestral Thebes, behold this Oedipus,
him who knew the famous riddles and who was a man most great.
It was I alone put down the murdering power of the Sphinx.
Now it's I who go dishonored in sad exile from the land.
Yet why do I lament these things and mourn for them in vain?
The constraint the gods lay on us we mortals all must bear.

Chorus
O great Victory, stay with me all my life.
Nor cease to give me crowns!

# Oedipus

## Seneca

### Characters

OEDIPUS, king of Thebes
JOCASTA, queen of Thebes
CREON, brother of Jocasta
TIRESIAS, a blind prophet
MANTO, daughter of *Tiresias*
OLD MAN, messenger from Corinth
PHORBAS, former shepherd of King Laius
MESSENGER
CHORUS of Theban Elders

OEDIPUS: Rising resignedly through smears of grey,
the sun slinks back to drive the dark away.
To houses stricken with this ravenous plague
it brings a lurid light:
each dawn uncovers wreckage from last night.
Who would want to be a king, I ask—
horrors heaped behind a grinning mask!
Rocks that jut out into the open sea
are drubbed by breakers on the quietest day,
vulnerable and naked as a king
daily exposed to every passing thing.
I shunned the scepter that my sire would leave me.
Exiled and bold, without a care to grieve me,
I wandered; and—I swear it by the sky!—
blindly stumbled into royalty.
Oh God, unspeakable the things I fear—
by my own hand somehow to kill my sire,
or so the Delphic oracle gives out.
And something even worse is hinted at

than murdering my father—some vile curse
too foul to speak of. Phoebus in my eyes
flashes the bed where my own father lies!
This threatening image made me leave the place.
My life at home was innocent, I say;
my effort was forever to obey
the laws of Nature. But when what you fear
is so enormous, though it may appear
impossible, you shudder all the time:
*Can I, could I commit this dreadful crime?*
Yes, Fate's concocting something just for me,
now, now this instant!
                    How can this not be,
when right and left my kinsmen are mown down?
Some special hell's reserved for me alone.
The city crumbles—fodder fresh at hand
for Death's forever hungry maw. I stand
safe and sound as far as I can see,
but still a doomed man, still Apollo's prey,
marked by the aura of foreboding fate:
the very life I've lived pollutes the state.
We burn with fever, but no breezes cool
our faces, and the August sun adds fuel
to feed the summer's flames. The streams dry up
and the thin grass grows colorless with drought.
Dirce's depleted, Ismenus so low
that through its sluggish waters bare banks show.
Down a dark sky the sun's pale sister slinks;
daylight dwindles to a feeble wink.
Even on clear nights, no stars appear;
a black miasma shrouds the atmosphere.
Heaven's happy houses, palaces of gods,
look dim, diminished. Grain within the pod
nods its golden top, then dries and dies.
No group's immune from such calamities:
all ages and both sexes are cut down.
The dreadful plague joins babies and. old men,
parents and children. A shared funeral pyre
is common: for each family, one fire.
Few are the survivors left to mourn;
most of them are ash within the urn.
All funeral rites now are abbreviated.
Who's left to weep? The city's decimated.
The monstrousness of what's befallen us
keeps us from weeping. Tears are little use
when a bewildered father lifts his son

onto the pyre. The mother, crazed, brings one,
then scurries back again to fetch another
for the same flames that just consumed his brother.
Lamentations may be at their height;
they're interrupted as fresh griefs break out.
Pyres people have reserved for their own use
are loaded with another family's corpse.
Fire is precious now, so people steal it.
Shame? In our wretchedness we do not feel it.
We lack the graves to cover up the bones.
Fire is sufficient—yet it hardly burns
more than a fraction truly through and through.
Earth is lacking, timber's lacking too
for mounds and pyres. And no prayer or skill
can help the sick; the healers too fall ill.
I kneel in supplication. Let me die
before this town collapses utterly!
Let me not be the last to linger on,
let not the final funeral be mine!
Oh savage gods, oh Fate on your black throne,
does death say no to me and me alone,
that death so greedy for my countrymen?
Oh, leave this place polluted by your past!
Death is your legacy, a single vast
infection stretching up into the sky!
Oh sinister sojourner! Who but I
visited you upon this wretched town?
Years ago I should have left for home.

JOCASTA: Oedipus, why lament so wretchedly?
It would be kinglier, if you ask me,
to stand firm, look your problems in the eye.
As the state of things gets slippery,
all the more firm should your comportment be.
It's hardly brave to turn your back on fate.

OEDIPUS: The charge of cowardice is far-fetched, remote;
our royal nature knows no pangs or qualms.
Should bristling Mars be facing me in arms,
I'd be audacious, I would fight back
even at giants leading the attack.
The Sphinx, that riddling monster, I defied,
who wove the web where many others died.
I faced that prophet with her bloody gums
and stood my ground—ground that was white with bones!
When from the cliff's edge she loomed over me,

already slavering for her future prey,
her wings were poised for flight, her tensile tail
a waiting whiplash. Fearful, all in all!
And yet I posed my riddle. Next, a shriek—
and her impatient claws ripped at the rock
and not my entrails. But that tangled mess,
her dark enigma, I solved nonetheless
*(Aside) [Some editors give the following brief speech to Jocasta.]*
What foolishness, the death you now implore!
It would have been appropriate before.
You killed the Sphinx, this scepter is your meed:
But still she fights against me! Even dead,
she drags the city down with her to hell.
One way remains; Phoebus alone can tell.

CHORUS: People are dying all over the city.
Empty fields. Where are the farmers?
This is how it used to be:
Theban armies galloping East
to pitch their tents in the land of dawn
saw the Arabs rich with spices,
Parthians who shot behind their backs;
got as far as the Red Sea
where hot sun burns the natives brown.
Our forebears were unconquered people;
we are dying. Savage doom
grinds us down. Every hour
a fresh procession moves along,
slowly shuffling toward Death.
Mournful parade, marking time:
seven gates gaping are too narrow
for travelers flocking toward the tomb.
For the sad survivors, gridlock!
Funeral blocks funeral.
First to fall sick were sleepy sheep:
poisonous pasturage they cropped.
Hand held high for the fatal blow
stands the priest; the gold-horned bull
slowly sinks. The neck-gash gapes
under the massive ax's blow;
but not by blood the steel is stained.
Black pus oozes from the wound.
The horse collapses on the track;
off his side the rider tumbles.
Abandoned cattle lie down to die.
Herds are shrinking, bulls are sick,

shepherds fail their feeble flocks,
dying leave livestock doomed to die.
No longer do wolves frighten deer;
lions' roars dwindle into whimpers.
Stored-up viper venom dries,
clots, so serpents choke and strangle.
Boughs of trees no longer pour
shadows onto bluish hills;
arable land turns hard and dry;
grapevines no longer droop with fruit.
All's plague-stricken, all's plague-sickened:
the plague lays waste to everything.
A mob of Furies, torches smoking,
has smashed the gates of the world below.
Hell's hot river, flowing fire,
changes course and waters us.
Dank Death opens wide his jaws,
spreads his wings. The ferryman
poles his boat on the murky stream—
tough old man, but his arms are weary,
so many victims to row over.
They say the mastiff Cerberus
has broken loose and haunts the living.
Earth herself's been heard to howl;
hypertrophied phantoms stalk
our woodlands, where the trembling trees
shake down snow from their branches.
The river Dirce's gummed with blood;
hounds are heard to bay by moonlight.
Worse than death, new forms of dying!
Heavy languor weighs the limbs,
faces flush, a rash breaks out,
heads are scorched by burning fever,
cheeks swell with a flux of blood,
ears are ringing, blackish bile
drains through nostrils, ruptures veins.
Guts are wrung by a rattling retch.
They hug cold stones against their chests.
A gleam of freedom for the sick
when the nurse feetfirst is carted out:
they rush to fountains, scarf down water.
Over the altars sufferers sprawl
to pray for death—the kindest gods
may grant so much. Shrines are piled high
with offerings not to please the gods
but to allay their endless hunger.

OEDIPUS: Who is that approaching hastily?
The noble Creon, so it seems to me,
or my sick spirit spins some fantasy.

CHORUS: Creon! The answer to the city's prayer.

OEDIPUS: I shudder, wondering which way Fate will steer.
My shaky mood could waver either way.
When joys and griefs so close together lie,
the mind is doubtful. How much should one see?
How much is best to know? I'm dubious.
Brother-in-law, do you bring help to us?
Let me hear it now, if there's good news!

CREON: The answer's tangled and ambiguous.

OEDIPUS: Half-hearted help in time of suffering
is no help.

CREON: But god's words are riddling.

OEDIPUS: Speak! I can deal with ambiguity.
Solving riddles is my specialty.

CREON: Laius's murder—such is god's command—
must be avenged by exile from our land;
only then can skies turned clear once more
give us our fill of unpolluted air.

OEDIPUS: Who was our great king's killer? Answer me!
Whom Phoebus named—he pays the penalty.

CREON: May I make bold to speak of things so vile
to sight and hearing that my guts congeal,
my limbs go numb?
All reverence, I trod
into the holy precinct of the god
and raised my pious hands in ritual prayer.
Parnassus' peaks responded with a roar!
Apollo's laurel shook as in a gale,
and the Castalian springs stood stony-still.
The wild-haired priestess, in the grip of god,
shrieked out supernaturally loud:
Kind stars will shine on Thebes once more;
First show this regicide the door!
King-killer, your identity

Apollo knows, and perfectly.
Short-lived will all your triumph be
And war will be your legacy
To the same city whence you came,
And to the sons you leave behind,
Mother-lover, doomed and blind.

OEDIPUS: What heaven now is urging me to do
was owed to Laius' ashes long ago,
to shield his scepter from all insolence.
Kings must look out for kings—it's common sense
to fear the living and ignore the dead.

CREON: But greater fears thrust piety aside.

OEDIPUS: What fear absolved you from such pious debts?

CREON: It was the baleful Sphinx and all her threats.

OEDIPUS: Let that old crime be expiated now!
Whatever god is good to us below—
Jupiter, who celestial laws ordains; I
Phoebus Apollo, whose bright beauty shines,
who rules by revolution twelve great signs;
night-wandering Phoebe, sun's fair sister moon;
and in his roving chariot Neptune;
and you, Lord Pluto, guardian of night,
whose dwelling places only lack for light,
listen! May he who cut King Laius down
no shelter find in countryside or town.
Disgraced by incest and its tainted brood,
may he trudge an exile's weary road,
may he slay his own father! That's my curse,
the very fate I've fled. What could be worse?
By both my kingdoms—present, past—I swear
he will find no forgiveness anywhere!
By my childhood faith I swear it too;
and, father Neptune, let me mention you,
who wash my Corinth with your double tide.
Apollo, witness all that I've just said.
So may my father end his days in peace,
and Merope know only his embrace.
Nothing can free the culprit from my grip!
But where did the appalling crime take place?
He fell—in battle? Or into a trap?

CREON: He was en route to the Castalian wood.
Overgrown and dark with leaves, the road
divides into three branches on the plain.
One leads to Phocis, town the god of wine
favors. Twin-peaked Parnassus from that place
gently rises into heaven's space;
next toward the Isthmus and its double sea
the second goes; and then, meanderingly,
the third through fields and valleys takes its course
and finally arrives at Elis' source,
a chilly stream. Here, unsuspecting, he
was set upon by robbers suddenly.
They were armed, and no one saw the crime.
Aha! Tiresias, in the nick of time!
Trembling and slow, yet summoned here by god,
by his daughter Manto he is led.

OEDIPUS: Please, confidant of gods, Apollo's friend:
name the victim whom the gods demand!

TIRESIAS: Sire, if I crave delays, if my tongue's slow,
let not this come as a surprise to you.
Much truth lies hidden from a sightless man.
But since both god and country spur me on,
I follow. Let us pick the Fates apart!
If warm blood only flowed into my heart,
then from my breast Apollo could have spoken.
Well then! Drive to the altar an unbroken
heifer, and a bull of gleaming white.
My daughter, who supplies your father's sight,
describe each step of the prophetic rite.

MANTO: A perfect victim waits for sacrifice.

TIRESIAS: Then call upon the gods with reverent voice
and sprinkle incense on the altars now.
Heap it high!

MANTO: What you command, I do.

TIRESIAS: And are there flames now to devour their prey?

MANTO: A light flashed suddenly, then died away.

TIRESIAS: But did the flame seem steadfast, bright, and clear?
Did it point straight upward in the air

unfolding its high crest, or did it falter,
so murky smoke wound all about the altar?

MANTO: As Iris makes her many colors one,
yet separate, when she brings in the rain,
curving her bow across a thunderhead,
so you would hesitate to name this shade.
The flame was many-faced and mutable:
deep blue with orange patches for a while,
then red as blood, then blackness. Finally
it snuffed Out to invisibility.
But now the angry flame is splitting—see!—
the sparks of sacred fire shun one another.
Father, as I stare at it, I shudder!
The wine's poured out and turns at once to blood;
thick smoke enwraps the king's head like a shroud
and, denser by the minute, blocks his sight
as a dark cloud effaces wan daylight.
Father, what does this mean?

TIRESIAS: I stand amazed
Confusion tugs my reeling mind both ways.
What shall I say? The signs are bad, not good,
but too obscure to be well understood.
The gods—who like to make their anger clear-
are undecided now, it would appear;
their wish is both to threaten and conceal.
Shame for some unknown cause is what they feel.
Drive bullocks to the altar speedily!
Do they allow rough handling placidly?

MANTO: Head held high, the bull was facing East,
then shrank in terror from the sun's bright face.

TIRESIAS: How many blows are needed for the kill?

MANTO: The heifer shoved herself against the steel
and thus with but a single blow she fell.
The bull, though twice struck, wanders here and there,
bleeding his listless soul into thin air.

TIRESIAS: Does the blood spurt from just one narrow cut
or from a larger wound ooze slowly out?

MANTO: From the wide chasm of its cloven breast,
a rapid flood of gore streams from one beast.

The other's wound, though deep, is nearly dry;
the blood runs backward, spilling out through eye
and mouth.

TIRESIAS: Ill-omened sacrifice of dread!
Describe the entrails now to me instead.

MANTO: Father! The entrails are not gently shaking,
but with a violence that sets me quaking,
splashed with fresh blood. The heart lies deep within;
rot and infection run through every vein.
The one-lobed liver oozes with black bile,
and—for a single ruler this bodes ill—
identically bulging twin heads grow,
on both of them transparent membranes through
which things best hidden are allowed to show.
Sturdy and thick, the side that means bad luck
has seven veins. A ridge that runs, oblique,
behind these, blocks them. Everything is wrong!
The organs lie where none of them belong.
On the right-hand side a lung lies bleeding,
unable to expand enough for breathing;
on the left side no heart, a gaping hole,
no soft-stretched membrane covering it all.
Anarchic creature, lawless in the womb!
And where does this protuberance come from?
Oh, monstrous! In this virgin animal
a fetus grows—deformed, unnatural,
ectopic pregnancy! With a bawling moan
it tries to urge its twitching limbs along.
All the entrails are stained with lurid gore.
Carcasses heave, straining to rise once more;
a disemboweled bullock tries to wound
the priest! I let the guts fall to the ground.
This growl you hear, now rising to a roar:
fire, altar, hearth are giving voice to fear!

OEDIPUS: Tell me the worst. I am prepared to hear
instructions from portents truly dire.
Somehow disasters often calm one's thought.

TIRESIAS: You'll wish woes back whose remedies you sought!

OEDIPUS: Tell me—the gods want me to know it too—
someone is stained with regicide, but who?

TIRESIAS: Nor birds that slice the sky in airy flight
nor sacrificial guts can drag to light
the buried name. We'll find some other way:
from gloomy shores unvisited by day
summon the king, who, freed for this from hell,
his murderer's identity will tell.
We'll unseal Hades, and the shades we'll ask
to rise from death and help.
Whose is this task?
Not yours; for royalty it is profane
to glimpse that kingdom where the dead souls reign.

OEDIPUS: Creon, successor to my kingdom, who
is better suited to this task than you?

TIRESIAS: Then let the people roar their Bacchic hymn
while we approach Death's kingdom dark and dim.

CHORUS: Tie back your flowing hair with ivy bands
and grasp the thyrsus in your soft white hands.

Here, come here, heavenly brightness.
Bacchus, come! Thebes implores you.
Toward us turn your fresh face,
radiant beauty! Conquer clouds,
hungry Fate, threats of doom.
Wreathe your head with spring flowers,
Eastern veils, ivy berries;
toss your hair, then twist it back.
For fear of furious Juno once
long ago you changed your shape,
dressed as a girl with golden hair,
a sash around your saffron gown,
and ever since you've sighed for softness,
long loose robes flowing down.
Easterners who drink the Ganges,
Northerners who break the ice
of Araxes saw you seated,
long-robed lions close beside you,
in your chariot of gold.
Disreputable old Silenus
trails behind you on a donkey;
ivy frames his flabby face.
His followers begin to dance!
Wild feet stamping to the beat,
Bassarids prance along behind you,

mountaintop to mountaintop,
till the women of this town
suddenly behold a Maenad,
holy fawnskin wrapped around her,
brandishing the Bacchic wand.
Frenzied women tear their hair;
then Pentheus is ripped apart,
the spell is broken. Did this happen?
Glossy Bacchus' foster mother,
Ino, wreathed with rings of sea nymphs,
lives in caves beneath the ocean;
a brand-new boy-child rules the waves,
divine Palaemon, Bacchus' cousin.
Tyrrhenian troops kidnapped you,
but Nereus soothed the swelling seas,
Turned blue depths to verdant meadows.
Plane trees put out bright green foliage,
Apollo's laurel flourishes,
loud birds chatter in the branches.
Around the oars ivy clings;
around the mast grapevines twine.
At the prow a lion roars;
at the stern a tiger crouches.
Into the sea the pirates dive.
Once in the water, transformation!
Their arms drop off; chests and bellies
meet in the middle, merge to one;
from their flanks wee hands dangle;
curved backs slide into the water;
tails like crescents slice the sea.
A school of dolphins swims after the fleet.
In Lydia the Pactolus
river's rich waves carry you
past burning banks in a float of gold.
Massagetes who drink milk and blood
unstring their bows, lay down their arrows.
Lands of Lycurgus who wields the ax
have also known the power of Bacchus.
The Zalaces know when he passes
as do tribes of wind-blown nomads
washed in the waters of cold Maeotis
and those beneath Arcadian stars.
Scattered Gelonians he has tamed;
he has disarmed the Amazons!
Their faces fell; they bit the dust,
laid down their arrows on the ground,

and metamorphosed into Maenads.
Then Pentheus was torn asunder;
holy Cithaeron ran with blood;
into the woods the women fled.
And in his stepmother's despite,
Argos also worships Bacchus.
Naxos, jewel of the Aegean,
bestowed a virgin bride on him,
a better husband than her first,
that cruel deserter Theseus.
From the rocks wine spouted forth;
rivulets crisscrossed the meadows;
earth drank deep of sweetest liquors.
Snowy milk gushed in radiant streams
and old wine steeped in Lesbian thyme.
To highest heaven they lead the bride.
Long-haired Apollo chants the hymn;
twin Cupids twirl the wedding torches;
his fiery weapons Jupiter
lays down, abjures the thunderbolt
at Bacchus's epiphany.
While the bright stars run in their courses,
while river Ocean rings the globe,
while the full moon collects her fires,
while the Morning Star predicts each dawn,
while the Great Bear hangs over the sea,
we shall worship, worship Bacchus
of the clear and shining face!

OEDIPUS: You're horrified—I see it in your eyes.
Still, tell us whom god says to sacrifice.

CREON: What you command fear bids me to withhold.

OEDIPUS: Even if our town's disaster leaves you cold,
think of the fortunes of those kin to you!

CREON: Avid your hunger for such knowledge *now*,
but you will come to rue the things you know.

OEDIPUS: So ignorance of all catastrophe
and ostrich tactics are a remedy?

CREON: With such a bitter pill, who'd want a cure?

OEDIPUS: Say what you know! Or else you can be sure,

taught by tortures: kings' wrath reaches far.

CREON: Kings come to hate words they themselves have bidden.

OEDIPUS: Unless your words uncover what is hidden,
the underworld will soon receive your ghost!

CREON: Is staying silent too much to request?

OEDIPUS: Too much free speech spells danger for a king,
yet silence is still deadlier a thing.

CREON: Silence being criminal, what can a man do?

OEDIPUS: The man who will not speak subverts the law.

CREON: Well, let me speak. The words are wrung from me;
I beg that you will hear them patiently.

OEDIPUS: Who's forced to speak should pay no penalty.

CREON: A somber grove of trees stands far from town
near Dirce's valley; rivulets run down.
One cypress, loftiest in all that place,
clasps the whole forest in its green embrace;
like open arms an ancient oak holds out
its great curved branches, riddled now with rot.
Great chunks of one long years have nibbled at;
another's crooked, split clear to the root.
In this place bitter-berried laurels grow,
and slender linden trees, and myrtle too;
alders whose timber sails the seven seas
and knotty pine exposed to every breeze.
Amidst all these trees, an enormous one
shades the smaller saplings from the sun.
Its giant branches, spreading far and wide,
furnish a kind of fort for all the wood.
Beneath this tree, untouched by light of day,
an icy river wends its sluggish way.
Spongy swamps are everywhere about.
When the old priest approached this gloomy spot
forever veiled in its peculiar night,
a ditch was swiftly dug, and glowing coals
flung into it (snatched first from funerals).
The priest, now garbed in a funereal gown,
takes a branch and waves it up and down.

Cloaked in deep mourning, the old man moves on;
his inky robes are trailing on the ground,
his white hair tied with sprigs of deadly yew.
Black-fleeced sheep and oxen of dark hue
are dragged away. The fed flames leap and thrive
as in their ghastly fire the victims writhe.
Dead spirits and their king the priest invokes
first; then the keeper of Lake Lethe's lock;
chants magic spells; and, foaming at the mouth,
repeats a charm that has the power to soothe
or to compel the shades that flit about.
Next upon the altar he pours out
blood; burns whole victims; fills the trench with gore.
Then a stream of snowy milk he pours
and, with his left hand, wine; and calls again
upon the spirits in a wilder tone.
Hecate's hounds were howling, and the sound
three times made the whole valley floor resound.
"They hear me!" cries the priest. "What I have said
has burst blind Chaos and released the dead."
The whole wood cringed; its leaves stood up like hair.
Stout oaks split open, forests quaked with fear,
the earth shrank back and gave a dreadful groan.
Indignant at this breach of Acheron,
or else travailing to give passage to
the dead, she shrieked, all barriers burst through!
Or triple Cerberus it might have been,
angrily worrying his massive chain.
Then earth yawned. An enormous gulf spread wide.
And I beheld the shadowy pools inside,
and pallid gods of quintessential night.
My thick blood clotted in my veins with fright
as troops of savage creatures leaped out, stood
in arms before me—that whole snaky brood
of brothers sprung once from the dragon's teeth.
Then grim Erinys and blind Fury shrieked,
and Horror, and whatever teeming forms
in such eternal darkness breed by swarms—
hair-tearing Grief, and Sickness, her poor head
scarcely upright; Old Age, and looming Dread;
and hungry Plague, who gobbles nations up.
At such a spectacle our spirits stop.
Even the girl, who from her father knew
such necromancy, was astonished too.
But her undaunted sire Tiresias
summoned the bloodless throng of ghosts to us.

Like clouds they float, and the fresh air drink in.
More than the leaves of autumn whirling down,
more than spring flowers massed in fullest bloom
among which a great globe of bees appears,
more than the waves that wash Ionian shores,
more than the birds that, fleeing winter chills,
crisscross the skies, exchanging snow for Nile's
warm waters—far more numerous than all
these were the ghosts responsive to his call.
Trembling, they flock where shade is to be found.
Zethus first emerges from the ground,
clutching a fierce bull by the horns. And then,
a lyre in his left hand, comes Amphion,
the sweetness of whose melodies split stone.
Then Niobe, safe now among her sons,
with haughty gaze re-counts her ghostly brood;
then Agave, a far worse mother, mad
and raving still. Along with her she brings
the Maenad troops who tore apart the king.
And mutilated Pentheus follows them,
still furiously angry, threatening doom.
Repeatedly called forth, a certain shade
far from the others lifts his guilty head
and tries to hide. The priest renews his pleas
and finally we glimpse the hidden face—
Laius! I shudder at the very sound.
The sight was fearful: blood was all around,
his filthy hair was matted in a mass. He raged at us:
"Oh Cadmus' horrid house,
ever rejoicing to shed kindred blood,
brandish your thyrsus, savage your own brood
sooner than commit what is the true
desire of every man in Thebes to do—
sleep with his mother! Not heavenly wrath, my town,
no, nothing but your own crimes drags you down!
You suffer—not from stormwinds from the south,
nor from earth parched by a destructive drought,
but from your king, who bought his reign with blood
and occupies the bed his father should—
appalling offspring of the monstrous womb
that bore him first, then swelled again by him.
Returning to the source from which he'd come,
he did a deed that even wild beasts shun,
himself begetting brothers of his own—
a knottier tangle than the Sphinx by far!
You wield that blood-stained scepter; I, your sire,

still unavenged, will haunt you everywhere.
Fury as bridesmaid keeps me company—
her hissing whiplash cracks resoundingly.
Your whole incestuous household I'll lay low,
plotting violence for its overthrow.
So take your king and fling him far from here,
an exile, to whatever land can bear
his poisoned presence. Once he leaves this place,
it will recapture springtime's verdant grace,
life-giving air we'll once again breathe deep
as in the forests beauty wakes from sleep.
Plague, death, destruction, labor, waste, and pain,
exiled with him, will never come again.
And even as he hastens to find ways
of quick escaping, I'll concoct delays.
With nothing but a staff to guide each step,
a wavering path of blackness he shall grope.
You Theban elders, exile is for you
to force on him; I'll darken his sky too."

OEDIPUS: My arms and legs, my bones begin to freeze—
I've done the dreaded deed. Or so he says;
yet Merope, still Polybus's spouse,
rinses the stain of incest from my house,
and Polybus is living! So you see
the crime of murder can't be laid on me.
From either charge each parent clears my name,
from murder, incest—no room's left for crime.
All Thebans mourned their good king Laius' loss
long before I set foot in this place.
A god is angry, or the old priest lies—
no, you're conspiring right under my nose.
The prophet blames the gods for my disgrace
and meanwhile plots for you to take my place.

CREON: And see my sister driven from the throne?
If kinship's sacred bonds were, on their own,
not strong enough to hold me safely here,
then fortune's pinnacle of sheer desire
would scare me off. But you must prudently
lay down this burden, let yourself go free.
Retire from kingship, and be more secure
henceforth living in a humbler sphere.

OEDIPUS: Resign the kingship—that's what you advise?

CREON: Advice is for those who still have a choice.
For you no way is open but your fate.

OEDIPUS: It never fails! Those hungry to be great
praise leisure and repose and moderation
as if these never masked a man's ambition.

CREON: So all my years of loyalty to you prove nothing?

OEDIPUS: Loyalty helps traitors too!

CREON: I'm free of royal burdens, yet to me
things royalty delights in wend their way.
Crowds of people mill about my gate,
and not a single day succeeds to night
that lacks in a munificent selection
of tokens of your powerful affection.
Rich food and clothing, every kind of aid—
with such fine fortune, what else could I need?

OEDIPUS: The thing you lack. There are no bounds for greed.

CREON: Condemned, defenseless, then, am I to fall?

OEDIPUS: But did you show regard for me at all,
you and Tiresias listen to my side?
I'm guilty—no! I follow where you lead.

CREON: And if I'm innocent?

OEDIPUS: You might as well
learn now—kings fear whatever's possible
as well as what is certain.
CREON: Any king
frightened by phantoms merits the real thing.

OEDIPUS: But once he is set free, the guilty man
responds with hatred. Kill him if you can.

CREON: And so breed hatred.

OEDIPUS: Who's afraid of hate
fails to see fear guards the royal gate.

CREON: Harsh rulers with fierce scepters in their hand
fear those they terrorize; don't understand

the way fears haunt us, always coming back.

OEDIPUS: Shut up the miscreant in a hollow rock!
And guard him there with vigilance, while I
go to the palace, seat of royalty.

CHORUS: Oedipus, you are not to blame,
but ancient grudges of the gods
against the house of Labdacus.
Castalia's grove was kind to Cadmus,
Dirce's stream cooled colonists
out of the East, when Agenor's son,
tired of tracking Jupiter's
thieveries throughout the world,
rested, trembling, beneath our trees,
kowtowing to the kidnapper.
Apollo's advice to him: Forever
follow the path of a straying heifer
never broken to yoke or plough.
But giving up the chase, he named
our race for that unlucky creature.
From that time on our land has teemed
with monsters. In valleys vipers rise
higher than oaks and pine trees, hissing,
dark blue heads above the treetops,
bodies stretched along the ground.
Or boiling with its bloody breed,
Earth spills over with men in arms.
Horns and trumpets bray for battle,
new lips and tongues are put to use
first to utter a battle cry.
The fields are full of kindred folk.
Worthy of the seed they spring from,
their lives last a single day:
after the morning star they rise,
before the evening star they fall.
Mother Earth shuddered at such creation,
feared her bellicose new brood
until the generation gave
away, and Earth saw her offspring—
bodies now—back in her bosom.
May the civil strife be done with!
May Thebes know no other battles!
And Actaeon, Cadmus' grandson—
his own forehead sprouted horns,
as pursued by his own hounds

headlong over woods and mountains
fled Actaeon, swiftly, swiftly,
crashing through groves, over boulders,
trembling at fluttering feather lures,
escaping snares he'd set himself.
In a peaceful mountain pool
finally he saw himself—
saw the antlers, saw the face
of an animal, in that same
tranquil pool where the goddess
savage in her chastity
had bathed her gleaming arms and legs.

OEDIPUS: Worries and fears are spinning in my head.
Through no one's deed but mine is Laius dead,
or so the gods of heaven and hell proclaim.
And yet my mind feels guiltless all the same.
Better than the gods know me, I know
myself. Yet memory yields up this dim clue:
a man my staff has struck ... and down he goes,
given over to the gods below,
but not before he shoulders me aside
(he older and I younger): "Off the road!"
All this was not nearby but far away,
near Phocis, where the road divides in three.
*(Enter* JOCASTA; OEDIPUS *addresses her)*
Wife and companion, answer this for me.
When Laius died, how old a man was he?
Bowed down by years of age, or in his prime?

JOCASTA: Between the two, yet near the older time.

OEDIPUS: And did great throngs cling closely to his side?

JOCASTA: Many of them mistook the path and strayed;
a faithful few contrived to keep close by.

OEDIPUS: Of those good friends, did no one die but he?

JOCASTA: One gave his life through faith and loyalty.

OEDIPUS: *(Aside)* Now I have him! Number, place agree-
but tell me when.

JOCASTA: Ten harvests have gone by.
*(Enter* OLD MAN)

OLD MAN: Sire, Corinth's people call upon you now
to rule them. Death has laid your father low.

OEDIPUS: Fortune's attacking me from every side!
Tell me exactly how Polybus died.

OLD MAN: His aged spirit drifted off in dreams.

OEDIPUS: My father was not murdered then, it seems.
Clean hands I now raise heavenward, and swear
they're free at last of any libelous smear.
Yet of my fears the greater part remain.

OLD MAN: Such cares will vanish once you're on the throne.

OEDIPUS: My father's kingdom willingly I take;
the image of my mother makes me quake.

OLD MAN: You fear the mother who so anxiously
awaits your coming?

OEDIPUS : Out of piety.
OLD MAN: And leave her widowed and abandoned?

OEDIPUS: There
you touch upon the very thing I fear.

OLD MAN: This buried fear that tortures you must be
spoken! No secret will leak out through me.

OEDIPUS: Warned by the Delphic Oracle, I dread
to pollute my mother's marriage bed.

OLD MAN: Reject such fears—they never can come true.
Merope did not give birth to you.

OEDIPUS: I was adopted? What good could this do?

OLD MAN: The sons of kings keep watch on loyalty.

OEDIPUS: How did you learn my secret history?

OLD MAN: These very hands passed you, an infant, on
to her who gave you birth.

OEDIPUS: My mother's son

you handed to her? Who gave me to you?

OLD MAN: A shepherd in high Mount Cithaeron's snow.

OEDIPUS: That wild place? What brought you there that day?

OLD MAN: A herdsman follows livestock as they stray.

OEDIPUS: Now name whatever marks you know I bear.

OLD MAN: Your feet were pierced with iron. From that scar
and the resulting swelling, you are lame;
the wound that makes you limp gave you your name.

OEDIPUS: And who was he—for I still want to know—
who gave my person as a gift to you?

OLD MAN: The royal herdsman, under whom a whole
flock of minor shepherds served as well.

OEDIPUS: His name?

OLD MAN: An old man's early memory grows
faint and flabby, fading with disuse.

OEDIPUS: But could you recognize the fellow's face?

OLD MAN: Perhaps I might. What's buried in the space
of bygone years some little mark can show.

OEDIPUS: Then towards the altars all our herds must go
together with their shepherds—quickly, too.
The leaders of each flock—slaves, call them out!

OLD MAN: Whether the cause is chance or foresight, let
those things stay hidden which have seen no light
for many years! We seek to lay truth bare,
but often what we find is sheer despair.

OEDIPUS: What evil worse than this is there to fear?

OLD MAN: Terrible woe, of that you can be sure.
The people's welfare and the king's meet here
in equal balance. Don't touch either one;
leave fate unchallenged to unfold alone.

OEDIPUS: I'd never meddle when the state's serene;
if anarchy's at hand, I intervene.

OLD MAN: What more than royal blood can tempt you so?
Beware; the parentage you learn, you'll rue.

OEDIPUS: Whoever I may be, I need to know!
Here comes old Phorbas, weighted down with years:
King Laius' flocks were all once in his care.
*(To* OLD MAN*)*
Are they familiar, this man's face or name?

OLD MAN: I think I recognize him. All the same,
his face is strange—and yet not quite unknown.
*(To* PHORBAS*)*
Was it you who during Laius' reign
drove his rich herds along Cithaeron's plain?
PHORBAS: Cithaeron's pastureland was always prime.
I'd feed my flocks there in the summertime.

OLD MAN: Do you know me?

PHORBAS: My memory isn't clear.

OEDIPUS: Did you once give a boy to this man here?
Speak up! You're blushing, fumbling for ways
to shape your words, but truth hates such delays.

PHORBAS: You stir up waters that for years have lain
stagnant.

OEDIPUS: Must torture force you to speak plain?

PHORBAS: I did give him the child. No gift—a blight
that never could have lived to see the light.

OLD MAN: Ill-omened words! He lives—and will, I pray,
live on.

OEDIPUS: Why should he perish, as you say?

PHORBAS: An iron rod pierced both his feet, and bound
his legs together; the resulting wound
foully festered. He was at death's door.

OEDIPUS: *(Aside)*
Fate's close at hand. Why question any more?
*(To* PHORBAS)
Who was that baby? Tell me.

PHORBAS: Loyalty
forbids an answer.

OEDIPUS: Bring fire, somebody!
Flames will drive such fidelity away.

PHORBAS: Must truth be sought by such a cruel path?
Pardon, I beg.

OEDIPUS: I may seem full of wrath,
but vengeance lies right within your reach.
Whose was that boy? I want a truthful speech.
What woman's child?

PHORBAS: Your own wife gave him birth.

OEDIPUS: Ah, open up and swallow me, oh earth!
Father of shadows, blast with blackest curses
that man who roles of son and sire reverses.
Stones at my head, you citizens, let fly;
take arms against me. Father, son will vie
to injure me. Husbands and brothers—let
them arm themselves against me! Let the poor
sick populace snatch brands from every pyre
to hurl at me. For my whole generation
I'm a miasma, harm for civilization.
Hated by the gods from that vile day
I first drew breath and feebly tried to cry,
what else am I now fit for but to die?
*(Aside)*
But summon up your spirits now. It's time
to dare atrocities that match your crime.
Back to the palace! Let Jocasta preen;
her dynasty's enriched by many a son.

CHORUS: If I could fashion my own fate,
I'd glide along caressing winds.
No violent gales would capsize me.
Let gentle breezes push my boat
while cautiously I steer my life
along the path of moderation.

Young Icarus feared the king of Crete,
yet boldly reached out for the stars;
he tried to order his false wings
to vie with skimming birds in flight.
Now deep waters bear his name;
nothing else is left of him.
Daedalus, the old survivor,
halted halfway up the sky
waiting for his winged son
(as a bird flees from the hawk
to gather up her fear-flung brood)
till, damned by his attempt to soar,
his hands entangled in false wings,
the boy splashed down into the sea.
All that exceeds the norm is left
hanging on the edge of doom.
What is this noise outside the door?
A stricken servant of the king
hammers a fist against his head.
What news?

MESSENGER: Once Oedipus perceived the whole foul dread
that was his birthright, onto his own head
he showered curses, and with hurrying feet
sped to the palace, mulling on his fate.
A savage lion on the Libyan plain
rages and roars and tosses its gold mane;
so, wild of eye, distorted by his passion,
he groaned—no, howled. An icy perspiration
covered his body, as a foaming tide
of long quiescent sorrows overflowed.
Some appalling stroke is in his mind
to match his fate—and bring it to an end.
"Why am I waiting? Why delay?" he moans.
"Stab me, someone! Shatter me with stones,
or let a fire consume my sins to ash!
Tigers and vultures, batten on my flesh!
Accursed Cithaeron, lair of nothing good,
send out wild beasts against me from your wood,
set a pack of slavering hounds on me
or the ferocious queen, mad Agave!
My soul, death's nothing fearful, no offense;
death preserves the good man's innocence."
These were his words. He drew his sword, and then:
"Is this the way? Such dreadful crimes with one
blow to be dissolved, the penalty

forever paid? Yes, for your father die—
punishment enough for that. But not
for her who bore you, on whom you begot
an evil breed of offspring—not for her!
If you're the sinner, she's the sufferer,
utterly ruined. And your country bleeds!
Suicide can't atone for these misdeeds.
No, let that nature who in fashioning me
forsook her laws and standards utterly
transform herself once more on my behalf
to punish me with freakish shapes of wrath.
Let me live a brand new life, then die,
only to be reborn to misery,
"a never-ending cycle. This takes thought:
some unique form of punishment stretched out,
some death continual, lingering; some way
where, shunned by live and dead alike, I'll stray
toward slow extinction, not a sudden end.
How can you shrink from such a sentence, friend?"
Sobs like a sudden rainstorm wet his face.
"Weeping is useless, tears a mere disgrace.
Ah, but if my eyes themselves I scrape
out of their sockets, then—like tears in shape—
they can rain down. Gods of connubial night,
let this be your sacrifice: my sight!"
These were his words. Cheeks blazing fiery red,
delirious, eyes starting from his head,
of desperation's violent power full,
he groaned. His fingers clawed into his skull.
His eyes wait, avid, ready for his hands,
and rush to meet them, eager for the wound.
His nails rake out all lingering shreds of light,
ripping loose the very roots of sight.
All blind and empty! Still, his hand's employed
scraping the hollow, picking at the void.
His maddened ravings too go on and on,
but somehow their immediacy is gone.
Now that he is finally free of sight,
he lifts his head to catch a glimpse of night.
Scanning the heavens with his empty eyes,
he rips away a lingering ribbon, cries
to all the gods triumphantly: "I pray
you, spare Thebes now! I've paid the penalty;
I've found a sure way to make old wrongs right.
My dark past matches this unending night."
Now from his mangled face a shower of gore

bursts out afresh, blood spraying everywhere.

CHORUS: By fate propelled, to fate we yield.
No fussy gestures set us free.
It is decreed, our human doom,
all from above. Lachesis' laws
(tightly she grasps them) point one way.
Through narrow channels our lives move:
our first day singles out our last.
No god can cause events to swerve
which, meshed in motives, roll along;
each life proceeds untouched by prayer.
To some men, fear's the greatest bane:
afraid of what is fated, blind,
they blunder right into their fate.
Listen, the door! The king himself—
eyeless, unguided—gropes this way.

OEDIPUS: All is well, the deed is done at last.
I've paid the penalty for my murderous past.
How sweet the shadows are! Some grateful god
has poured a cloud of blackness on my head,
pardoned my crimes. The sun's unwinking lid
I have escaped. It's not, you parricide,
to any exercise of your own might
that you owe this deliverance. Rather, light
shuns you.
I finally have a truthful face.

CHORUS: Here comes Jocasta at a frantic pace,
beside herself, delirious, like the queen
who, frenzied, tore the head from her own son
and understood too late what she had done.
She hesitates to speak to him. In her,
desire and pity alternate with fear.
Though such calamities must banish shame,
her voice still falters as she speaks to him.

JOCASTA: What shall I call you? Son? You are, I know,
a son who will not speak to me, or show
his empty features.

OEDIPUS: Leave me, let me be!
What enemy would restore my sight to me?
My mother's voice—I recognize the tone—
means that all my efforts are in vain.

For us to meet again is blasphemy.
Our crimes should be divided by some sea
as vast as our own sins; some country far
from here should shelter us, strange as a star.
Only a planet alien to this place
(if there is any) could be home to us.

JOCASTA: You are not guilty! Fate's to blame, not you!

OEDIPUS: Oh mother, spare your breath, and my ears too—
by my mutilated face I plead
and by the hideous mingling of our blood
and by our double kinship, fair and foul.

JOCASTA: What are you waiting for, oh coward soul?
You were his crime's companion, yet he
alone now faces punishment. Why not me?
Incestuous creature, through whose dreadful deed
every human decency lies dead,
end it! Free your ill spirit with a blade!
Not even if god were thundering at my head
with all his glittering bolts aimed straight at me
could I ever pay the penalty,
hellish mother that I am. I see
no way but death—and death will find a way.
*(to* OEDIPUS*)*
Come, parricide; your mother needs a stroke
to kill her too. Come and complete your work!
*(She grabs his sword)*
Better to seize the sword that struck him down,
my husband—no, my husband was his son!—
the sword I'll plunge into my breast or neck.
Come on, sword, quickly! Choose a place to strike.
I know the place: I'll pierce that fruitful womb
that brought to birth a husband and a son.

*(Stabs herself)*

CHORUS: Her cold hand heavy on the wound,
she lies. Blood forces out the sword.

OEDIPUS: Oh god in charge of truth, what have you done?
Another death? My father was the one
I owed to fate, but—doubly guilty now—
I've killed my father and my mother too.
She never would have perished but for me.

Lying Apollo, in my cruelty
I surpass my own vile destiny!
With trembling fingers, wandering through the gloom
with hands outstretched and groping, you must roam—
and quickly, too—one foot before the other—
but careful lest you stumble on your mother!
All you with bodies burdened by disease
and fighting for your lives, I leave this place.
Look up! For even as I move away,
a gentler spirit animates the sky.
Whoever at death's door somehow lives on,
let him now gulp great draughts of oxygen.
Go offer hope to those resigned to die;
the pestilence leaves Thebes along with me.
Destructive Fates and sickness' trembling fear,
wasting, black plague, dementia—come here,
be my companions! All to me are dear.
*(Exit)*

# Oedipus el Rey

Luis Alfaro

Time
Now

Settings
California State Prison, 2737 W. Cecil Ave, North Kern State, Delano, CA
Highway 99, between McFarland & Famoso Districts, Kern County, CA
*Farmacia* Million Dollar, 301 S. Broadway, Downtown L.A., CA
*La Casa*, 1324 Toberman Street, Pico-Union, L.A., CA

Characters

| | |
|---|---|
| Coro | [a chorus of inmates] |
| | |
| Oedipus | [a young king] |
| Laius | [an old king] |
| Jocasta | [a wife] |
| Creon | [a brother-in-law] |
| Tiresias | [a blind servant] |
| | |
| El Sobador | [a healer who uses touch] |
| El Huesero | [a healer who realigns bones] |
| El Curandero | [a shaman who cures spiritual illness] |
| El Mistico | [a mystic] |
| | |
| Los Tecolotes | [an oracle in the form of owls] |
| Esfinge | [a sphynx] |
| Esfinge #2 | [sphnyx 2nd head/her sister] |
| Esfinge #3 | [sphnyx 3rd head/her sister] |
| Coatlicue | [an oracle in the form of the aztec mother] |
| Coyolxauhqui | [an oracle in the form of the aztec moon] |

A company of seven, with the chorus playing all the secondary characters.

The songs are oldies (ala art laboe) and it is a theatrical idea that they would be sung by the Coro. If that is not possible, they could serve as a musical landscape heard in their original recordings. If royalties become a problem—well, they were a great idea.

PAGEANT
***Look Upon***

The ambient sound of a desolate landscape.

An empty stage stripped of decoration—hollow and hallowed. Its emptiness should feel religious. A delineated square is center.

An elevated row of simple identical chairs surround the square on three sides. Upstage center, a single chair sits slightly spaced apart from the others. The elevation should give a sense of spectator quality.

The sound of an occasional car passing through a lonely highway interrupts the quiet. We are out in the middle of Kern County, heading into Central California, off Highway 99.

A pageant begins. The song of the highway rises and begins to fill the space.

From the audience, Oedipus leads a blind Tiresias, (*Cholo* cool wearing black shades and holding a white stick in his hands), his hand on Oedipus' shoulder as they make their way toward the stage.

Oedipus has a disability and it is clear from watching him that he once could not walk, but has managed to not let this deformity get in his way.

The rest of the company follow and take their place on stage. The ritual to a story often told.

A moment of silence, prayer, preparation.

Okay, let's begin.

PROLOGUE
***Let Every Man Consider***

[The soundtrack of our pageantry is violently interrupted by the loud sound of prison doors slamming shut. There is a sudden change in the light and tone of our world. In the air, three convicts each throw a *chifle* (a whistle), one after another from their cells. A sort of call and response of whistling, *los tres chifles* echo as they sing the beginning of the CORO.]

CORO #1
***Oye!***

CORO #2
***Que!***

CORO #1
***Oye!***

CORO #2 & #3 & #4
***Que!***

CORO #1
***Oye!***

CORO #2 & #3 & #4 & #5
***Que!***

CORO #1
***Oye!***

CORO
**Who is this man?**

CORO #2
**Who is this man—**

CORO #3
**that we should consider—**

CORO #4
**his story?**

CORO #5
***Quien es este hombre—***

CORO #1
**this man—**

CORO #2
***con su* story?**

CORO #3
**Who is this man—**

CORO #4
**who will teach us a lesson?**

CORO #5
**Teach US a lesson?**

CORO #1
**(That's what I said.)**

CORO #2
**Who is this man—**

CORO #3
**living in prison—**

CORO #4
**raised in 'the yard'?**

CORO #5
**Who is this man—**

CORO #1
**feared by many—**

CORO #2
**yet one of our own?**

CORO #3
**Who is this man—**

CORO #4
**who lives like an orphan—**

CORO #5
**even with a father at his side?**

CORO #1
**Who is this man—**

CORO #2
**who throws the first punch—**

CORO #3
**and stays for the last kick?**

CORO #4
**Who is this man—**

CORO #5
**they call Oedipus—**

CORO #1
**a.k.a. *Patas Malas?***

CORO #2
**Who is this man—**

CORO #3
**always talking about fate?**

CORO #4
**Fate, bro . . .**

CORO #5
**Who is this man—**

CORO #1
**who makes the prison library—**

CORO #2
**his territory?**

CORO #3
**(No shit—the prison library?)**

CORO #4
***Quien es este hombre—***

CORO #5
**who gets high—**

CORO #1
**on thought?**

CORO #2
**Thought?**

CORO #3
**That's what I said, *foo!***

CORO #4
***Quien es este hombre—***

CORO #5
**a *chamaco* we call—**

CORO #1
***El Rey Juvenil.***

CORO #2
**Wants to be a king.**

CORO #3
**A what?**

[They begin to laugh.]

CORO #4
**Wants to be noble.**

CORO #5
**Yes, this *cabron* is noble.**

[They all laugh.]

CORO #1
**Lots of good it does him in here!**

[It's not so funny . . .]

CORO #2
**Here . . .**

CORO #3
**Yes, a man—**

CORO #4
**who wants to be something more.**

CORO #5
**More?**

CORO #1
***El rey.***

CORO #2
**A man of principle.**

CORO
***Como no!***

CORO #3
**A reputable man.**

CORO
***Como no!***

CORO #4
**A hard-headed man.**

CORO
***Como no!***

CORO #5
**A man with no limits.**

CORO
***Como no!***

CORO #1
**A man who doesn't forget.**

CORO
***Como no!***

CORO #2
**A man who doesn't forgive.**

CORO
***Como no!***

CORO #3
**A man with 'issues'.**

CORO
***Como no!***

CORO #4
**A man destined to be.**

CORO
***Como no!***

CORO #5
**Destined.**

CORO #1
**To be.**

CORO #2
***El rey.***

CORO
**Destined ...**

[Silence. The actor who is playing TIRESIAS rises.]

TIRESIAS
***Yo soy.***

[TIRESIAS takes his white stick and unfolds it to reveal his blind-man's cane. He stands with stick in hand, looking like a *Loteria* card.]

**I am the father.**

CORO #1
***El papa de* Oedipus.**

CORO #2
**The old man.**

CORO #3
***Tiresias.***

CORO #4
**Servant to God in all ways.**

CORO #1
**And even he—**

CORO #2
**an *alleluia*—**

CORO #3
**has not escaped the lord's wrath.**

CORO #4
**He believes.**

CORO #1
**Believes in the mysterious ways.**

CORO #2
**A *mistico.***

CORO #3
**Always looking—**

CORO #4
**for the divine intervention.**

CORO #1
**I go to him.**

CORO #2
**Me too.**

CORO #3
**And he gives me *consejo.***

CORO #4
**Counsels me.**

CORO #1
**Like in church.**

CORO #2
**Tells me what's coming.**

CORO #3
**How I ended up here.**

CORO #4
**He knows.**

CORO #1
**Oh yes, he knows.**

CORO #2
**But I'm angry.**

CORO #3
**I don't listen.**

CORO #4
**No, I don't.**

CORO #1
**I don't listen because he can't see!**

CORO #2
**That's messed up, dude ...**

CORO #3
**How can you be a seer—**

CORO #4
**if you can't see?**

CORO #1
**Slowly going blind.**

CORO #2
**Everyday gets darker.**

CORO #3
**Sunlight toward sunset.**

CORO #4
**For the old man ...**

CORO #1
**Everyday the *ojos* eclipse.**

CORO #2
**It's not even funny.**

CORO #3
**No, it's sad, *ese*.**

CORO #4
**Sits in his cell.**

CORO #1
**Waiting for God.**

CORO #2
**While his son studies to be *un rey*.**

CORO #3
**Been so long.**

<u>CORO #4</u>
**What's he in for?**

<u>CORO #1</u>
**He won't say.**

<u>CORO #2</u>
***Misticos* don't talk much.**

<u>CORO #3</u>
**Silence for the old man!**

[They bow their heads in deference. Beat. The actress playing JOCASTA rises from her seat.]

<u>CORO #4</u>
**To lose the gift.**

<u>CORO #1</u>
**To see beauty.**

<u>CORO #2</u>
**So sad.**

<u>CORO #3</u>
**He must have done something.**

<u>CORO #4</u>
**Something bad.**

<u>CORO #1</u>
**Something terrible.**

<u>CORO #2</u>
**Worse than what I did.**

<u>CORO #3</u>
**To live in silence.**

<u>CORO #4</u>
**With permanent night-time.**

<u>CORO #1</u>
***Puede ser mal, ese cabron.***

<u>CORO #2</u>
**What he must have done—**

CORO #3
**to lose the light.**

[TIRESIAS sits. A beat.]

CORO #4
**To see beauty.**

CORO #1
**That's all I got sometimes.**

CORO #2
**Sometimes,**

CORO #3
**that's all I got.**

CORO #4
**A chance to see something beautiful.**

CORO #1
**The sky.**

CORO #2
**The yard.**

CORO #3
**The lady guard with the big ass.**

[They laugh recognition. A sigh.]

CORO #4
**Seriously, though, dude.**

CORO #1
**Serious, *ese***

CORO #2
**Something beautiful.**

CORO #3
**That I can see.**

CORO #4
**A woman …**

[Silence. JOCASTA faces upstage, lifts her blouse and exposes a large tattoo of angel wings that cover her back.]

JOCASTA
**I am.**

[The wings glow. She slowly pulls her blouse back down.]

**That woman.**

CORO #1
**Beauty.**

CORO #2
**Yes, beauty.**

CORO #3
**I remember.**

CORO #4
**Soft.**

CORO #1
**Gentle.**

CORO #2
**Skin.**

CORO #3
**Smooth.**

CORO #4
**Smell.**

CORO #1
**Beauty.**

CORO #2
**'Jean Nate'.**

CORO #3
**Remember …**

CORO #4
**But she's taken.**

CORO #1
**Damn!**

CORO #2
**Yes, taken.**

CORO #3
**By a man.**

CORO #4
**Not worthy of her.**

[JOCASTA sits.]

CORO #1
**That's always the woman I want.**

CORO #2
**I need.**

CORO #3
**I could live for.**

CORO #4
**The one that's—**

CORO #1
**taken.**

CORO #2
**A lived-in woman.**

CORO #3
**Lived.**

CORO #4
**A woman not afraid.**

CORO #1
**Not afraid to be yours.**

CORO #2
**Taken.**

CORO #3
**Taken from you.**

CORO
**Taken.**

[Silence. The actor playing LAIUS rises and looks out at the audience.]

LAIUS
**I am that man.**

[He looks out and nods his head.]

**A king.**

CORO #1
**Who has the woman.**

CORO #2
**Who makes the rules.**

CORO #3
**Who turns us against each other.**

CORO #1
**Who others follow.**

CORO #2
**Who is ruthless.**

CORO #3
**A politician.**

CORO #1
**Yes, a *politico*.**

CORO #2
**Rules with a *firme* hand—**

CORO #3
**Earns his respect.**

CORO #1
**Should know better—**

CORO #2
**but doesn't care.**

CORO #3
**Never learns lessons—**

CORO #1
**from God.**

CORO #2
**But no ...**

CORO #3
***Pinche* gods ...**

CORO #1
**They made a *Rey*—**

CORO #2
**who is—**

CORO
**destined ...**

[A long *chifle* echoes down a cell block neighborhood. LAIUS, JOCASTA and EL SOBADOR all make their way to the playing area.]

SCENE ONE
***Wise In The Ways Of God***

[*La casa*. An old *viejo*, EL SOBADOR is rubbing JOCASTA'S stomach, LAIUS stands over them watching. A restless JOCASTA pulls EL SOBADOR's hands off her.]

LAIUS
**You know something, but you're not saying.**

EL SOBADOR
**This is the work of God—he speaks in poems.**

LAIUS
**You telling me you don't understand his language?**

EL SOBADOR
**It's hard to understand what he means sometimes.**

LAIUS
**Try ...**

[Beat. EL SOBADOR looks at JOCASTA, nodding for LAIUS to leave. EL SOBADOR keeps his eyes on JOCASTA.]

EL SOBADOR
**Tell him to leave …**

[LAIUS suddenly grabs EL SOBADOR by the throat, taking him down to the floor as he chokes him.]

LAIUS
**Tell God I am ready to hear what he has to say!**

JOCASTA
**Laius, don't!**

LAIUS
**Tell him!**

JOCASTA
**Stop it! You'll curse the baby.**

EL SOBADOR
(struggling for breath) ***Senor,* please …**

[LAIUS to JOCASTA.]

LAIUS
**Get out. NOW!**

[JOCASTA reluctantly runs out, as LAIUS lets go of EL SOBADOR]

**Now, speak, or I'll take that tongue out so that you never translate another word from God again.**

[EL SOBADOR, struggling for breath and humiliated, begins to get up. He takes a beat to compose himself.]

EL SOBADOR
**That baby is going to kill you.**

LAIUS
**What!**

EL SOBADOR
**The poem was clear.**

LAIUS
**What are you talking about?**

EL SOBADOR
**You are cursed to be killed by your own son.**

LAIUS
**A son …**

EL SOBADOR
**Who will grow up to be *un rey*.**

[As he wipes the blood off his nose …]

**And like *todo los reyes*, he will be ruthless.**

LAIUS
**You're full of shit.**

EL SOBADOR
**Can I speak the truth, *Senor Bruto*?**

LAIUS
**You haven't already?**

EL SOBADOR
***That* was God.**

LAIUS
**Speak then.**

EL SOBADOR
**To your son, you will be the only obstacle in this *barrio* and its territories.**

LAIUS
**Just proves how merciless God is.**

EL SOBADOR
***Es* destiny. *Esta* willed and your son must follow it.**

LAIUS
***Me va matar …***

EL SOBADOR
**At your last breath, he will look you in the eye … and you will know. *Te lo prometo*.**

LAIUS
***Como?***

EL SOBADOR
**I don't know, *Senor*, it's a poem, it's vague.**

LAIUS
**When?**

EL SOBADOR
**I am just interpreting. I am not a calendar.**

[He begins to go.]

***Es todo.* The *curandero* will do a *limpia* of your house tomorrow—buy a chicken and a broom.**

[LAIUS sits on the floor, suddenly terrified. EL SOBADOR notices this.]

***Lo siento, Senor.* When he is born I will make sure his *huesos* are aligned. You can pay me then.**

[EL SOBADOR walks away. LAUIS is suddenly quite terrified.]

LAIUS
**Maybe … you misunderstood the poem?**

[EL SOBADOR notices LAIUS' fear. It satisfies him.]

EL SOBADOR
**Cash only, no checks …**

SCENE TWO
***Soliloquy***

[A light up on a very pregnant JOCASTA. She is sitting, smoking a cigarette. She looks down, as she rubs her belly.]

JOSCASTA
**You're a pain in the ass you know that?**

***Ay*, Stop all that damn kicking!**
**What do you got to be restless about, huh?**
**All you're doing is sitting there, watching *All My Children*.**

[She looks down at her belly.]

**What are you waiting for?**

**Come on, come out.**

**I need someone.**
**To keep me company.**
**To protect me.**
**To love me.**

[She takes a hit on her cigarette.]

**Hurry, *cabron*.**
**You're killing my back.**

[Restless, she exhales.]

SCENE THREE
***Sound of Lamentation***

[Night. The CORO sing The Five Satins *"In The Still of the Night"*. While they sing TIRESIAS goes back in time to center stage and waits, while JOCASTA gives birth and hands the baby to LAIUS.]

CORO
***So before the light***
***Hold me again***
***With all of your might***
***In the still of the night***
***In the still of the night***

SCENE FOUR
***Life At His Death***

[LAIUS enters with a small bloody bundle. A younger TIRESIAS runs to him.]

TIRESIAS
**At your service, *mi comandante!***

LAIUS
**Thank you, *Tiresias,* my *mas* loyal. I have an *orden* for you.**

TIRESIAS
**Without question, *carnal*.**

[LAIUS vulnerable to TIRESIAS for the first time.]

LAIUS
**Don't look badly on me.**

[LAIUS opens the bloody cloth as TIRESIAS looks in and gasps.]

TIRESIAS
***Santo Jesus!***

LAIUS
**I have to kill my son.**

TIRESIAS
***Porque?***

LAIUS
**He's been cursed, to destroy me.**

TIRESIAS
***No puede ser.***

LAIUS
**God is demanding of those who dare to challenge him.**

TIRESIAS
**But, *jefe*, I thought you didn't care about God?**

LAIUS
**And he knows it, that's why he pulls shit like this on me!**

TIRESIAS
**Maybe you should apologize.**

LAIUS
***Yo no*! God's a grudge-holder. They all think he's up there on his cross making it easier for everybody. These days he's sitting on a recliner with the remote, making my life miserable.**

[TIRESIAS looks at the bundle.]

TIRESIAS
**He's just a baby.**

LAIUS
**Who could be *el rey*.**

TIRESIAS
**A child.**

LAIUS
**A murderer! Don't get *sentimental* on me, *compadre*.**

TIRESIAS
***Maestro, con todo respeto*—I can't do this.**

LAIUS
**Yes you can. You've done worse. We have to do it now before it takes to my wife's *chi-chi*.**

TIRESIAS
***Jocasta* ...**

LAIUS
**She doesn't know. I got her so doped up she thinks she's on a *novela*.
I'll be honest with her later—I'll tell her it stopped breathing ...**

TIRESIAS
**I've never hurt a child, *compadre*.**

LAIUS
**It's a tiny death. We'll laugh about it later.**

[LAIUS hands him the child.]

**Here, take it.**

[TIRESIAS takes the bundle.]

TIRESIAS
**Why is he bleeding?**

LAIUS
**I cut the bottoms of his feet. I don't want him chasing me in the afterlife.**

TIRESIAS
**I thought you didn't believe?**

LAIUS
**I don't, but just enough ...**

**Let's scare the gods. Go to Griffith Park and hang him from a tree. Like a *chivo*. Let the life drain from him. The *coyotes* will do the rest.**

TIRESIAS
**Why cause him pain when he hasn't sinned?**

LAIUS
***Ya callate* and stop with the *alleluia*!**

TIRESIAS
**But how can you kill your son?**

LAIUS
**I didn't say I was good father. Go!**

[They look at each other and part ways.]

SCENE FIVE
***Eternal Pain***

[The actors playing LAIUS and TIRESIAS return to the Coro. Silence. All the actors cover their faces with their hands, except JOCASTA, who realizes what has just happened and screams as she weeps … ]

JOCASTA
***NOOOOOOOOOO!***
***Por favor, Santo Jesus!***
***Mi hijo …***
***Mi hijo …***

[She covers her face as the actors lower their hands.]

SCENE SIX
***Time Comes***

[A variation on the *Tres chifles* return. While OEDIPUS goes center stage and begins a series of exercises. LAIUS and JOCASTA each change out of their outfits into older versions of themselves.]

CORO #1
**Time comes.**

CORO #2
***El tiempo viene.***

CORO #3
**A boy becomes a man.**

CORO #4
**You become the thing you are.**

CORO #5
**Through a glass darkly.**

CORO #1
**Try to make it stop.**

CORO #2
**But it can't be.**

CORO #3
**Someone is chosen.**

CORO #4
**Time comes.**

CORO #5
**And the world changes.**

CORO #1
**Passes you by.**

CORO #2
**No windows.**

CORO #3
**Just bars.**

CORO #4
**Time comes.**

CORO #5
**And all your dreams.**

CORO #1
**Hide from you.**

CORO #2
**Like time.**

CORO #3
***El tiempo.***

CORO #4
***El tiempo.***

CORO #5
***El tiempo.***

CORO #1
**Time . . .**

CORO #2
**Nothing**

CORO #3
**And everything**

CORO #4
**Change …**

[The chorus begins to breathe and puff in rapid succession.]

SCENE SEVEN
***A Memory Without Pain***

[The breathing continues and bleeds into OEDIPUS in the prison yard, young, tough and working out. He is powerful as he rips through a blazing round of his exercises with a fixed intensity. He grunts with each rep. The chorus blows a last breath as he stops.]

OEDIPUS
**I am the one they call Oedipus.**

CORO
**Oedipus.**

OEDIPUS
**My old man gave me my name.**
**You know how the Chinese always give their babies beautiful names like—**

OEDIPUS/CORO
***…Shao wen***

OEDIPUS
**and—**

OEDIPUS/CORO
***…Yin ha.***

OEDIPUS
**They always sound like soft names for different kinds of winds.**
**But underneath, they always mean something else, like—**

OEDIPUS/CORO
**Rotten tree—**

OEDIPUS
**or—**

OEDIPUS/CORO
**Smelly egg.**

OEDIPUS
**I have a Chinese name.**
**It means *Swollen Foot*.**

CORO
**Oedipus.**

OEDIPUS
**My father says the day I learned to walk—I ran into an alley.**
**When they found me, the bottoms of my feet were tore up from walking on broken glass.**

**I'm not crippled enough to be crippled.**
**Even though I've been like this since I was a baby.**

CORO
**Oedipus.**

OEDIPUS
**The only son of the widowed *Tiresias*.**

CORO
**Tiresias.**

OEDIPUS
**I never knew my mother.**
**She left me to a life of picking pockets, selling pot and juvenile detention.**
**Mothers sometimes do that.**

CORO
**Yes they do.**

OEDIPUS
**I always want to dream her. But I can't.**

CORO
**Never.**

OEDIPUS
**It's not good to dream in here.**

CORO
**No sir!**

OEDIPUS
**To wish for things.**
**It makes you soft.**

CORO
**Soft.**

OEDIPUS
**It makes you crazy.**

CORO
**Crazy.**

OEDIPUS
**It makes you sad.**

CORO
**Sad.**

OEDIPUS
**There's nothing in my night, but sleep.**
**No Tinkerbell or fluffy cloud.**
**Just deaf night.**

[Suddenly it is night. The Coro makes the sound of sleep. Only Oedipus is fully awake.]

**Tonight an oracle appeared …**

[The CORO appear as a parliament of owls. The *tecolote* stare is defined by the turns of their heads.]

TECOLOTE #1
**What's up, *ese*?**

[Oedipus tries to stare them down.]

TECOLOTE #2
**Dude, don't try to stare us down,**

TECOLOTE #3
**that's our nature.**

TECOLOTE #4
**And your's,**

TECOLOTE #1
**well, yours …**

[They all look at each other.]

TECOLOTE #2
**We have some wise old philosophy for you;**

TECOLOTE #3
***'Cuando el tecolote canta …***

TECOLOTE #4
**(When the owl cries …)**

TECOLOTE #1
***El Indio muere.***

TECOLOTE #2
**(The Indian dies.)**

OEDIPUS
**I'm gonna die?**

TECOLOTE #3
**No, your father, *puto*.**

OEDIPUS
**My father?**

TECOLOTE #4
**At your hands.**

OEDIPUS
**Never!**

TECOLOTE #1
**Don't worry.**

TECOLOTE #2
**It'll be brief.**

TECOLOTE #3
**And probably not your fault.**

TECOLOTE #4
**We won't hold it against you.**

TECOLOTE #1
**It's your nature.**

TECOLOTE #2
**Just like this is ours …**

[They turn their heads like owls in one synchronized move.]

TECOLOTE #3
**Count your blessings.**

TECOLOTE #4
**Your parole is up!**

TECOLOTE #1
**Life is a mystery isn't it?**

[They do one collective hoot. Oedipus falls to his knees.]

TECOLOTE #2
**Make amends while you can, *joven*.**

TECOLOTE #3
**For you are the accursed.**

[The oracle disappears. Suddenly it is day. Oedipus stands, reaches for a jump rope as he plows through an intense rep.]

OEDIPUS
**I am the accursed …**

CORO
**The accursed.**

[Double the speed. He stops and breathes.]

OEDIPUS
**That's why I have to leave.**
**Sometimes you do things in here that are not really you.**

CORO
**Leave.**

OEDIPUS
**I wouldn't hurt my dad.**
**Even if it was my destiny.**

CORO
**Destiny**

OEDIPUS
***Tiresias Gomez*, my dad, the blind *mistico*, who broke the law, so that he could be in here and raise me. Father's sometimes do that.**

CORO
**Yes they do.**

OEDIPUS
**But one day he woke and blindness started to become permanent evening for him.**
**So he opened his eyes and started to look for the light inside.**

CORO
**Inside.**

OEDIPUS
**He's got sins that I don't know about.**
**Sins that he has to pay for.**

CORO
**Everybody pays.**

OEDIPUS
**Everyday, my dad and I, go to the prison library—**
**SECTION 6:**

OEDIPUS/CORO
**R-A-Y to R-E-L.**

OEDIPUS
**The library is like a church—empty and quiet.**
**That's where me and my old man spend our days—**
**SECTION 6:**

OEDIPUS/CORO
**R-A-Y to R-E-L.**

OEDIPUS
**And we study-**

OEDIPUS/CORO
**R-E-L-I-G-I-O-N.**

[TIRESIAS speaks from his seat.]

TIRESIAS
**The only thing that needs healing is the soul—**

OEDIPUS
**...he says.**

TIRESIAS
**...everything else can go to *mierda*.**

[TIRESIAS laughs to himself.]

OEDIPUS
***Misticos*, they don't really do much.**
**They just want to be in the presence of God.**

CORO
**Presence.**

OEDIPUS
**Everyday we read about him.**

OEDIPUS/CORO
**G-O-D.**

[OEDIPUS mimes doing Braille.]

OEDIPUS
**He 'Stevie Wonders' it.**
**And I read the old-fashioned way.**

[The CORO whispers the Hail Mary, while OEDIPUS speaks.]

CORO
***Hail Mary, full of grace,***
***the Lord is with thee;***
***blessed art thou among women,***
***and blessed is the fruit of thy womb, Jesus.***
***Holy Mary, Mother of God, pray for us sinners,***
***now and at the hour of our death. Amen.***

*OEDIPUS*
**White People God.**
**Chino God.**
**Muslim God.**
**Hindu God.**
**Everybody wants a God.**

**Not me!**

[The CORO abruptly stops the prayer at this revelation.]

OEDIPUS
**I don't want God.**
**He's like a teacher or a boss—**
**wanting you to do everything exactly the way he says or he'll punish you—**
**for the rest of your life!**

**I can do better than God.**

CORO
**Ssh!**

OEDIPUS
**His ego's too big.**

CORO
***Callate!***

OEDIPUS
**But while I 'm here—**
**that is a belief that has to live in the silence of me.**

CORO
**That's right!**

OEDIPUS
**For me—**
**up there, there is no heaven—**
**just sky, chunky blue sky.**

CORO
**Heaven.**

OEDIPUS
**My father's journey is contemplation.**
**Mine is to be something more …**

CORO
**Ah …**

OEDIPUS
**Why not, right?**

CORO
**Try.**

OEDIPUS
**My old man, he wants balance—**

OEDIPUS/CORO
***Pingheng***

OEDIPUS
**he wants to understand—**

OEDIPUS/CORO
***Jie***

OEDIPUS
**and he wants to accept—**

OEDIPUS/CORO
***Jieshou***

OEDIPUS
**He must be a *Chino*,**
**because he loves the 'I Ching'.**

TIRESIAS
***Ai, chingao!***

[OEDIPUS laughs an affectionate laugh. It sparks a memory. Sadness.]

OEDIPUS
**I won't kill him.**
**He is my life.**
**I owe him my breath.**

[The CORO let out a big breath.]

**Tomorrow I'm going to be released.**
**I'll say goodbye right before I go. Not one minute before.**

**One cold quick prick to the heart, that's the way it works in here.**

**He'll go inside of himself.**
**Or maybe he'll go to—SECTION 6:**

OEDIPUS/CORO
**R-A-Y to R-E-L.**

OEDIPUS
**Or maybe God has already told him how to deal with it ...**

[One last rep of an exercise. Breath. Breath. Breath.]

SCENE EIGHT
***Until He Find***

[LAIUS and JOCASTA on one side of the playing area. TIRESIAS and OEDIPUS on the other.]

LAIUS/OEDIPUS
**I gotta go ...**

JOCASTA/TIRESIAS
**Where you going?**

LAIUS/OEDIPUS
**To change our future.**

[JOCASTA and TIRESIAS both laugh and nod to themselves.]

LAIUS
**An old friend of ours is up north.**
**I knew he was there, but I didn't think it mattered.**
**Until now.**
**He's the reason I have this bad luck.**

JOCASTA
**Who is it?**

LAIUS
**Don't worry about it.**
***Vieja*, why do I always have to kill my friends?**

JOCASTA
**Let it go, Laius ...**

LAIUS
**He's gonna make a deal with God for me, and then I'm gonna get our *negocios* together and we'll make some real *dinero*. We'll move out of the *barrio* and up to 'burbs, like all the Mexicans.**

JOCASTA
**Maybe this is good enough.**

LAIUS
**Don't be stupid.**

[beat]

**We can finally have a baby.**

[JOCASTA laughs out loud.]

JOCASTA
**Are you kidding? We're too old for that.**

LAIUS
**No, we're not, *vieja*.**

JOCASTA
**What do we want a kid for? To pass along your good luck?**

[LAIUS reaches over and slaps her hard across the face. She falls. He looks away.]

LAIUS
**If anything happens to me, get off your ass and do some work. I leave you all of this.**
**Don't give any of it to that idiot brother of yours.**

[LAIUS leaves without looking back. The blind TIRESIAS stands downstage looking inside, while OEDIPUS looks at him for a sign.]

OEDIPUS
**Tell me something.**

TIRESIAS
**What?**

OEDIPUS
**Give me a head start.**

TIRESIAS
**There's a man waiting for you in McFarland. With a car. It's cheap, but it rides good.**

OEDIPUS
***Gracias, papa.***

[Beat]

**What else?**

TIRESIAS
**What else you want? That's a lot.**

OEDIPUS
**Come on, old man.**
**Throw me a prophecy.**

TIRESIAS
**I don't know . . .**

OEDIPUS
***Viejo*, don't make it any harder for me than it has to be . . .**

[A moment. A conjuring. TIRESIAS looks up at the sky, a light bounces off his shades, *muy mistico*.]

TIRESIAS
**Go south.**

OEDIPUS
**South?**

TIRESIAS
***Pero, cuidate!***

OEDIPUS
**You know I will.**

TIRESIAS
**There's a territory . . . It's weak.**
***Se llama* Pico/Union.**

OEDIPUS
**Pico/Union?**

TIRESIAS
**A ruler, envious *y de mal humor*.**

OEDIPUS
**Weak.**

TIRESIAS
**An easy kingdom.**

OEDIPUS
**Easy.**

TIRESIAS
***Pero*, he's just the puppet. There's a welcome committee. *Esfinge*.**

OEDIPUS
***Esfinge?***

TIRESIAS
**The Sphinx. She's a total *bruja*.**

OEDIPUS
**Yeah?**

TIRESIAS
**She has a lot of control, and she's intellectual, so don't go all crazy on her.**

OEDIPUS
**I'll surprise her with my visit.**

TIRESIAS
**She's so smart she already knows your coming.**

OEDIPUS
**And what will I get?**

TIRESIAS
**What she controls.**

[Beat. TIRESIAS reaches out for OEDIPUS, who goes to him. TIRESIAS hugs him so hard that it feels like *el mundo* might split. OEDIPUS has never seen his father do this. He doesn't know how to respond.]

OEDIPUS
**If I could stay ...**

[He waits, but when it becomes unbearable, he pulls his father's arms off. He stands back and takes off his dad's shades. He looks deeply into his eyes and then kisses each one.]

**Ah, they're sweet! Papa, you always said tears we're salty. But they're sweet ...**

[He puts the shades back on the old man. He turns away from him and calms himself. OEDIPUS looks at him for a last time. Instinctually, they give each other a *veterano* nod.]

**Later ...**

[The CORO form a royal line as OEDIPUS begins to take off his prison clothes and folds them into a neat pile, which is passed down the line. When he is down to his boxers and wife-beater : a parade of civilian clothes make their way back down the line. He puts them on. When he is finished dressing, he begins to walk down the line as each member of the CORO gives him a *'later, ese'* bow of the head. The sound of prison doors opening. OEDIPUS goes to the playing area and is followed by LAIUS. The doors close.]

SCENE NINE
***Weep No More***

[A sudden shift in the world. The sound of a car screeching to a halt. Two headlights face each other, creating a blazing swath of harsh white light that cuts across the center of the stage. It looks like the roar in the middle of a boxing ring. LAIUS and OEDIPUS step into the center of this cold white space.]

LAIUS
**What the fuck is wrong with you?**

OEDIPUS
**Are you talking to me?**

LAIUS
**Who do you think I'm talking to, you fucking idiot.**

OEDIPUS
**Get back in your car, sir.**

LAIUS
**You see another car coming—you pull over.**

OEDIPUS
**It's one lane.**

LAIUS
**Yeah, mine.**

OEDIPUS
***You* pull over.**

LAIUS
**You king of the road, you little bitch?**

OEDIPUS
**Watch your tongue, old man.**

LAIUS
**Old man? I can take out a little *mocoso* like you with one hand.**

OEDIPUS
**Then do it.**

LAIUS

**This is no place to act *como si eres un rey*. *Mira*, take my advice, little *niña*, I could bury you out here and *nadie* would ever know where to find you.**

[OEDIPUS holds his ground.]

**Move *esa* piece of shit *carro* out of the way!**

[A beat.]

OEDIPUS

**You move it.**

LAIUS

**What did you say?**

OEDIPUS

**You heard me.**

LAIUS

**Let me tell you something, asshole, I have a problem with my temper.**

OEDIPUS

**We have something in common.**

LAIUS

**I can't control it.**

OEDIPUS

**Then we are more alike than you realize.**

LAIUS

**I don't think someone with an 85 Honda Civic should be acting like he owns the road.**

OEDIPUS

**This close, *viejo*.**

[Beat. They glare at each other. OEDIPUS doesn't move. LAIUS sizes him up.]

LAIUS

**When did you get out?**

OEDIPUS

**I don't know what you're talking about.**

LAIUS

**You're so obvious, *pendejo*.**

**North Kern, right? You got convict written all over you, *baboso*.**

[OEDIPUS knows to say nothing.]

**I'm on my way there now. Anybody you want me to say hello to, a boyfriend?**

[OEDIPUS fumes, suddenly feeling very self-conscious and showing his age.]

**Ah … You don't know the outside, do you?**

**Wow, *ese*, you threw me for a *momento*, I thought you were an *hombre*, but you're just a little boy.**

[LAIUS laughs.]

**Wow, wouldn't that be crazy if you went right back in? I could do that. Make a call, Highway Patrol, tell them you got some sort of road rage, a *rabia* from being locked in a cage for so long. Danger to society, *y todo eso*. Send you back before you got a *taco*—or some pussy.**

**Unless you don't like *tacos* …**

**Or pussy …**

[LAIUS laughs again.]

**What's the matter, *gato* got your tongue?**

[LAIUS dismisses the little boy and reaches for a cigarette pack in his shirt pocket. Without warning, OEDIPUS lunges and takes him down. It is scary and primal. Over him, OEDIPUS begins to punch LAIUS in the face repeatedly, with an absolute savagery and lack of emotion. It's hard and quick, like in a prison yard. With each blow—the CORO begins to chant.]

CORO

***Asi.***
***Asi.***
***Asi.***
***ASI.***
***ASI.***
***ASI.***

[With the last of his strength, LAIUS reaches up and grabs the hand that is pummeling him, stopping him for just a moment. LAIUS recognizes the moment that was prophesized so long ago, spitting on OEDIPUS' face, spraying him with blood, as he howls …]

LAIUS
**My son ...**

[It doesn't register to OEDIPUS, who resumes his assault with a workmanlike ferocity. The CORO continue their call, but this time they chant ...]

EL CORO
***Eso.***
***Eso.***
***Eso.***
***ESO.***
***ESO.***
***ESO.***

[The headlights fade and OEDIPUS stops punching. All we can hear is his heavy breathing. He walks away like an opponent in a boxing match.

After a quiet moment, the CORO lift and carry the dead LAIUS to JOCASTA.

A member of the CORO goes to OEDIPUS and trades his shirt with a dried bloody one.

We hear the screech of a car taking off and into a busy street. We are in the middle of downtown. We start to hear the sound of Broadway—people, music and cars.]

SCENE TEN
***This Is The King Who Solved The Famous Riddle***

[OEDIPUS approaches the *Farmacia* Million Dollar on Broadway. ESFINGE, the vendor, an older, *pero* sexy, *mujer* wearing a *poncho* and sucking on a *saladito*, stands behind a glass case filled with saints, *polvos* and a live chicken.]

OEDIPUS
**I'm here.**

ESFINGE
***Ya veo*. And what can I offer you, love potion or something for maturity?**

[She giggles *muy fea* to herself.]

OEDIPUS
**Don't tease me, *mujer*.**

ESFINGE
***Ai jovencito*, you talk like an adult!**

OEDIPUS

***Como dicen*; childhood is short—maturity is forever.**

ESFINGE

***Ai, que* wise! *Puedo ver que* you got consciousness, little boy. But that shirt! *Tan obvio*. I'll sell you a *camisa* and we can put your favorite saint on it.**

OEDIPUS

**I want to talk to *Esfinge*.**

ESFINGE

***Esfinge*? What's that?**

OEDIPUS

**You tell me.**

ESFINGE

**Wouldn't you rather have a little *polvo* to help you grow, *chaparrito*?**

[She laughs *muy fuerte*.]

OEDIPUS

**Are we gonna flirt all night long?**

ESFINGE

**I have a little something for that too!**

OEDIPUS

***Señora*, I haven't wasted my life on growing 'up'—but rather, 'in'.**

[ESFINGE can't disguise the pleasure this intellectual tingle gives her. She fans herself.]

ESFINGE

***Ay, se calento … Un filosofo* are you?**

[She looks around to make sure no one is listening. Looking for foreplay, she runs the *saladito* down her chest.]

***Dime*, what do you know about wisdom?**

[On to her, OEDIPUS obliges.]

OEDIPUS

***Pues*, wisdom is to question *todo*, and in the end, to accept.**

ESFINGE
**I'm sorry, *senor*, but even I can tell you don't believe your own philosophy.**

OEDIPUS
**I don't have to—I'm *un rey*!**

[Wow, that hit the G spot. ESFINGE puts on a sexy face and voice.]

ESFINGE
**Young *Rey*. Well why didn't you say so? Would you like to come inside?**

OEDIPUS
**My pleasure.**

ESFINGE
**Mine first!**

[She laughs to herself as she exits. We hear the sound of her front metal door rolling down. The sound of the city disappears. OEDIPUS doesn't let this throw him. When she re-appears, she is behind a glass case holding her arms out with a head in each hand.]

ESFINGE
**These are my *hermanas*.**

ESFINGE #1
***Hola!***

ESFINGE #2
***Que tal!***

ESFINGE #1
***Ay Dios*, you didn't say he was *tan guapo*!**

ESFINGE #2
***Y tan macho!***

ESFINGE #1
***Miralo.***

ESFINGE #2
***Me encanta!***

ESFINGE #1
**So young.**

ESFINGE #2
**So fresh.**

ESFINGE #1
**Untouched.**

ESFINGE #2
**A natural born leader.**

[They stare at him and smile. They smack their lips in hunger.]

ESFINGE
**That one is your past.**

ESFINGE #1
***Pasada.***

ESFINGE
**This one is your future.**

ESFINGE #2
***Futura.***

OEDIPUS
**I know my past.**

ESFINGE / ESFINGE #1 / ESFINGE #2
**So do we!**

[All three heads laugh.]

***Ai, hermanas,* que funny *son!***

OEDIPUS
**And what are you?**

ESFINGE
**I'm your present!**

[All three crack up at the double entendre.]

**Would you like to unwrap me now?**

[They laugh even more.]

OEDIPUS
**I don't want to know my future.**

[He punches HEAD #2. It falls off her hand. Serious, they quickly turn on him like serpents.]

ESFINGE
***Ai, que monstro!***

[OEDIPUS laughs, but they hiss.]

ESFINGE #1
**What are you going to do …**

ESFINGE
**murder us in the middle of a road …**

ESFINGE #1
**…in the middle of the night?**

[This catches OEDIPUS off-guard. HEAD #2 re-appears again, but in a little bit of pain.]

ESFINGE #2
**Yeah …**

OEDIPUS
**How did you know about that?**

ESFINGE
**Don't worry about it.**

ESFINGE #1
***Este animal,***

ESFINGE #2
**we thought he had a conscience.**

ESFINGE #1
**But he shows us he doesn't.**

ESFINGE #2
**So, maybe he is *un rey*!**

ESFINGE #1
***Que caliente* it makes him!**

ESFINGE #2
**I like your attitude!**

ESFINGE #1 & #2
**So delicious ...**

OEDIPUS
**I hear you can't control a man with no conscience?**

ESFINGE
**But we can give you other things.**

ESFINGE #2
**Dreams.**

ESFINGE #1
**Remember those?**

OEDIPUS
***Hermanas, no sean malas ...***

ESFINGE
**Or you can avoid our curse by answering a question.**

OEDIPUS
**You know I don't like questions.**

ESFINGE / ESFINGE #1 / ESFINGE #2
**We know!**

[They look at each other in triumph.]

OEDIPUS
**Let's get to it. I got a territory to conquer.**

ESFINGE
**If you get it right ...**

ESFINGE #1
**...you will have proven that you are *un rey* ...**

ESFINGE #2
**...of great *inteligencia.***

ESFINGE #1
**A thinker.**

ESFINGE #2
**A man who understands the world.**

ESFINGE
**Capable of being a ruler.**

OEDIPUS
**What do I get?**

ESFINGE #1
**It's not what you get.**

ESFINGE #2
**It's what we don't.**

OEDIPUS
**What happens to you?**

ESFINGE
**We die.**

ESFINGE #1
**We eat each other.**

ESFINGE #2
**We're starved!**

OEDIPUS
**You're not scared?**

ESFINGE
**Oh no.**

ESFINGE #1
**No one's ever answered correctly.**

ESFINGE #2
**You should be scared.**

ESFINGE
**We've been around since the beginning.**

ESFINGE #1
**You should be asking what happens to you.**

ESFINGE #2
**Some people don't want to know.**

OEDIPUS
**Well?**

ESFINGE
**We give you a conscience.**

ESFINGE #1
**A real nice one.**

ESFINGE #2
**Like all your neighbors.**

ESFINGE #1
**Heavy.**

ESFINGE #2
**and guilty.**

ESFINGE
**Very Catholic.**

ESFINGE #1
**And then we kick back,**

ESFINGE #2
**and watch your people destroy you,**

ESFINGE
**It's a wonderful to sight to see.**

ESFINGE #1
**And you have to service us.**

ESFINGE #2
**He does?**

ESFINGE #1
**Yes, I just added that.**

ESFINGE
**For as long as we like.**

ESFINGE #1
**And remember.**

ESFINGE #2
**We been around ...**

ESFINGE #1
**A long time ...**

ESFINGE #2
**We take our *tiempo* ...**

[They laugh as they stare him down.]

OEDIPUS
**And the question is?**

[The heads get focused.]

ESFINGE
***Hermanas, listas?***

ESFINGE #1
***Lista!***

ESFINGE #2
**I was born ready!**

[They adjust themselves in a sphinx like ritual. They purr and make guttural hungers sounds to throw him off.]

ESFINGE
***Senor*, what is the creature that walks on four legs *en la manana* ...**

ESFINGE #1
**...two legs *en la tarde* ...**

ESFINGE #2
**...and three legs *en la noche*?**

OEDIPUS
**Hm.**
**What is the creature that walks on four legs in the morning,**
**two in the afternoon,**
**and three in the evening?**

ESFINGE
**Let me remind you, *señor* …**

ESFINGE #1
**…that to understand the riddle—**

ESFINGE #2
**…is to understand humanity.**

[They look at him with the confidence *que este pendejo* would never guess the answer. OEDIPUS takes a moment and looks out at the audience, as if seeing them he can see the answer to humanity in their faces. Behind him, the image he conjures up appears. It is TIRESIAS, who slowly stands at his place. He mimes holding a baby.]

OEDIPUS
**A man walks on four legs in the morning of his life.**

[TIRESIAS stands with his arms at his side. The three heads lose their smile.]

**Two legs in the afternoon of his youth.**

[TIRESIAS pulls out his stick and unfolds it to the full-length walking cane. The three heads put on a frown.]

**And three legs at the end of his evening.**

[OEDIPUS smiles with confidence. The three heads are in shock.]

**A child.**
**A man.**
**A *viejo*.**

**Humanity.**

[TIRESIAS sits. Beat.]

ESFINGE #1
**Uh …**

ESFINGE #2
**Oh.**

ESFINGE / ESFINGE #1 / ESFINGE #2
***HIJO DE LA CHINGADA MADRE!***

[The heads begin to scream.]

ESFINGE
**Prison may have set you free ...**

ESFINGE #1
**...but freedom will imprison you forever ...**

ESFINGE #2
***cabron*!**

[They begin to hiss as they advance on one another.]

SCENE ELEVEN
***Count No Man Happy***

[In the air we hear three *gritos* echo as the *CORO* begin a new song. CREON goes on stage and looks out, as if he can see OEDIPUS, who is approaching.]

CORO
**Why?**
**Why, oh Lord?**

CORO #1
**Does someone else get to be *El Rey*?**

CORO #2
**Why don't the rich go hungry?**

CORO #3
**Why don't the greedy ever fill up?**

CORO #4
**Why does someone else always win the lotto?**

CORO
**Why?**

CORO #1
**Why is it someone else who escapes untouched?**

CORO #2
**Why is it someone else your wife wants to fuck?**

CORO #3
**Why is it someone else everyone loves?**

CORO #4
**Yeah, why is that?**

CORO
**Why?**

CORO #1
**Why doesn't God pick me?**

CORO #2
**So mean this God.**

CORO #3
**He doesn't listen.**

CORO #4
**No he doesn't.**

CORO
**Why?**

CORO #1
**Why do the less worthy—**

CORO #2
**the less loyal—**

CORO #3
**the undeserving—**

CORO #4
**get rewarded with your mercy?**

CORO #1
**I believe.**

CORO #2
**I love.**

CORO #3
**I try.**

CORO #4
**I take what's mine.**

CORO #1
**You also did that.**

CORO #2
**Don't lie God!**

CORO #3
**I read it.**

CORO
**Mysterious ways.**

CORO #4
**So,**

CORO #1
**Come on,**

CORO #2
**man,**

CORO
**Why?**

CORO #3
**If it's just fate ...**

CORO #4
**...then why don't you ...**

CORO
**...pick me?**

[The CORO leave as CREON and OEDIPUS are left alone to face each other.]

SCENE TWELVE
***This Is and Was***

[*La Casa*. CREON and OEDIPUS face off, maybe echoing the pose with Laius earlier. They look at each other for a moment.]

CREON
**You think you're all bad cause you killed *Esfinge*?**

[Beat]

OEDIPUS
**That's the welcome I get?**

CREON
**What were you expecting, a parade?**

OEDIPUS
***Hermano …***

CREON
***Hermano?* Why are you here, Oedipus?**

OEDIPUS
**No where else to go.**

CREON
**You're peeps.**

OEDIPUS
**I'm hoping that's you …**

[This throws off CREON. OEDIPUS extends his arms, CREON knows better than to ignore the gesture. He goes to OEDIPUS and hugs him coldy.]

CREON
**You just get out?**

OEDIPUS
**Yeah.**

CREON
**Thought you'd be there forever.**

OEDIPUS
**Always and forever …**

[OEDIPUS does a little laugh, CREON doesn't.]

**You miss it?**

CREON
**Locked up?**

[CREON thinks about it.]

**I miss the grilled cheese—but I like being my own boss more.**

OEDIPUS
**Oh, you the boss?**

[CREON looks at OEDIPUS directly.]

CREON
**Yeah.**

**Oedipus, listen, you were like a brother to me once. I wouldn't have made it in the *Pinche* California Youth Authority without you—but we don't got room for visitors.**

OEDIPUS
**I won't stay long.**

CREON
**Naw, it's just that, *con todo respeto*, I can't have any problems here.**

OEDIPUS
**You won't. I gotta land somewhere. Not forever, just for now.**

[Beat]

CREON
**You can stay a week, tops.**

OEDIPUS
**I appreciate it, *hermano*.**

CREON
**This is my sister's pad. I live with her.**

OEDIPUS
**You have a sister? You never told me that.**

CREON
**She takes good care of me.**

OEDIPUS
**What do you do?**

CREON
**Got a shop I run for my brother-in-law.**

OEDIPUS
**You live with a family?**

CREON
**Naw, she's a widow.**

OEDIPUS
**Okay … Got a job for me?**

CREON
**It's not really a shop, it's more like a Wal-Mart, if you know what I mean. I sell a lot of different kind of 'merchandise'…**

OEDIPUS
**Ah. I don't got no money.**

CREON
**Don't worry. We got food and good weed. It's just a week, right?**

OEDIPUS
**Thanks, man.**

[Beat]

CREON
**Listen, my sister …**

OEDIPUS
**What about her?**

CREON
**She's not doing too good right now. Her husband just died. She keeps to herself.**

OEDIPUS
**That's cool. We don't have to know each other.**

CREON
**Just be cool around her. Don't mention her old man, okay?**

OEDIPUS
**What happened to him?**

CREON
**That's one of the things you shouldn't talk about.**

[Beat]

**You respect me, right?**

OEDIPUS
**Give me a reason not to.**

[CREON holds his gaze on OEDIPUS.]

**Of course.**

CREON
**Just so we're clear ...**

OEDIPUS
**Come right out.**

CREON
**She's not available.**

OEDIPUS
**I wouldn't do that.**

CREON
**She's doing time herself.**

OEDIPUS
**She locked up?**

CREON
**No, she's punishing herself.**

OEDIPUS
**She an *alleluia*?**

CREON
**No, but here, people still believe things in this *barrio*. About what happens to us. Our fate. Prophecy. Prediction. Oracles. We're very Old-School here.**

OEDIPUS
**And you?**

[He thinks about it.]

CREON
**Yeah, me too.**

OEDIPUS
**Like what?**

[JOCASTA speaks from another part of the room.]

JOCASTA
**Like we get punished for losing faith.**

[They are both surprised to see her there. OEDIPUS keeps his eyes on her.]

CREON
**Dammit, don't sneak up on me like that!**

OEDIPUS
**Hey.**

[JOCASTA doesn't answer him.]

**Is this your sister?**

JOCASTA
**What do I look like, his mother?**

CREON
**You been here the whole time?**

[She glares at CREON.]

JOCASTA
**Yup …**

[They look at OEDIPUS.]

**So, you don't believe in punishment?**

OEDIPUS
**You talking to me?**

JOCASTA
**Who the hell do you think I'm talking to?**

OEDIPUS
**Cause if you are, I didn't say anything.**

JOCASTA
**You didn't have to.**

OEDIPUS
**I don't think God punishes you unless you want him to.**

JOCASTA
**You saying we look for pain?**

OEDIPUS
**Do you?**

[Tense silence. They stare at each other. Beat.]

CREON
**Okay, so, uh …**

JOCASTA
**What do you mean?**

OEDIPUS
**I'm just saying that for some people, God is a stick they use to beat themselves up with.**

JOCASTA
**And how do you know what people think?**

OEDIPUS
**I don't know what people think.**

JOCASTA
**That's right, you don't.**

OEDIPUS
**But I can look at them and tell how beat up they are.**

[Ouch.]

JOCASTA
**You think the people in this *barrio*, the elders, the healers, *los hueseros,* beat them selves up with a 'God Stick'?**

OEDIPUS
**I don't know the people in this *barrio*.**

JOCASTA
**That's right, you don't.**

OEDIPUS
**But I can see how beat up you are.**

JOCASTA
**Fuck you, asshole!**

[Beat. Trying to diffuse the moment.]

CREON
**Oedipus, man … Let me just show you your room.**

[Beat. OEDIPUS keeps his eyes on JOCASTA.]

OEDIPUS
**I'm sorry.**

CREON
**It's over here …**

JOCASTA
**You should be, you're arrogant.**

OEDIPUS
**I thought I knew what you were feeling.**

JOCASTA
**What are you, psychic? We're people of faith, shithead.**

OEDIPUS
**Yeah, I can tell by the way you talk.**

JOCASTA
**Don't mess with me, little boy!**

CREON
**I gotta go.**

OEDIPUS
**Go ahead, please, believe.**

[OEDIPUS doesn't move, although CREON would like him to.]

CREON
**Whatever, I'm going to work …**

JOCASTA
**What do you believe?**

[CREON's had enough.]

[As he leaves, he looks at OEDIPUS.]

**A week.**

[As he exits, he shouts ...]

**Don't kill each other!**

[OEDIPUS turns to JOCASTA.]

OEDIPUS
**Sorry about your old man.**

[CREON shakes his head in disgust as he exits. He mutters to himself.]

CREON
**Dammit! ...**

JOCASTA
**Maybe it's what God wanted ...**

OEDIPUS
**What did you want?**

JOCASTA
**Who cares what I wanted?**

[Beat]

OEDIPUS
**Why are you so angry?**

[An irritated JOCASTA.]

JOCASTA
***Who* are you?**

OEDIPUS
**My name is Oedipus.**

[JOCASTA takes a beat.]

JOCASTA
**What kind of retarded name is that?**

OEDIPUS
**It means …**

JOCASTA
**I know what it means. Was it a joke? Is it your real name?**

OEDIPUS
**My father gave it to me.**

JOCASTA
**Why would he name you after something so bad?**

OEDIPUS
**It's who I am. If it's me, why would it be bad?**

JOCASTA
**Hm. I'm Jocasta.**

OEDIPUS
**No shit?**

JOCASTA
**Shit.**

OEDIPUS
**Well, it's a beautiful name.**

JOCASTA
**It is?**

OEDIPUS
**It has a lot of beautiful letters in it.**

[This throws her for a moment.]

**It sounds like it has a lot of history.**

JOCASTA
**Yeah, it's old. I don't know what it means.**

OEDIPUS
**It can mean what you want it to.**

[She dismisses him, but is amused.]

**I would say it means 'beautiful letters'.**

[Beat. He looks at her intensely.]

**How long you been this lonely?**

JOCASTA
**Shut up!**

OEDIPUS
**You just look really sad to me.**

JOCASTA
**Maybe I am, maybe I'm not.**

OEDIPUS
**Angry.**

JOCASTA
**I have a right!**

OEDIPUS
**We all do.**

JOCASTA
**Not like me.**

OEDIPUS
**You don't get to own it, Jo-cas-ta.**

[He likes the way it sounds in his mouth, but he stays with her.]

**I got sadness too.**

JOCASTA
**Don't give me the comfort bullshit, okay?**

OEDIPUS
**I'm not, I was just telling you my truth.**
**That I can relate.**

[Beat]

JOCASTA
**How old are you?**

OEDIPUS
**Old enough.**

JOCASTA
**Uh huh. Are you older than eighteen?**

OEDIPUS
**Yeah …**

JOCASTA
**Well, that's good. At least we got ourselves an adult.**
**How long were you locked up?**

OEDIPUS
**Almost all my life.**

[This might throw her a bit.]

JOCASTA
**You another animal or you got rules?**

OEDIPUS
**Yeah, I got rules. I got a lot under my belt.**

JOCASTA
**What you got?**

OEDIPUS
**I got my G.E.D.**

[JOCASTA feigns impression.]

JOCASTA
**Oh …**

OEDIPUS
**I didn't cheat. It took me a while, but I got through it.**
**I also got some training in things.**

JOCASTA
**Like?**

OEDIPUS
**Serving food. Fixing cars. Cooking. Cleaning. Manners. Talking.**

JOCASTA
**Talking?**

<u>OEDIPUS</u>
**Yeah. Being a leader.**

<u>JOCASTA</u>
**Oh? And how you get that?**

<u>OEDIPUS</u>
**Same way you did ...**

[Beat]

<u>JOCASTA</u>
**So what are you running from?**

<u>OEDIPUS</u>
**Stuff.**

<u>JOCASTA</u>
**Uh huh, everybody is. What's your stuff?**

<u>OEDIPUS</u>
**Does it matter?**

<u>JOCASTA</u>
**It matters if you're some kind of pervert or some shit like that.**

<u>OEDIPUS</u>
**I'm not.**

<u>JOCASTA</u>
**You got dreams?**

<u>OEDIPUS</u>
**I don't dream.**

<u>JOCASTA</u>
**Hm, I don't either.**

<u>OEDIPUS</u>
**See, I knew we'd have something in common.**

<u>JOCASTA</u>
**You're very young to be so serious.**

<u>OEDIPUS</u>
**So are you.**

JOCASTA
**You don't know me.**

OEDIPUS
**You don't know me.**

[Beat]

**What happened to your old man?**

[She looks at him. This is the first time she's talked about him.]

JOCASTA
**He was cursed. He had been dead for a long time before he died.**

OEDIPUS
**He was?**

JOCASTA
**Do you know how hard it is to live when you're afraid?**

OEDIPUS
**No.**

JOCASTA
**Do you know what it means to live without God?**

OEDIPUS
**Yeah.**

JOCASTA
**What are you, some kind of atheist bullshit or something?**

OEDIPUS
**No.**

JOCASTA
**You an annoying Jehovahs?**

OEDIPUS
**No.**

JOCASTA
**Then what do you believe in?**

[Beat]

OEDIPUS
**Me.**

JOCASTA
**What?**

OEDIPUS
**I believe in my power.**

JOCASTA
**Well you know what, don't run around telling that to the people here. We're border people. We've always been. It's who we are. We're the stuff underneath the cement. Do you get that?**

OEDIPUS
**I guess.**

JOCASTA
**This city—it's just borders and beliefs. It's about the old ways here.**

**In this *barrio*—we still lay hands and kill chickens and go to church and do what the *shaman* says. Look at the way we look, like our ancestors. We haven't changed. This ain't downtown—it's the borderlands. This is the way we live.**

**You might think you have the power to make the world you want to make, but there's someone upstairs pulling your strings.**

**You think you got here on your own? We all got destiny. We all got a story that was written for us a long time ago. We're just characters in a book. We're already history and we just started living. Our story has already been told. Were fated.**

[He smiles.]

**Don't laugh at me!**

OEDIPUS
**I'm not.**

[She keeps looking at him. He loses the smile.]

**I'm not.**

JOCASTA
**So, that's your whole religion—that you can kick ass?**

OEDIPUS
**No, it's that I am more powerful than God.**

JOCASTA
**Shame on you!**

OEDIPUS
**You're just saying that because you think you should.**

[She doesn't respond.]

**One day I am going to be a God.**

[She smiles.]

**Don't laugh at me.**

JOCASTA
**I'm not. It's just that, challenging God—it's a little boy thing.**
**When you get older, you're going to beg for him.**

OEDIPUS
**I won't need his help.**

JOCASTA
**Not help—comfort.**

[She knows this feeling well.]

**When it's you and the darkness—that's when you're going to want to speak with him. So don't offend him so early in your game.**

OEDIPUS
**I'm not. I just want him to see me.**

[This surprises her.]

JOCASTA
**Why?**

OEDIPUS
**I'm missing something …**
**A history.**

[He's vulnerable, but he likes the feeling.]

JOCASTA
**You got one.**

<u>OEDIPUS</u>
**I need a new one.**

[He looks at her and takes something from inside her.]

**So do you.**

<u>JOCASTA</u>
**What?**

<u>OEDIPUS</u>
**You heard me.**

**I know you do.**
**Don't stop looking at me.**

**Please.**

[Beat]

<u>JOCASTA</u>
**You can't just invent one.**

<u>OEDIPUS</u>
**Why not?**

<u>JOCASTA</u>
**It's not the way it's done.**

<u>OEDIPUS</u>
**I'm not interested in the way things are done. Neither are you.**

<u>JOCASTA</u>
**Stop talking to me like you know me.**

<u>OEDIPUS</u>
**But I do. I look at you and I feel like a sentence just got finished. I don't know why.**
**It's not a feeling. It's right here.**

[OEDIPUS points to his chest.]

**Like a hole got filled.**

[Silence. A beat filled with heat.]

JOCASTA
**You ever been with a woman?**

[OEDIPUS nods his head no.]

**You're not embarrassed about that?**

OEDIPUS
**When it happens, I want it to mean so much that it will make me a man.**

JOCASTA
**You ever cried so hard that everything inside you came floating out like the L.A. River when it rains?**

[He thinks about it.]

OEDIPUS
**Yeah.**

JOCASTA
**You ever lost something?**

OEDIPUS
**Yeah.**

JOCASTA
**Something that destroyed you?**

OEDIPUS
**I don't know ...**

JOCASTA
**You ever killed a man?**

[He doesn't say anything.]

**Oh ...**

**I should have known, it's all power hungry bullshit.**

[She gets up to leave, but he grabs her by the hand. He looks at her and she returns the stare. There is such longing between them, but it's also a gulf. They look at each other too long. As she stands there, she allows herself to be torn open, but the thought makes her sad.]

**Why, young man, do you want to be *un Rey*?**

[He caresses her hand.]

OEDIPUS
**I want things.**

JOCASTA
**Things ...**

OEDIPUS
**Anything.**

**That I can hold on to.**

**I want it so bad.**

[He puts her hand on his face.]

**Don't you want something?**

**Other than that sadness?**

[He catches her. She starts to cry. He watches her cry for a moment. He reaches out to touch her face. She lets him. He does the only he knows how to do—he kisses each eye. Her tears are as sweet as his father's. He kneels before her.]

**Teach me.**

[He grabs her by the waist and kisses her breast.]

**Teach me.**

[He rests his head on her belly.]

**Teach me.**

[He pulls her down. They begin to make love as the CORO begins to sing The Shirelles, 'Will You Still Love Me Tomorrow'.]

***Tonight you're mine completely***
***You give your love so sweetly***
***Tonight the light of love is in your eyes***
***But will you love me tomorrow?***

SCENE THIRTEEN
***So, Being Mortal***

[OEDIPUS and JOCASTA lay on stage undressing each other. CREON stands pissed, looking at them, while the CORO recites.]

CORO #1
**Time passes.**

CORO #2
***El tiempo pasa.***

CORO #3
**They stay in bed.**

CORO #1
**Stay *en la cama.***

CORO #1
**For three months.**

CORO #2
**Three months?**

CORO #3
**Must be good.**

CORO #2
**Must be …**

CORO #1
**What do they have …**

CORO #2
**…to stay *en la cama* …**

CORO #3
**…for three months?**

CORO #3
**Damn!**

CORO #1
**One day they decide.**

CORO #2
**While they're in bed …**

CORO #3
**There needs to be a new *rey*.**

CREON #1
**Who is going to rule.**

CORO #1
**Out here we need kings.**

CORO #2
**And systems.**

CORO #3
**To operate *under* the system.**

CORO #2
**And he starts going out.**

CORO #1
**While she is sleeping.**

CORO #2
**Checking out the territory.**

CORO #3
**Shaking some hands.**

CORO #3
**And cutting some deals.**

CORO #1
**Brings her back some *churros*.**

CORO #2
**And Twinkies.**

CORO #3
**Her favorite.**

CORO #1
**But there's trouble.**

CORO #1
**Trouble to come.**
CORO #2
**You knew it wasn't easy.**

CORO #3
**No way.**

CORO #2
**Because time passes.**

CORO #1
***El tiempo pasa.***

CORO #2
**And there are deals to be made.**

CORO #3
**And territories to protect.**

CORO #3
**And kingdoms to conquer.**

CORO
**But you don't want to get out of bed …**

SCENE FOURTEEN
***Drowned In A Sea Of …***

[OEDIPUS and JOCASTA in their underwear. She gets up and starts to put on her clothes.]

OEDIPUS
**Don't.**

JOCASTA
**Why?**

OEDIPUS
**I want to see you.**
**Like you are.**

JOCASTA
**In a different light—I look better.**

OEDIPUS
**I like it like that.**

JOCASTA
**Like how?**

OEDIPUS
**Like real.**

[JOCASTA laughs.]

JOCASTA

**That's because you're young. Real is hot when you're young. Then you get older and you say that word to yourself—'real'—and it's never a good word again.**

OEDIPUS

**I wish I had that.**

JOCASTA

**What, seriousness? You have too much of it.**

OEDIPUS

**Experience.**

JOCASTA

**You have more than you think. Why do you need it anyway?**

OEDIPUS

**Honest?**

JOCASTA

**What do you think we're being?**

OEDIPUS

**I wonder … if you're just killing time with me.**

JOCASTA

**What?**

[She kisses him tenderly.]

I'm filling up with you.

Doesn't that sound strange?
Even thinking it makes me feel …

All the empty spaces inside of me, it's as if they were always yours.
The touch of your skin, your smile, the way you look at me.
They complete me.

**I know I sound like some teenage *puta*, but it's different, I swear to you. When a woman my age says that to a man—it's different.**

OEDIPUS

**Why?**

JOCASTA
**Because it means more when you've been through something.**
**Lived.**

**You're a part of me.**
**I don't know why.**

[He kisses her. They look at each other as she runs a finger over the tattoo on his chest.]

**Who were your people?**

OEDIPUS
**You mean my father?**

JOCASTA
**Yeah.**

OEDIPUS
**I'm a Gomez.**

JOCASTA
**Gomez.**

OEDIPUS
**His name is *Tiresias*.**

JOCASTA
***Tiresias Gomez?***

OEDIPUS
**You know him?**

JOCASTA
**Yeah, I know him!**

OEDIPUS
**You do?**

JOCASTA
**He worked with my husband.**

OEDIPUS
**My dad? Here?**

JOCASTA
**Yes. He was an associate.**

***Tiresias* and his loyalty.**
**He had very strong beliefs.**
**He loved to read.**

OEDIPUS
**I know.**
**Are you kidding me about this?**

JOCASTA
**No. He never told you his life?**

OEDIPUS
**He didn't.**

JOCASTA
**What did he say about his past?**

OEDIPUS
**Nothing.**

JOCASTA
**You didn't talk about your family? Your histories?**

OEDIPUS
**No. My father, he was … inside.**
**I mean, he raised me, but we never talked about the past.**

[This gives her pause.]

**What's the matter?**

JOCASTA
**Nothing …**
**What about your mother?**

OEDIPUS
**She died when I was a baby.**

JOCASTA
**But did you know who she was?**

OEDIPUS
**Yeah.**

[That helps.]

***Maria Gomez.***
**She died in the fields.**
**She was a farm worker.**

[He reaches for his pants and pulls out his wallet and a worn picture. He shows it to her.]

**I look at it a lot.**

[She stares at the picture.]

**What?**

JOCASTA
**Nothing.**

**Wow, our friend *Tiresias*.**
**He always seemed a little bit of a monk to me, you know?**

OEDIPUS
**That's him.**

JOCASTA
**I can't believe he had a kid.**
**And he raised you?**

OEDIPUS
**Sort of.**
**I started getting in trouble when I was little.**
**They put me in the Youth Authority.**
**I was there until I was seventeen.**

JOCASTA
**Ah, Creon …**

OEDIPUS
**Yup.**
**By then, I didn't know how to live on the outside.**
**So, one day—I robbed a Costco!**

JOCASTA
**You did?**

OEDIPUS
**Yeah. I didn't want the money or anything.**
**I didn't even have a gun.**
**I just went outside and waited for the cops.**

**And they put me in the Penn.**
**It was a place I knew …**

**And then my dad, he did something …**
**Broke the law.**
**To be with me.**
**And that's when we became something.**
**Something real.**

**Like us.**

JOCASTA
**And he's still up there—at North Kern?**

OEDIPUS
**Yup.**

JOCASTA
**I can't believe it.**

[She stops for a moment and tries to think. Put pieces of puzzles together.]

OEDIPUS
**And your people?**

JOCASTA
**I don't talk to them.**

OEDIPUS
**Do you have a picture?**

JOCASTA
**I don't keep pictures.**

OEDIPUS
**Why?**

JOCASTA
**I don't have any good memories, why would I want to look at that?**

OEDIPUS
**You have Creon.**

JOCASTA
**Yes, that's all I ever had.**
**But he's like a baby that needs his tit every few hours.**

OEDIPUS
**He can't help it.**
**He's insecure.**

JOCASTA
**He always wanted to be something. More.**
**But that's not his destiny.**

OEDIPUS
**Now you got me.**

[She looks at him.]

**You never wanted no kids?**

JOCASTA
**I had a baby.**

OEDIPUS
**You did?**

JOCASTA
**But he died when he was born.**

OEDIPUS
**You miss him?**

JOCASTA
**I don't know.**
**I remember him, here, on my chest.**

**The thought of him was killing me, so I had to let him go.**
**In my mind.**

**See, in this *barrio*, they do that to you—the dead—they can get into your head and make you stop living, even from the grave.**

**I think they all hate being over there at Forest Lawn.**
**The sound of the freeway day and night.**

OEDIPUS
**Is that where he is?**

JOCASTA
**I don't know.**
**They took him from me.**

<u>OEDIPUS</u>
**Who did?**

<u>JOCASTA</u>
**It doesn't matter.**
**It won't bring him back.**

**It's part of the life.**
**You choose to live this kind of life, you have to accept the rules.**

**But I do have a loud sister that lives at Forest Lawn.**
**She's a bitch.**

[He laughs.]

**I bring her flowers—she wilts them.**
**I visit her,—it rains.**
**She hates her plot.**
**She complains about everything.**

<u>OEDIPUS</u>
**Maybe one day we'll find him and you can go see him?**

<u>JOCASTA</u>
**No. We won't.**

**Listen, we can't talk about him no more.**

<u>OEDIPUS</u>
**Okay.**

[Beat]

<u>JOCASTA</u>
**You fill that space.**

<u>OEDIPUS</u>
**I do?**

<u>JOCASTA</u>
**You fill the space that was his.**

[They lay back down, his head on her chest.]

SCENE FIFTEEN
***Like Wind Suddenly Ruffling A Stretch Of Calm Sea***

[Night. The Oracle of owls appear, shifting their heads from side to side. CREON seems to be the leader of the parliament. He stands directly over a sleeping OEDIPUS and JOCASTA. The other owls leave, only CREON stays.]

SCENE SIXTEEN
***Envied On His Pedestal***

[JOCASTA suddenly wakes to see CREON standing over them. She is embarrassed and wraps herself in a sheet.]

JOCASTA
**What?**

CREON
**Nothing.**

JOCASTA
**Don't start anything!**

[She goes off. CREON kicks OEDIPUS with his foot. He is jolted awake. CREON stares at him. This makes OEDIPUS uncomfortable and he starts to get dressed.]

OEDIPUS
**What do you want?**

CREON
**Did *La Senora* at *La Curacao* give you a package?**

[Beat]

OEDIPUS
**She did.**

CREON
**Why?**

OEDIPUS
**Your sister asked me to pick it up.**

CREON
**Jocasta asked you to do my work?**

OEDIPUS
**She didn't say that.**

[CREON tries to brush it off.]

CREON
***El Pinguino* saw you at Lucy's Tacos asking the *viejos* about the territory.**

OEDIPUS
**He's thinking about somebody else.**

CREON
**Naw, he still goes to Latin Mass, he doesn't lie.**

OEDIPUS
**What do you care?**

CREON
**You're like the mayor without a nice suit, but for what, I wonder?**

OEDIPUS
**It's not CSI, don't speculate so much, dude.**

[JOCASTA enters.]

CREON
**You don't think I know what's going on?**

JOCASTA
**What's going on?**

[CREON ignores her.]

CREON
**Have you forgotten our agreement?**

OEDIPUS
**That wasn't an agreement. That was a request.**

[CREON grabs OEDIPUS by his shirt.]

CREON
**This is mine. I've been waiting a long time for it. I haven't been able to take a wife. You are not going to fuck this up for me.**

OEDIPUS
**Take your hands off me.**

JOCASTA
**Creon, let him go!**

[He does.]

CREON
**Listen, little boy, I'm not lost in your crooked teeth smile.**

[CREON looks at JOCASTA.]

**Where's your head?**

OEDIPUS
**What's he talking about?**

JOCASTA
**He's talking out of his ass, calm down, Creon.**

CREON
**I know you were grieving, but what the hell is this? I told him he could stay a week. It's been three months and now he's on the payroll?**

JOCASTA
**And what's wrong with that? He's earning his keep.**

CREON
**He must be a good lay.**

JOCASTA
**Don't talk to me like that!**

CREON
**What do you know about him?**

JOCASTA
**Creon, you're being ridiculous. *Mi hermano*, do you think I would abandon you?**

[She goes to him and puts his hand on her heart.]

**You always have a place here.**

[CREON pulls his hand away.]

CREON
**There's no room left in there.**

JOCASTA
**There's room for all of us.**

CREON
**When was the last time you were out there?**

OEDIPUS
**I've been taking care of business for her.**

CREON
**Yeah, thanks, I see that.**

OEDIPUS
**People ask me for help. Should I not help?**

CREON
**Help is my business, *brother*.**

OEDIPUS
**I'm not trying to take a piece of your pie, so chill out.**

CREON
**If you're not asking for money then what are you asking for?**

[Slight pause. Why lie?]

OEDIPUS
**Loyalty.**

CREON
**You think I'm an idiot?**

JOCASTA
**Creon, *por favor*! There's enough business for everybody. What you should be doing is helping each other.**

CREON
**Each other? What's his investment?**

[OEDIPUS and JOCASTA look at each other. CREON watches them.]

**What?**

OEDIPUS
**Let's not mess this up for anybody. Let's keep it within the family.**

CREON
**Family?**

[Beat. CREON looks at JOCASTA.]

JOCASTA
**We're getting married.**

CREON
**What are you talking about?**

JOCASTA
**Just simple. In the backyard.**

CREON
**When were you going to tell me?**

[She can't look at him.]

**Do you know what they say about him?**

OEDIPUS
**Nothing!**

CREON
**Nothing, right. Have you ever heard these people say nothing? How do you think this community survives? That's how they keep the myths alive. Even the damn blind kid selling Chiclets talks shit about you.**

OEDIPUS
**They're liars.**

CREON
**You're so arrogant you misjudged their smiles.**

JOCASTA
**Creon, *por favor*, don't make *pleito*. This is for all of our good. These people they need their *reyes*. They're tied to their history. That's what we give them. We don't make the rules, we just get around them.**

CREON
**Why not me?**

[There is silence.]

JOCASTA
***Creon, con todo mi corazon*, please don't ask me this.**

CREON
**You're not being honest with me. Are you honest with him?**

[She looks at OEDIPUS. She can't look at CREON.]

JOCASTA
**It's not your calling, *mi hermano*.**

CREON
**How do you know that?**

OEDIPUS
**You know it too.**

[CREON looks down, ashamed, but his anger builds.]

CREON
**They think he's cursed.**

JOCASTA
**What?**

CREON
**All the healers feel it. *El Mistico* swears by it.**

[EL MISTICO stands from his place.]

EL MISTICO
***En mi corazon!***

CREON
**And so does *El Curandero*—**

[EL CURANDERO and stands.]

EL CURANDERO
***Yo tambien.***

[He points to his heart.]

***Aqui lo siento.***

CREON
**And *El Huesero, pues* that *pendejo* doesn't like being left out—**

[EL HUESERO, appears, unsure.]

EL HUESERO
***Yo siento algo ...***

[They all sit.]

CREON
**Have a great wedding!**

[CREON leaves. JOCASTA looks at OEDIPUS, troubled. He goes to her and kisses her. She smiles for him.]

SCENE SEVENTEEN
***This Is No Time For Petty Personal Bickering***

[A ritual begins. OEDIPUS goes to one side of the stage and JOCASTA goes to the other, as they walk towards each other in a stylized *homeboy* version of a wedding march. As OEDIPUS passes, each member of the CORO extends a hand with an open palm and throws a *bendicion* on the soon-to-be. OEDIPUS and JOCASTA come together, center stage. The CORO place a traditional wedding cord over them. They begin a slow dance to a classic old school song.]

CORO
***Always and forever***
***Each moment with you***
***Is just like a dream to me***
***That somehow came true.***

***And I know tomorrow***
***Will still be the same***
***Cuz we got a life of love***
***That won't ever change.***

[JOCASTA teaches OEDIPUS how to dance. He is overjoyed to learn and she is quickly becoming light and young.]

SCENE EIGHTEEN
***May I Never Enjoy Life, But Perish Under A Curse***

[Three CORO members appear before the dancing couple as EL MISTICO, EL CURANDERO and EL HUESERO. OEDIPUS and JOCASTA stop dancing. He whispers into her ear and she walks away.]

OEDIPUS
***Señores, gracias* for your work. Jocasta appreciates all that you do.**

**So, tell me, what is it that you do?**

[The healers all look at each other quizzically.]

ALL
**We heal.**

OEDIPUS
**Yeah, but like how?**

EL MISTICO
***Pues*, I see *lo que viene*.**

OEDIPUS
**You're a seer?**

EL MISTICO
***Senor*, I don't name it, I just do it.**

EL HUESERO
**I look at your bones and heal your wounds.**

OEDIPUS
**You're a chiropractor?**

EL HUESERO
**Yes, but without the license.**

OEDIPUS
**And you?**

EL CURANDERO
**I just heal.**

OEDIPUS
**That's it?**

EL CURANDERO
**That's a lot!**

OEDIPUS
**I see. So how may I help you?**

ALL
**The question is, young king, how can we help you?**

OEDIPUS
**I'm glad you asked, *veteranos*. Can I be *directo*?**

ALL
**Honesty is our business.**

OEDIPUS
**Good, each one of you is going to pay me a percentage of what you make.**

ALL
***Que?***

OEDIPUS
**An operating fee for working in the *barrio*.**

ALL
**What you are asking for is against our *tradiciones*.**

OEDIPUS
**How can I charge the Taco Truck owners for providing their *servicios* and not you?**

ALL
**We do the work of God!**

OEDIPUS
**If God wants to heal someone, let him do it himself!**

ALL
***Respeto!***

OEDIPUS
**Kings are only respectful to other kings.**

ALL
**You are very young.**

OEDIPUS
**Don't forget, I'm the one that got rid of *Esfinge*! People like their leaders young these days. There can only be one God in this *barrio*, and that is me.**

ALL
**Fear him, little boy!**

OEDIPUS
**I don't got no fear! This life took it away from me. That don't mean I don't like nice and tender and feelings and shit, but I can turn them off, because if you want to live in this world, you have to.**

ALL
**Bow your head in reverence!**

OEDIPUS
**EVERYONE IS GOING TO RESPECT ME!**

ALL
**What happened to you?**

OEDIPUS
**I'm drunk. With power. I'm not afraid to say it. I'm sure you've all felt this way. Don't worry, I'm going to use it for good too. Clean up some of these corners. Give the *chamacos* a basketball court and all that stuff. But don't get me wrong, old men, I'm gonna take what's mine too.**

ALL
**We will pray for you.**

OEDIPUS
**Don't pray for me.**
**Pray to me!**

[OEDIPUS walks through the group of healers, pushing them aside.]

SCENE NINETEEN
***Foremost OF All The Gods***

[OEDIPUS, with the boundless energy of youth, begins to run around the stage. He is working out, but more recklessly. He runs up against a wall and does a somersault. He is pure energy. He starts doing push ups with one hand.]

OEDIPUS
**I am the accursed.**

**Oedipus.**

**A lord.**

**A God.**

**An almighty!**

[He begins to laugh, very pleased with himself. He continues his regimen.

In another part of the stage, JOCASTA is holding her white wedding bible, a veil still on her head. She stands and looks out, full of doubt. She brushes it off and throws away the bible on stage. OEDIPUS runs to where the bible is and picks it up.]

**SECTION 2: B-E-E to B-I-E.**

**B-I-B-L-E.**

[Slowly he begins to rip pages out of the bible. He throws them up in the air defiantly. They fall to the floor like confetti and litter the stage.]

**Goodbye Genesis.**

**Goodbye Judges.**

**Goodbye Psalms.**

**Goodbye Proverbs.**

**Goodbye Matthew.**

**Goodbye James.**

**Goodbye Corinthians.**

**Goodbye Peter.**

**Goodbye John.**

**Goodbye Revelations.**

[He angrily rips out a big stack of pages and throws them up.]

**Bye, bye!**

[The stage is covered in confetti of scripture.]

<u>SCENE TWENTY</u>
***What Should A Man Fear?***

[JOCASTA makes her way to the stage. The CORO form a circle around her.]

<u>CORO #1</u>
**There was a time.**

<u>CORO</u>
**Time.**

<u>CORO #2</u>
**When I crossed a line.**

CORO
**Line.**

CORO #3
**Went too far.**

CORO
**Far.**

CORO #1
**Said too much.**

CORO
**Much.**

CORO #2
**Wanted it all.**

CORO
**All.**

CORO #3
**But now I see.**

CORO
**See.**

CORO #1
**Was blind**

CORO
**Blind.**

CORO #2
**But now I see.**

CORO
**I.**

CORO #3
**But that was a long time ago.**

CORO
**Time**

CORO #2
**When I was young.**

CORO
**Young.**

CORO #3
**I was free.**

CORO
**Free**

[CREON enters the circle and he and JOCASTA face each other.]

CORO #3
**One day.**

CORO
**Day.**

CORO #1
**Time catches up with you.**

CORO
**You.**

CORO #2
**And you have to be honest.**

CORO
**Honest.**

CORO #3
**With yourself.**

CORO
**Yourself.**

[The CORO part to reveal CREON and JOCASTA.]

SCENE TWENTY-ONE
***Presume On His Good Fortune***

[CREON and JOCASTA *en la casa.*]

JOCASTA
***Hermano*, what do they say about me?**

CREON
**It doesn't matter.**

JOCASTA
**It always did, why wouldn't it now?**

CREON
**Because it's too late, you've given him everything, including his noose to hang himself.**

JOCASTA
***Callate!***

CREON
**You can lie to yourself, but I will never lie to you, *mi hermana*.**

JOCASTA
**What I gave him, Creon, was my love and everything that comes with a marriage.**

CREON
**And the kingdom …**

JOCASTA
**I never shut you out, Creon.**

CREON
**I know, but you opened the door, to your heart, and he took advantage.**

JOCASTA
**Would you have preferred to see me die alone?**

CREON
**You weren't alone …**

JOCASTA
**Creon …**

CREON
**This was mine.**

JOCASTA
**No, it wasn't.**

CREON

**He's exactly like Laius—he won't be happy with what he has. I know him. He'll take and take until he leaves you dry, like a desert. That boy has a hunger and he never knows when to stop.**

JOCASTA

**Is that what they say?**

CREON

**That's what I say.**

JOCASTA

**Then you don't understand what it means to be *un rey*. Show me a king who doesn't get seduced by the power of being a God? It's natural. He aspires to something.**

CREON

**What is it with you and your choice in men?**

JOCASTA

**Stop it!**

CREON

**You're not acting like a queen, you're acting like a *puta*!**

[She slaps him.]

JOCASTA

**DON'T TALK TO ME THAT WAY!**

[CREON turns away.]

CREON

**Sister, when did you become so blind?**

JOCASTA

**I'M NOT BLIND! I am holding on to what little we have left. How will we live without a king? In exile? We would die, *hermano*. You can barely wipe your own ass!**

[They've stopped looking at each other.]

**I didn't choose him. He chose me! He came into my life. He saved me. I was dead before him. Stop being so ungrateful.**

CREON

**Ungrateful? I'm the one who took him in. I practically dragged him to your bed. I only have myself to blame.**

JOCASTA
**What do you want, Creon?**

CREON
**We have to kill him …**

JOCASTA
**What!**

CREON
**You have to let him go.**

JOCASTA
**I can't.**

**He's … mine.**

CREON
**He's a boy!**

JOCASTA
**He's our *rey*!**

CREON
**They're going to destroy him. The old school way. A *chisme* will become a belief. A belief will become a motive. A motive will be justified.**

**They'll isolate you. They'll force you out of here. Where will you go?**

JOCASTA
**My poor brother, your jealousy is suffocating you.**

CREON
**My poor sister, your love has made you blind.**

[OEDIPUS quietly steps in.]

JOCASTA
**Tell me what they know.**

CREON
**I won't lie to you, but I also won't destroy you.**

JOCASTA
**You'd rather see me die alone.**

OEDIPUS
**What do you know, *chismoso*?**

[JOCASTA and CREON both turn to see OEDIPUS.]

CREON
**You should ask your father in prison.**

JOCASTA
**Don't listen, he's full of venom today.**

OEDIPUS
**What do you know about my father?**

CREON
**HIS SON KILLED OUR KING!**

JOCASTA
**Don't listen to him!**

[OEDIPUS starts to move towards CREON, but JOCASTA steps in between them.]

JOCASTA
**Don't, please don't.**

OEDIPUS
**YOU'RE A TRAITOR! And I don't care that you're family.**

JOCASTA
**You've brought terrible lies into this house, Creon.**

OEDIPUS
**You'll pay for that!**

CREON
**That worries me, as I hear your anger is uncontrollable and the reason for Laius' death.**

OEDIPUS
**Why are you doing this? You're a poison, brother-in-law …**

CREON
**You mean trying to save the kingdom?**

OEDIPUS
**Trying to tear us apart.**

[OEDIPUS looks at JOCASTA.]

**Are you in on this with him?**

JOCASTA
**What? Of course not!**

[OEDIPUS pulls back from them both.]

OEDIPUS
**How can you stand to be in the same room with this traitor when you know he tells lies against me?**

JOCASTA
**He's my brother!**

OEDIPUS
**Only an accomplice would do that.**

JOCASTA
**Oedipus, *por favor*, calm down.**

OEDIPUS
**How can I trust you when you choose the loyalty of your brother over our bond?**

JOCASTA
**Don't do this to us.**

[She looks at CREON.]

**Why Creon, why do you bring such sadness into this house? Did we push so far away?**

OEDIPUS
**Did I steal your money?**

CREON
**No. Just my family.**

[Suddenly OEDIPUS screams as he rushes for CREON, taking him down to the floor where they wrestle and fight.]

JOCASTA
**Stop it! STOP IT!**

[CREON screams as he tries to fight OEDIPUS off.]

CREON
**You can't kill everyone who holds a secret against you!**

JOCASTA
**Let him go, Oedipus. Please, let him go!**

[JOCASTA tries to pull OEDIPUS off of CREON, but he is *en rabia* like a bulldog and won't let go. He begins to choke CREON.]

**DON'T! I COULDN'T BEAR ANOTHER DEATH IN MY FAMILY. PLEASE ...**

[OEDIPUS is enraged and out of his head, he digs his hands deeper into CREON's neck. JOCASTA leans over Oedipus, and with her knee, kicks into Oedipus, who falls over, out of breath and grabbing his ribs. CREON chokes for breath. Jocasta weeps. They all stop, as their breath fills the space. A beat.]

**Why Creon? Why destroy us?**

[Beat. CREON, regaining his breath, but not his emotions.]

CREON
**Don't you see? It's not me. It's ...**

[He points up to the heavens.]

**Them ...**

[A small earthquake trembles. They all stand, looking up at the sky.]

**An oracle appeared today.**
**Not to one, but to all.**
**Not in private, but in public.**
**Our past spoke to our future.**

**Why would the earth speak to the moon?**

[Jocasta gasps.]

***Coatlicue*, the mother under our feet,**
**spoke to the daughter she murdered, *Coyolxauhqui*,**
**the moon in the sky.**

**It stopped the rush hour traffic on the boulevard.**
**Everyone heard it.**
**From the *Panadero* to the *Paletero*.**

[The sound of the city suddenly surrounds them. The CORO speak in the voice of an *indìgena*, while OEDIPUS, JOCASTA and CREON look up at the sky in witness.]

COATLICUE
***Un hombre—***

COYOLXAUHQUI
**A man—**

COATLICUE
***que es un nino—***

COYOLXAUHQUI
**who is a boy—**

COATLICUE
***viviendo en su inocencia—***

COYOLXAUHQUI
**living in his innocence—**

COATLICUE
***pero perdido en su colera—***

COYOLXAUHQUI
**but lost in his anger—**

COATLICUE
***mata a un desconocido—***

COYOLXAUHQUI
**kills a stranger—**

COATLICUE
***en media noche—***

COYOLXAUHQUI
**in the middle of the night—**

COATLICUE
***en medio de un camino—***

COYOLXAUHQUI
**in the middle of a road—**

COATLICUE
***no realizando—***

COYOLXAUHQUI
**not realizing—**

COATLICUE
***que él ha asesinado un rey—***

COYOLXAUHQUI
**that he has murdered a king—**

COATLICUE
***y destruido su familia.***

COYOLXAUHQUI
**and destroyed his family.**

COATLICUE
***En el mismo tiempo—***

COYOLXAUHQUI
**at the same time—**

COATLICUE
***un rey destruye un rey.***

COYOLXAUHQUI
**a king destroys a king.**

COATLICUE
***Puede ser verdad.***

COYOLXAUHQUI
**can it be true.**

[The sound of the city dies away. CREON leaves.]

SCENE TWENTY-TWO
***And Towered Up***

[OEDIPUS and JOCASTA are left alone in space. He goes to her, but does not touch her.]

OEDIPUS
**Do you believe him?**

[Beat]

JOCASTA
**In the end, it's all we have isn't it—our beliefs?**

OEDIPUS
**Do we have to believe everything they tell us?**
**Even if I killed a man ...**

JOCASTA
**You killed a man.**

OEDIPUS
**If he was a king ...**

JOCASTA
**My husband.**

OEDIPUS
**I wouldn't have known.**

JOCASTA
**That's right, you wouldn't have.**

OEDIPUS
**So, it can't be my fault.**

JOCASTA
**Does it matter?**

[OEDIPUS reaches for her hand and JOCASTA takes his. He leans his head on her, vulnerable.]

**He pulls strings so tight, this God, how can we move when we're trapped?**

OEDIPUS
**Why does he cause such hurt?**

JOCASTA
**He's petty. He just happens to be God. Maybe he suffers our weakness as well?**

OEDIPUS
**What are we going to do?**

JOCASTA
**He'll destroy us, unless we own up to our sins.**

OEDIPUS
**You don't believe them do you?**

[Beat]

**Oh …**

[He's hurt, but tries to think of an option.]

**I'll find the curse and break it.**

JOCASTA
**You can't.**

OEDIPUS
**Why can't I?**

JOCASTA
**We are the curse …**

[OEDIPUS refusing to believe. He pulls away.]

OEDIPUS
**I saved these people once. I can save them again.**

JOCASTA
**Maybe you can.**

OEDIPUS
**It's a lie. I'll prove it. *Chula,* I can do it.**

JOCASTA
**I know …**

OEDIPUS
**Then?**

JOCASTA
**Talk to your father, Oedipus.**

[JOCASTA turns away. OEDIPUS walks away as we hear the sound of a car speeding down a highway. TIRESIAS makes his way to two chairs downstage that face each other.]

SCENE TWENTY-THREE
***Most Powerful Of Men***

[The sound of the car is cut off by the sound of bars opening on a prison door. OEDIPUS enters and sees TIRESIAS sitting at a chair waiting. OEDIPUS goes and sits. They face each other in silence for a moment. Finally, OEDIPUS gets up and goes to TIRESIAS. He takes off his glasses and kisses each eye. He sits again.]

TIRESIAS
**What colors did you see on the way up?**

OEDIPUS
**Oh, I saw some greens. A lot of brown. A few yellows!**

TIRESIAS
***Amarillos?***

OEDIPUS
**Yeah.**

**I saw a house with a weird kind of dark reddish burnt color that had a tree with a lot of fruit hanging from it. I was going to get off and pick some, but there was a sign that said, "Nothing is free".**

[TIRESIAS laughs.]

TIRESIAS
**That's true. But greedy.**

OEDIPUS
**How are the books?**

TIRESIAS
**Oh, the books are fine. They love to talk.**
**Everyday they want to tell me something new.**
**Some days I have to tell them to slow down.**

**I moved.**

OEDIPUS
**You did?**

TIRESIAS
**Yeah. SECTION 8: T-A-O to T-E-M.**

OEDIPUS
**How's everybody?**

TIRESIAS
**Well, everybody, you know.**

**Some of them died.**
**Some of them left.**
**Not always when they wanted to.**
**Cycles, you know.**

[A desperate beat.]

OEDIPUS
**What do you know?**

TIRESIAS
**If I told you what I knew, it would destroy you.**

OEDIPUS
**I am already being destroyed.**
**You have to tell me what the Gods say to you.**

**Was the man in the middle of the road …**

TIRESIAS
**Yes.**

OEDIPUS
**Oh no!**

**I have to break this curse.**
**I have to defy him and show him that I can't be fucked with!**

TIRESIAS
**We don't defy the Gods.**

OEDIPUS
**Not in here, *papa*, but out there …**

TIRESIAS
**My son, don't you see?**
**In here is out there.**

OEDIPUS
**You don't understand.**
**You can't see how it is.**

[TIRESIAS points at OEDIPUS' head.]

TIRESIAS
**You are still inside, *mi hijo*.**

OEDIPUS
**I have to go …**

[As OEDIPUS starts to get up, TIRESIAS reaches for his hand.]

TIRESIAS
**You haven't heard everything he wants to say.**

OEDIPUS
**I don't care to hear anything more from his poisoned tongue!**

TIRESIAS
**Then, hear from mine.**

OEDIPUS
**And what do you have to say that he doesn't already say through you?**

TIRESIAS
**That I once was a man who defied him.**
**And because of that, he punished me by taking away the colors.**

**I saved a life.**
**But it was not mine to save.**

**I defied destiny.**

[Beat]

**And that life was yours.**

OEDIPUS
**Yes, you did.**
**You gave me all that is good in my life.**

TIRESIAS
**But it was not mine to give.**

OEDIPUS
**What do you mean?**

[Beat]

TIRESIAS
**I took you from your father.**

OEDIPUS
**My father?**

TIRESIAS
**The man in the middle of the road . . .**

[TIRESIAS bows his head.]

OEDIPUS
**Say it.**
***Papa*, please say it.**

**SAY IT!**

TIRESIAS
**His name is Laius.**
**He is your father.**

OEDIPUS
**If he is my father,**
**then she . . .**

[OEDIPUS falls to his knees.]

**Why?**

TIRESIAS
**Because I wanted you to live.**
**Isn't that what every father wants for his son?**

OEDIPUS
**But you're not my father.**

TIRESIAS
**You think a father is made of blood?**

**A father is a made of sweat—**
**running to keep up in your youth,**
**and praying that you'll survive when you're older.**

**A father is made of bruises—**
**from taking your punches,**
**and then kicking himself for the things he never did.**

**A father is made of breath—**
**from blowing into your lungs the ideas of life,**

**and gasping in fear at what you'll do with them.**

<u>OEDIPUS</u>
**I never gave my father that chance!**

<u>TIRESIAS</u>
**He didn't want it.**

<u>OEDIPUS</u>
**How do you know?**

**You vicious old man!**

**You filled me with stories that should have been his to tell.**
**You gave me lessons that you were not yours to give.**
**You held me in my fear knowing that the wrong hands were in place.**

**Fuck you!**

**Playing out a power trip with my life.**
**You steal me from my father and then leave me at the mercy of a God who loves punishment.**

<u>TIRESIAS</u>
**He didn't want you!**

<u>OEDIPUS</u>
**What were you doing all this time?**

**You didn't learn anything in SECTION 6: R-A-Y to R-E-L.**

**You didn't learn anything.**

**The books don't talk to you because you don't listen.**

**I mistook your silence for meditation.**
**But you were sleeping the whole time.**

**I just want to know if you were laughing at me?**
**Because I'm fucked!**

I dared to open my heart to someone and God tricks me into perversion.

I did exactly what he wanted, didn't I?
**I played out his version.**
**My weakness was his plotting.**

[His is a desperate confession.]

**Can't you see?**

**I wanted to make a new story.**
**Something no one had ever seen.**

**I wanted to tell it my way.**
**And I wanted to be able to control my own destiny.**

**But I never had the chance because all of this was decided way before I got here.**

**Isn't that right?**

**Is this the way the lesson looks?**
**Like me?**

**Am I the lesson?**

**AM I THE WAY THE LESSON LOOKS?**

TIRESIAS
**I don't know.**

**I can't see …**

[OEDIPUS, in his rage, lunges at TIRESIAS and begins to choke him. TIRESIAS, in true *mistico* form, does not resist. All we can hear is OEDIPUS struggling against tears and TIRESIAS choking. Maybe because of his lack of resistance, OEDIPUS looks at his father and comes to his senses, letting go. TIRESIAS struggles for breath. OEDIPUS realizing that he has hurt his adopted, quickly hugs him. He begins to cry with abandon.]

OEDIPUS
**Father.**
**My father.**
**Please.**
**Please …**

[It's too much. Too much to take. He runs out. The sound of the prison bars closing. TIRESIAS quietly goes back to his chair, sitting and talking to OEDIPUS, as if he was still there, sitting across from him.]

TIRESIAS
**I took you when he gave you to me. I didn't have the heart. The heart to see history play itself out the way the Gods wanted.**

**I made a new story. That story was you. I gave it the best chance I knew how, to make sure it lived.**

**But I'm not a God,**
**I'm not a creator.**
**I'm just a man.**

**A weak man,**
**who looks inside now,**
**for all of his answers.**

**I can not see them in the world.**

**So, I look inside.**

**For the answers.**

**The stories.**

**Inside . . .**

[TIRESIAS stays in his chair looking off for the rest of the play.]

SCENE TWENTY-FOUR
***Consider His Last Day***

[OEDIPUS stands just off stage, in the audience.]

OEDIPUS
**I am the accursed.**

CORO
**Accursed.**

OEDIPUS
**I am Oedipus.**

CORO
**Oedipus.**

OEDIPUS
**The son of royalty.**
**But the product of mortal man.**

CORO
**Mortal man.**

OEDIPUS
**Tonight I have seen,**

CORO
**Seen.**

OEDIPUS
**that I have been the fool.**

CORO
**Fool.**

OEDIPUS
**I'm just a bit player,**
**in a story you all know too well.**

CORO
**Too well.**

OEDIPUS
**Why couldn't I see it when it played out in front of me?**

**I was arrogant.**
**I was a kid in a man's body.**
**I treated people unkindly.**
**And those who loved me most,**
**I never really trusted.**

**I saw too much.**

CORO
**Too much.**

OEDIPUS
**And now I have to pay for that.**

CORO
**Pay.**

OEDIPUS
**I am the accursed.**

**I am Oedipus.**

CORO
**Oedipus …**

[The CORO begin to sing James Brown's *It's a Man's Man's Man's World*. OEDIPUS makes his way towards the stage, where JOCASTA stands on an opposite side of him.]

***This is a man's world,***
***this is a man's world***
But it wouldn't be nothing,
nothing without a woman or a girl

He's lost in the wilderness
***He's lost in bitterness***

SCENE TWENTY-FIVE
***No Mortal Eyes***

[OEDIPUS and JOCASTA face each other. Neither advances on the other. The distance between them should feel like a gulf.]

OEDIPUS
**It's true.**

[Beat]

JOCASTA
**I know.**

OEDIPUS
**Everything? Tell me what they told you.**

JOCASTA
**It's not what they told me. It's what I should have known.**

OEDIPUS
**You couldn't have.**

JOCASTA
**We're all guilty of the lies we live with. The ones we choose to believe.**

[Beat]

**You filled spaces. Spaces that were yours. I should have known.**

[Beat]

OEDIPUS
**I won't see you again.**

JOCASTA
**I know.**

OEDIPUS
**I can't bear the weight. I cursed you. I cursed myself.**

JOCASTA
**The curses of my life came before you.**

**I was afraid. To fight him. Fear. That I would kill him.
But now I see that Laius has killed me.**

**To think I thought myself greater than the Gods. I lied to myself for so long.**

[Beat]

OEDIPUS
**Take these eyes from me.**

JOCASTA
**Never.**

OEDIPUS
**All that I have seen. The darkness and the light. Take them from me.**

JOCASTA
**No.**

OEDIPUS
**I beg of you.**

JOCASTA
**Please, Oedipus.**

OEDIPUS
**Let me live in a memory, without pain. You must.**

***Mama*, please.**

**God will forgive you. He will grant you mercy in your violence.**

JOCASTA
**Please …**

OEDIPUS
**I promise. I won't scream. I won't cry.
Do it because you love me.
You must.**

**You must.**
**You must.**

[He goes to her and kneels in front of her. They look at each other. He pulls her hands to his eyes.]

**Do it!**

[She reaches in and blinds him.]

JOCASTA
***Mi hijo …***

[She gives him a kiss on each eye.]

OEDIPUS
**Now go.**
**Go to your destiny.**
**I am going to mine.**
**Go.**
**To your memories.**

[She pulls back and OEDIPUS shanks her with a small hand-made prison knife. At first she resists, then she stops and pushes back in to his blade, never taking her eyes off him. He turns the blade into her stomach until she falls.]

EPILOGUE
***Yet In The End***

[The CORO stand. We hear *los tres chifles* in the air.]

CORO
***Oye, gente!***
**Look at this *hombre*.**
***Todos* who live here.**

**This is Oedipus.**
**The young *vato* who defeated *Esfinge*.**
**Who took the crown and swore himself in,**
**as *un rey*.**

***Oye gente!***
**Look upon Oedipus.**
***Un rey* who could not escape his destiny.**

**Who found a way.**

**To come back.**
**To his beginning.**

**Let him live.**
**Roam in his memories.**
**However few.**

**No man is *feliz,***
**until he's six feet under.**

***Pero* for now,**
**Let him be.**

**Free.**

[The last *tres chifles*. OEDIPUS stands. He puts on a pair of old *cholo* shades. He pulls out a blind man's cane and begins to use it as he walks. TIRESIAS stands. All we hear is the sound of the clickety-clack of their canes roaming around the stage. They find each other. OEDIPUS puts his hand on his father's shoulder as TIRESIAS slowly leads him back to prison. The sound of prison doors closing.]

- FIN—

# Agamemnon

## Aeschylus

### Characters

*Watchman*
*Clytaemestra*
*Herald*
*Agamemnon*
*Cassandra*
*Aegisthus*
*Chorus of Argive Elders*
*Attendants of Clytaemestra: of Agamemnon: bodyguard of Aegisthus (all silent parts)*
*Time, directly after the fall of Troy.*

SCENE: *Argos, before the palace of King Agamemnon. The Watchman, who speaks the opening lines, is posted on the roof of the palace. Clytaemestra's entrances are made from a door in the center of the stage; all others, from the wings.*

*(The Watchman, alone.)*

I ask the gods some respite from the weariness
of this watchtime measured by years I lie awake
elbowed upon the Atreidae's roof dogwise to mark
the grand processionals of all the stars of night
burdened with winter and again with heat for men,
dynasties in their shining blazoned on the air,
these stars, upon their wane and when the rest arise.

I wait; to read the meaning in that beacon light,
a blaze of fire to carry out of Troy the rumor
and outcry of its capture; to such end a lady's
male strength of heart in its high confidence ordains.
Now as this bed stricken with night and drenched with dew
I keep, nor ever with kind dreams for company;
since fear in sleep's place stands forever at my head

against strong closure of my eyes, or any rest:
I mince such medicine against sleep failed: I sing,
only to weep again the pity of this house
no longer, as once, administered in the grand way.
Now let there be again redemption from distress,
the flare burning from the blackness in good augury.

*(A light shows in the distance.)*
Oh hail, blaze of the darkness, harbinger of day's
shining, and of processionals and dance and choirs
of multitudes in Argos for this day of grace.
Ahoy!
I cry the news aloud to Agamemnon's queen,
that she may rise up from her bed of state with speed
to raise the rumor of gladness welcoming this beacon,
and singing rise, if truly the citadel of Ilium
has fallen, as the shining of this flare proclaims.
I also, I, will make my choral prelude, since
my lord's dice cast aright are counted as my own,
and mine the tripled sixes of this torchlit throw.

May it only happen. May my king come home, and I
take up within this hand the hand I love. The rest
I leave to silence; for an ox stands huge upon
my tongue. The house itself, could it take voice, might speak
aloud and plain. I speak to those who understand,
but if they fail, I have forgotten everything.

*(Exit. The Chorus enters, speaking.)*

Ten years since the great contestants
of Priam's right,
Menelaus and Agamemnon, my lord,
twin throned, twin sceptered, in twofold power
of kings from God, the Atreidae,
put forth from this shore
the thousand ships of the Argives,
the strength and the armies.
Their cry of war went shrill from the heart,
as eagles stricken in agony
for young perished, high from the nest
eddy and circle
to bend and sweep of the wings' stroke,
lost far below
the fledgelings, the nest, and the tendance.
Yet someone hears in the air, a god,
Apollo, Pan, or Zeus, the high
thin wail of these sky-guests, and drives

late to its mark
the Fury upon the transgressors.
So drives Zeus the great guest god
the Atreidae against Alexander:
for one woman's promiscuous sake
the struggling masses, legs tired,
knees grinding in dust,
spears broken in the onset.
Danaans and Trojans
they have it alike. It goes as it goes
now. The end will be destiny.
You cannot burn flesh or pour unguents,
not innocent cool tears,
that will soften the gods' stiff anger.

But we; dishonored, old in our bones,
cast off even then from the gathering horde,
stay here, to prop up
on staves the strength of a baby.
Since the young vigor that urges
inward to the heart
is frail as age, no warcraft yet perfect,
while beyond age, leaf
withered, man goes three footed
no stronger than a child is,
a dream that falters in daylight.

*(Clytaemestra enters quietly. The Chorus continues to speak.)*

But you, lady,
daughter of Tyndareus, Clytaemestra, our queen:
What is there to be done? What new thing have you heard?
In persuasion of what
report do you order such sacrifice?
To all the gods of the city,
the high and the deep spirits,
to them of the sky and the market places,
the altars blaze with oblations.
The staggered flame goes sky high
one place, then another,
drugged by the simple soft
persuasion of sacred unguents,
the deep stored oil of the kings.
Of these things what can be told
openly, speak.
Be healer to this perplexity
that grows now into darkness of thought,

while again sweet hope shining from the flames
beats back the pitiless pondering
of sorrow that eats my heart.

I have mastery yet to chant the wonder at the wayside
given to kings. Still by God's grace there surges within me
singing magic
grown to my life and power,
how the wild bird portent
hurled forth the Achaeans'
twin-stemmed power single hearted,
lords of the youth of Hellas,
with spear and hand of strength
to the land of Teucrus.
Kings of birds to the kings of the ships,
one black, one blazed with silver,
clear seen by the royal house
on the right, the spear hand,
they lighted, watched by all
tore a hare, ripe, bursting with young unborn yet,
stayed from her last fleet running.
Sing sorrow, sorrow: but good win out in the end.

Then the grave seer of the host saw through to the hearts divided,
knew the fighting sons of Atreus feeding on the hare
with the host, their people.
Seeing beyond, he spoke:
"With time, this foray
shall stalk the castle of Priam.
Before then, under
the walls, Fate shall spoil
in violence the rich herds of the people.
Only let no doom of the gods darken
upon this huge iron forged to curb Troy—
from inward. Artemis the undefiled
is angered with pity
at the flying hounds of her father
eating the unborn young in the hare and the shivering mother.
She is sick at the eagles' feasting.
Sing sorrow, sorrow: but good win out in the end.
Lovely you are and kind
to the tender young of ravening lions.
For sucklings of all the savage
beasts that lurk in the lonely places you have sympathy.
Grant meaning to these appearances
good, yet not without evil.

Healer Apollo, I pray you
let her not with cross winds
bind the ships of the Danaans
to time-long anchorage
forcing a second sacrifice unholy, untasted,
working bitterness in the blood
and faith lost. For the terror returns like sickness to lurk in the house;
the secret anger remembers the child that shall be avenged."
Such, with great good things beside, rang out in the voice of Calchas,
these fatal signs from the birds by the way to the house of the princes,
wherewith in sympathy
sing sorrow, sorrow: but good win out in the end.

Zeus: whatever he may be, if this name
pleases him in invocation,
thus I call upon him.
I have pondered everything
yet I cannot find a way,
only Zeus, to cast this dead weight of ignorance
finally from out my brain.

He who in time long ago was great,
throbbing with gigantic strength,
shall be as if he never were, unspoken.
He who followed him has found
his master, and is gone.
Cry aloud without fear the victory of Zeus,
you will not have failed the truth:

Zeus, who guided men to think,
who has laid it down that wisdom
comes alone through suffering.
Still there drips in sleep against the heart
grief of memory; against
our pleasure we are temperate
From the gods who sit in grandeur
grace comes somehow violent.

On that day the elder king
of the Achaean ships, no more
strict against the prophet's word,
turned with the crosswinds of fortune,
when no ship sailed, no pail was full,
and the Achaean people sulked
fast against the shore at Aulis
facing Chalcis, where the tides ebb and surge:

and winds blew from the Strymon, bearing
sick idleness, ships tied fast, and hunger,
distraction of the mind, carelessness
for hull and cable;
with time's length bent to double measure
by delay crumbled the flower and pride
of Argos. Then against the bitter wind
the seer's voice clashed out
another medicine
more hateful yet, and spoke of Artemis, so that the kings
dashed their staves to the ground and could not hold their tears.

The elder lord spoke aloud before them:
"My fate is angry if I disobey these,
but angry if I slaughter
this child, the beauty of my house,
with maiden blood shed staining
these father's hands beside the altar.
What of these things goes now without disaster?
How shall I fail my ships
and lose my faith of battle?
For them to urge such sacrifice of innocent blood
angrily, for their wrath is great—it is right. May all be well yet."

But when necessity's yoke was put upon him
he changed, and from the heart the breath came bitter
and sacrilegious, utterly infidel,
to warp a will now to be stopped at nothing.
The sickening in men's minds, tough,
reckless in fresh cruelty brings daring. He endured then
to sacrifice his daughter
to stay the strength of war waged for a woman,
first offering for the ships' sake.

Her supplications and her cries of father
were nothing, nor the child's lamentation
to kings passioned for battle.
The father prayed, called to his men to lift her
with strength of hand swept in her robes aloft
and prone above the altar, as you might lift
a goat for sacrifice, with guards
against the lips' sweet edge, to check
the curse cried on the house of Atreus
by force of bit and speech drowned in strength.

Pouring then to the ground her saffron mantle

she struck the sacrifices with
the eyes' arrows of pity,
lovely as in a painted scene, and striving
to speak—as many times
at the kind festive table of her father
she had sung, and in the clear voice of a stainless maiden
with love had graced the song
of worship when the third cup was poured.

What happened next I saw not, neither speak it.
The crafts of Calchas fail not of outcome.
Justice so moves that those only learn
who suffer; and the future
you shall know when it has come; before then, forget it.
It is grief too soon given.
All will come clear in the next dawn's sunlight.
Let good fortune follow these things as
she who is here desires,
our Apian land's singlehearted protectress.

*(The Chorus now turns toward Clytaemestra, and the leader speaks to her.)*

I have come in reverence, Clytaemestra, of your power.
For when the man is gone and the throne void, his right
falls to the prince's lady, and honor must be given.
Is it some grace—or otherwise—that you have heard
to make you sacrifice at messages of good hope?
I should be glad to hear, but must not blame your silence.

Clytaemestra

As it was said of old, may the dawn child be born
to be an angel of blessing from the kindly night.
You shall know joy beyond all you ever hoped to hear.
The men of Argos have taken Priam's citadel.

Chorus

What have you said? Your words escaped my unbelief.

Clytaemestra

The Achaeans are in Troy. Is that not clear enough?

Chorus

This slow delight steals over me to bring forth tears.

Clytaemestra

Yes, for your eyes betray the loyal heart within.

Chorus
Yet how can I be certain? Is there some evidence?

Clytaemestra
There is, there must be; unless a god has lied to me.

Chorus
Is it dream visions, easy to believe, you credit?

Clytaemestra
I accept nothing from a brain that is dull with sleep.

Chorus
The charm, then, of some rumor, that made rich your hope?

Clytaemestra
Am I some young girl, that you find my thoughts so silly?

Chorus
How long, then, is it since the citadel was stormed?

Clytaemestra
It is the night, the mother of this dawn I hailed.

Chorus
What kind of messenger could come in speed like this?

Clytaemestra
Hephaestus, who cast forth the shining blaze from Ida.
And beacon after beacon picking up the flare
carried it here; Ida to the Hermaean horn
of Lemnos, where it shone above the isle, and next
the sheer rock face of Zeus on Athos caught it up;
and plunging skyward to arch the shoulders of the sea
the strength of the running flare in exultation,
pine timbers flaming into gold, like the sunrise,
brought the bright message to Macistus' sentinel cliffs,
who, never slow nor in the carelessness of sleep
caught up, sent on his relay in the courier chain,
and far across Euripus' streams the beacon flare
carried to signal watchmen on Messapion.
These took it again in turn, and heaping high a pile
of silvery brush flamed it to throw the message on.
And the flare sickened never, but grown stronger yet
outleapt the river valley of Asopus like
the very moon for shining, to Cithaeron's scaur

to waken the next station of the flaming post.
These watchers, not contemptuous of the far-thrown blaze,
kindled another beacon vaster than commanded.
The light leaned high above Gorgopis' staring marsh,
and striking Aegyplanctus' mountain top, drove on
yet one more relay, lest the flare die down in speed.
Kindled once more with stintless heaping force, they send
the beard of flame to hugeness, passing far beyond
the promontory that gazes on the Saronic strait
and flaming far, until it plunged at last to strike
the steep rock of Arachnus near at hand, our watchtower.
And thence there fell upon this house of Atreus' sons
the flare whose fathers mount to the Idaean beacon.
These are the changes on my torchlight messengers,
one from another running out the laps assigned.
The first and the last sprinters have the victory.
By such proof and such symbol I announce to you
my lord at Troy has sent his messengers to me.

Chorus

The gods, lady, shall have my prayers and thanks straightway
And yet to hear your story till all wonder fades
would be my wish, could you but tell it once again.

Clytaemestra

The Achaeans have got Troy, upon this very day.
I think the city echoes with a clash of cries.
Pour vinegar and oil into the selfsame bowl,
you could not say they mix in friendship, but fight on.
Thus variant sound the voices of the conquerors
and conquered, from the opposition of their fates.
Trojans are stooping now to gather in their arms
their dead, husbands and brothers; children lean to clasp
the aged who begot them, crying upon the death
of those most dear, from lips that never will be free.
The Achaeans have their midnight work after the fighting
that sets them down to feed on all the city has,
ravenous, headlong, by no rank and file assigned,
but as each man has drawn his shaken lot by chance.
And in the Trojan houses that their spears have taken
they settle now, free of the open sky, the frosts
and dampness of the evening; without sentinels set
they sleep the sleep of happiness the whole night through.
And if they reverence the gods who hold the city
and all the holy temples of the captured land,
they, the despoilers, might not be despoiled in turn.

Let not their passion overwhelm them; let no lust
seize on these men to violate what they must not.
The run to safety and home is yet to make; they must turn
the pole, and run the backstretch of the double course.
Yet, though the host come home without offence to high
gods, even so the anger of these slaughtered men
may never sleep. Oh, let there be no fresh wrong done!

Such are the thoughts you hear from me, a woman merely.
Yet may the best win through, that none may fail to see.
Of all good things to wish this is my dearest choice.

Chorus

My lady, no grave man could speak with better grace.
I have listened to the proofs of your tale, and I believe,
and go to make my glad thanksgivings to the gods.
This pleasure is not unworthy of the grief that gave it
O Zeus our lord and Night beloved,
bestower of power and beauty,
you slung above the bastions of Troy
the binding net, that none, neither great
nor young, might outleap
the gigantic toils
of enslavement and final disaster.
I gaze in awe on Zeus of the guests
who wrung from Alexander such payment.
He bent the bow with slow care, that neither
the shaft might hurdle the stars, nor fall
spent to the earth, short driven.

They have the stroke of Zeus to tell of.
This thing is clear and you may trace it.
He acted as he had decreed. A man thought
the gods deigned not to punish mortals
who trampled down the delicacy of things
inviolable. That man was wicked.
The curse on great daring
shines clear; it wrings atonement
from those high hearts that drive to evil,
from houses blossoming to pride
and peril. Let there be
wealth without tears; enough for
the wise man who will ask no further.
There is not any armor
in gold against perdition
for him who spurns the high altar

of Justice down to the darkness.

Persuasion the persistent overwhelms him,
she, strong daughter of designing Ruin.
And every medicine is vain; the sin
smolders not, but burns to evil beauty.
As cheap bronze tortured
at the touchstone relapses
to blackness and grime, so this man
tested shows vain
as a child that strives to catch the bird flying
and wins shame that shall bring down his city.
No god will hear such a man's entreaty,
but whoso turns to these ways
they strike him down in his wickedness.
This was Paris: he came
to the house of the sons of Atreus,
stole the woman away, and shamed the guest's right of the board shared.
She left among her people the stir and clamor
of shields and of spearheads,
the ships to sail and the armor.
She took to Ilium her dowry, death.
She stepped forth lightly between the gates
daring beyond all daring. And the prophets
about the great house wept aloud and spoke:
"Alas, alas for the house and for the champions,
alas for the bed signed with their love together.
Here now is silence, scorned, unreproachful.
The agony of his loss is clear before us.
Longing for her who lies beyond the sea
he shall see a phantom queen in his household.
Her images in their beauty
are bitterness to her lord now
where in the emptiness of eyes
all passion has faded."

Shining in dreams the sorrowful
memories pass; they bring him
vain delight only.
It is vain, to dream and to see splendors,
and the image slipping from the arms' embrace
escapes, not to return again,
on wings drifting down the ways of sleep.
Such have the sorrows been in the house by the hearthside;
such have there been, and yet there are worse than these.
In all Hellas, for those who swarmed to the host

the heartbreaking misery
shows in the house of each.
Many are they who are touched at the heart by these things.
Those they sent forth they knew;
now, in place of the young men
urns and ashes are carried home
to the houses of the fighters.

The god of war, money changer of dead bodies,
held the balance of his spear in the fighting,
and from the corpse-fires at Ilium
sent to their dearest the dust
heavy and bitter with tears shed
packing smooth the urns with
ashes that once were men.
They praise them through their tears, how this man
knew well the craft of battle, how another
went down splendid in the slaughter:
and all for some strange woman.
Thus they mutter in secrecy,
and the slow anger creeps below their grief
at Atreus' sons and their quarrels.
There by the walls of Ilium
the young men in their beauty keep
graves deep in the alien soil
they hated and they conquered.

The citizens speak: their voice is dull with hatred.
The curse of the people must be paid for.
There lurks' for me in the hooded night
terror of what may be told me.
The gods fail not to mark
those who have killed many.
The black Furies stalking the man
fortunate beyond all right
wrench back again the set of his life
and drop him to darkness. There among
the ciphers there is no more comfort
in power. And the vaunt of high glory
is bitterness; for God's thunderbolts
crash on the towering mountains.
Let me attain no envied wealth,
let me not plunder cities,
neither be taken in turn, and face
life in the power of another.

*(Various members of the Chorus, speaking severally.)*

From the beacon's bright message
the fleet rumor runs
through the city. If this be real
who knows? Perhaps the gods have sent some lie to us.

Who of us is so childish or so reft of wit
that by the beacon's messages
his heart flamed must despond again
when the tale changes in the end?

It is like a woman indeed
to take the rapture before the fact has shown for true.

They believe too easily, are too quick to shift
from ground to ground; and swift indeed
the rumor voiced by a woman dies again.

Now we shall understand these torches and their shining,
the beacons, and the interchange of flame and flame.
They may be real; yet bright and dreamwise ecstasy
in light's appearance might have charmed our hearts awry.
I see a herald coming from the beach, his brows
shaded with sprigs of olive; and upon his feet
the dust, dry sister of the mire, makes plain to me
that he will find a voice, not merely kindle flame
from mountain timber, and make signals from the smoke,
but tell us outright, whether to be happy, or—
but I shrink back from naming the alternative.
That which appeared was good; may yet more good be given.

And any man who prays that different things befall
the city, may he reap the crime of his own heart.

*(The Herald enters, and speaks.)*

Soil of my fathers, Argive earth I tread upon,
in daylight of the tenth year I have come back to you.
All my hopes broke but one, and this I have at last.
I never could have dared to dream that I might die
in Argos, and be buried in this beloved soil.
Hail to the Argive land and to its sunlight, hail
to its high sovereign, Zeus, and to the Pythian king.
May you no longer shower your arrows on our heads.
Beside Scamandrus you were grim; be satisfied
and turn to savior now and healer of our hurts,
my lord Apollo. Gods of the market place assembled,
I greet you all, and my own patron deity

Hermes, beloved herald, in whose right all heralds
are sacred; and you heroes that sent forth the host,
propitiously take back all that the spear has left.
O great hall of the kings and house beloved; seats
of sanctity; divinities that face the sun:
if ever before, look now with kind and glowing eyes
to greet our king in state after so long a time.
He comes, lord Agamemnon, bearing light in gloom
to you, and to all that are assembled here.
Salute him with good favor, as he well deserves,
the man who has wrecked Ilium with the spade of Zeus
vindictive, whereby all their plain has been laid waste.
Gone are their altars, the sacred places of the gods
are gone, and scattered all the seed within the ground.
With such a yoke as this gripped to the neck of Troy
he comes, the king, Atreus' elder son, a man
fortunate to be honored far above all men
alive; not Paris nor the city tied to him
can boast he did more than was done him in return.
Guilty of rape and theft, condemned, he lost the prize
captured, and broke to sheer destruction all the house
of his fathers, with the very ground whereon it stood.
Twice over the sons of Priam have atoned their sins.

Chorus
Hail and be glad, herald of the Achaean host.

Herald
I am happy; I no longer ask the gods for death.

Chorus
Did passion for your country so strip bare your heart?

Herald
So that the tears broke in my eyes, for happiness.

Chorus
You were taken with that sickness, then, that brings delight.

Herald
How? I cannot deal with such words until I understand.

Chorus
Struck with desire of those who loved as much again.

Herald
You mean our country longed for us, as we for home?

Chorus
So that I sighed, out of the darkness of my heart.

Herald
Whence came this black thought to afflict the mind with fear?

Chorus
Long since it was my silence kept disaster off.

Herald
But how? There were some you feared when the kings went away?

Chorus
So much that as you said now, even death were grace.

Herald
Well: the end has been good. And in the length of time
part of our fortune you could say held favorable,
but part we cursed again. And who, except the gods,
can live time through forever without any pain?
Were I to tell you of the hard work done, the nights
exposed, the cramped sea-quarters, the foul beds—what part
of day's disposal did we not cry out loud?
Ashore, the horror stayed with us and grew. We lay
against the ramparts of our enemies, and from
the sky, and from the ground, the meadow dews came out
to soak our clothes and fill our hair with lice. And if
I were to tell of winter time, when all birds died,
the snows of Ida past endurance she sent down,
or summer heat, when in the lazy noon the sea
fell level and asleep under a windless sky—
but why live such grief over again? That time is gone
for us, and gone for those who died. Never again
need they rise up, nor care again for anything.
Why must a live man count the numbers of the slain,
why grieve at fortune's wrath that fades to break once more?
I call a long farewell to all our unhappiness.
For us, survivors of the Argive armament,
the pleasure wins, pain casts no weight in the opposite scale.
And here, in this sun's shining, we can boast aloud,
whose fame has gone with wings across the land and sea:
"Upon a time the Argive host took Troy, and on
the houses of the gods who live in Hellas nailed

the spoils, to be the glory of days long ago."
And they who hear such things shall call this city blest
and the leaders of the host; and high the grace of God
shall be exalted, that did this. You have the story.

Chorus

I must give way; your story shows that I was wrong.
Old men are always young enough to learn, with profit.
But Clytaemestra and her house must hear, above
others, this news that makes luxurious my life.
I raised my cry of joy, and it was long ago
when the first beacon flare of message came by night
to speak of capture and of Ilium's overthrow.
But there was one who laughed at me, who said: "You trust
in beacons so, and you believe that Troy has fallen?
How like a woman, for the heart to lift so light."
Men spoke like that; they thought I wandered in my wits;
yet I made sacrifice, and in the womanish strain
voice after voice caught up the cry along the city
to echo in the temples of the gods and bless
and still the fragrant flame that melts the sacrifice.

Why should you tell me then the whole long tale at large
when from my lord himself I shall hear all the story?
But now, how best to speed my preparation to
receive my honored lord come home again—what else
is light more sweet for woman to behold than this,
to spread the gates before her husband home from war
and saved by God's hand?—take this message to the king:
Come, and with speed, back to the city that longs for him,
and may he find a wife within his house as true
as on the day he left her, watchdog of the house
gentle to him alone, fierce to his enemies,
and such a woman in all her ways as this, who has
not broken the seal upon her in the length of days.
With no man else have I known delight, nor any shame
of evil speech, more than I know how to temper bronze.

*(Clytaemestra goes to the back of the stage.)*

Herald

A vaunt like this, so loaded as it is with truth,
it well becomes a highborn lady to proclaim.

Chorus

Thus has she spoken to you, and well you understand,
words that impress interpreters whose thought is clear.

But tell me, herald; I would learn of Menelaus,
that power beloved in this land. Has he survived
also, and come with you back to his home again?

Herald
I know no way to lie and make my tale so fair
that friends could reap joy of it for any length of time.

Chorus
Is there no means to speak us fair, and yet tell the truth?
It will not hide, when truth and good are torn asunder.

Herald
He is gone out of the sight of the Achaean host,
vessel and man alike. I speak no falsehood there.

Chorus
Was it when he had put out from Ilium in your sight,
or did a storm that struck you both whirl him away?

Herald
How like a master bowman you have hit the mark
and in your speech cut a long sorrow to brief stature.

Chorus
But then the rumor in the host that sailed beside,
was it that he had perished, or might yet be living?

Herald
No man knows. There is none could tell us that for sure
except the Sun, from whom this earth has life and increase.

Chorus
How did this storm, by wrath of the divinities,
strike on our multitude at sea? How did it end?

Herald
It is not well to stain the blessing of this day
with speech of evil weight. Such gods are honored apart.
And when the messenger of a shaken host, sad faced,
brings to his city news it prayed never to hear,
this scores one wound upon the body of the people;
and that from many houses many men are slain
by the two-lashed whip dear to the War God's hand, this turns
disaster double-bladed, bloodily made two.
The messenger so freighted with a charge of tears

should make his song of triumph at the Furies' door.
But, carrying the fair message of our hopes' salvation,
come home to a glad city's hospitality,
how shall I mix my gracious news with foul, and tell
of the storm on the Achaeans by God's anger sent?
For they, of old the deepest enemies, sea and fire,
made a conspiracy and gave the oath of hand
to blast in ruin our unhappy Argive army.
At night the sea began to rise in waves of death.
Ship against ship the Thracian stormwind shattered us,
and gored and split, our vessels, swept in violence
of storm and whirlwind, beaten by the breaking rain,
drove on in darkness, spun by the wicked shepherd's hand.
But when the sun came up again to light the dawn,
we saw the Aegaean Sea blossoming with dead men,
the men of Achaea, and the wreckage of their ships.
For us, and for our ship, some god, no man, by guile
or by entreaty's force prevailing, laid his hand
upon the helm and brought us through with hull unscarred.
Life-giving fortune deigned to take our ship in charge
that neither riding in deep water she took the surf
nor drove to shoal and break upon some rocky shore.
But then, delivered from death at sea, in the pale day,
incredulous of our own luck, we shepherded
in our sad thoughts the fresh disaster of the fleet
so pitifully torn and shaken by the storm.
Now of these others, if there are any left alive
they speak of us as men who perished, must they not?
Even as we, who fear that they are gone. But may
it all come well in the end. For Menelaus: be sure
if any of them come back that he will be the first.
If he is still where some sun's gleam can track him down,
alive and open-eyed, by blessed hand of God
who willed that not yet should his seed be utterly gone,
there is some hope that he will still come home again.
You have heard all; and be sure, you have heard the truth.

(The Herald goes out.)

Chorus

Who is he that named you so
fatally in every way?
Could it be some mind unseen
in divination of your destiny
shaping to the lips that name
for the bride of spears and blood,
Helen, which is death? Appropriately
death of ships, death of men and cities

from the bower's soft curtained
and secluded luxury she sailed then,
driven on the giant west wind,
and armored men in their thousands came,
huntsmen down the oar blade's fading footprint
to struggle in blood with those
who by the banks of Simoeis
beached their hulls where the leaves break.

And on Ilium in truth
in the likeness of the name
the sure purpose of the Wrath drove
marriage with death: for the guest board
shamed, and Zeus kindly to strangers,
the vengeance wrought on those men
who graced in too loud voice the bride-song
fallen to their lot to sing,
the kinsmen and the brothers.
And changing its song's measure
the ancient city of Priam
chants in high strain of lamentation,
calling Paris him of the fatal marriage;
for it endured its life's end
in desolation and tears
and the piteous blood of its people.

Once a man fostered in his house
a lion cub, from the mother's milk
torn, craving the breast given.
In the first steps of its young life
mild, it played with children
and delighted the old.
Caught in the arm's cradle
they pampered it like a newborn child,
shining eyed and broken to the hand
to stay the stress of its hunger.

But it grew with time, and the lion
in the blood strain came out; it paid
grace to those who had fostered it
in blood and death for the sheep flocks,
a grim feast forbidden.
The house reeked with blood run
nor could its people beat down the bane,
the giant murderer's onslaught.
This thing they raised in their house was blessed

by God to be priest of destruction.

And that which first came to the city of Ilium,
call it a dream of calm
and the wind dying,
the loveliness and luxury of much gold,
the melting shafts of the eyes' glances,
the blossom that breaks the heart with longing.
But she turned in mid-step of her course to make
bitter the consummation,
whirling on Priam's people
to blight with her touch and nearness.
Zeus hospitable sent her,
a vengeance to make brides weep.

It has been made long since and grown old among men,
this saying: human wealth
grown to fulness of stature
breeds again nor dies without issue.
From high good fortune in the blood
blossoms the quenchless agony.
Far from others I hold my own
mind; only the act of evil
breeds others to follow,
young sins in its own likeness.
Houses clear in their right are given
children in all loveliness.

But Pride aging is made
in men's dark actions
ripe with the young pride
late or soon when the dawn of destiny
comes and birth is given
to the spirit none may fight nor beat down,
sinful Daring; and in those halls
the black visaged Disasters stamped
in the likeness of their fathers.

And Righteousness is a shining in
the smoke of mean houses.
Her blessing is on the just man.
From high halls starred with gold by reeking hands
she turns back
with eyes that glance away to the simple in heart,
spurning the strength of gold
stamped false with flattery.

And all things she steers to fulfilment.

*(Agamemnon enters in a chariot, with Cassandra beside him. The Chorus speaks to him.)*

Behold, my king: sacker of Troy's citadel,
own issue of Atreus.
How shall I hail you? How give honor
not crossing too high nor yet bending short
of this time's graces?
For many among men are they who set high
the show of honor, yet break justice.
If one be unhappy, all else are fain
to grieve with him: yet the teeth of sorrow
come nowise near to the heart's edge.
And in joy likewise they show joy's semblance,
and torture the face to the false smile.
Yet the good shepherd, who knows his flock,
the eyes of men cannot lie to him,
that with water of feigned
love seem to smile from the true heart.
But I: when you marshalled this armament
for Helen's sake, I will not hide it,
in ugly style you were written in my heart
for steering aslant the mind's course
to bring home by blood
sacrifice and dead men that wild spirit.
But now, in love drawn up from the deep heart,
not skimmed at the edge, we hail you.
You have won, your labor is made gladness.
Ask all men: you will learn in time
which of your citizens have been just
in the city's sway, which were reckless.

Agamemnon

To Argos first, and to the gods within the land,
I must give due greeting; they have worked with me to bring
me home; they helped me in the vengeance I have wrought
on Priam's city. Not from the lips of men the gods
heard justice, but in one firm cast they laid their votes
within the urn of blood that Ilium must die
and all her people; while above the opposite vase
the hand hovered and there was hope, but no vote fell.
The stormclouds of their ruin live; the ash that dies
upon them gushes still in smoke their pride of wealth.
For all this we must thank the gods with grace of much
high praise and memory, we who fenced within our toils

of wrath the city; and, because one woman strayed,
the beast of Argos broke them, the fierce young within
the horse, the armored people who marked out their leap
against the setting of the Pleiades. A wild
and bloody lion swarmed above the towers of Troy
to glut its hunger lapping at the blood of kings.

This to the gods, a prelude strung to length of words.
But, for the thought you spoke, I heard and I remember
and stand behind you. For I say that it is true.
In few men is it part of nature to respect
a friend's prosperity without begrudging him,
as envy's wicked poison settling to the heart
piles up the pain in one sick with unhappiness,
who, staggered under sufferings that are all his own,
winces again to the vision of a neighbor's bliss.
And I can speak, for I have seen, I know it well,
this mirror of companionship, this shadow's ghost,
these men who seemed my friends in all sincerity.
One man of them all, Odysseus, he who sailed unwilling,
once yoked to me carried his harness, nor went slack.
Dead though he be or living, I can say it still.

Now in the business of the city and the gods
we must ordain full conclave of all citizens
and take our counsel. We shall see what element
is strong, and plan that it shall keep its virtue still.
But that which must be healed—we must use medicine,
or burn, or amputate, with kind intention, take
all means at hand that might beat down corruption's pain.
So to the King's house and the home about the hearth
I take my way, with greeting to the gods within
who sent me forth, and who have brought me home once more.
My prize was conquest; may it never fail again.

*(Clytaemestra comes forward and speaks.)*

Grave gentlemen of Argolis assembled here,
I take no shame to speak aloud before you all
the love I bear my husband. In the lapse of time
modesty fades; it is human.
What I tell you now
I learned not from another; this is my own sad life
all the long years this man was gone at Ilium.
It is evil and a thing of terror when a wife
sits in the house forlorn with no man by, and hears
rumors that like a fever die to break again,

and men come in with news of fear, and on their heels
another messenger, with worse news to cry aloud
here in this house. Had Agamemnon taken all
the wounds the tale whereof was carried home to me,
he had been cut full of gashes like a fishing net.
If he had died each time that rumor told his death,
he must have been some triple-bodied Geryon
back from the dead with threefold cloak of earth upon
his body, and killed once for every shape assumed.
Because such tales broke out forever on my rest,
many a time they cut me down and freed my throat
from the noose overslung where I had caught it fast.
And therefore is your son, in whom my love and yours
are sealed and pledged, not here to stand with us today,
Orestes. It were right; yet do not be amazed.
Strophius of Phocis, comrade in arms and faithful friend
to you, is keeping him. He spoke to me of peril
on two counts; of your danger under Ilium,
and here, of revolution and the clamorous people
who might cast down the council—since it lies in men's
nature to trample on the fighter already down.
Such my excuse to you, and without subterfuge.

For me: the rippling springs that were my tears have dried
utterly up, nor left one drop within. I keep
the pain upon my eyes where late at night I wept
over the beacons long ago set for your sake,
untended left forever. In the midst of dreams
the whisper that a gnat's thin wings could winnow broke
my sleep apart. I thought I saw you suffer wounds
more than the time that slept with me could ever hold.

Now all my suffering is past, with griefless heart
I hail this man, the watchdog of the fold and hall;
the stay that keeps the ship alive; the post to grip
groundward the towering roof; a father's single child;
land seen by sailors after all their hope was gone;
splendor of daybreak shining from the night of storm;
the running spring a parched wayfarer strays upon.
Oh, it is sweet to escape from all necessity!

Such is my greeting to him, that he well deserves.
Let none bear malice; for the harm that went before
I took, and it was great.

Now, my beloved one,

step from your chariot; yet let not your foot, my lord,
sacker of Ilium, touch the earth. My maidens there!
Why this delay? Your task has been appointed you,
to strew the ground before his feet with tapestries.
Let there spring up into the house he never hoped
to see, where Justice leads him in, a crimson path.

In all things else, my heart's unsleeping care shall act
with the gods' aid to set aright what fate ordained.

*(Clytaemestra s handmaidens spread a bright carpet between the chariot and the door.)*

Agamemnon

Daughter of Leda, you who kept my house for me,
there is one way your welcome matched my absence well.
You strained it to great length. Yet properly to praise
me thus belongs by right to other lips, not yours.
And all this—do not try in woman's ways to make
me delicate, nor, as if I were some Asiatic
bow down to earth and with wide mouth cry out to me,
nor cross my path with jealousy by strewing the ground
with robes. Such state becomes the gods, and none beside.
I am a mortal, a man; I cannot trample upon
these tinted splendors without fear thrown in my path.
I tell you, as a man, not god, to reverence me.
Discordant is the murmur at such treading down
of lovely things; while God's most lordly gift to man
is decency of mind. Call that man only blest
who has in sweet tranquillity brought his life to close.
If I could only act as such, my hope is good.

Clytaemestra

Yet tell me this one thing, and do not cross my will.

Agamemnon

My will is mine. I shall not make it soft for you.

Clytaemestra

It was in fear surely that you vowed this course to God.

Agamemnon

No man has spoken knowing better what he said.

Clytaemestra

If Priam had won as you have, what would he have done?

Agamemnon
I well believe he might have walked on tapestries.

Clytaemestra
Be not ashamed before the bitterness of men.

Agamemnon
The people murmur, and their voice is great in strength.

Clytaemestra
Yet he who goes unenvied shall not be admired.

Agamemnon
Surely this lust for conflict is not womanlike?

Clytaemestra
Yet for the mighty even to give way is grace.

Agamemnon
Does such a victory as this mean so much to you?

Clytaemestra
Oh yield! The power is yours. Give way of your free will.

Agamemnon
Since you must have it—here, let someone with all speed
take off these sandals, slaves for my feet to tread upon.
And as I crush these garments stained from the rich sea
let no god's eyes of hatred strike me from afar.
Great the extravagance, and great the shame I feel
to spoil such treasure and such silver's worth of webs.

So much for all this. Take this stranger girl within
now, and be kind. The conqueror who uses softly
his power, is watched from far in the kind eyes of God,
and this slave's yoke is one no man will wear from choice.
Gift of the host to me, and flower exquisite
from all my many treasures, she attends me here.

Now since my will was bent to listen to you in this
my feet crush purple as I pass within the hall.

Clytaemestra
The sea is there, and who shall drain its yield? It breeds
precious as silver, ever of itself renewed,
the purple ooze wherein our garments shall be dipped.

And by God's grace this house keeps full sufficiency
of all. Poverty is a thing beyond its thought.
I could have vowed to trample many splendors down
had such decree been ordained from the oracles
those days when all my study was to bring home your life.
For when the root lives yet the leaves will come again
to fence the house with shade against the Dog Star's heat,
and now you have come home to keep your hearth and house
you bring with you the symbol of our winter's warmth;
but when Zeus ripens the green clusters into wine
there shall be coolness in the house upon those days
because the master ranges his own halls once more.

Zeus, Zeus accomplisher, accomplish these my prayers.
Let your mind bring these things to pass. It is your will.

*(Agamemnon and Clytaemestra enter the house. Cassandra remains in the chariot. The Chorus speaks.)*

Why must this persistent fear
beat its wings so ceaselessly
and so close against my mantic heart?
Why this strain unwanted, unrepaid, thus prophetic?
Nor can valor of good hope
seated near the chambered depth
of the spirit cast it out
as dreams of dark fancy; and yet time
has buried in the mounding sand
the sea cables since that day
when against Ilium
the army and the ships put to sea.

Yet I have seen with these eyes
Agamemnon home again.
Still the spirit sings, drawing deep
from within this unlyric threnody of the Fury.
Hope is gone utterly,
the sweet strength is far away.
Surely this is not fantasy.
Surely it is real, this whirl of drifts
that spin the stricken heart.
Still I pray; may all this
expectation fade as vanity
into unfulfilment, and not be.

Yet it is true: the high strength of men
knows no content with limitation. Sickness
chambered beside it beats at the wall between.

Man's fate that sets a true
course yet may strike upon
the blind and sudden reefs of disaster.
But if before such time, fear
throw overboard some precious thing
of the cargo, with deliberate cast,
not all the house, laboring
with weight of ruin, shall go down,
nor sink the hull deep within the sea.
And great and affluent the gift of Zeus
in yield of ploughed acres year on year
makes void again sick starvation.

But when the black and mortal blood of man
has fallen to the ground before his feet, who then
can sing spells to call it back again?
Did Zeus not warn us once
when he struck to impotence
that one who could in truth charm back the dead men?
Had the gods not so ordained
that fate should stand against fate
to check any man's excess,
my heart now would have outrun speech
to break forth the water of its grief.
But this is so; I murmur deep in darkness
sore at heart; my hope is gone now
ever again to unwind some crucial good
from the flames about my heart.

*(Clytaemestra comes out from the house again and speaks to Cassandra.)*

Cassandra, you may go within the house as well,
since Zeus in no unkindness has ordained that you
must share our lustral water, stand with the great throng
of slaves that flock to the altar of our household god.
Step from this chariot, then, and do not be so proud.
And think—they say that long ago Alcmena's son
was sold in bondage and endured the bread of slaves.
But if constraint of fact forces you to such fate,
be glad indeed for masters ancient in their wealth.
They who have reaped success beyond their dreams of hope
are savage above need and standard toward their slaves.
From us you shall have all you have the right to ask.

Chorus

What she has spoken is for you, and clear enough.
Fenced in these fatal nets wherein you find yourself

you should obey her if you can; perhaps you can not.

Clytaemestra
Unless she uses speech incomprehensible,
barbarian, wild as the swallow's song, I speak
within her understanding, and she must obey.

Chorus
Go with her. What she bids is best in circumstance
that rings you now. Obey, and leave this carriage seat.

Clytaemestra
I have no leisure to stand outside the house and waste
time on this woman. At the central altarstone
the flocks are standing, ready for the sacrifice
we make to this glad day we never hoped to see.
You: if you are obeying my commands at all, be quick.
But if in ignorance you fail to comprehend,
speak not, but make with your barbarian hand some sign.

Chorus
I think this stranger girl needs some interpreter
who understands. She is like some captive animal.

Clytaemestra
No, she is in the passion of her own wild thoughts.
Leaving her captured city she has come to us
untrained to take the curb, and will not understand
until her rage and strength have foamed away in blood.
I shall throw down no more commands for her contempt.

*(Clytaemestra goes hack into the house.)*

Chorus
I, though, shall not be angry, for I pity her.
Come down, poor creature, leave the empty car. Give way
to compulsion and take up the yoke that shall be yours.

*(Cassandra descends from the chariot and cries out loud.)*

Oh shame upon the earth!
Apollo, Apollo!

Chorus
You cry on Loxias in agony? He is not
of those immortals the unhappy supplicate.

Cassandra

Oh shame upon the earth!
Apollo, Apollo!

Chorus

Now once again in bitter voice she calls upon
this god, who has not part in any lamentation.

Cassandra

Apollo, Apollo!
Lord of the ways, my ruin.
You have undone me once again, and utterly.

Chorus

I think she will be prophetic of her own disaster.
Even in the slave's heart the gift divine lives on.

Cassandra

Apollo, Apollo!
Lord of the ways, my ruin.
Where have you led me now at last? What house is this?

Chorus

The house of the Atreidae. If you understand
not that, I can tell you; and so much at least is true.

Cassandra

No, but a house that God hates, guilty within
of kindred blood shed, torture of its own,
the shambles for men's butchery, the dripping floor.

Chorus

The stranger is keen scented like some hound upon
the trail of blood that leads her to discovered death.

Cassandra

Behold there the witnesses to my faith.
The small children wail for their own death
and the flesh roasted that their father fed upon.

Chorus

We had been told before of this prophetic fame
of yours: we want no prophets in this place at all.

Cassandra

Ah, for shame, what can she purpose now?

What is this new and huge
stroke of atrocity she plans within the house
to beat down the beloved beyond hope of healing?
Rescue is far away.

Chorus

I can make nothing of these prophecies. The rest
I understood; the city is full of the sound of them.

Cassandra

So cruel then, that you can do this thing?
The husband of your own bed
to bathe bright with water—how shall I speak the end?
This thing shall be done with speed. The hand gropes now, and the other
hand follows in turn.

Chorus

No, I am lost. After the darkness of her speech
I go bewildered in a mist of prophecies.

Cassandra

No, no, see there! What is that thing that shows?
Is it some net of death?
Or is the trap the woman there, the murderess?
Let now the slakeless fury in the race
rear up to howl aloud over this monstrous death.

Chorus

Upon what demon in the house do you call, to raise
the cry of triumph? All your speech makes dark my hope.
And to the heart below trickles the pale drop
as in the hour of death
timed to our sunset and the mortal radiance.
Ruin is near, and swift.

Cassandra

See there, see there! Keep from his mate the bull.
Caught in the folded web's
entanglement she pinions him and with the black horn
strikes. And he crumples in the watered bath.
Guile, I tell you, and death there in the caldron wrought.

Chorus

I am not proud in skill to guess at prophecies,
yet even I can see the evil in this thing.
From divination what good ever has come to men?

Art, and multiplication of words
drifting through tangled evil bring
terror to them that hear.

Cassandra
Alas, alas for the wretchedness of my ill-starred life.
This pain flooding the song of sorrow is mine alone.
Why have you brought me here in all unhappiness?
Why, why? Except to die with him? What else could be?

Chorus
You are possessed of God, mazed at heart
to sing your own death
song, the wild lyric as
in clamor for Itys, Itys over and over again
her long life of tears weeping forever grieves
the brown nightingale.

Cassandra
Oh for the nightingale's pure song and a fate like hers.
With fashion of beating wings the gods clothed her about
and a sweet life gave her and without lamentation.
But mine is the sheer edge of the tearing iron.

Chorus
Whence come, beat upon beat, driven of God,
vain passions of tears?
Whence your cries, terrified, clashing in horror,
in wrought melody and the singing speech?
Whence take you the marks to this path of prophecy
and speech of terror?

Cassandra
Oh marriage of Paris, death to the men beloved!
Alas, Scamandrus, water my fathers drank.
There was a time I too at your springs
drank and grew strong. Ah me,
for now beside the deadly rivers, Cocytus
and Acheron, I must cry out my prophecies.

Chorus
What is this word, too clear, you have uttered now?
A child could understand.
And deep within goes the stroke of the dripping fang
as mortal pain at the trebled song of your agony
shivers the heart to hear.

Cassandra

O sorrow, sorrow of my city dragged to uttermost death.
O sacrifices my father made at the wall.
Flocks of the pastured sheep slaughtered there.
And no use at all
to save our city from its pain inflicted now.
And I too, with brain ablaze in fever, shall go down.

Chorus

This follows the run of your song.
Is it, in cruel force of weight,
some divinity kneeling upon you brings
the death song of your passionate suffering?
I can not see the end.

Cassandra

No longer shall my prophecies like some young girl
new-married glance from under veils, but bright and strong
as winds blow into morning and the sun's uprise
shall wax along the swell like some great wave, to burst
at last upon the shining of this agony.
Now I will tell you plainly and from no cryptic speech;
bear me then witness, running at my heels upon
the scent of these old brutal things done long ago.
There is a choir that sings as one, that shall not again
leave this house ever; the song thereof breaks harsh with menace.
And drugged to double fury on the wine of men's
blood shed, there lurks forever here a drunken rout
of ingrown vengeful spirits never to be cast forth.
Hanging above the hall they chant their song of hate
and the old sin; and taking up the strain in turn
spit curses on that man who spoiled his brother's bed.
Did I go wide, or hit, like a real archer? Am I
some swindling seer who hawks his lies from door to door?
Upon your oath, bear witness that I know by heart
the legend of ancient wickedness within this house.

Chorus

And how could an oath, though cast in rigid honesty,
do any good? And still we stand amazed at you,
reared in an alien city far beyond the sea,
how can you strike, as if you had been there, the truth.

Cassandra

Apollo was the seer who set me to this work.

Chorus
Struck with some passion for you, and himself a god?

Cassandra
There was a time I blushed to speak about these things.

Chorus
True; they who prosper take on airs of vanity.

Cassandra
Yes, then; he wrestled with me, and he breathed delight.

Chorus
Did you come to the getting of children then, as people do?

*Cassandra*
I promised that to Loxias, but I broke my word.

Chorus
Were you already ecstatic in the skills of God?

Cassandra
Yes; even then I read my city's destinies.

Chorus
So Loxias' wrath did you no harm? How could that be?

Cassandra
For this my trespass, none believed me ever again.

Chorus
But we do; all that you foretell seems true to us.

Cassandra
But this is evil, see!
Now once again the pain of grim, true prophecy
shivers my whirling brain in a storm of things foreseen.
Look there, see what is hovering above the house,
so small and young, imaged as in the shadow of dreams,
like children almost, killed by those most dear to them,
and their hands filled with their own flesh, as food to eat.
I see them holding out the inward parts, the vitals,
oh pitiful, that meat their father tasted of . . .
I tell you: There is one that plots vengeance for this,
the strengthless lion rolling in his master's bed,
who keeps, ah me, the house against his lord's return;

my lord too, now that I wear the slave's yoke on my neck.
King of the ships, who tore up Ilium by the roots,
what does he know of this accursed bitch, who licks
his hand, who fawns on him with lifted ears, who like
a secret death shall strike the coward's stroke, nor fail?
No, this is daring when the female shall strike down
the male. What can I call her and be right? What beast
of loathing? Viper double-fanged, or Scylla witch
holed in the rocks and bane of men that range the sea;
smoldering mother of death to smoke relentless hate
on those most dear. How she stood up and howled aloud
and unashamed, as at the breaking point of battle,
in feigned gladness for his salvation from the sea!
What does it matter now if men believe or no?
What is to come will come. And soon you too will stand
beside, to murmur in pity that my words were true.

Chorus

Thyestes' feast upon the flesh of his own children
I understand in terror at the thought, and fear
is on me hearing truth and no tale fabricated.
The rest: I heard it, but wander still far from the course.

Cassandra

I tell you, you shall look on Agamemnon dead.

Chorus

Peace, peace, poor woman; put those bitter lips to sleep.

Cassandra

Useless; there is no god of healing in this story.

Chorus

Not if it must be; may it somehow fail to come.

Cassandra

Prayers, yes; they do not pray; they plan to strike, and kill.

Chorus

What man is it who moves this beastly thing to be?

Cassandra

What man? You did mistake my divination then.

Chorus

It may be; I could not follow through the schemer's plan.

Cassandra

Yet I know Greek; I think I know it far too well.

Chorus

And Pythian oracles are Greek, yet hard to read.

Cassandra

Oh, flame and pain that sweeps me once again! My lord,
Apollo, King of Light, the pain, aye me, the pain!
This is the woman-lioness, who goes to bed
with the wolf, when her proud lion ranges far away,
and she will cut me down; as a wife mixing drugs
she wills to shred the virtue of my punishment
into her bowl of wrath as she makes sharp the blade
against her man, death that he brought a mistress home.
Why do I wear these mockeries upon my body,
this staff of prophecy, these flowers at my throat?
At least I will spoil you before I die. Out, down,
break, damn you! This for all that you have done to me.
Make someone else, not me, luxurious in disaster ...
Lo now, this is Apollo who has stripped me here
of my prophetic robes. He watched me all the time
wearing this glory, mocked of all, my dearest ones
who hated me with all their hearts, so vain, so wrong;
called like some gypsy wandering from door to door
beggar, corrupt, half-starved, and I endured it all.
And now the seer has done with me, his prophetess,
and led me into such a place as this, to die.
Lost are my father's altars, but the block is there
to reek with sacrificial blood, my own. We two
must die, yet die not vengeless by the gods. For there
shall come one to avenge us also, born to slay
his mother, and to wreak death for his father's blood.
Outlaw and wanderer, driven far from his own land,
he will come back to cope these stones of inward hate.
For this is a strong oath and sworn by the high gods,
that he shall cast men headlong for his father felled.
Why am I then so pitiful? Why must I weep?
Since once I saw the citadel of Ilium
die as it died, and those who broke the city, doomed
by the gods, fare as they have fared accordingly,
I will go through with it. I too will take my fate.
I call as on the gates of death upon these gates
to pray only for this thing, that the stroke be true,
and that with no convulsion, with a rush of blood
in painless death, I may close up these eyes, and rest.

Chorus
O woman much enduring and so greatly wise,
you have said much. But if this thing you know be true,
this death that comes upon you, how can you, serene,
walk to the altar like a driven ox of God?

Cassandra
Friends, there is no escape for any longer time.

Chorus
Yet longest left in time is to be honored still.

Cassandra
The day is here and now; I can not win by flight.

Chorus
Woman, be sure your heart is brave; you can take much.

Cassandra
None but the unhappy people ever hear such praise.

Chorus
Yet there is a grace on mortals who so nobly die.

Cassandra
Alas for you, father, and for your lordly sons.
Ah!

Chorus
What now? What terror whirls you backward from the door?

Cassandra
Foul, foul!

Chorus
What foulness then, unless some horror in the mind?

Cassandra
That room within reeks with blood like a slaughter house.

Chorus
What then? Only these victims butchered at the hearth.

Cassandra
There is a breath about it like an open grave.

Chorus

This is no Syrian pride of frankincense you mean.

Cassandra

So. I am going in, and mourning as I go
my death and Agamemnon's. Let my life be done.
Ah friends,
truly this is no wild bird fluttering at a bush,
nor vain my speech. Bear witness to me when I die,
when falls for me, a woman slain, another woman,
and when a man dies for this wickedly mated man.
Here in my death I claim this stranger's grace of you.

*Chorus*

Poor wretch, I pity you the fate you see so clear.

*Cassandra*

Yet once more will I speak, and not this time my own
death's threnody. I call upon the Sun in prayer
against that ultimate shining when the avengers strike
these monsters down in blood, that they avenge as well
one simple slave who died, a small thing, lightly killed.

Alas, poor men, their destiny. When all goes well
a shadow will overthrow it. If it be unkind
one stroke of a wet sponge wipes all the picture out;
and that is far the most unhappy thing of all.

*(Cassandra goes slowly into the house.)*

Chorus

High fortune is a thing slakeless
for mortals. There is no man who shall point
his finger to drive it back from the door
and speak the words: "Come no longer."
Now to this man the blessed ones have given
Priam's city to be captured
and return in the gods' honor.
Must he give blood for generations gone,
die for those slain and in death pile up
more death to come for the blood shed,
what mortal else who hears shall claim
he was born clear of the dark angel?

*(Agamemnon, inside the house.)*

Ah, I am struck a deadly blow and deep within!

Chorus

Silence: who cried out that he was stabbed to death within the house?

Agamemnon

Ah me, again, they struck again. I am wounded twice.

Chorus

How the king cried out aloud to us! I believe the thing is done.
Come, let us put our heads together, try to find some safe way out.

*(The members of the Chorus go about distractedly, each one speaking in turn.)*

Listen, let me tell you what I think is best to do.
Let the herald call all citizens to rally here.

No, better to burst in upon them now, at once,
and take them with the blood still running from their blades.

I am with this man and I cast my vote to him.
Act now. This is the perilous and instant time.

Anyone can see it, by these first steps they have taken,
they purpose to be tyrants here upon our city.

Yes, for we waste time, while they trample to the ground
deliberation's honor, and their hands sleep not.

I can not tell which counsel of yours to call my own.
It is the man of action who can plan as well.

I feel as he does; nor can I see how by words
we shall set the dead man back upon his feet again.

Do you mean, to drag our lives out long, that we must yield
to the house shamed, and leadership of such as these?

No, we can never endure that; better to be killed.
Death is a softer thing by far than tyranny.

Shall we, by no more proof than that he cried in pain,
be sure, as by divination, that our lord is dead?

Yes, we should know what is true before we break our rage.
Here is sheer guessing and far different from sure knowledge.
From all sides the voices multiply to make me choose
this course; to learn first how it stands with Agamemnon.

*(The doors of the palace open, disclosing the bodies of Agamemnon and Cassandra, with Clytaemestra standing over them.)*

Clytaemestra

Much have I said before to serve necessity,
but I will take no shame now to unsay it all.
How else could I, arming hate against hateful men
disguised in seeming tenderness, fence high the nets
of ruin beyond overleaping? Thus to me
the conflict born of ancient bitterness is not
a thing new thought upon, but pondered deep in time.
I stand now where I struck him down. The thing is done.
Thus have I wrought, and I will not deny it now.
That he might not escape nor beat aside his death,
as fishermen cast their huge circling nets, I spread
deadly abundance of rich robes, and caught him fast.
I struck him twice. In two great cries of agony
he buckled at the knees and fell. When he was down
I struck him the third blow, in thanks and reverence
to Zeus the lord of dead men underneath the ground.
Thus he went down, and the life struggled out of him;
and as he died he spattered me with the dark red
and violent driven rain of bitter savored blood
to make me glad, as gardens stand among the showers
of God in glory at the birthtime of the buds.

These being the facts, elders of Argos assembled here,
be glad, if it be your pleasure; but for me, I glory.
Were it religion to pour wine above the slain,
this man deserved, more than deserved, such sacrament.
He filled our cup with evil things unspeakable
and now himself come home has drunk it to the dregs.

Chorus

We stand here stunned. How can you speak this way, with mouth
so arrogant, to vaunt above your fallen lord?

Clytaemestra

You try me out as if I were a woman and vain;
but my heart is not fluttered as I speak before you.
You know it. You can praise or blame me as you wish;
it is all one to me. That man is Agamemnon,
my husband; he is dead; the work of this right hand
that struck in strength of righteousness. And that is that.

Chorus

Woman, what evil thing planted upon the earth
or dragged from the running salt sea could you have tasted now
to wear such brutality and walk in the people's hate?
You have cast away, you have cut away. You shall go homeless now,
crushed with men's bitterness.

Clytaemestra

Now it is I you doom to be cast out from my city
with men's hate heaped and curses roaring in my ears.
Yet look upon this dead man; you would not cross him once
when with no thought more than as if a beast had died,
when his ranged pastures swarmed with the deep fleece of flocks,
he slaughtered like a victim his own child, my pain
grown into love, to charm away the winds of Thrace.
Were you not bound to hunt him then clear of this soil
for the guilt stained upon him? Yet you hear what I
have done, and lo, you are a stern judge. But I say to you:
go on and threaten me, but know that I am ready,
if fairly you can beat me down beneath your hand,
for you to rule; but if the god grant otherwise,
you shall be taught—too late, for sure—to keep your place.

Chorus

Great your design, your speech is a clamor of pride.
Swung to the red act drives the fury within your brain
signed clear in the splash of blood over your eyes.
Yet to come is stroke given for stroke
vengeless, forlorn of friends.

Clytaemestra

Now hear you this, the right behind my sacrament:
By my child's Justice driven to fulfilment, by
her Wrath and Fury, to whom I sacrificed this man,
the hope that walks my chambers is not traced with fear
while yet Aegisthus makes the fire shine on my hearth,
my good friend, now as always, who shall be for us
the shield of our defiance, no weak thing; while he,
this other, is fallen, stained with this woman you behold,
plaything of all the golden girls at Ilium;
and here lies she, the captive of his spear, who saw
wonders, who shared his bed, the wise in revelations
and loving mistress, who yet knew the feel as well
of the men's rowing benches. Their reward is not
unworthy. He lies there; and she who swanlike cried
aloud her lyric mortal lamentation out

is laid against his fond heart, and to me has given
a delicate excitement to my bed's delight.

Chorus

O that in speed, without pain
and the slow bed of sickness
death could come to us now, death that forever
carries sleep without ending, now that our lord is down,
our shield, kindest of men,
who for a woman's grace suffered so much,
struck down at last by a woman.
Alas, Helen, wild heart
for the multitudes, for the thousand lives
you killed under Troy's shadow,
you alone, to shine in man's memory
as blood flower never to be washed out. Surely a demon then
of death walked in the house, men's agony.

Clytaemestra

No, be not so heavy, nor yet draw down
in prayer death's ending,
neither turn all wrath against Helen
for men dead, that she alone killed
all those Danaan lives, to work
the grief that is past all healing.

Chorus

Divinity that kneel on this house and the two
strains of the blood of Tantalus,
in the hands and hearts of women you steer
the strength tearing my heart.
Standing above the corpse, obscene
as some carrion crow she sings
the crippled song and is proud.

Clytaemestra

Thus have you set the speech of your lips
straight, calling by name
the spirit thrice glutted that lives in this race.
From him deep in the nerve is given
the love and the blood drunk, that before
the old wound dries, it bleeds again.

Chorus

Surely it is a huge
and heavy spirit bending the house you cry;

alas, the bitter glory
of a doom that shall never be done with;
and all through Zeus, Zeus,
first cause, prime mover.
For what thing without Zeus is done among mortals?
What here is without God's blessing?

O king, my king
how shall I weep for you?
What can I say out of my heart of pity?
Caught in this spider's web you lie,
Your life gasped out in indecent death,
struck prone to this shameful bed
by your lady's hand of treachery
and the stroke twin edged of the iron.

Clytaemestra

Can you claim I have done this?
Speak of me never
more as the wife of Agamemnon.
In the shadow of this corpse's queen
the old stark avenger
of Atreus for his revel of hate
struck down this man,
last blood for the slaughtered children.

Chorus

What man shall testify
your hands are clean of this murder?
How? How? Yet from his father's blood
might swarm some fiend to guide you.
The black ruin that shoulders
through the streaming blood of brothers
strides at last where he shall win requital
for the children who were eaten.

O king, my king
how shall I weep for you?
What can I say out of my heart of pity?
Caught in this spider's web you lie,
your life gasped out in indecent death,
struck prone to this shameful bed
by your lady's hand of treachery
and the stroke twin edged of the iron.

Clytaemestra

No shame, I think, in the death given
this man. And did he not
first of all in this house wreak death
by treachery?
The flower of this man's love and mine,
Iphigeneia of the tears
he dealt with even as he has suffered.
Let his speech in death's house be not loud.
With the sword he struck,
with the sword he paid for his own act.

Chorus

My thoughts are swept away and I go bewildered.
Where shall I turn the brain's
activity in speed when the house is falling?
There is fear in the beat of the blood rain breaking
wall and tower. The drops come thicker.
Still fate grinds on yet more stones the blade
for more acts of terror.

Earth, my earth, why did you not fold me under
before ever I saw this man lie dead
fenced by the tub in silver?
Who shall bury him? Who shall mourn him?
Shall you dare this who have killed
your lord? Make lamentation,
render the graceless grace to his soul
for huge things done in wickedness?
Who over this great man's grave shall lay
the blessing of tears
worked soberly from a true heart?

Clytaemestra

Not for you to speak of such tendance.
Through us he fell,
by us he died; we shall bury.
There will be no tears in this house for him.
It must be Iphigeneia
his child, who else,
shall greet her father by the whirling stream
and the ferry of tears
to close him in her arms and kiss him.

Chorus

Here is anger for anger. Between them

who shall judge lightly?
The spoiler is robbed; he killed, he has paid.
The truth stands ever beside God's throne
eternal: he who has wrought shall pay; that is law.
Then who shall tear the curse from their blood?
The seed is stiffened to ruin.

Clytaemestra
You see truth in the future
at last. Yet I wish
to seal my oath with the Spirit
in the house: I will endure all things as they stand
now, hard though it be. Hereafter
let him go forth to make bleed with death
and guilt the houses of others.
I will take some small
measure of our riches, and be content
that I swept from these halls
the murder, the sin, and the fury.

*(Aegisthus enters, followed at a little distance by his armed bodyguard.)*

Aegisthus
O splendor and exaltation of this day of doom!
Now I can say once more that the high gods look down
on mortal crimes to vindicate the right at last,
now that I see this man—sweet sight—before me here
sprawled in the tangling nets of fury, to atone
the calculated evil of his father's hand.
For Atreus, this man's father, King of Argolis—
I tell you the clear story—drove my father forth,
Thyestes, his own brother, who had challenged him
in his king's right—forth from his city and his home.
Yet sad Thyestes came again to supplicate
the hearth, and win some grace, in that he was not slain
nor soiled the doorstone of his fathers with blood spilled.
Not his own blood. But Atreus, this man's godless sire,
angrily hospitable set a feast for him,
in seeming a glad day of fresh meat slain and good
cheer; then served my father his own children's flesh
to feed on. For he carved away the extremities,
hands, feet, and cut the flesh apart, and covered them
served in a dish to my father at his table apart,
who with no thought for the featureless meal before him ate
that ghastly food whose curse works now before your eyes.
But when he knew the terrible thing that he had done,
he spat the dead meat from him with a cry, and reeled

spurning the table back to heel with strength the curse:
"Thus crash in ruin all the seed of Pleisthenes."
Out of such acts you see this dead man stricken here,
and it was I, in my right, who wrought this murder, I
third born to my unhappy father, and with him
driven, a helpless baby in arms, to banishment.
Yet I grew up, and justice brought me home again,
till from afar I laid my hands upon this man,
since it was I who pieced together the fell plot.
Now I can die in honor again, if die I must,
having seen him caught in the cords of his just punishment.

Chorus

Aegisthus, this strong vaunting in distress is vile,
You claim that you deliberately killed the king,
you, and you only, wrought the pity of this death.
I tell you then: There shall be no escape, your head
shall face the stones of anger from the people's hands.

Aegisthus

So loud from you, stooped to the meanest rowing bench
with the ship's masters lordly on the deck above?
You are old men; well, you shall learn how hard it is
at your age, to be taught how to behave yourselves.
But there are chains, there is starvation with its pain,
excellent teachers of good manners to old men,
wise surgeons and exemplars. Look! Can you not see it?
Lash not at the goads for fear you hit them, and be hurt.

Chorus

So then you, like a woman, waited the war out
here in the house, shaming the master's bed with lust,
and planned against the lord of war this treacherous death?

Aegisthus

It is just such words as these will make you cry in pain.
Not yours the lips of Orpheus, no, quite otherwise,
whose voice of rapture dragged all creatures in his train.
You shall be dragged, for baby whimperings sobbed out
in rage. Once broken, you will be easier to deal with.

Chorus

How shall you be lord of the men of Argos, you
who planned the murder of this man, yet could not dare
to act it out, and cut him down with your own hand?

Aegisthus

No, clearly the deception was the woman's part,
and I was suspect, that had hated him so long.
Still with his money I shall endeavor to control
the citizens. The mutinous man shall feel the yoke
drag at his neck, no cornfed racing colt that runs
free traced; but hunger, grim companion of the dark
dungeon shall see him broken to the hand at last.

Chorus

But why, why then, you coward, could you not have slain
your man yourself? Why must it be his wife who killed,
to curse the country and the gods within the ground?
Oh, can Orestes live, be somewhere in sunlight still?
Shall fate grown gracious ever bring him back again
in strength of hand to overwhelm these murderers?

Aegisthus

You shall learn then, since you stick to stubbornness of mouth
and hand.
Up now from your cover, my henchmen: here is work for you to do.

Chorus

Look, they come! Let every man clap fist upon his hilted sword.

Aegisthus

I too am sword-handed against you; I am not afraid of death.

Chorus

Death you said and death it shall be; we take up the word of fate.

Clytaemestra

No, my dearest, dearest of all men, we have done enough. No more
violence. Here is a monstrous harvest and a bitter reaping time.
There is pain enough already. Let us not be bloody now.
Honored gentlemen of Argos, go to your homes now and give way
to the stress of fate and season. We could not do otherwise
than we did. If this is the end of suffering, we can be content
broken as we are by the brute heel of angry destiny.
Thus a woman speaks among you. Shall men deign to understand?

Aegisthus

Yes, but think of these foolish lips that blossom into leering gibes,
think of the taunts they spit against me daring destiny and power,
sober opinion lost in insults hurled against my majesty.

Chorus

It was never the Argive way to grovel at a vile man's feet.

Aegisthus

I shall not forget this; in the days to come I shall be there.

Chorus

Nevermore, if God's hand guiding brings Orestes home again.

Aegisthus

Exiles feed on empty dreams of hope. I know it. I was one.

Chorus

Have your way, gorge and grow fat, soil justice, while the power is yours,

Aegisthus

You shall pay, make no mistake, for this misguided insolence.

Chorus

Crow and strut, brave cockerel by your hen; you have no threats to fear.

Clytaemestra

These are howls of impotent rage; forget them, dearest; you and I
have the power; we two shall bring good order to our house at least,

*(They enter the house. The doors close. All persons leave the stage.)*

# Eumenides

## Aeshcylus

### Characters

THE PYTHIA—priestess of Apollo at Delphi
APOLLO—son of Zeus, god of prophecy and purificaticon
ORESTES—son of Agamemnon and Clytemnestra
CLYTEMNESTRA—killed by Orestes, now a ghost
CHORUS—of the Erinyes of Clytemnestra
ATHENA—daughter of Zeus, patron goddess of Athens
ATHENIAN CITIZEN-JURORS
ATHENIAN WOMEN

*The scene is at Delphi, before the oracular temple of Apollo. His priestess, the* PYTHIA, *enters from the right.*
PYTHIA

PYTHIA Among the gods I honor in my prayer,
I give first place to the first prophet, Earth,
and second place to Themis, the second one
to hold her mother's seat of prophecy,
or so the story goes. Then third in line,
by Themis' own choice and not by force,
another Titaness took her place: Phoebe,
child of earth, and she in turn gave it
to Phoebus for his birthday, which is why
he added her name to his own.
Leaving
the pool and spiny ridge of Delos, he sailed
into the ship-hive coast of Pallas and came here
to this land to make his home on Mount Parnassus.
The children of Hephaestus, road-makers
who tamed the land that was untamed before,
escorted him with deepest reverence.

The people honored him greatly at his coming,
as Delphus did, the country's king and helmsman.
And Zeus infused him with the prophet's art,
and put him as the fourth seer on this throne.
Apollo, then, is spokesman for his father Zeus.

I make these gods the prelude of my prayer,
yet in all I say I also honor Pallas
whose shrine stands there, apart, and revere the
    Nymphs
whose dwelling is the hollowed Corycian rock,
sweet haunt of birds and spirits lingering.
And Bromius too (I don't forget) has held
sway in this region ever since the day
he, in his true form, led his troop of women,
his wild bacchants, to hunt down Pentheus,
to snare him like a hare in a net of death.
I call on the streams of Pleistus in the gorge below,
and on Poseidon's power, and on Zeus,
who brings all to fulfillment, the Most High.
And as I take my seat to prophesy,
may they all grant me foresight that exceeds
whatever foresight I have had before.
If there are any Greeks here, let them enter
in order of the lots they drew, as the custom is.
My prophecies will follow where the god leads.

*The* PYTHIA *enters the temple, then immediately returns, but now crawling at first on hands and knees.*

Terror for tongue to tell of, for eyes to see,
sheer terror has driven me away, again,
from Apollo's house, so that my strength falters,
and I can't stand on my own two legs, and
I go on all fours, trembling, inch by inch,
because a terrified old woman's nothing
at all, no better than a child.
                                        I was
making my way into the inner chamber
where the air glows green from the garlands left there
when I saw a man polluted before the gods
sitting the way a suppliant would sit
on the navel stone, blood dripping from his hands,
blood also dripping from his just drawn sword;
he held a tall branch of an olive tree
wreathed as it should be with a shock of wool,
the white fleece radiant—this I can say for sure.

But an astounding gang of women sleeps
around him, all slouched in chairs. Women?
No, not women. Gorgons maybe, but, no,
not even Gorgon shapes could do them justice.
I saw a painting once of flying female-
creatures snatching food from Phineus,
but this gang has no wings, and they're all black,
disgusting, and their phlegmy snores spew out
a stink that blinds and repels, and their eyes drip
a sickening ooze. Their dark rags, too, aren't fit
to wear before the statues of the gods,
or even right to bring into the house.
I've never seen the tribe this crew belongs to,
or known a land that could rear a brood like this
and not be damaged and regret the labor.
How this will end up now is his concern,
the master of the house, great Loxias
himself, the wily one. He is the prophet,
the healer; he scans the signs to see what is
to come; he has the power to purify.

*The* PYTHIA *exits to the tight.* APOLLO *and* ORESTES *enter from the temple.*

APOLLO
I won't betray you. Your guardian to the end,
both when I'm here with you and far away—
I won't ease up against your enemies.
See how I've tamed, for now, these crazed hags,
lulled them to sleep, these maidens of filth, these wrinkled
children no god, or man, or any beast
would want to touch: born evil, born for evil,
their only dwelling place the evil darkness
of the deepest underground, despised
alike by men and all the gods above.
They're tamed for now. But flee them, don't let up,
for they will dog you, there at your heels, as you run
on from horizon to horizon, fast
at your pounding heels, over the vast mainland,
and across the sea to sea-encircled cities.
Don't tire or lose heart till you've shepherded
your hard task all the way to Pallas Athena's
city. Once there, sit as a suppliant,
holding her age-old image in your arms.
And we'll have judges for your case, and words
that spellbind; we will find the means to free you
from this toil you've been caught in, once and for all.
For I persuaded you to kill your mother.

ORESTES

My lord Apollo, you know how not to be
unjust; learn, too, how not to be neglectful.
Your strength assures me of your power for good.

APOLLO

Remember, don't let fear overtake you.
Now, Hermes, my brother, son of my father too,
watch over him; be your own namesake and
escort him, guide him well, for he's my suppliant,
and Zeus honors the rights of outcasts who are blessed
with such a guide back to the world of men.

ORESTES *exits to the left and* APOLLO *enters the temple. After a brief pause,* CLYTEMNESTRA'S *ghost appears, perhaps on the roof of the stage building.*

CLYTEMNESTRA

Keep sleeping! You there! Ah, what good are you
to me asleep? Because of you I go go
dishonored among the other dead. The spirits
of those I killed won't stop accusing me,
I wander in disgrace. I tell you, day
and night they hector me with blame. And though
I too have suffered from my blood relations,
none of the gods is angry on my behalf,
though I was slaughtered by my own son's hands.
Picture my wounds in your heart (for the sleeping mind
can see more clearly than the mind awake).
Remember where they came from, and don't forget
how many offerings I made to you,
how you would lap them up, the wineless pourings,
sober propitiations, holy feasts
burned in a hearth pit in the darkest recess
of the night, at an hour not shared by other gods —
And all for what? To see my offerings trampled
while I watch him slip away so easily
and vanish like a fawn, watch him leap free
out from the middle of your net, and taunt you,
mock you, winking, as he bounds off? Hear me!
My very being hinges on my plea.
Wake up now, goddesses from beneath the ground,
for I am Clytemnestra, the dream that calls you.

*(whining from within the temple)*

The more you whine, the farther away he gets, .
for his friends, unlike mine, know how to help.

*(more whining)*

More sleep's in you than pity for my pain.
Orestes, who ran me —his mother!—through, is gone.

*(moaning)*

How can you sleep and moan like this? Get up!
Get up! Ruin's the job you're meant to do!

*(more moaning)*

Sleep and exhaustion, those arch-conspirators,
have drained the poison from the dread snake's tooth.

CHORUS *(moaning twice as loud, still from within)* Get him!
Get him! Get him! There! Over there!

CLYTEMNESTRA The quarry you keep hunting's just a dream,
and yet you still bay like a hound that can't
stop sniffing out the bloodtrail. What are you doing?
Get up! Don't let exhaustion overcome you!
Don't let sleep slacken your pace, make you forget
my misery! Let my just accusations
sting your heart awake, for they are sharp
goads to the sensible. Breathe over him the blood-
reek of your breath, shrivel him in the sizzling
gust of your belly's fire! Get after him,
wither him away with a. fresh pursuit!

(CLYTEMNESTRA'S GHOST DISAPPEARS. *The* CHORUS *enters from the temple by ones and twos.)*

CHORUS Up now! Wake her, just as I wake you!
Still sleeping? Come on, get up! Kick sleep away,
let's see if this dream is a truthful prelude.

IOU! IOU! POPAX *Strophe 1*
Wronged, sorely wronged, my sisters,
Oh I have suffered so much, and for what?
  Yes we have suffered
such searing pain, oh yes, a hurt
  no one could bear,
the beast has slipped free of the net and vanished:
sleep took me, and the prey is lost.
O child of Zeus, you thief! So young *Antistrophe 1*

yet you have trampled down the gray gods
by guarding the suppliant,
the godless, the mother-hating man.
A god yourself,
you've spirited away the mother-killer.
Could anyone call these actions just?

Blame came to me in my dream —over
and over *Strophe* 2
it struck me like a charioteer,
with the goad gripped
tight in his fist; in the heart, in the guts,
it struck, and I feel
the cold sting of the scourger's cruel
quick public lash.

This is what all of you do, you younger
gods, *Antistrophe* 2
your power knows no bounds, respects none.
Gore oozes over
Apollo's throne, from the top, to the bottom,
it drips, and I see
the earth's stone navel smeared with filth
from bloody deeds.

A prophet himself, he's dirtied his own
shrine, *Strophe* 3
defiled his hearth
at no one's bidding but his own,
invited blight
by placing men above the god-
set limits, breaking
the age-old power of the fates.

Although he hurts me too, he still won't
save *Antistrophe* 3
Orestes, never;
for even hid beneath the earth,
this suppliant
will not escape, but come stained,
cursed, to where
a new avenger will rise against him.

APOLLO *enters from the temple.*

APOLLO Get out of this house, right now, I order you!

Away from my temple's deep prophetic chamber
or you'll be bitten by a flying snake
shot from my bowstring's beaten gold, and retch
in agony, coughing up all the black
scum sucked from men, the clotted gore you guzzled.
You have no rights here, no business in this house,
your jurisdiction is where heads are lopped off
in retribution, eyes gouged out, throats slashed;
where the manhood of mere boys is cut away,
their seed squandered, and men—their hands, their feet,
their ears and nose —are maimed, and they are stoned
to death, and where they feel the sharp stake driven
into their backs and groan out loud and long.
Don't you hear then what sort of feasts you crave
that make the gods despise you? Your very shape
and dress explain it. Creatures like you belong
in caves with blood-befouled, blood-lapping lions;
you have no business in this prophetic place,
rubbing your stinking dirt off on those near you.
Get out of here, you herd without a herdsman!
No god would ever tend a flock like this.

CHORUS LEADER It's your turn now to listen, lord Apollo.
You are no mere accessory to this crime;
From start to finish, the blame is yours alone.

APOLLO How so? Say just enough to make it clear.

CHORUS LEADER You told your guest-friend he should kill his mother.

APOLLO I told him to avenge his father. What else?

CHORUS LEADER You took him in, blood still wet on his hands.

APOLLO I told him to come for cleansing to this shrine.

CHORUS LEADER And you malign us for serving as his escort?

APOLLO You aren't fit creatures to come near my house.

CHORUS LEADER But we as well have our appointed task …

APOLLO Appointed? You? Crow on about this noble job.

CHORUS LEADER We hound all mother-killers from their houses.

APOLLO
And what about a wife who kills her husband?

CHORUS LEADER
That isn't killing one's own flesh and blood.

APOLLO
Why, then, you spit on, treat as less than nothing,
the solemn vows of Hera, the fulfiller,
and of Zeus; and Aphrodite, too, is thrown
away like something worthless by your words,
yes, Aphrodite who gives to humankind
the deepest and most intimate bond of all.
Marriage is a thing of destiny,
greater than any oath, and Justice guards if.
And so if you let spouses kill each other
and overlook it, neither punishing them
nor looking on them with a wrathful vigilance,
then I maintain this hounding of Orestes
isn't just. It's clear to me you're stirred
to utter outrage by the one crime while
the other doesn't move you in the least.
But Pallas, goddess of wisdom that she is,
will oversee the issue of this case.

CHORUS LEADER
We'll never stop harassing him, not ever.

APOLLO
Go on, then. Make more trouble for yourself.

CHORUS LEADER
Don't try to steal our rights with clever words.

APOLLO
If someone gave me your rights, I wouldn't take them.

CHORUS LEADER
Why should you, high and mighty as you seem
near Zeus's throne? But the scent of motherblood drives us,
and we will hunt the man down, get our justice.

*The* CHORUS *exits to the left.*

APOLLO
And I will help my suppliant and save him.
A suppliant's wrath's a dreadful thing for gods
and men alike. I never will betray him.

APOLLO *exits into the temple. There is a brief pause. The scene is now set in Athens.* ORESTES *enters from the left.*

ORESTES
Queen Athena, I have come at Apollo's
command. Receive me graciously, a cursed,

a hounded man, but one no longer stained,
my hands now clean, my guilt's keen edge now dulled,
worn down to nothing by the crowded paths
I've traveled, by the homes I've sheltered in.
Holding a firm course over both sea and land,
obedient to Apollo's orders, I've come
at last, goddess, here to your house, your image,
watching and waiting for justice to be fulfilled.

*The* CHORUS *enters by ones and twos, miming hounds tracking a scent.*

CHORUS LEADER

So, finally, a clear sign of the man.
Here, this way, this is where the voiceless snitch
is leading! Like a blood hound on the scent
of a wounded fawn, we track him by this trail
of blood drops. And he's panting out his guts
from all the endless deadly labors, driven
like a sheep over every stretch of land
while we flew wingless, faster than any ship,
across sea after sea, pursuing. I know
he's cowering somewhere near here, for the scent
of blood is like the warm smile of an old friend.

CHORUS

Look! Look again!
Check everywhere —
don't let the mother-killer slip through our clutches
and get away unpunished.

There he is, himself, there in the flesh!
   and once again
protected, his arms around the image
   of the immortal goddess,
eager to stand trial for his crime.
But that won't happen. Once a mother's blood
   is spilled on the ground,
it can't return again, not ever.
   POPOI! The red
stream pools there, seeps into earth, and then
   it's gone for good.
You'll have to pay with your own blood for hers,
   you'll feel me suck the half-
caked gore out of your living flesh;
   swill from your very veins
the vile dregs of the drink I crave.
I'll shrivel you up and drag you, still alive,

into the underworld
where you will pay in currencies of torment
for the murder of your mother.
And there you'll see all other mortal sinners,
the ones who flout
the honor owed to gods or guests,
or loving parents—
you'll see them get the justice they deserve.
For Hades holds men mightily to a strict
accounting down below the earth;
he sees all things, inscribes them
within the book
of his remembering.

ORESTES

I have been schooled by my own suffering:
I've learned the many ways of being purged.
I know where words are proper, and when silence is,
and that on this occasion a wise teacher
has ordered me to speak. For the blood drowses,
sloughs from my hand, the stain of having killed
my mother has been entirely washed away:
when it was still fresh at Apollo's hearth,
he cast it out by sacrificing swine.
My story would be a long one if I told it
right from the start, the many men I met
and mingled with, not one of whom was' harmed.
Time cleanses what it touches over time.
So now with clean lips and well-omened words
I call Athena, this land's queen, to be
my savior. Not by force of spear or sword,
she'll claim me, my land, and all the people of Argos,
as her true allies till the end of time.
Wherever she is—whether in distant Libya,
there by the stream of Triton where she was born,
enthroned or on the march to help her friends,
or whether like a dauntless leader she over-
sees the Phlegrean plain —O let her come
(a god can hear even from far away),
and save me from the troubles that hound me still.

CHORUS LEADER

No, not Apollo's, not Athena's strength
can save you, keep you from going down in disgrace,
forgotten, no place in your heart for joy, all blood
sucked from your body till it's nothing but
death's vaporous feedbag, shadowy husk of air.

So you have nothing to say? You just spit at my words —
calf fattened all for me, my living feast,
my calf not butchered first over any altar?
Hear the spell we sing to bind you fast:

CHORUS

Let's dance as well as sing around him,
  hand in hand,
and let's reveal the terrifying
power of our dark melody
and tell the way our company
fulfills the offices assigned
  to us, our given
right to guide the lives of men.
We keep straight on the path of justice,
  that's our belief:
our wrath is never aimed at the one
who holds up hands no blood has stained—
for *that* one lives out his life unharmed.
But the man, like this one here before us,
  who tries to keep
his red hands hid, yet reeks of guilt,
will find us ever at his side,
  bearing witness
truthfully for those who died,
the court of last appeal, the final
  blood avengers.

*Strophe 1*

Mother, O mother Night,
who bore me as a scourge
to those under the sun,
and those in sunlessness,
hear me. Leto's child,
Apollo, steals my honor,
he's trying now to steal
out of my rightful grasp
this trembling hare whose blood
alone is the atonement
for the motherblood he spilled.

*Refrain 1*

Over our victim's head,
this is the song we sing,
this is the maddening song,
the raging song of fear
that twists the brain, that binds it,
the lyre-shunning song
of the Erinyes, draining,

withering life away.

When Fate, the all-directing, *Antistrophe 1*
spun the unchangeable, ever-
piercing thread of life,
this was the task she gave
us to be ours forever:
those whom rage seizes, who
willfully kill their own
kin with their own hands, we
will hound them, drive them down
beneath the earth, and even
in death they'll find scant freedom.
Over our victim's head, *Refrain 1*
this is the song we sing,
this is the maddening song,
the raging song of fear
that twists the brain, that binds it,
the lyre-shunning song
of the Erinyes, draining,
withering life away.

Yes, at our birth, we were given this holy task. *Strophe 2*
So the high gods steer clear of us, and we of them.
None of them would feast with us at the same table;
we have no part in festivals where white robes are worn.

The calling I've made my own *Refrain 2*
is the destruction of houses
when the spirit of Ares, reared,
tamed, pampered in the home,
cuts down a loved one. Then
we hunt the doer down,
strong though he is, we suck
his blood away to nothing
for all the blood he shed.

We are all keen to Spare others these troubling
cares, *Antistrophe 2*
keen, too, to keep the gods from meddling with our prayers.
But Zeus despises our band as being soaked in blood
and calls us unworthy to be part of his high company.

The calling I've made my own *Refrain 2*
is the destruction of houses
when the spirit of Ares, reared,

tamed, pampered in the home,
cuts down a loved one. Then
we hunt the doer down,
strong though he is, we suck
his blood away to nothing
for all the blood he shed.

But the self-preening conceits of men, swelling
so big *Strophe* 3
under the sun, rot away into earth, all dishonored, driven
down by the gale of our black robes rushing upon
them,
by the quick kicks of our raging dance.

For leaping from a great *Refrain* 3
height I bring the full
force of my foot down
more heavily upon him;
unseen, I thrust out my leg
and even the swiftest runner
stumbles and falls down
to ruin beyond enduring.

But as he falls, his mind so crazed he doesn't know
it— *Antistrophe* 3
this the miasmal dark that hovers about the man,
and rumor passes its groan from voice to voice to say
that a dense fog has shrouded his house.

For leaping from a great *Refrain* 3
height I bring the full
force of my foot down
more heavily upon him;
unseen, I thrust out my leg
and even the swiftest runner
stumbles and falls down
to ruin beyond enduring.

This stands fixed. Adept at devising, *Strophe* 4
unmatched alike in remembering wrong done
as in repaying it;
awful to men, deaf to their pleas,
detested and dishonored we fulfill
our given office; cut off
from the gods, we in the dark slime make
the path rough both for those who live in sunlight

and for those in sunlessness.

Who among mortals is immune *Antistrophe* 4
to feeling awe and fear when I describe
the covenant that fate
assigned me, that the gods made final?
My privileges, ancient as they are,
remain still no less mine.
And I am no less honored for
the station that I hold beneath the ground
deep in the sunless slime.

ATHENA *enters from the left, in full armor and wearing her aegis.*

ATHENA
From the Scamander far away I heard
your call for help, as I took possession there
of land that the Achaean chieftains gave me,
all completely and forever mine,
a rich allotment from the spoils of war,
and a precious gift for Theseus' sons.
From there I sped, my stride unwearied, wingless
but for the flap and billow of the folds
my aegis made.
But now I see a strange
and motley crew of visitors to this land.
Though I feel no fear, my eyes grow wide with wonder.
Who are you? I mean all of you together—
you stranger with your arms around my image,
and you who look like nothing ever born—
not seen by gods among the goddesses,
or shaped in any human form. But, no,
it isn't just to speak ill of another
when he's done nothing wrong; Right won't abide it.

CHORUS LEADER
Daughter of Zeus, you'll learn all, in a few words:
we are the children of the never-dying Night.
In our homes beneath the earth we're known as "Curses."

ATHENA
I now know your descent, and your true names.

CHORUS LEADER
And soon you'll learn our privileges as well.

ATHENA
I will, yes, if you tell them to me plainly.

CHORUS LEADER
We hound from home the ones who kill their own.

ATHENA
Do you chase the killer to some final place?

CHORUS LEADER A place where all joy is unknown to him.

ATHENA And this man here, you howl him on that far?

CHORUS LEADER Yes, since he thought it right to kill his mother.

ATHENA Was he made to do it, fearing some other anger?

CHORUS LEADER What spur's so sharp to make one kill his mother?

ATHENA The case has two sides; so far we've heard just one.

CHORUS LEADER He won't swear he's innocent, or yield if I swear to his guilt.

ATHENA So you would rather seem just than act with justice?

CHORUS LEADER How so? Tell me. For you are rich in wisdom.

ATHENA Injustice shouldn't triumph on an oath.

CHORUS LEADER Then question him yourself. And judge him fairly.

ATHENA You'd take my verdict as the final one?

CHORUS LEADER Yes. We pay you the respect you pay to us.

ATHENA It's your turn, stranger. How will you answer them?
Say first where you come from, who your family is.
Explain your circumstances, and then refute
these accusations. If you're sure you sit
in justice near my hearth, clutching my image —
as a holy suppliant, like Ixion before you,
then answer clearly, so I understand.

ORESTES Queen Athena, let me speak first
to the keen anxiety your last words hold.
I'm not a suppliant in need of cleansing.
When I took my seat here at your image,
my hands weren't stained with blood. And I can prove
my claim with powerful evidence: by law,
a killer is forbidden to speak a word
till someone with the power to purify
has washed away his blood-guilt with the blood
of a young beast. I have been long since purged
at other houses, both in the blood of sucklings

slain to cleanse me, and in clear-running streams.
My hands are clean. Put your mind at ease.
Now I can tell you straight out where I come from,
who my family is: I am from Argos,
and my father, Agamemnon, you know well
as warlord of the fleet who helped you turn
the city of Troy into no city at all.
When he came home, he died an ugly death:
my black-hearted mother cut him down,
wrapped him in her subtle net, a net that
bore witness to the blood bath of his murder.
So I returned, after my years of exile,
and killed the very woman who gave me life—
I don't deny it—killed her for killing him,
the father I loved —although Apollo, too, had
an equal hand in this, for he had goaded
me on with warnings of heart-piercing pain
if I failed to get revenge on the murderers.
But it's all up to you now to decide
whether I've acted justly or not. However
the case turns out, I will accept your ruling.

ATHENA

This case is too hard for one man to judge.
No, even I don't have the right to rule
on a murder trial like this one, one
that calls down such fierce anger either way,
especially as you've come here to my house
a proper suppliant who's clean, who bears
no danger to us, and I welcome you.
And yet these, too, have their appointed task
that can't be shrugged off lightly. If they fail
to get their way, the poison of their outrage,
dripping on the land, will soon become
'a deadly everlasting sickness. But since
the problem's up to me to solve, I'll choose
a panel of judges to preside at murder
trials like this, and put them under oath,
and so set up a court to last forever.
Now call your witnesses, prepare your proofs,
bring forth whatever evidence you have
that best supports your case. Meanwhile, I'll pick
my ablest citizens, and then return
to deal with this matter fairly, once and for all.

ATHENA *exits to the right.* ORESTES *stands aside during the following song.*

CHORUS

*Strophe 1*

Catastrophes will come,
disasters of new laws, if
the mother-killer's mayhem-
making plea prevails.
This deed, from this time on,
will make men poised for any
and all outrageousness.
Truly, parents will await
in time to come the keen
edge of a blade thrust
home by their own child's hand.

*Antistrophe* 1

And we, wild revelers, who keep
a close watch over all
men do, will never again
attack them in anger. We'll
let any murder pass:
and one man, seeing his neighbor
suffer, will ask another,
"When will the sickness ease,
or end?" Poor wretch, the balm
he hopes heals evil won't,
and he'll hope in vain.

*Strophe 2*

From now on let no one
struck by disaster cry
for help, call out in terror:
"O Justice! O Erinyes,
enthroned in majesty!"
Caught unaware by pain,
some father or mother now
will cry like this, because
the house of Justice falls.

*Antistrophe 2*

There is a place where dread
is good, and must abide
to keep watch over all
men think. It's for the best
that wisdom comes from wailing.
What man, or.city even,
whose heart's not fed on fear,.
would ever again pay Justice
the reverence she's owed?

*Strophe* 3

Praise no life that no law reins,
no life a tyrant rules.

God gives
victory always to the middle way,
even while seeing to it
differently in different spheres.
Be moderate, I say:
truly, sacrilege
gives birth to recklessness,
but a well, mind breeds
what we all love and pray for—
a lasting, a rich well-being.

I tell you, then, revere, *Antistrophe* 3
in all you do, the altar
of Justice.
don't kick it over in a wild forgetfulness,
fixing your hungry gaze
on some brief gain beyond it.
Vengeance will track you down.
The inevitable waits.
Knowing this, first honor
your parents, then respect
the guest you welcome in.

And doing this you will be just *Strophe* 4
by choice, not by compulsion, and never lack
well-being—you and yours
will never be dragged down into dirt.
But the wild man, I tell you, shamelessly defiant
in the face of justice, hauling
his plunder off—he'll be compelled,
in time, to lower his sails when the storm grips him
and his yardarm snaps and shatters.

He calls to those who will not hear him *Antistrophe* 4
as he wrestles to get a grip on whirling water,
and the god howls with laughter
to see him there, the bold and cocky man
who'd brag that no bad thing could ever touch him
and now flails, battered by sorrows,
waves rising insurmountably around him.
His lifelong wealth breaks up on the reef of Justice,
and he sinks, unwept, unseen.

ATHENA *enter from the rights, accompanied by a group of Athenian citizen-jurors.*

ATHENA

Herald, declare the court in session, call
the people to their places, and let the piercing
Etruscan trumpet, dense with human breath,
blare out its shrill voice to the assembly.
While the court is filling, it is right
that everyone be silent, so that both
the city and these jurors learn the laws
I've fashioned for all time; in that way those
who stand here will receive a just decision.

APOLLO *enters from the left.*

My lord Apollo, take charge of your own affairs:
What role have you played in this matter? Tell us.

APOLLO

I am here as a witness: when this man
came in supplication to my house
and hearth, as is the custom, I purged him
of the blood he shed. And I am also here
to represent him, for I ordered him
to kill his mother. I am responsible.
Now start the trial, Athena. Take it in hand,
as you know how to do, and set it right.

ATHENA

The case is now before us. Plaintiffs speak first.
It's only right you should, for the pursuer,
telling the story from beginning to end,
can best explain the nature of the case.

CHORUS LEADER

Though we are many, we'll keep our speeches short.

*(addressing* ORESTES*)*

Answer our charges, each one, as we present it:
First, did you kill your mother? Yes or no.

ORESTES

Yes, I killed her. I never said I didn't.

CHORUS LEADER

The first fall goes to us. Two more to go.

ORESTES

Or so you boast, but no one's thrown me yet.

CHORUS LEADER

Then tell us how you killed her, since you must.

ORESTES

Yes. I drew my sword and slit her throat.

CHORUS LEADER

By whose persuasion? By whose sage advice?

ORESTES By this god's oracle. He is my witness.

CHORUS LEADER The god taught you it's right to kill your mother?

ORESTES Yes, and till now I have nothing to complain of.

CHORUS LEADER But when the verdict snares you, you'll change your tune.

ORESTES I trust him; and my father will help me from the grave.

CHORUS LEADER Good, kill your mother, and then trust in corpses!

ORESTES Yes, I killed her since she was doubly defiled.

CHORUS LEADER How exactly? Explain it to the judges.

ORESTES She killed my father when she killed her husband.

CHORUS LEADER Death freed her from her guilt, but you're still living.

ORESTES Why didn't you hunt her down while she still lived?

CHORUS LEADER The man she killed was not her flesh and blood.

ORESTES You think I have the same blood as my mother's?

CHORUS LEADER How else could she have fed you in her womb,
you killer? You spurn the mother blood you live by?

ORESTES Now testify, Apollo, on my behalf
and teach the law to show whether I did
or didn't act with justice when I killed her—
for I did kill her, that I don't deny.
But you determine whether or not this blood
was justly shed, so I can make my case.

APOLLO I say to all of you, to this high court
established by Athena, he acted justly.
I am a prophet; I can never lie.
Not once from my far seeing throne have I
said anything concerning a man, a woman,
or even a city that Zeus himself, father
of the Olympians, did not command.
Be mindful of how powerful this plea
for justice is. Follow my father's will.
No oath is stronger than almighty Zeus.

CHORUS LEADER

So you want us to believe that Zeus gave you
this oracle to pass on to Orestes,
told him to avenge his father's murder
and, in the process, cast aside, trample
to nothing, the respect he owed his mother?

APOLLO

Yes, I do. For it's a different thing
entirely when a noble man who holds
the scepter Zeus bestows is murdered, struck down
not even by the far-shot arrow of
some Amazon, but by a woman's hand,
and in a manner I'll describe to you,
Athena, and to all you seated here
to judge the case by vote. Once he returned
from war where he did well enough, on balance,
the woman made a show of being kind,
seemed anxious to please him, fuss over him like a wife,
until, as he was stepping from the bath,
there at the very end, she swaddled him
in a winding cloth, tangling him up from head
to toe within the endless fold on fold
of the embroidered robe, then struck him down.
This is how wretchedly he died, a man
all men revered, commander of the fleet.
I've spoken as I have to whip up anger
in you who are called to set this matter right.

CHORUS LEADER

So it's your view that Zeus's main concern
is for a father's death. Yet didn't he
himself chain up his aged father, Cronus?
How do you square this with your argument?
Heed what you just heard, judges. Remember it.

APOLLO

You stinking, hideous filth, shunned by the gods,
we can break bonds, we can slip out of shackles! There's
a cure for ills like those, yes, countless ways
of getting free. But once a man is dead,
and the ground has sucked dry all his blood,
nothing can ever raise him up again.
My father made no healing spell for that,
though he can turn all other things, at will,
inside and out, and not pant from the effort.

CHORUS LEADER

See where your way of pleading for this man
has led you: he has spilled his mother's dear
blood on the ground —so how can he live in Argos,

take possession of his father's house?
What public altars could he use? How can he touch
the cleansing water at his kinsmen's shrine?

APOLLO

I'll tell you something else, to show how right
I am: the so-called mother of the child
isn't the child's begetter, but only a sort
of nursing soil for the new-sown seed.
The man, the one on top, is the true parent,
while she, a stranger, fosters a stranger's sprout,
if no god blights it. And I can prove it to you:
a father can give birth without a mother.
And here before us is our witness, child
of Olympian Zeus, daughter who never fed
and grew within the darkness of a womb,
a seedling that no goddess could bring forth.
In all things, Pallas, and with all my power,
I'll glorify your people and your city;
for that's the very reason I sent this man
here to your house and hearth so he could be
a constant friend to you for all time to come,
a friend and ally, goddess, he and his heirs,
each one of their descendents who will keep
this sacred bond, this covenant forever.

ATHENA

Have we now heard enough? Should I tell these judges
to cast their votes where they think justice lies?
apollo Our quiver's empty, all our arrows shot.
I'll wait to see which way the trial goes.

ATHENA

*(turning to the* CHORUS*)*

And what must I do now to avoid your reproach?

CHORUS LEADER

You've heard what you've heard, and as you vote, my friends,
with all your heart respect the oath you've sworn.

ATHENA

Now hear my ordinance, you men of Athens,
you who have been chosen to decide
this first trial ever for the shedding of blood.
Now and in future time, this court of judges
will continue to exist for the people of Aegeus,
here on this hill of Ares where the Amazons
pitched their tents when they invaded, armed,
and angry at King Theseus, raised up
against the city the towering walls of their

own battlements, and slit the throats of beasts
in sacrifice to Ares. This is why
we call this place the rock and hill of Ares.
Here the people's awe and innate fear
will hold injustice back by day, by night,
so long as the people leave the laws intact,
just as they are, and never alter them
with foul infusions: muddy the cleanest spring,
and all you'll have to drink is muddy water.
I urge my people to follow and revere
neither tyranny nor anarchy,
and to hold fear close, never to cast it out
entirely from the city. For what man
who feels no fear is able to be just?
And if you fear and justly revere this court,
then you will have a bulwark for your land,
the city's guardian, the like of which
nobody else on earth possesses, not even
the law-abiding Scythians, or Spartans.
This council I establish will be immune
from greed, majestic, poised for wrath, the country's
wakeful watchman over those who sleep.

I've given this long advice to all my people—
it's for the future. But now you must stand up,
take up your ballots and decide the case,
respecting your sacred oath. My speech is done.

*During the following exchange, the jurors arise,
proceed to the voting urns, deposit their ballots,*
and return to their seats.

CHORUS LEADER I warn you all —if you dishonor us,
we'll be a crushing burden on your land.

APOLLO And I tell you to fear the oracles,
Zeus's and mine. Don't keep them from bearing fruit.

CHORUS LEADER You honor bloody crimes that aren't your business.
Your oracles will never now be pure.

APOLLO So Zeus made a mistake when Ixion,
the first to kill, appealed to him for help?

CHORUS LEADER You said it, I didn't. But if I don't get justice,
I will come back to crush this land forever.

APOLLO How so? You have no honor among gods,

young or old. I will win this case.

CHORUS LEADER

You did the same thing, too, in Pheres' house:
you persuaded the Fates to let men hide from death.

APOLLO

Is it unjust to treat someone so kindly,
someone that pious, in his time of need?

CHORUS LEADER

You overturned the age-old covenant
by duping those ancient goddesses with wine.

APOLLO

And when you lose this trial, you'll vomit all
your venom at the ones you hate —quite harmlessly.

CHORUS LEADER

Young one, since you would trample down your elders,
I'll have to wait to hear if the court will give me
justice, or the city feel my wrath.

ATHENA

My office makes me last to judge this case.
And I will cast my ballot for Orestes.
No mother gave me birth, and in all things
but marriage I wholeheartedly approve
the male —I am entirely my father's child.
And this is why the killing of a woman
who killed her husband, guardian of the house,
can have no overriding claim on me.
Orestes wins, even if the votes be equal.

*(turning to the jurors)*

You jurors, who have this duty to fulfill,
quickly spill out the ballots from the urns.

*Two jurors return to the urns and begin the count*
ATHENA *takes a place behind the urns.*

ORESTES

Phoebus Apollo, how will it be decided?

CHORUS LEADER

Black Night, our mother, are you watching this?

ORESTES

It's time now—to feel the noose, or see the light!

CHORUS LEADER

To be disgraced, or forever keep our honors!

APOLLO

Count up the spilled out votes precisely, friends,
make no mistake, be sure the sum is just.
Out of bad judgment comes catastrophe,

But when the judgment's sound, a single vote
can reestablish order in a house.

ATHENA

*(examining the ballots)* This man's acquitted on the charge of murder—
the number of votes for both sides is the same.

ORESTES

O Pallas Athena, you have saved my house!
When I was stripped bare of my homeland,
you gave it back to me. Now Greeks will say:
"The man is Argive once again; he lives
among his father's holdings by the grace
of Pallas and Apollo, and of the third,
the savior, he who brings all to fulfillment."
Yes he, himself, gave due weight to the way
my father died, and has delivered me
to safety from my mother's advocates.

And now before I leave for home, I swear
to your country and your people, now and forever,
up to the fullest ripening of time
that no helmsman of my realm, spear poised for battle,
will come against them. Even from my tomb,
I'll torture the transgressors of this oath
with failure and befuddlement. I'll sap
the spirit from their marches, and beset
their way with ominous wingbeats, so that they
regret they ever did what they have done.
But only if they keep an upright course,
and give enduring honor to the city
of Pallas with their loyal spears, will I
remain a blessing to them.

And so goodbye
to you, and to the people of your city.
May the hold you get on all your enemies
allow them no escape, and keep you safe,
and if war comes bring you the victory.

ORESTES *exits to the left, accompanied by* APOLLO.

CHORUS

IOU! IOU! You young gods—you *Refrain 1*
have trampled down the age-old laws,
ripped them out of my hands!
My honor stripped away, enraged,
aggrieved, now I
will squeeze out all the poison in my heart

against the land for all I've suffered,
yes, poison now will ooze and drip
unbearably into the soil.
   And out of it pale fungus
blighting leaf and child (O justice!)
   will quicken across
the land to cover it and all the people
   in a miasmal fog of
killing illnesses. Sorrow!
What can I do? Mocked! Spit on
   by the citizens!
We suffer the insufferable,
   luckless daughters of Night
who have been wronged, stripped of our honor!

ATHENA

Let me persuade you not to shoulder such
a burden of grief—because you weren't defeated,
the voting in the trial was truly equal;
you haven't been disgraced, no. After all,
the evidence from Zeus shown clear, and he
who gave the oracle bore witness that
Orestes should not be harmed for what he did.
So don't be angry; no longer aim your out-
rage on this land, or send out blight against it,
the piercing vapors that eat up the seeds.
I swear wholeheartedly to you, in justice,
that you will have your seat in a vast cavern
deep in this land of justice, and there you will sit
on gleaming thrones beside your sacred altars,
forever honored by my citizens.

CHORUS

IOU! IOU! You young gods— you *Refrain 1*
have trampled down the age-old laws,
   ripped them out of my hands!
My honor stripped away, enraged,
   aggrieved, now I
will squeeze out all the poison in my heart
against the land for all I've suffered,
yes, poison now will ooze and drip
unbearably into the soil.
   And out of it pale fungus
blighting leaf and child (O justice!)
   will quicken across
the land to cover it and all the people
   in a miasmal fog
of killing illnesses. Sorrow!

What can I do? Mocked! Spit on
by the citizens!
We suffer the insufferable,
luckless daughters of Night
who have been wronged, stripped of our honor!

ATHENA

Not stripped of honor, no. You're goddesses,
don't in a rush of anger blast the land
of mortals. I have Zeus on my side and—
why even bring it up? —I'm the only one
among the gods who knows where he keeps the key
to the chamber in which the lightning bolt is sealed.
No, we won't have need of that. Please,
let me persuade you not to spew from foolish
lips such curses against the land as make
all things that bear fruit shrivel up and die.
Soothe into sleep the black wave of your rage,
its bitter surging: for you'll be honored here,
and worshipped, and share my home. And when
you receive the first fruits of this great land
offered up to you in hope of children
and for the fulfillment of the marriage rite,
you'll thank me for this advice I've given you.

CHORUS

That they would do this to me! *Refrain 2*
Force me, with all my age-old wisdom,
under this earth
like some defiled contaminated thing!
I'm breathing rage, sheer rage.
OTOTOTOI POPOI! DA!
What torture slides down over me
and through my brain!
Hear me O mother Night—the gods'
sleight of hand has snatched
my ancient rights away and made me
less than nothing.

ATHENA

I'll put up with your anger, for you are much
older than I am —and, therefore, so much wiser.
But Zeus has given me a keen mind too,
and if you leave here for a foreign country
I warn you now you'll long just like a lover
for this country you have left behind.
For time as it flows forward will bring great
and greater honors to the people here,
And honorably seated near the house

of Erechtheus, you'll receive from long
processionals of men and women more gifts
than any other place on earth could give.
Don't set the inciting whetstone of bloodshed spinning
throughout my land, sharpening the hearts of young
men till they're seized by a wildness not of wine.
Don't make their hearts seethe like the seething hearts
of fighting cocks, infusing in my people
a war lust they'll turn inward on each other.
May all their warfare be with foreigners,
and may the wars be plentiful enough
to sate their fiercest hunger for renown.
There's nothing brave about a cock who fights
inside the nest.
So it is your choice now
to take what I am holding out to you:
to do well and receive well and, well honored,
have your own share of this land the gods love well.

CHORUS

That they would do this to me! *Refrain 2*
Force me, with all my age-old wisdom,
under this earth
like some defiled contaminated thing!
I'm breathing rage, sheer rage.
OTOTOTOI POPOI! DA!
What torture slides down over me
and through my brain!
Hear me O mother night—the gods'
sleight of hand has snatched
my ancient rights away and made me
less than nothing.

ATHENA

I'll never tire of telling you the benefits
I'm offering, so you can never say
that you, an elder goddess, have been disgraced
and driven into exile from this country,
either by me, a younger goddess, or by
the mortal keepers of the city. No!
But if you hold in awe Persuasion's glory,
the power of my tongue to soothe and enchant,
you might live here with us. Still, if you don't,
if you choose not to, it would not be right
to bring the riot of your raging hate
against the city, to harm the people. The way
is free for you to be a landholder here,
enjoying honor justly and forever.

CHORUS LEADER What kind of place would be mine, Queen Athena?

ATHENA One free of pain. Will you make it yours?

CHORUS LEADER And if I do, what honor will I have?

ATHENA No house will ever grow without your blessing.

CHORUS LEADER You'd make me as powerful as that?

ATHENA We'll swell the fortunes of your followers.

CHORUS LEADER You promise me this power's mine forever?

ATHENA I wouldn't promise what I won't fulfill.

CHORUS LEADER You might persuade me; I feel my anger easing.

ATHENA Live with me here, and you'll have more friends, new friends.

CHORUS LEADER What blessings would you have my chant call forth?

ATHENA Blessings that bring victory without dishonor,
blessings that come from earth, and from the water
of the sea, and from the sky that make the air
across the land breathe out in sunlit breezes;
blessings that make the earth's yield swell, and the thick
herds grow more bountiful as time goes on
and never fail my people. Their seed, too,
you'll bless and protect, and may you favor most
the purest among them, make them prosper most.
I'm like a gardener, caring for the stock
of these just men, keeping them safe from sorrow.
These are the blessings that are yours to give
while I will shower glory on their battles,
and never fail to let the city's fame
for victory resound in every land.

CHORUS I will accept a home *Strophe 1*
here in the house of Pallas,
and won't dishonor the city
ruled by Zeus all-mighty
and Ares as the fortress
of the gods, protector of
the altars of the Greeks,
city that all rejoice in,

city for which I pray
and lovingly foretell
that the bright rays of the sun
will make the earth bring forth
in rich profusion all
the good things that foster life.

ATHENA

Since my heart is filled with tenderness
for all my people,
I have ensconced these powerful,
demanding goddesses here among them,
goddesses whose task it is
to oversee the lives of men.
And any man
they train their hate on doesn't know

from where the flurry of hard blows
crashes against
his life. Ancestral crime pulls him down
before their judgment seat, and while
he brags out loud, silently
their crushing hatred hits him, their
implacable rage
grinds him completely down to dust.

CHORUS

*Antistrophe*

May no fierce wind blast the trees —
these are my words of grace—
and may no heat that sears
the plants and kills their buds,
cross this land's boundary.
May no blight waste the crops. May Pan swell the swarming
flocks, double their yield
at the appointed time.
And may the land's children
find veins of wealth within
the soil and honor the gods
with sacrifice for the luck
of their discoveries.

ATHENA

Jurors, bulwark of the city,
do you hear what blessings
she'll bring about? The power of the great
Erinyes awes the gods above
and those below, achieves their ends
for all to see, bringing bright
joyous life

to some, life blind with tears to others.

CHORUS

*Strophe 2*

I ban, too, the untimely
killing of young men;
and you gods who possess
the power to do so, let
young girls find husbands —
especially you Fates,
our sisters from one mother,
goddesses whose share is just,
who have a hand in every
home, whose force weighs
heavily in every season,
whose reckoning, exact
in all ways is in all
ways honored by the gods.

ATHENA

They bless my land so lovingly
  that my heart swells.
I'm glad Persuasion's eye watched over
my lips and tongue when I first faced
their brutal "No!" But Zeus who guides
men's speech won out. Our rivalry
  in doing good
gives victory to good forever.

CHORUS

*Antistrophe 2*

I pray that the crazed voice
of civil strife that feeds
on evil and is never full
may never roar through this land.
And may the earth not guzzle
down the black blood of its people,
and then, hot for revenge,
welcome the city's ruin,
murder paid back with murder.
Instead let citizens
give joy for joy,
loving the common good,
hating a common foe:
they'll cure most ills this way.

ATHENA

These women, have they the wisdom to find
  a path of blessing?
Then I discern in their dread faces
great gain for all my people. Revere them,
be kindly to these kindly ones,

and you will keep the land and city
on the straight path
of justice, and shine in everything.

CHORUS *Strophe* 3

Farewell! Rejoice amid
the wealth you've earned! Goodbye,
you people of the city
dwelling near the throne
of Zeus, loving the goddess
who loves you well, wiser
with every passing day,
safe in the wings of Pallas
whose father honors you.

ATHENA

Goodbye to you! I'll go before you
and show you to
your chambers by the sacred light
these escorts hold. Now go, and take
with you these holy offerings.
Hurry beneath the ground and hide
down deep within it
whatever's harmful to the city;.

whatever's to the city's gain
send up, so she
may always be triumphant! You sons
of Cranaus, keepers of the city,
lead the way for them, our new
inhabitants, and may the people
receive with good
hearts all the goodness they are given.

CHORUS *Antistrophe* 3

Farewell! Goodbye again
I say, to everyone
within the city, gods
as well as mortals. Watch over
Athena's city well,
revere my dwelling here
among you, and the lives
you lead will give you nothing
ever to complain of.

*A group of women equal in number to the Chorus enters, carrying crimson robes, preceded by torchbearers, and followed by one or more sacrificial animals led by attendants.*

ATHENA

I thank you for the blessings you have spoken.
I'll lead you by the dancing light of torches
to your deep chamber underneath the earth,
accompanied by my attendants, the women appointed
in justice to guard my image. I invite you
into the very heart of Theseus' land.
And now, you honorable band of young
girls, women, aged ladies, dress them
as suits their dignity in purple robes,
and let the torches flare and dance, so that
they'll always show their kindness to the land
in blessings that bring glory to our men.

*The* ESCORT, *made up of the jurors and the band of women and led by the torchbearers, accompanies the Erinyes to the right.*

ESCORT

Go on to your new home, you awesome children
of Night, you aged children,
childless children, covetous of honor,
under a kind escort.
Hush now, people, all of you, speak well,
only auspicious words.
Deep in earth's oldest caverns, you'll be graced
with worship and sacrifices—
Hush now, citizens, all of you, speak well,
only auspicious words.
Gracious and favoring the land that favors you,
come this way, venerable ones,
radiant in the torch-devouring flame,
rejoicing as you go.
Lift up a joyous cry in rhythm to our song.
There will be peace forever
among the people of Pallas. All-seeing
Zeus and Fate have helped
us make it so. Lift up a joyous cry
together and crown our song!

EUMENIDES

1–156 / 1–139 *Prologue* Substantially longer than the prologues (defined simply as the portion of the play before the Chorus makes its entrance) of the first two plays of the trilogy, this is really a sequence of separate scenes with a remarkable cumulative impact. First, there is a scene-setting speech by the Pythia (1–40/1–33), who exits only to return with a kind of messenger speech, an agitated report of the presence in the temple of Orestes and the Erinyes (41–76/3–63). In the next scene, Apollo promises Orestes his continues protection and prescribes the journey to Athens through which Orestes will win release from his troubles (77–108/64–93) He has put the Erinyes to sleep, and Orestes is able to make his escape. In the final scene of the Prologue, the ghost of Clytemnestra awakens her Erinyes and stir them into pursuit of Orestes (109–156/94–139). Taken as a whole, this sequence presents the essential outlines of the coming struggle clearly and with dramatic force.

1–76 / 1–63 Structurally, the Pythia's speech resembles the two preceding prologues in that all three are intersected by a startling sight that changes the speaker's mood. In this case, the initial mood is markedly different from that which prevailed in the final scene of *Libation Bearers,* since the Pythia's prayers emphasize the order and peace of the shrine at Delphi, and the harmony among the gods associated with it (see on 6/5) The Pythia's report of what she has seen in the temple, on the other hand, directly continues the situation and tenor at the end of the preceding play.

2 / 2 *the first prophet, Earth* There was a shrine to Earth in the sanctuary at Delphi through its active history, and her importance, to the site is presumably reflected in the story that Delphi was found to be the center of the earth when the two eagles Zeus sent out from either side of the earth met there.

6 / 5 *by her own choice and not by force* Aeschylus explicitly rejects the standard account, in which Apollo used force to capture Delphi from a chthonic predecessor, usually the monstrous serpent Pytho, occasionally Earth or Themis. See further the Introduction, pp. 22–23. This picture of peaceful succession helps bridge the gap between the violence of the past (the succession of crimes in the house of Atreus; the violent overthrow of Zeus's predecessors, leaving them unnamed and without honor *[Agamemnon,* 189–99/168–75]) and the more pacific order to come (Orestes' acquittal and the end of the curse on the house; the reconciliation of Olympian and chthonic deities, with continued powers and honors given to the latter).

7/7 *Phoebe* Not otherwise associated with Delphi, Phoebe is apparently given her place here to make the picture of harmonious relations among the generations and orders of divinity more complete. In addition to being Themis' sister in the Titan generation, Phoebe was Leto's mother (He-siod, *Theogony* 404–6), and thus Apollo's grandmother. Aeschylus also establishes an etymological connection between the cult name Phoebus ("bright one") and Delphi, since he has Apollo adopt it in gratitude for Phoebe's gift.

12 / 10 *the ship-hive coast of Pallas* I.e., the coast of Attica, whose patron god is Pallas Athena. This version of Apollo's journey seems designed to honor Athens (cf. on 14/13); a number of other sources have him landing in Boeotia; to the north.

14/13 *The children of Hephaestus A* reference to the Athenians, who regarded themselves as descended from Hephaestus through their early king Eri-chthonius, born of seed that fell to earth when Hephaestus attempted to rape Athena. The reference to the Athenians as road builders is explicated by a fragment of the fourth-century historian Ephorus, who says that Apollo first traveled to Delphi along the road that the Athenians still use to send their delegation to the Pythian Festival (a quadrennial Panhellenic competition like the Olympics, but featuring musical and poetic as well as athletic contests). Aeschylus is here alluding to (or perhaps even inventing) the story of how that road came to be built.

21 / 19 *spokesman for his father Zeus* The implication of this statement is that Zeus, the great ruler of the gods, stands behind Apollo's oracles, including the demand that Orestes kill his mother and the promise of protection when the deed is done.

23–34 / 21–28 The Pythia's prayer concludes with mention of a rather disparate group of gods, major Olympians and local nature deities, in no apparent order, except for reserving the final place for Zeus "who brings all to fulfillment" (see on 33–34/28). All the gods, however, have connections to Delphi: Athena's shrine that "stands there, apart" (24/21) gives her cult at Delphi the name *pronaia,* "before the temple," because it is some distance from the temple of Apollo, and would be reached by the approaching traveler before they entered his precinct. The Cory-cian cave (25/22), sacred like many others to the Nymphs, lies on the slopes of Parnassus above Delphi. Bromius (27/24) is a cult name of Dionysus, who was thought to take up residence at Delphi during the three winter months when Apollo visited the Hyperboreans (see on *Libation Bearers,* 425–26/373). Pleistus (32/27), god of the river that flows below Delphi, was the father of the Corycian Nymphs. Poseidon (33/27) was the father of Delphus, the eponymous king at the time of Apollo's arrival (18/16), and had an altar within Apollo's temple, indicating a long-standing association with the shrine (in one tradition, he originally shared the shrine with Earth).

29–30 / 25–26 *led his troop of women / ... to hunt down Pentheus* This story, best known to us from Euripides' *Bacchae,* was also enacted in a lost Aeschylean trilogy. Dionysus, who was born in Thebes, wished to establish his cult there when he returned to Greece after a long absence. King Pentheus tried to ban.'this new form of worship, but Dionysus drove a group of his maenads, led by Pentheus' own mother, to tear him to pieces on Mount Cithaeron, near Thebes. Here, the tale serves to explain when worship of Dionysus began at Greece —when he returned to Thebes and established his cult in Greece—but it sits uncomfortably in an otherwise peaceful prayer. The effect seems willed: the detail that Pentheus was snared like a hare (31/26) reminds us of the omen of a hare torn apart by eagles that led to the sacrifice of Iphigenia {*Agamemnon,* 129–57/108–38), and his "net of death" evokes the slaughter of Agamemnon.

33–34 / 28 *Zeus, / who brings all to fulfillment* This is Zeus *teleios* (see on *Agamemnon* 1115–18/972–74), he who fulfills prayers, and who may or may not show the way to fulfillment and finality here. (Like others before them in the trilogy, the Erinyes in this play will see themselves as *teleoi* [see on 370–73/ and 463/382].)

39 / 32 *in order of the lots they drew* Ordinarily, after purification and sacrifice, those admitted to consult the oracle drew lots to determine the order in which they would approach and put their questions.

40 / 33 The Pythia now enters the temple to perform her duties, and the audience awaits the arrival of another character or the entrance song of the Chorus. Exits such as this that leave the stage completely empty are rare, but there is no parallel at all in tragedy for the disappearance and reappearance of the same character. The shock is increased by the manner of her reentry, so terrified by what she has seen that she can. only crawl on all fours (44–47/36–38).

51 / 41 *sitting the way a suppliant would sit* A suppliant must be in physical contact with a sacred object, of which he becomes in effect an extension, i.e., the inviolable property of the god to whom the

object belongs. Here, that object is the "navel stone" (52/40), the sacred stone that stood in the inner chamber of the temple to mark the center of the earth. He may be sitting on it (as we have translated the phrase) or beside it—the Greek can indicate either, and vase paintings show both—but he must be touching it with his hand or a suppliant branch such as he was carrying when he left Argos *(Libation Bearers,* 1172/1035).

57 / 47 *sleeps* Why this ferocious gang has fallen asleep around their prey remains a mystery until Apollo tells us the answer at 80–81/67–68.

61–62 / 50–51 *flying female- / creatures* These are the Harpies, represented in fifth-century vase painting as winged women. The Pythia, having compared the Erinyes to Gorgons (as did Orestes, at *Libation Bearers,* 1187–89/1048–50), finds the likeness inadequate, and tries again by recalling an image she has seen of the hideous creatures who persecuted Phi-neus, King of Thrace. The Harpies ("Snatchers") swooped down and snatched his food whenever a table had been set for him. (Aeschylus wrote a *Phineus,* performed in 472 along with his *Persians.)*

66 / 55 *Their dark rags* The Erinyes, as daughters of Night and dwellers in darkness, dress in the color of mourning, inappropriate and inauspicious for wearing in a temple. The Pythia, as a priestess of Apollo, will be wearing white.

77–108 / 64–93 Apollo assures Orestes of his continued support and sends him on his way to Athens, guided by Hermes. For possible ways of staging this scene, see on 109–56/94–139.

77 / 64 J *won't betray you* Cf. *Libation Bearers,* 303/269, "Apollo's great oracle will never betray me," and 1169/1030–32, [Apollo] "told me I could do this guiltlessly." Apollo here makes his promise more explicit, offering his protection "to the end" *(dia telous,* i.e., until the goal is reached).

95 / 80 *holding her age-old image in your arms* The venerable and venerated olive wood statue of Athena Polias, which was ceremonially given a new embroidered robe at the Great Panathenaea, the major Athenian festival in honor of Athena. Again, the suppliant is to maintain physical contact with the sacred object (see on 51/41).

96 / 81 *we'll have judges for your case* The first inkling that resolution will come in the form of a trial, although there is no indication that the judges will be mortals rather than gods. But the promised resolution will be worked by persuasion ("words / that spellbind," 96–97/81–82; cf. on 1032/886), and it will bring Orestes permanent release from his troubles.

105 / 90 *be your own namesake* Hermes is given his title "the escorter" *(pompaios)* and asked to be true to its meaning. Although it is often supposed that Hermes must be present on stage there is no need to assume that Hermes appears in this scene, and no reason to think he reappears with Orestes in Athens. Apollo calls his brother, who can hear him even from afar (cf. 342/297) and asks him to protect and guide Orestes, again something he can do without appearing on the scene.

109–56 / 94–139 Clytemnestra's ghost appears and exhorts the sleeping Erinyes to rouse themselves and pursue their escaping prey. Ghosts were far from common on the Greek stage; among extant tragedies, we find only the ghosts of the Persian king Darius, in Aeschylus' *Persians,* and of Hecuba's treacherously slain son, Polydorus, in Euripides' *Hecuba.* Clytemnestra's ghost has, the additional oddity of coming to her intended audience, the Erinyes, as a dream (156/139), whereas the theater audience witnesses her appearance as a real event. The scene completes preparations for the great confrontation to come. Apollo has seen to Orestes' escape and provided protection and instruction; now Clytemnestra charges her agents of retribution to follow Orestes and give him no quarter.

Regarding staging, although it is impossible to know precisely how Clytemnestra's entrance was handled, several satisfactory ways can be imagined. The real problem is to decide at what point the audience sees the sleeping Erinyes. The main choices seem to be these: (1) Before 77/64, the temple door opens, and the *ekkyklema* (see on *Agamemnon,* 1563/1372) rolls, out, with Orestes seated among at least a small group of sleeping Erinyes. Apollo then appears from behind the *ekkyklema,* eventually guiding Orestes out into the orchestra, sending him on his way and reentering the temple after 109/93. Clytemnestra then appears from one of the side entrances, or through a subterranean entrance (if the theater had one: see Taplin, *Stagecraft of Aeschylus,* 447–48), or perhaps most appropriately and effectively, since she is a dream-apparition, on the roof of the stage building. (2) Apollo and Orestes exit from the temple in the usual way, and play their scene, with Orestes departing to the side at the end and Apollo reentering the temple. The door then opens again, and a tableau with Clytemnestra's ghost among a group of sleeping Erinyes rolls into view on the *ekkyklema.* At the end of the scene, Clytemenestra exits to the side and the Erinyes on the *ekkyklema,* urged on by the Chorus Leader, enter the orchestra, joined, as the parodos begins, by others who had been out of sight inside the stage building. (3) Apollo and Orestes perform their scene as in 2; Clytemnestra appears in any of the ways listed in 1 and performs her scene with no Erinyes to be seen, although they begin to be heard after 133/116. Clytemnestra exits in the same way she entered, the temple door opens, and the Erinyes enter the orchestra at the urging of the Chorus leader as the parodos begins. Each of these stagings has advantages and disadvantages, but we are persuaded to opt for 3 by the considerations suggested in Taplin, *Stagecraft of Aeschylus,* 369–74. Withholding the actual sight of the Erinyes until Clytemnestra has departed prevents visual distractions in the prologue scenes and builds expectations for the moment when they take over the orchestra, heightening the dramatic effect of their appearance when the doors are opened at last.

110–17 / 95–102 Clytemnestra has two separate complaints: she suffers dishonor in the world below because her Erinyes have not yet exacted vengeance for her death, and in addition she has to endure the constant reproaches of her own victims. The implied connection between these complaints is that the lack of any show of divine anger for the wrongs she suffered makes her vulnerable to their attacks. Giving and receiving due honors will be an important theme of *Eumenides.* The Erinyes in particular are incensed that the younger generations gods want to deny them their honors and, after Orestes' acquittal, they will have to weigh the honors they have lost against the new ones that Athena offers them instead.

120–25 / 106–9 For the notion that offerings are made in the understanding that they will be reciprocated with favor, see on *Libation Bearers* 290/257. Although wine was the regular medium of drink offering, the Erinys were among the deities honored with libations of water and honey. The burnt offerings might be cakes or animal sacrifices.

127 / 110 *my offerings trampled* A phrase reminiscent of other images of trampling down what ought to be sacred, and of the image's enactment when Agamemnon treads on the sacred embroideries

*(Agamemnon* 1038–96/ 905–57. The Erinyes in turn will complain that their ancient rights are being trampled by the younger gods (165–66/149–50, 850/731, 903–5/ 808–9).

129 / 112 *out from the middle of your net* Aeschylus again uses one of the leading images of the trilogy. Zeus's net was cast over Troy so that no one could escape *(Agamemnon* 410–15/357–61), and Clytemnestra set hers "so high no one can over- / leap them" *(Agamemnon* 1568–69/1376); only Orestes, the leaping fawn, has leapt free from the hunting net the Erinyes set. The Chorus takes up the metaphor at 163–64/147–48.

134 / 118 Preceding this line and 136/121, the manuscripts carry the onomatopoeic expression for whining, *mugmos.* Before 138/124 and 140/127, we have a similar expression for moaning, *ôgmos,* and before 142/130, "high, repeated *mugmos.*" These are among the few "stage directions" that come down in ancient dramatic texts. Whether or not they stem from Aeschylus himself, they represent the needed response of the Erinyes. It is perhaps significant that the response starts as soon as Clytemnestra says her name.

141 / 128 *the poison from the dread snake's tooth* The image of the serpent, applied to the trilogy's stealthy murderers Clytemnestra *(Libation Bearers,* 281/ 248–49 and 1123–25/994–95; cf. 1186/1047) and Orestes *(Libation Bearers,* 603–11/526–34 and 627–28/549–50; cf. 1057/928), is especially appropriate to the Erinyes. In art, they were often represented as serpents, and when Orestes first saw them, he described "snakes swarming all over them, / braiding and unbraiding" *(Libation Bearers,* 1188–89/1049–50).

157 / 142 *let's see if this dream is a truthful prelude* Did the dream give, like the introductory section of a musical performance, a foretaste of what is to come? The Chorus Leader is asking whether the dream truly predicts that Orestes has escaped.

158–99 /143–78 *Parodos* The chorus express their horror at having let Orestes escape and their passionate condemnation of Apollo for aiding a murderer whose very presence has polluted his shrine. It is not clear whether the entire Chorus is already in the orchestra when the parodos begins. A scholiast (an ancient or medieval commentator whose annotations are included in our manuscript tradition) suggests that the first strophe is divided among individual members of the Chorus, and this is all the more likely if, as it seems, the Chorus enters from the stage building by ones and twos, and may hold for the antistrophe as well.

158 / 143 *IOU! IOU! POPAX* An expression of horror at the recognition that Orestes is nowhere to be found. (It seems likely that the Chorus Leader and those who immediately follow him into the orchestra briefly mime a search before the song itself begins.)

165–71 / 149–54 These lines contain the essential elements of the Erinyes' quarrel with Apollo: he is a young upstart who has no respect for their seniority and has denied them their rights; although he is a god, he protects as a suppliant a mortal who has violated the gods' laws; and he has not acted in accord with justice *(dikaiôs).* The disrespect of the younger (male) gods will only be set right by Athena's persistence in showing the ancient female deities due deference (987–88/848–49,1025–30/881–84). Supplication will be vindicated, but (like purification, its partner in eliminating blood-guilt) it will be shown to be inadequate in this difficult case (see on 266/237). Indeed, it will only be a new way of working *dikê* —the establishments of a court of law—that will at last allow the quarrel to come to an end.

176–78 / 160–61 The Erinyes liken their pain to that of a criminal submitting to a public flogging.

181–92 / 164–73 "The Chorus's charge that Apollo has polluted his own sanctuary is a pendant to their objection to his receiving suppliants guilty of murder. Their picture of Apollo's throne and earth's navel stone dripping with blood gains effectiveness from the notion of blood pollution as a kind of contagion that spreads by contact (cf. 219/195). But, as Orestes will point out (531–38/448–52), it is only by undergoing rites of purification that a suppliant guilty of shedding blood can be freed from pollution. Apollo's answer is that the Erinyes themselves are the ones polluting his sanctuary by their presence (206/185, 231/207).

192 /172 *the age-old power of the fates* the Erinyes are referring to the ancient dispensation (one meaning of *moira)* that gives them their function. But they are half-sisters of the divine *Moirai,* the Fates, by their mother Night (1122–23/961–62); and they are closely associated with them as agents of the retributive justice over which the Fates preside. The Fates might be thought of in this context as the bookkeepers of justice, making sure that in the end the accounts are brought into balance; cf. the invocation of the Fates as accomplishers of justice, along with Zeus, at *Libation Bearers* 352–61/306–14.

199 /177 *a new avenger* When Orestes goes to the world below, his punishment will continue. See 305–18/267–75, where the Chorus threatens to drag Orestes to the underworld still living, and it is explicit that the "new avenger" who holds transgressors to a strict accounting is Hades himself.

200–263 / 179–234 *First episode.*

202 /181 *a flying snake* Apollo's arrow is given an image used of the Erinyes themselves, and of the trilogy's chief murderers (see on 141/128).

207 / 186 *your jurisdiction* Apollo describes a set of customs involving mutilation, torture, and killing, all of which would be regarded by Greeks as abhorrent cruelties practiced by barbarians. Almost all can be paralleled by descriptions of Persian customs in Herodotus's *Histories.* The one exception is stoning, which was used by Greeks as a form of execution in which a whole community could participate, and was therefore reserved for those who had injured the whole community. Public stoning is the punishment foretold by the Chorus of *Agamemnon* for Aegisthus (1864–65/1615–16). Perhaps it is included here simply as an example of mob violence.

217 / 194 *blood-lapping lions* The lion has appeared in the trilogy as a symbol of fierce strength, as a ruthless killer, and even (in Cassandra's sardonic description of Aegisthus, *Agamemnon,* 1399/1224) as a coward skulking in the bedroom. In its final appearance, the lion is reduced to a monstrous creature, dwelling in darkness like the Erinyes —who will make the imagery of bloodsucking their own at 300–4/264–66.

221 / 197 No *god* Somewhat hyperbolic, since this "herd" is itself divine, but Apollo is clearly talking about respectable Olympians, like himself. See further on 413–15/350–52.

222 / 198 *It's your turn to listen* Thus, appropriately, begins a debate that suggests how disputes can be pursued without bloodshed. The Chorus accuses Apollo of responsibility both for Orestes' crime and of shielding him from punishment (223–28/199–204). Apollo challenges their exclusive concern for mother-killers, which he regards as doing dishonor to Hera, Aphrodite, and the bonds of marriage (234–42/210–16). Although the debate unsurprisingly leads to no agreement, Apollo sets out the means, if not the content, of a peaceful settlement: Athena will "oversee the issue of this case" (253/224; in Greek, Apollo uses a plural form of *dike, dikas,* which can mean "legal proceedings").

230 / 206 *And you malign us for serving as his escort?* The irony of this defense lies in the use of a word *(propompoi)* that suggests a ceremonial procession—the Chorus uses it of "marching" to Agamemnon's grave *(Libation Bearers,* 27/23) —or a guard of honor—the Athenian citizens who escort the Erinyes-Eumenides to their new home are called *propompoi* in a scholion (later annotation included in our manuscript tradition)—rather than the pursuit of fleeing prey by relentless hunters.

235–36 / 211–12 Apollo's question is reminiscent of Clytemnestra's objection at *Agamemnon,* 1612–21/1412–18 that the Elders should have condemned Agamemnon for his slaughter of Iphigenia. Orestes will raise Apollo's question again, and receive the same answer, at 702–3/604–5. Here, Apollo accuses the Erinyes of insufficient regard for another sacred bond, the sexual union of a man and a woman. There, he will intervene to argue the case that mother and son are not in fact related by blood at all.

238 / 214 *the solemn vows of Hera the fulfiller* Marriage vows *(pistomata,* pledges of trust) sacred to Hera *teleia,* who both alone and in the company of her consort Zeus *teleios* is the patron deity of marriage. This cult name derives from the use of *telos* to designate religious rites in general, and Zeus *teleios* is "the fulfiller" in a broader sense as well (see on *Agamemnon* 1115–18/972–74).

243–49 / 217–21 Apollo emphasizes the sacredness of marriage and its claim on justice to show the injustice of the Erinyes' pursuit only of killers within the bloodline.

24 / 218 *greater than any oath* An oath would ordinarily be the strongest form of pledge or promise, but Apollo argues that marriage vows are even stronger. He will later say the same thing of the will of Zeus (722/621), which perhaps suggests how bold Apollo's claim here is. Apollo makes his case for the special sacrality of marriage in part simply by calling it "a thing of destiny," which does not imply what we mean by "a match made in heaven" (Agamemnon's and Clytemnestra's clearly was not), but rather that it is the allotted portion of men and women to unite in marriage.

258–63 / 229–34 The Chorus Leader and Apollo cap the scene with three lines each in which they state the equally intransigent positions from which the trial will begin. The effect is clearest if the Chorus depart immediately as soon as their Leader has spoken, and Apollo, who cannot stop them but is resolved to defeat their plans, delivers his lines after they leave the orchestra.

260 / 230–31 *get our justice* The Erinyes use the same word, *dikas,* that Apollo used at 253/224 to indicate that Athena would oversee Orestes' trial. In their mouths, however, *dikas* still means the old retributive justice of blood for blood.

262–63 / 233 *a dreadful thing for gods / and men alike* This is one of several passages in *Eumenides* that suggest the gods' respect for mortals and sense of responsibility to them (see on 882–84/760–61,

1169/1002). There is also the implication here that the gods seek to avoid the anger or displeasure of mortals by shirking their responsibilities (see further on 558–61/470–72).

264–352 / 235–306 *Second episode* No choral ode separates the second episode from the first. None is possible because the Chorus has left the orchestra, which makes possible the change of scene that now occurs. Instead of an act-dividing stasimon, there is a momentary pause before Orestes enters, alone. There need be little change to the playing space —simply the removal of props (if there were any) that identified the setting as Delphi and their replacement by a wooden statue of Athena (cf. on 95/80, and see 290–92/258–59). From Orestes' first words we understand that he has reached Athens, as Apollo ordered. This sort of change of scene is rare in Greek drama. (The closest parallel, Sophocles' *Ajax,* 815, also involves the Chorus disappearing from view.) The Erinyes reappear, apparently again by ones and twos, miming bloodhounds following a scent, and sing what is usually referred to as an "epiparo-dos," or second entry song (285–318/254–75). The remainder of the episode is a pair of speeches (not an exchange —see 349/303; Orestes will not address the Erinyes until his trial) for Orestes and the Chorus Leader.

266 / 237 *but one no longer stained* Orestes has been purified from blood-guilt and his hands are no longer stained. In this passage, the cleansing appears to have happened in the course of his journey, but at 326–27/282–83, Orestes explicitly states that he was purified by Apollo at Delphi; apparently we are to understand that both the Delphic rite and the trials of his wanderings were necessary for his cleansing. Orestes mentions multiple purifications again at 535–37/451–52. Most important, however, although Orestes repeatedly insists that his formal purity has freed him to have normal contact with others (268–69/238–39, 329–30/285, 528–30/445–46), it does nothing to placate the Erinyes or make them abandon their pursuit.

273 / 243 *waiting for justice to be fulfilled* literally, "guarding the final outcome of justice." Two of the trilogy's most powerful words, *telos* (finality, fulfillment) and *dike* (justice, judgment) are combined in this phrase. Orestes is praying for Athena's intervention, but it will not come until after the Erinyes have found him and we have witnessed their attempt to get him in their power.

275 / 245 *the voiceless snitch* a riddle in the form of a kenning, whose answer is given as "blood drops" at 278/247.

284 / 253 *the warm smile of an old friend* In Greek, the verb *prosgelai,* "smiles on," can simply mean "greets me," but the Erinyes' delight in blood gives the image its grotesque charge.

285–318 / 254–75 *Epiparodos* (second entry song) The Erinyes sing and mime their hound-like pursuit of Orestes and threaten terrible violence, their own and that in the world below. This passage is in lyric verse reminiscent of the Chorus's first entry song (parodos, 158–99/143–78), but without the usual strophic responsion, presumably indicating a freer and perhaps less elaborate choreography.

290–91 / 258 *once again / protected* As at Delphi, so in Athena's shrine, Orestes is safe in the deity for protection. The Erinyes can threaten, but they cannot attack.

296 / 262 *it can't return again, not ever* This phrase resonates with a series of statements and images throughout the trilogy, in some of which the blood disappears (e.g., *Agamemnon* 1160–62/1017–21), and in others remains as a source of disease and suffering (e.g., *Libation Bearers* 54–55/48 and 76–79/66–67).

Here, the emphasis is on the debt of blood that Orestes owes for the mother's blood he has shed, but Apollo will later use the same argument in defense of Orestes' actions (756–58/647–48), and the Eriynes-Eumenides will repeat it in a political context in their prayer against violent civil strife (1143–45/979–80).

305–6 / 267 *drag you, still alive / into the underworld* The Chorus has already said that Orestes' punishment will continue among the dead (195–99/175–8); now, the terrible threat to suck his blood and shrivel him (300–305/ 264–67) is figured as a preliminary for the tortures of the underworld. The repeated notion of payment (300/264, 307/268), however, reminds us that this is also the Erinyes' exaction of justice for Orestes' murder of his mother (see on 313/272).

311–12 / 270–71 *honor owed to gods, guests, / or loving parents* This corresponds to the three "ordinances of Justice" set out in Aeschylus' *Suppliants* 701–9 and expresses basic precepts of Greek popular morality. The Erinyes do not here claim that they themselves enforce all three, and elsewhere they systematically ignore the claims of Orestes' other parent and of Apollo, but traditionally Erinyes are associated with punishing infractions on all these counts. The Erinyes' recognition here of the larger values of which they see their own "appointed task" (232/208) in part prepares for the new role they agree to undertake at the end of the play. See also on 639–41/545–49.

313 / 272 *you'll see them get the justice they deserve* The Chorus in effect answers Apollo's proposal of a court overseen by Athena (252–53/224) with just punishment meted out in a strict accounting by Hades himself.

320 / 277 *the many ways of being purged* Cf. on 266/237.

327 / 283 *by sacrificing swine* This was a standard form of purification, involving a kind of homeopathy or sympathetic magic. A young pig's throat was cut over the head of the person to be purified, so that its blood flowed down his body and carried off blood-guilt with it. Swine were sacrificed particularly to chthonic powers, and there is evidence of swine-purification at the great sanctuary of Demeter at Eleusis, the Attic deme that was home to Aeschylus' family.

336 / 291 as *her true allies* The offer of an alliance with Athena in return for his safety (for this kind of bargain with the gods, see on *Libation Bearers,* 290/257) is in effect an offer of alliance between his city, Argos, and hers, Athens. This is the first of three references to such a pact, reflecting one recently concluded between the two cities: see 782–87/669–73 and 885–98/762–74 (with note).

337 / 292 *wherever she is* This is a standard prayer formula, no doubt reflecting the widespread influence of the divinity, but, more important, assuring that the prayer will reach the right destination. In this case, Aeschylus is also preparing us for the lack of an immediate response that permits the Erinyes' attempt to get Orestes in their power. We learn at 480–81/397–98 that Athena was at Troy when she heard Orestes' prayer, thus confirming Orestes' belief that "a god can hear even from far away" (342/297).

*Libya* A natural place to mention in this context because of the tradition of Athena's birth there, but perhaps made more pointed because of an Athenian military expedition still ongoing in Libya at the time the *Oresteia* was produced. Thucydides reports in his History *of the Peloponnesian War,* 1, 104, that the Athenians had, a year or two before Aeschylus wrote the trilogy, sent an expedition of some two hundred ships to Egypt to help King Inarus of Libya free Egypt from Persian domination.

This expedition eventually met with disaster, but only several years later. An Athenian audience in 458, hearing of Athena in Libya "on the march to help her friends," would surely think of this ambitious and dangerous undertaking.

341 / 295 *the Phlegrean plain* The site of the great battle between the Olympian gods and the giants, in which Athena played a major part. There does not seem to be a contemporary allusion in this reference, but it is appropriate in a number of other ways: it expresses the wide extent of Athena's influence, taking her far to the north as Libya took her far to the south. It shows her once again in her military aspect, aiding her allies in struggle. And this battle between Olympians and dangerous and primitive children of Earth is emblematic in much Greek art and literature for the struggle between the forces of civilization and those of brutalitiy and barabarism.

350–51 / 304–5 A shocking perversion of sacrificial rite. Orestes is a choice animal, fattened for sacrifice, who will be eaten before the sacrifice can take place.

352 / 306 *the spell we sing to bind you fast* Orestes has just asked Athena to set him free. The Chorus Leader replies that, on the contrary, the Erinyes will cast a spell over him to hold him fast. The choral song that follows, then, is more closely integrated than usual into the action of the drama. Binding spells were part of ancient magical practice, and a large number of these have been found, inscribed for the most part on lead curse tablets. Faraone, "Aeschylus' *hymnos desmios,*" suggests that the Erinyes' song shares some motifs with a class of such tablets designed to provide magical superiority over one's opponent in a trial.

353–479 / 307–96 *First stasimon,* The Erinyes' "Binding Song" The Chorus sings and dances, hoping to bind and madden Orestes in their spell. He continues to clasp the image of Athena and remain impassive (as he evidently did at 349/303), knowing as he does when silence is proper (321/277–78). The earlier choruses of this play began unconventionally with the Chorus entering in small groups, miming their pursuit of Orestes. This song, on the other hand, displays a high level of formality within which to display its images of horror and madness. As at *Agamemnon,* 407–22/355–66, there is a chanted prologue (353–74/307–20) in marching anapests (see on *Agamemnon,* 48–123/40–103), even though the Chorus is already in the orchestra. The ode that follows uses repeated refrains, a formal feature that befits its ritual character. The manuscript tradition repeats only the first of these refrains (385–92 = 404–11/328–33 = 341–46), but we have followed many editors in repeating the two other nonresponding stanzas (416–24 = 429–37/354–59 and 442–49 = 454–56/372–76).

370–73 / 318–20 The language here uses terms familiar from the Athenian judicial system to describe the Erinyes' pre-legal justice. They invoke the notion of finality, associated elsewhere in the trilogy with the dispensation of Zeus, by appropriating the adverb *teleos* (here rendered by the adjectives "last" and "final") to describe their authority. For the Erinyes' further appropriation of this language, see on 463/382.

374 / 321 *Mother, O mother Night* These enforcers of a mother's rights begin their song with the invocation of their own mother, and will refer to her again several strategic points in the course of the play (499/416, 865/ 745, 921/791–92 = 956/821–22, 983/844–45 = 1021/876–77; and cf. 1123/ 962 and 1207–9/1033). They never mention their father, given by Sophocles as Skotos (Darkness), and

elsewhere as Cronus or Acheron, a river of the underworld. In this sense, they are the complete opposite of Athena, who has a father, but no mother (see on 855/736).

382 / 325–26 this *trembling hare* The memorable image of the trembling victim from the omen at Aulis ("her father's flying blood- / hounds eating in sacrifice / the trembling hare," *Agamemnon,* 154–56/136–37) now attaches itself to Orestes.

390 / 332–33 *the lyre-shunning song* See on *Agamemnon,* 735/645.

393 / 335 *Fate* Once again, the notion of a fixed dispensation *(moira)* that gives the Erinyes their function is combined with a personification of their half-sisters by mother Night, the *Moirai* (see on 192/172).

413–15 / 350–52 The Erinyes express the mutual aversion between them and the Olympian gods (see also 427–28/365–66, and cf. the scorn expressed by Apollo at 221/197). Black is the color of the gods whose home below ground, white that of the gods of Olympus (see on 66/55).

418–19 / 355–56 *the spirit of Ares, reared /... in the home* The war god's name can be used to refer to violence even if it is not military. The image of violence "reared / ... in the home" recalls the story of the lion cub that was raised as a pet but grew up to reveal its true nature *(Agamemnon,* 818–43/717–36).

438 / 368 *self-preening conceits* Literally, "awesome (self-) regard," a phrase made almost sarcastic by the transfer of the Erinyes' Attic cult name *Semnai,* "the Awesome Ones," to mortals who feel that they can escape punishment for their transgressions. The Erinyes will shortly reclaim their title by describing themselves as "awful *(semnai)* to men" (465/383).

441 / 370–71 *the quick kicks of our raging dance* This phrase and the following stanza, which has been read as a grim perversion of normal dance patterns, may give some clue to the wildness of the choreography here.

463 / 382 *unmatched* In the Greek, the Erinyes call themselves *teleioi* (370–73/318–20), fully accomplished, but also accomplishers of finality, of the definitive requiting of wrongs. The epithet picks up the assertion of authority in *teleos* ("last ... final") at 372/320 and looks forward to the assertion of power that "the gods made final *(teleon),*" 474/393.

478 / 395 *beneath the ground* The Erinyes[1] will be offered a very different home beneath the ground in Athens, and will finally accept it when they understand that it, too, will bring them honor.

480–578 / 397–489 *Third episode* Athena enters in answer to Orestes' prayer and asks first the Erinyes, then Orestes to explain their presence at her shrine. Both ask her to decide their dispute, but she prefers to have it tried by a jury of Athenian citizens, whom she goes off to select. The manner of Athena's entry has been a source of much discussion. We agree with most modern commentators in deleting a line (405 in the Greek, following on our 488a) that suggests that she arrives in the orchestra in a horse-drawn chariot. This is an alternative that probably found its way into the text when the producer of a revival of the trilogy decided to give Athena an entrance to match that of Agamemnon in the first play. Athena's description of her journey (486–88/403–4) suggests wingless flight, so it is possible that she entered on the stage crane *(mechane),* a device that permitted actors to be swung through the air and onto the stage or the roof of the stage building. There is nothing in the text, however, that necessitates her entering in anything other than the usual way, though presumably at a faster than usual clip.

480–85 / 397–402 Athena has been at Troy, taking possession of land awarded to her, i.e., to "Theseus' sons," the Athenians. Her temporary absence made possible the Erinyes' binding song, but why this particular journey? Aeschylus uses it to underline (once more; see on 336/291) the easy identification of Athena with her city and its people, who are never far from her mind. He also brings the Trojan War into the ambit of successful Athenian undertakings rewarded by grateful allies, i.e., into a kind of model for the role Athens had chosen for herself since taking the lead in opposing Persian expansion in the early part of the fifth century. There may, however, be a more specific allusion here. We know that there was conflict between Athens and Mytilene in the sixth century over the town of Sigeum in the Troad, and that it ended with Sigeum in Athens' possession (see Herodotus, *Histories,* 5, 94–95). Herodotus also tells us (5, 63) that Sigeum fell into the hands of the Peisistratid family when their tyranny was overthrown and they were driven from Athens in 510, and must have been in the orbit of Persia for some time thereafter. By 465/64 Athenians were involved in fighting there, and an inscription of 451/50 makes it clear that Sigeum is by then a member of the Athenian alliance. In short, this was a place in which Athens had a special interest, and the suggestion that it was part of a grant by the Achaeairs that made it "completely and forever" a dependency of Athens might well allude- to whatever events had recently led or were then leading to Sigeum's absorption into the Athenian sphere of influence.

488 / 404 *my aegis* A regular attribute of Athena, a goatskin garment, often depicted with a fringe of snakes around it and the head of the Gorgon that Perseus killed at its center.

500 / 417 *"Curses"* The curse launched on a wrongdoer from the grave sends the Erinyes out to seek vengeance, and in this sense they are indeed embodied curses.

512 / 429 *He won't swear he's innocent, or yield if I swear to his guilt* In Athenian legal practice, if the parties agreed to employ the so-called "evidentiary oath," the trial opened with the accuser taking an oath that the defendant had committed the deed, 'and the defendant that he had not. Orestes here will not agree, since of course he did kill his mother, but the critical issue is not the deed, but whether it was justified. Athena recognizes this, distinguishing between seeming to be just by relying on an oath and doing justice by examining the merits of the case (513–15/430–32).

517 / 434 *the final one* the Greek phrase *aitias telos,* literally, the "endpoint of guilt" or the "completion of the case," is reminiscent in its use of the language of fulfillment and finality of Orestes' "waiting for justice to be fulfilled" *(telos dikes);* see on 273/243.

518 / 435 The Erinyes here, and Orestes at 555–57/468–69, both accept Athena as sole judge of the case, making her decision not to do so but to appoint a jury of Athenians all the more remarkable.

524 / 441 Ixion See Glossary for details, and cf. on 835–36/717–18.

528–38 / 445–53 This is Orestes' most elaborate statement of his ritual purity, and Athena acknowledges its importance in her response (562–64/473–74). For the claim, see on 266/237.

558–61 / 470–72 Despite the agreement of both parties to accept her decision, Athena demurs. She explains her reluctance in terms of the burden, too great even for her, to judge a case that will produce so much anger however it is decided. She does indeed face a genuine dilemma, since her verdict must either damage her suppliant Orestes (see further on 563/474) or expose her beloved city to the poisonous wrath of the Erinyes (see on 566–69/477–79). The dilemma is very like that of King Pelasgus in an earlier play of Aeschylus, the *Suppliants.* Pelasgus must decide whether to accept the supplication of the Danaids, who are fleeing unwanted marriage to their cousins, the sons of Aegyptus, and risk a terrible war, or reject it and risk the wrath of Zeus, who protects the rights of suppliants. He, too, refuses to decide by himself and brings the issue before his people to gain their support. One difference here, of course, is that Athena is a great deity herself. The comparison thus underlines the fact that, notwithstanding the enormous disparity in power, gods seek to avoid the anger or displeasure of mortals by failing to meet their responsibilities to those to whom they have bonds of obligation or friendship.

563 / 474 *a proper suppliant* Athena explicitly acknowledge that Orestes' status as a suppliant who is ritually pure and brings no harm makes it grievous for her to reject his plea of innocence (cf. 262–63/233–34), and legitimate for him to feel wronged if she should do so.

566–69 / 477–79 To reject the Erinyes is dangerous for Athens, dearest of all places' to Athena's heart (see on 480–85/397–402), and therefore a threat to her, too. These lines foreshadow threats that the Erinyes will make as soon as Orestes is acquitted (906–17 = 941–52/780–87 = 810–17).

570–71 / 483–84 *I'll choose / a panel of judges* Athena, having decided that judgment in this case cannot be rendered by a mortal or by herself alone, decides to judge it together with a chosen body of Athenians, establishing a tribunal for the purpose over which she will preside and in which she will, as it turns out, have the deciding vote. Here, however, she mentions only her role to choosing the jurors and emphasizes she is founding "a court to last forever" (573/484). Thus, this exceptional case leads not only to the first murder trial (797/682), but to an institution Aeschylus' audience still knows.

577 / 487 *my ablest citizens* This translates a phrase, *aston emon ta beltista,* that does not necessarily imply high social standing. Like the members of the Areopagus Council in Aeschylus' day, however, Athena's jury was not chosen democratically by election or lot. (See Wallace, *The Areopagos Council,* 94–97.

579–659 / 490–565 *Second stasimon* The Chorus presents itself, and its case, in a new and surprising light. Orestes' fate was at the center of the previous song, as the Chorus sang and danced its binding web around him. Here, his crime is only the starting point for a reflection that moves outward to encompass the importance of fear for the well-being of society, and the role of justice —the retributive justice of the Erinyes, needless to say—in the lives of individuals and communities. The Erinyes no longer present themselves as relentless bloodhounds or bloodsucking monsters; they are agents of a stern morality that makes them sound in places like the Elders of *Agamemnon* (see below on 614/520–21, 626–27/533, 633–35/539–42, 646–59/553–65 ), and will later be echoed by Athena (see on 610–20/517–28). The ode reminds us, just before the trial begins, that the Erinyes' case cannot easily be dismissed, despite their own repulsiveness. It is perilous in the extreme to leave the demands of justice unmet.

593–94 / 502 *We'll / let any murder pass* The Erinyes depict the spread of violent crime as their own refusal, should they be dishonored by Orestes' acquittal, to continue to fulfill their function. They identify their work so completely with that of justice (604–5/511–12), that for them the survival of justice in human society hangs in the balance at Orestes' trial.

609 / 516 *the house of Justice falls* In the previous ode, the Erinyes identified their task as "the destruction of houses" (417/354–55) in which injustice has held sway; here, they imagine a world in which they no longer do their work as one in which the house of Justice itself is destroyed.

610–20 / 517–28 These ideas will be repeated in very similar terms by Athena at 813–17/696–99.

614 / 520–21 *Wisdom comes from wailing* Literally, "prudence from duress," but our version makes use of the homophony of *stenos* "straits" and *steno,* "groan." The idea is very similar to *Agamemnon,* 200–10/176–83.

626–27 / 533 *sacrilege / gives birth to recklessness* Cf. *Agamemnon,* 868–70/758–59. Lines 626–30/533–37 as a whole echo *Agamemnon* 860–91/750–81, where the Elders are at pains to show that reckless behavior *(hybris)* is the result of wickedness, and that prosperity depends on respect for justice and the containing of ambitions and desires within sane boundaries. This view explains the seemingly paradoxical embrace of the "middle way" (622/530) by a band of "wild revelers" (590/500), whose attitude until now has hardly seemed moderate.

633–35 / 539–42 *the altar / of Justice, / don't kick it over* Cf. *Agamemnon,* 437–40/ 381–84.

639–41 / 545–49 These are two of the three prime ordinances set forth at 311–12/270–11. The third, honor the gods, is represented by the injunction to "revere /... the altar / of Justice" (632–34/539).

646–59 / 553–65 An extended parable, like the story of the lion cub *(Agamemnon,* 818–43/717–36), using nautical images familiar from *Agamemnon,* e.g., destruction by storm (745–49/653–57), jettisoning cargo (1152–56A008–13), striking a hidden reef (1151/1006–7).

660–902 / 566–777 *Fourth episode* There is another change of scene at this point, but it resembles the refocusing of attention from orchestra to stage building that marks the shift from Agamemnon's tomb to the palace in *Libation Bearers,* rather than the marked change of locale from Delphi to Athens earlier this play. As at 264/235, little change to the playing space is needed for the move from Athena's temple to the Areopagus, the hill of Ares where Orestes trial will take place—the removal of the wooden statue of Athena, perhaps, and the placement on stage of a table with voting urns, and probably of benches for the jurors (who are instructed to stand up to cast their votes, 827/708). This episode can be regarded as the turning point of the entire trilogy, since it enacts the institution of a new civic form of justice, replacing the old uncontrolled and unbounded pursuit of vengeance by a legal procedure whose verdict is binding on all parties, and therefore final. The long succession of crimes in the house of Atreus is brought to an end at last in Athens, and in the process the first trial by jury and the first court of law come into being there.

660 / 566 *Herald* No proclamation of the beginning of the trial appears in our text, and it may well be that no Herald appeared on stage. Taplin, *Stagecraft of Aeschylus,* 393, assumes that the trumpet call (661–62/567–68) is heard and amounts in effect to the Herald's summons, but it could equally well be that Athena's mention of proclamation and trumpet suffice to evoke them, so that their enactment is not required.

662 / 567–68 *Etruscan trumpet* Greek lore attributed the invention of this instrument to the "Tyrrhenians," whom we know as Etruscans, or alternatively considered it a gift to them from Athena.

665–66 / 572–73 *both I the city and these jurors* The treatment of jurors and city as separate groups has suggested to some commentators that at least a few extras, representing those who gather to see and hear the trial, have entered along with Athena and the jury. It seems likely, however, that Athena refers, with a sweeping gesture of her arms, to the spectators in the theater who do, in fact, represent the city.

669 / 574 *My lord Apollo* Apollo apparently enters silently and without announcement just before he is addressed, a procedure that is anomalous. The Chorus's greeting cuts short Athena's announced intention of expounding her laws (666/571) and changes the direction of the proceedings. Athena does not return to the establishment of her new ordinance until 795/681. Instead, the trial itself begins, and the inconclusive debate between Apollo and the Erinyes can only be settled when the jury votes. Athena's formal founding-speech for the new court is postponed until that moment is at hand.

680 / 583 *the pursuer* The Greek word *diokon* is the standard legal term for "plaintiff," but it literally denotes one who pursues, and thus describes as well the role that the Erinyes have been playing, and that is now being transformed from physical persecution to legal prosecution.

687 / 589 *Two more to go* There were three falls in a Greek wrestling match; see on *Libation Bearers* 386/339. Orestes replies that the Erinyes haven't thrown him at all, because he never denied that he did the deed, only that he has any guilt from it.

702–6 / 604–8 Orestes' first question and the Chorus Leader's answer correspond closely to the exchange at 235–36/211–12, but the subsequent dialogue moves in a new direction as Orestes' challenges the commonsense assumption that mother and son are blood relatives. He seems to have backed into a position he himself does not fully understand. He had earlier called the killing of his mother "blood- / shed that's my own," i.e., the shedding of blood he shared with her *(Libation Bearers,* 1175–76/1028), and his only answer to the Chorus Leader's indignant objection, is to turn to Apollo for help. Apollo will make the argument for him at 769–74/658–61.

722 / 621 No *oath is stronger than almighty Zeus* This is the culmination of an argument designed to make Orestes' deed tantamount to following the command of Zeus and thus obligate the jurors to acquit him if they are not themselves to flout Zeus's will. Apollo's statement is couched in general terms, as at 243–44/217–18, where marriage vows are said to be "greater than any oath," but it very generality disturbingly incorporates the oath the jurors took (572/483), and which Athena will enjoin them to respect when reaching their verdict (829/710).

731–32 / 627–28 *not even by the far-shot arrow of I some Amazon* To die in close combat brought glory (see, e.g., *Libation Bearers,* 395–98/345–48); to be killed from afar by an arrow was less glorious; to be killed by a woman, even in battle, would be inglorious; to be killed by a woman's arrow would be an even greater indignity. And, says Apollo, Agamemnon's death was far worse even than that. For the Amazons' battle against Athens, see on 800–6/685–90.

750 / 641 *chain up his ancient father, Cronus* For the myth of Zeus shackling Cronus and the Titans under ground after defeating them, alluded to already at *Agamemnon,* 189–96/168–72, see Hesiod,

*Theogony,* 664–735. Such treatment of a father by a child would be reprehensible by human standards, although of course the Chorus Leader neglects to mention Cronus' habit of swallowing his children the minute they were born *(Theogony,* 453–67). The Chorus Leader, however, is simply disputing Apollo's claim that Zeus ordained the priority of the father's rights over all others.

756–58 / 647–48 Apollo insists that the finality of death makes it entirely different from the imposition of chains; but his argument that "nothing can ever raise again" the man who has blood has been "sucked dry" by the ground is turned against him by the Chorus Leader's reminder that Orestes has spilled his own mother's blood on the ground (762–64/652–53). They insist, as they have all along, that such a pollution derived from kindred blood can never be purified (764–67/654–56). Now Apollo has no alternative but to present the argument that mothers do not share kindred blood with their children.

769–70 / 658–59 *the so-called mother of the child / isn't the child's begetter* This view, later supported by Aristotle (who ascribes it to the philosopher Anaxagoras, a younger contemporary of Aeschylus), cannot be regarded as the sole, or even the dominant, Greek view on the subject in Aeschylus' day. See further the Introduction, pp. 24–25. It is the conclusive argument not because we can be sure that Aeschylus' audience would have found it convincing, but because the Erinyes have no answer to offer. As for the play's "internal audience," Athena accepts Apollo's view as grounds for Orestes' acquittal (855–57/736–38), but the human jurors are evenly divided as to his guilt, and thus half of them appear to regard Apollo's argument as fallacious or inconclusive.

776 / 663–64 *And here before us is our witness* Apollo's proof is the exceptional case of Athena, born (in the version of the myth given here) entirely without a mother, although in Hesiod's account *(Theogony,* 886–900), she has a mother, Metis, who conceives her in the. usual way, only to be swallowed by Zeus. In both versions, however, Zeus brings Athena to birth himself.

785 / 671 *a friend and ally* The second of three references to an alliance between Argos and Athens; the first was at 335–36/289–91; see further on 885—98/762–74.

795 / 681 Now *hear my ordinance* This is the speech that Athena seemed about to give when Apollo entered at 669/574. In this position, it introduces and solemnizes the moment of the jurors' decision.

797 / 682 *this first trial ever for the shedding of blood* Aeschylus is departing from a well-known tradition that explained the name Aereopagus ("hill of Ares," 800/685) by making it the site of an earlier trial of Ares for murder before a jury of his fellow gods. See further the Introduction, pp. 19–20. The trial of Orestes in Athens may or may not have been Aeschylus' invention; that Orestes visited Athens after his matricide certainly was not. There is evidence for non-Aeschylean versions of the story in which relatives of Clytemnestra or Aegisthus were the plaintiffs and a jury made up only of gods or only of men decided the case. This evidence postdates the *Oresteia,* but it is likely that the variant versions predate it, since it is hard to see how they would arise once Aeschylus had given the story so definitive a form. In any case, we can be reasonably certain that it was Aeschylus who connected Orestes' trial with the founding of the Areopagus Council, and who made the first act of that body the first murder trial in history.

800–806 / 685–90 In line with his change in the foundation myth for murder trials on the Areopagus from a trial of Ares by gods to a trial of Orestes by what would become the Areopagus Council, Aeschylus substitutes a new explanation for the name "Hill of Ares." This he does by making the future site of Orestes' trial the encampment of the invading Amazons, a tribe of barbarian women warriors, who sacrificed to the war god. The Areopagus would in fact be the best place from which to attack the Acropolis, and was the Persians' base when they sacked it in 490. The tradition that the Amazons used it for their attack may well predate Aeschylus. For the possible significance of this allusion to the Amazons, see the Introduction, p. 24.

802 / 686 *angry at King Theseus* This may refer to the story that Theseus had attacked their territory and carried their queen, Antiope, back to Greece, but the phrase (which could also be translated "jealous of King Theseus") is vague enough to be compatible with the tradition that the invasion was unprovoked by any prior hostilities.

807–17 / 690–99 Athena emphatically endorses ideas expressed by the Erinyes at 610–20/517–28. Lines 807–12/690–95 have generated enormous controversy because they are capable of being interpreted as representing Aeschylus' opinion of the recent reform of the Areopagus Council (see the Introduction, pp. 19–20). The very variety of interpretations, however, suggests that Aeschylus is making no such direct political statement. The text leaves it open to scholars to argue that the laws Athena instructs the people to "leave intact" and "never alter ... with foul infusions" are the laws of Athens as a whole, or the laws concerning homicide, or the laws that governed the Areopagus Council itself. Similarly, some have argued that Aeschylus is condemning Ephialtes' reform of 462, and others that he is supporting the reform by suggesting that the state of affairs Ephialtes confronted, in which the Areopagus had assumed broad political authority, represents what happens when ill-considered changes "muddy the clearest stream." Nothing in Athena's words here, and nothing elsewhere in the trilogy, compels such choices.

822 / 703 *Scythians, or Spartans* Both peoples, one barbarian but "naturally" law-abiding, the other a Greek community whose long history of stable laws and good government helped them fend off tyranny, were considered models of successful self-government.

828 / 709 *take up your ballots and decide the case* The voting takes place during the following exchange. Assuming ten jurors, we can imagine that one juror reaches the urns and casts his ballot during each of the ten couplets at 830–49/711–30. (For other assumptions, see on 854/735.) The Chorus Leader's lines at 850–52/731–33 then mark the end of the voting, and during them Athena would proceed to a place behind the table with the urns. The "ballots" are tokens, usually pebbles (which is what the Greek word *psephos,* used here, literally means). In this instance, the jurors cast their ballots into one of two urns to vote for conviction or acquittal.

835–36 / 717–18 Apollo adduces the case of Ixion, the first murderer (and already mentioned as a suppliant at 524/441) as the precedent set by Zeus himself for the purification of blood-guilt. Apollo's rhetorical question as to whether Zeus made a mistake would raise eyebrows among those who remembered the whole story, in which Ixion went on to betray Zeus by attempting to seduce Hera (see Glossary for details). The Chorus Leader, however, answers with a noncommittal "You said it, not I" (837/719) and returns to threats of destruction if the Erinyes should lose.

842–47 / 723–28 The Erinyes supply their own mythological example to illustrate Apollo's devious tampering with fate. This is the story, familiar from Euripides *Alcestis,* that Apollo tricked the Fates into allowing Admetus, the son of King Pheres of Thessaly, to live beyond his allotted time if he could find someone else to die in his place. The Chorus leader says that Apollo got the "ancient goddesses" drunk to secure their agreement (a detail not found in Euripides), thus connecting this episode to the charge that "you would trample down your elders" (850/731).

854 / 735 I *will cast my ballot for Orestes* Precisely what role Athena has in the voting has been the subject of vigorous debate. The most important question is this: Were the jurors' votes tied (implying an even number of jurors), with the tie then broken by Athena; or was there an uneven number of votes (implying a majority of one to convict), with the tie, and thus acquittal, being achieved only by counting Athena's vote? Unfortunately, the evidence of our text yields no easy answer. The original audience would have seen a voting procedure that clarified the text, so that every solution makes assumptions about how the scene was staged. E.g., those who favor an uneven number of jurors generally assume that an eleventh juror votes during the first two of the Chorus Leader's final three lines (850–52/731–33), leaving the final line for Athena's approach to the voting urns. Most important for our purposes, the result of the vote was regarded as decisive and final by all parties, however it was reached, and there is no suggestion of any irregularity or impropriety, even on the part of the Erinyes.

We have adopted the view that the jurors cast an even number of votes, so that the vote of Athena (a term that becomes proverbial for just this situation) is actually a tiebreaker. This approach has the notable advantage of avoiding Athena's overturn of a majority vote by the human jurors. If one takes the view that Athena creates the tie with her vote, one must either deal with that anomaly as part of Aeschylus' plan, or else assume that for the purpose of the vote, at least, the audience will accept Athena as simply another member of the jury, with no distinction between her vote and that of her mortal colleagues, even though it is she who set up the court and will shortly make the rule that a tie acquits (861/741). On the other hand, the greatest impediment to the view we have adopted is that Athena says she will cast her vote for Orestes before, the votes are counted and a tie declared. A possible solution is that Athena does not actually put a voting token in the urn, so that her vote is notional and contingent on the tie that emerges from the counting completed between 864/744 and 873/752. This staging would in effect provide a sort of instantiation, in the foundation legend of the judicial system, of the Athenian practice that allowed a tie to result automatically in acquittal by invoking the purely notional "vote of Athena." Another, perhaps less persuasive, possibility is that she adds her vote only after she has announced the tie at 874/753-

855 / 736 *No mother gave me birth* Athena confirms what Apollo said about her (776–78/663–66), although without any indication that she subscribes to his general view about procreation. What she does assert is her predisposition to value the male, which constitutes the decisive reason for her vote. As a virgin goddess, Athena rejects the role of wife, but she does not share the antipathy for males felt by others who shun marriage bonds, such as the Amazons or the Erinyes. She does, however, share a strain of androgyny with them, and with Clytemnestra. And yet, since she is "entirely my father's child" (857/738), she also abhors Clytemnestra's overturning of patriarchal order, and she will not condemn her killing. Her inclinations are thus entirely opposed to those of the Erinyes, who have a mother but no father (cf. on 374/321).

862 / 743 *You jurors who have this duty to fulfill* We know that in the fourth century B.C.E., four jurors were chosen by lot to count the votes. This passage is evidence for a similar practice before the middle of the fifth century.

880–81 / 759–61 The final appearance in the trilogy of the motif of the third libation to Zeus Savior, with the Savior restored to his proper place of honor. Now, at last, he has shown himself to be both savior and *teleios* (the one who "brings all to fulfillment;" see on *Agamemnon,* 1115–18/972–74) for the house of Atreus. See further the Introduction, p. 34.

882–84 / 760–61 One of the passages in *Eumenides* (cf. on 262–63/233) that suggest the gods can feel respect and responsibility for mortals.

885–98 / 762–74 An alliance between Argos and Athens has been mentioned twice before in *Eumenides* (335–36/289–91 and 782–87/669–73). Now, as Orestes leaves for Argos, he solemnizes the alliance with an oath to maintain friendship between his land and Athens both in his lifetime, and thereafter from the grave. Aeschylus thus gives a patina of great antiquity to an alliance made very recently between Athens and Argos. In 462, at about the same time as the reforms to the Areopagus were being undertaken, Athens abandoned an alliance with Sparta that was dear to the more conservative elements of the city in favor of a thirty-year treaty with Sparta's enemy in the Peloponnese, Argos. To the extent that this alliance is part of the ascendancy of more democratic policies in Athens, as has often been suggested, Orestes' warm offer of friendship between Argos and Athens may provide a clue to Aeschylus' political sympathies.

889 / 767 *Even from my tomb* The long-standing belief that a hero continues to exercise power from his grave was an important element of the first half of *Libation Bearers,* set at Agamemnon's tomb. Here, Orestes takes a solemn oath to use that power after his death to protect his friends, the Athenians. Similar promises are made to Athens by Oedipus in Sophocles' *Oedipus at Colonus* and by Eurystheus in Euripides' *Children of Heracles.* That such beliefs were not confined to tragic poetry can be gauged from Herodotus' account of the importance that Sparta attributed to recovering the bones of Orestes from Tegea, where they had been buried and forgotten (Histories, 1, 67–8).

893 / 770 *with ominous wingbeats* The Greek *parornithas* literally means "contrary to bird [signs]," i.e., visited by bad omens.

900 / 776 *the hold you get on all your enemies* A final use of the wrestling metaphor. Orestes the wrestler (see 687–88/589–90 and *Libation Bearers,* 992–95/ 866–68) has in effect linked his victory with future victories for Athens.

902 / 777 With Orestes' exit, the great story of crime and retribution in the house of Atreus is over at last, and the curse that lasted through generations is finally lifted. Orestes is mentioned only once more in the remainder, of the play (929/799). Apollo's part in the story is over as well, but his exit is far more problematic, since it is entirely unmarked, which is irregular in Greek tragedy even for a minor character —much less for a major deity. Furthermore, Orestes hardly mentions Apollo in his final speech, despite the crucial part Apollo played, as purifier and defense attorney, in winning

his freedom. Nevertheless, the least jarring way for Apollo to exit seems to be in the company of Orestes.

903–1226 / 778–1047 The last third of the play is an extended scene for the Erinyes and Athena, capped by a short choral exodus sung by a group of Athenians as they escort the ancient goddesses to their new home below the Acropolis. Orestes' acquittal and disappearance leaves the Erinyes, who have repeatedly threatened to wreak terrible damage should their prosecution fail, ready to turn their full wrath against Athens. Athena uses her powers of persuasion to transform anger into benevolence and vengeance into blessing, and the Erinyes at last accept a new role in Athens as Eumenides ("kindly ones," see on 1158/992).

This scene is formally varied through alternation of song and speech, but its structure does not readily lend itself to the traditional divisions into episode and stasimon. The sequence begins with the strong act division of a choral song, which, however, turns out not to be the usual stasimon but the beginning of a kind of *kommos* (see on *Agamemnon* 1220–1348/1072–1177) in which the Chorus expresses its outrage in two stanzas, each repeated as a refrain between conciliatory speeches in dialogue verse by Athena (903–1024/778–880). There follows a short episode, again in spoken dialogue, in which Athena's persuasion works its magic as she explains the benefits she can offer the Erinyes in return for their blessings on the land and people of her city (1025–64/881–915). The process continues in a *kommos* (the Chorus singing, Athena responding in anapests, 1065–1194/916–1020) in which the Erinyes agree to accept new honors, new functions, and a new home in Athens, and then sing songs of blessing that in effect cancel and replace the songs of wrath with which the scene began. Athena then leads the Erinyes-Eumenides on their way to new dwellings in the Attic earth, accompanied by their Athenian escort (1195–1226/1021–47).

903–22 / 778–93 Repeated verbatim (and presumably with identical music and dance) at 938–57/808–23, as is 975–86/837–47 at 1013–24/870–80. This is an effective way of showing the stubborn intransigence that Athena's persistence in persuasion has to overcome.

906 / 780 *my honor stripped away* Concern for the loss of honor has been a recurrent theme of the Erinyes' complaints (see on 110–17/95–102), and has previously been expressed, as it is here, by the metaphor of young gods trampling down their elders (see on 127/110). The Erinyes emphasize this fear obsessively in their refrains, and Athena keeps attempting to reassure them that they will continue to be held in the highest honor (926/796, 937/807, 958/824, 969–70/833, 995–96/854–55, 1011–12/868–69, 1025–28/881–84).

910 / 782–83 *poison will now ooze and drip* Apollo alluded to the Erinyes' spewing of venom, only to dismiss it as harmless (848–49/729–30), but their threat of blighting the land is a real and terrible danger for Athens. Averting it will test Athena's powers of persuasion.

934 / 805 *your seat in a vast cavern* Chthonic deities were thought of as dwelling underground, and Aeschylus' audience would have known the grotto between the Areopagus and the Acropolis where Athens honored the Erinyes under the cult name *Semnai* (see on 1158/992).

961 / 826 *why even bring it up?* Athena can answer threat with threat, but she prefers to use persuasion. Violent struggles like those of the past are always possible, but now not inevitable. The threat is

dispelled immediately, and Zeus's lightning bolt is depicted as being kept under lock and key, in contrast to its unrestrained use at *Agamemnon*, 534–35/469–70 and 741/651 (with note).

965 / 829 *let me persuade you Peitho* (persuasion), which appeared in its negative incarnations as temptation and deception in the earlier plays, now finally emerges as a constructive force, the power to convince by reason rather than subdue by force —the power needed to govern a democratic polis.

972–73 / 835 *children /... the marriage rite* The earlier opposition between blood ties and bonds of marriage disappears in Athena's promise of offerings made to ensure the success of both childbirth and marriage vows. The Greek phrase translated "for the fulfillment of the marriage rite" *(pro ... gameliou telous)* alludes to the *proteleia* (sacrifice made before a marriage) that had appeared in distorted contexts of bloodshed in *Agamemnon* (see on 79–80/65, 260/226, 821/720) and is now shorn of any sinister connotations and restored at last to its normal signification.

976–77 / 871 Force *me ... / under this earth* The Erinyes associate Athena's offer of a new home underground with the dishonor and imprisonment of Cronus and the Titans, with which they reproached Zeus at 750/641.

991–92 / 852 *you'll long just like a lover / for this country* Although the Erinyes are invited to remain in Athens as resident aliens, Athena predicts that they will feel what the city ideally meant to Athenian citizens. The language is reminiscent of the exhortation that Thucydides will later put into the mouth of Pericles in the famous Funeral Oration to "see the city's power in practice day by day and become its passionate lovers" *(History of the peloponnesian War,* 2, 43.1).

999–1009 / 858–66 Although the desire to avert civil strife does not require special circumstances to motivate it (there is a similar prayer in Aeschylus, *Suppliants,* 678–83), the probability that Athenian political tensions were high in 458 (see the Introduction, footnote 12) may have made this theme more than usually urgent. The injunction to fight only foreign wars may reflect the ongoing Athenian expedition in Egypt (see on 337/292).

1008–9 / 866 *a cock who fights / inside the nest* In addition to the pugnaciousness of fighting cocks in general (cf. 1002–4/861–63), there is a suggestion here of the Greek belief that cocks were unusually prone to fight their kin. Cf. the image of Aegisthus, who has eliminated his rival and "brags on bravely, like a cock beside his hen" *(Agamemnon* 1932/1671). And since Athena's concern is for reckless young men, she may also be glancing at the idea that young birds consider it "a fine thing to bite and throttle their fathers" (Aristophanes, *Birds,* 1337–38).

1032 / 886 *the power of my tongue to soothe and enchant* Persuasion in its positive form has the same power of enchantment that in early Greek thought was held (perhaps paradoxically from our point of view) to guarantee the truth of great poetry. See Walsh, *Varieties of Enchantment.*

1042 / 895 No *house will ever grow without your blessing* A complete reversal of the Erinyes' earlier description of their "calling" as "the destruction of houses" (416–17/354–55).

1081–82 / 928–29 *these powerful, / demanding goddesses* In the midst of the Erinyes' blessings on Athens, Athena does not let the audience forget that they have power to curse as well (1085–94/932–37,

1116/954–55), and that they must be propitiated with due honors (1156–60/992–95). The Erinyes are transformed in the course of the play, but that does not mean that their old functions or danger have been completely forgotten.

1135–36 / 973 Zeus *who guides / men's speech* This is Zeus *agoraios,* the god who presides over the *agora,* the public meeting place where he had an altar, but also over *agora* in its broader sense of public meetings and the persuasive speech with which decisions are reached in the legislative and judicial assemblies of the polis.

1150–51 / 985–86 *loving the common good, / hating a common foe* This is the fundamental principle of Greek popular ethics, "helping friends and harming enemies," expressed in communal terms as the antithesis of destructive civil strife.

1158 / 992 *these kindly ones* Athena calls the Erinyes *euphrones,* in effect conferring upon them a new and auspicious name. They are actually nowhere called Eumenides in the play as we have it, but since both words mean "well-minded" or "well-disposed," it is possible that the title of the play (which need not stem from Aeschylus) came from a mis-citation of this line by the author of the "hypothesis" (synopsis) found in Our manuscript tradition. The synopsis says that Athena "having soothed the Erinyes, addressed them as 'Eumenides.' " Alternatively, it has been argued that a passage in which Athena gave them the actual title Eumenides has been lost. The title by which the Erinyes were worshipped at Athens, *Semnai Theai* (August or Awesome Goddesses), is used at 1218/ 1041 ("venerable ones" in our version).

1169 /1002 The most remarkable of the passages in *Eumenides* that suggest the gods can feel respect and responsibility for mortals (cf. on 262–63, 882–84/760–61. The verb used here, *azetai,* is usually used of the feelings of awe that mortals have for the gods.

1174 / 1006 *holy offerings Sphagion semnon* refers literally to sacrificial victims that are august or awesome (the same word as the Erinyes' Athenian cult title *Semnai;* see on 1158/992). The animal(s) to be sacrificed would presumably be a black cow and/or ewe, the animals of choice for sacrifice to chthonic goddesses. Athena's pointing out of "these ... offerings" appears to require that one or two be present on stage.

1182–83 / 1011 our new / *inhabitants Metoikoi* are literally "resident aliens." At *Libation Bearers,* 1096/971, the Erinyes are described as *metoikoi* who will be evicted from the house of Atreus; now, as Eumenides, they are offered a home in Athens (see further on 1203/1028).

1196 / 1022 *by the dancing light of torches* The torches present a visual conclusion and resolution for the trilogy's persistent imagery of light and dark. Light has been a symbol of hope from the beginning, when the Watchman saw the beacon fire he had been awaiting for so long, but just as persistently light yielded to darkness. Now the "dark" Erinyes move to their new home bathed in the light of Athenian torches to show that they are fully incorporated in the new civic order.

1198 / 1024 *my attendants* This group presumably includes the "escorts" referred to at 1172–73/1005 as holding the sacred light and perhaps Athena's priestess and one or more of the *arrephoroi,* maidens who carried the symbols of Athena's cult in procession.

1203 / 1028 *in purple robes* These robes —the final transformation of the seductive embroideries and blood-stained nets of the earlier plays —are what the *metoikoi,* Athens' resident aliens, wore in the great procession of the Panathenaea, the main Athenian festival in honor of Athena.

1208–9 / 1034 aged *children, / childless children* This translates the compact phrase *paides apaides,* literally, "children not children." This form of expression is particularly dear to the tragic poets (e.g., "city ... no city" *[polin ... apolin],* 543/457). Here it implies both that the goddesses are children and yet not children, because they are old; and that they are children who have no children, because they are virgins.

1211–12 / 1035 *and* 1215–16 / 1038 *Hush ... speak well, / only auspicious words* This translates a single Greek word, *euphameite,* which literally means "speak well." But is used before religious rites as a ritual injunction to say nothing except the words prescribed by ritual. Since an inauspicious word could spoil the rite, silence was the safest course.

1221 / 1043 AND 1225 / 1047 a joyous cry on Agamemnon 33–34/28.

# Orestes

## Euripides

### Characters

ELECTRA, daughter of Agamemnon and Clytemnestra
ORESTES, son of Agamemnon and Clytemnestra
HELEN, daughter of Tyndareus and wife of Menelaus
MENELAUS, brother of Agamemnon
TYNDAREUS, king of Sparta
PYLADES, loyal friend of Orestes
MESSENGER, an old peasant, retainer of Agamemnon
HERMIONE, daughter of Menelaus and Helen
PHRYGIAN, slave of Helen
APOLLO

CHORUS of Argive women

Scene: In front of Agamemnon's palace in Argos. ORESTES is lying on a couch, ELECTRA sitting on the ground by his side.

ELECTRA. It is scarcely an exaggeration to say that there is nothing terrible—no pain or god-given disaster—the burden of which human nature is not liable to endure. For instance, that happy man Tantalus (and I don't mean to slight his fate), said to be the offspring of Zeus, flies through the air in constant terror of the rock looming over his head.* This is his punishment—or so they say—because, a mortal man among gods, with equal honour at their shared table, he contracted the worst of diseases, an unbridled tongue. He was the father of Pelops, whose son was Atreus, and Atreus was the victim of designs spun by the goddess Strife, who made him engage in hostilities against his brother Thyestes.* But what need is there for me to rehearse these obscenities? Suffice it to say that Atreus killed Thyestes' children and gave them to him to eat. I pass in silence over what happened next,* and move on to Atreus' sons: glorious Agamemnon (if glorious he was) and Menelaus, children of Aerope of Crete.* Of these Menelaus married Helen, who was loathed by the gods,* and lord Agamemnon wedded Clytemnestra—a notable alliance in Greek eyes. To him she bore the three of us girls—Chrysothemis, Iphigenia, and me, Electra—and one boy, Orestes, children of the same mother, a woman so far gone in iniquity that she trapped her husband in the coils of an endless cloth* and killed him. Her motives it would be improper for a young woman like myself to mention;* I leave them veiled and forebear to go into them in public. Next, Phoebus—it is hard to accuse a god of injustice, but he persuaded Orestes to murder his mother, the woman who bore him.* Despite the fact that some would count the deed infamous, Orestes obeyed the god and killed her, and I did what a woman could to help him commit the murder.

The upshot is that poor Orestes lies here sick, ravaged by a fierce disease, prostrate on his bed, his mother's blood goading him with fits of insanity. I shrink, as you see, from naming the divine Eumenides,* who are striving to encompass his downfall with this horror. This is now the sixth day since our mother's corpse was purified with fire, following her slaughter, and in all this time he has neither taken food into his stomach nor bathed his body* Hidden inside his robes, he weeps when his body gains some respite from its disease and he is in his right mind; but sometimes he leaps up from his bed and runs around like a colt freed from the yoke.

By a decree of this city of Argos no one is to take us into hearth and home, nor speak to us, since we are matricides. And this is the decisive day on which the citizens of Argos will cast their vote for or against the proposal that we two are to be stoned to death.* But our hopes of avoiding death have been raised by the arrival of Menelaus here from Troy. On his way back from Troy he was driven well off course and strayed for a long time, but now he lies at anchor by the coast, filling the harbour of Nauplia* with his fleet. As for the mass-murderer Helen,* he waited for nightfall, in case any of those whose sons died at Troy should see her making her way there in the daytime and should take to hurling stones, and sent her on ahead to our palace. She is indoors, weeping for her sister and her family's misfortunes. But she does have something to alleviate her grief, because Hermione, the daughter Menelaus brought from Sparta and left at home in my mother's care when he sailed for Troy, gives her great pleasure and helps her to forget her woes.

I am looking in every direction, watching for Menelaus' arrival. We are in an extremely precarious situation, and he offers our only chance of safety. A house plagued by misfortune is a thing without resources.

Enter HELEN from the palace, carrying libation jugs and a lock of her hair.

HELEN. Electra, still unwed after all these years,* how are you, you poor thing? And how is your brother? I incur no pollution in addressing you,* because the fault lies with Phoebus, in my opinion. And yet I mourn the fate of my sister Clytemnestra. The last time I saw her was before I made that voyage of mine to Troy, driven in a fit of supernatural insanity by my destiny, and so in my bereavement I grieve for what has happened.

ELECTRA. Helen, why should I tell you what you can see with your very own eyes? Here I sit, keeping vigil beside a wretched corpse—I don't mean to slight his troubles, but his breath is so faint now that he might as well be a corpse. You and your husband, a happy couple, have arrived to find us in a miserable state.

HELEN. How long has he been lying here on his bed?*

ELECTRA. Ever since he carried out the slaughter of his mother.

HELEN. I feel sorry for him, and also for his mother. Look at the way she died!

ELECTRA. What's happened is that he has been overwhelmed by his woes.

HELEN. Electra, please may I ask you to do something for me?

ELECTRA. Yes, but I am busy keeping watch by my brother's bed.

HELEN. Would you go to my sister's tomb for me …

ELECTRA. You want me to go to my mother's tomb? What for?

HELEN. … and take these hair-trimmings of mine,* and some libations?

ELECTRA. Is it forbidden for you to go to the family tomb?

HELEN. I would be embarrassed to be seen by the Argives.

ELECTRA. Proper behaviour at last, but you had no sense of shame when you left your home that time.

HELEN. What you say is correct, even if unkind.

ELECTRA. But what is it about the Mycenaeans that makes you hold back?

HELEN. I'm afraid of the fathers of those who died at Troy.

ELECTRA. Yes, there's certainly something frightening about the way voices are raised about you in Argos.

HELEN. So you can free me of fear by doing me this favour.

ELECTRA. I couldn't bear to look on my mother's tomb.

HELEN. But it would be wrong for slaves to take these offerings there.

ELECTRA. Why don't you send your daughter Hermione?

HELEN. It's not right for young women to go about in public.

ELECTRA. But she would be repaying the dead woman for looking after her.

HELEN. Yes, that makes sense: I'll send my daughter. (She calls out) Hermione, dear, come out here to the front of the palace.

Enter HERMIONE from the palace.

Take these libations and trimmings from my hair, and go and pour out the honeyed milk and the frothy wine around Clytemnestra's tomb. Then stand on top of the mound* and say, 'These libations are a gift from your sister Helen, though fear of the people of Argos makes her too nervous to approach your tomb herself.' Ask her to look kindly upon me and you, and my husband, and this wretched pair here, brought low by a god, and assure her that I shall certainly be providing her with all the gifts it is appropriate for me to offer a dead sister. Quickly, child, off you go, and once you've poured the libations at the tomb see that you hurry back again.

Exit HERMIONE, with the jugs and hair.

Exit HELEN back into the palace.

ELECTRA. What a terrible thing a person's nature is! Did you see* how she has trimmed just the ends of her hair, to preserve her beauty? She's the same woman she always was. You have ruined not just my life and that of my brother, but the whole of Greece, and I pray that the gods may hate you for it!

Enter CHORUS.

Oh, no! Here come my friends again, who share my sorrow. Their singing will soon wake my brother here from his peaceful sleep, and start the tears flowing from my eyes when I see him raving. Good friends, come on tiptoes! No loud or harsh noises! I appreciate your friendship, but please be quiet all the same.

CHORUS {softly, while approaching ORESTES). Quietly!* Quietly now! Tread lightly on the ground! Make no harsh noise!

ELECTRA. No, over there, please! Keep well away from his bed!

CHORUS {moving away, but compensating by speaking louder).

There. I'm doing as you wish.

ELECTRA. No, no, my dear! Please keep your voice down, as soft as the breath of a gently blown pipe.

CHORUS (very softly). How about this? I'm singing as low as I would indoors.*

ELECTRA. Yes, that's perfect! Now come closer, closer—but quietly! Come quietly up to me, and tell me what brings you here. For at last he has lain down and fallen asleep.

CHORUS. How is he? Do tell me, dear. How am I to describe his condition?

ELECTRA. He breathes still, but it's very ragged and shallow.

CHORUS. Really? The poor boy!

ELECTRA. I'll be so upset if you make his eyelids flutter open, now that he's succumbed to the sweet boon of sleep!

CHORUS. The poor boy! I feel sorry for him. Look at the appalling deeds he has done, thanks to the gods.

ELECTRA. Oh, what he has had to endure! There was no justice in the god, no justice in the oracles he uttered that day, when on Themis' tripod Loxias decreed that murder should be paid for by the murder of my mother!*

ORESTES stirs restlessly.

CHORUS. Do you see how he tosses in his robes?

ELECTRA. Yes, for you've disturbed his sleep with your shouting, you wretch!

CHORUS. But I thought he was asleep.

ELECTRA. Why don't you leave us, leave the palace? Retrace your steps back to where you came from—but without making any noise.

CHORUS. He's asleep.

ELECTRA. I'm glad to hear it. Lady Night, you who give sleep to long-suffering mortals, come from Erebus!* Come, lady, come on wings to Agamemnon's palace! For overcome by grief and disaster we perish, we perish! Oh, no! You made a noise! Quietly, quietly! Take care not to raise your voice! Stay away from the bed, and afford him the gentle boon of sleep, please, my dear!

CHORUS. Tell me how he will find an end to his troubles.

ELECTRA. Through death, only through death! He has no desire even for food.

CHORUS. There's no doubt, then, what the future holds for him.

ELECTRA. We are the victims of Phoebus, for he sanctioned the piteous, unnatural murder of our mother, in retaliation for her murder of our father.

CHORUS. Justice demanded it …

ELECTRA (forcefully). But it was not right. Mother, who gave me life, you killed and died, and in destroying our father you destroyed these your children, born of your blood. We are lost, ruined, as good as dead! For my brother here is among the dead, and the greater part of my life has been spent on weeping and wailing and tears in the night, as without husband* or children I draw my pitiable life out into an interminable future.

CHORUS. Electra, since you're close beside him, please check whether your brother has died without your noticing it. The complete slackness of his body worries me.

ELECTRA inspects ORESTES. He stirs and struggles to sit up.

ORESTES. O Sleep, precious enchantment and ally against sickness! You came just when I needed you and your visit was so welcome! O lady Oblivion, through whom we forget our troubles, what skill you wield! You are indeed a goddess to whom those in distress should pray. (He looks about in surprise) But where have I come from? How did I get here? I can't remember: I have no recollection of the past.

ELECTRA. Darling, I was so glad that you fell asleep. Can you bear me to touch you? Shall I prop you up?

ORESTES. By all means, yes, please go ahead, and also wipe the sticky crust from my poor mouth and eyes.

She attends to him.

ELECTRA. There. I welcome the menial task and am glad to look after my brother's body with a sisterly hand.

ORESTES. Let me lean on you. And please brush the lank hair from my face, because I can't see clearly.

ELECTRA. Your poor head with its greasy hair! It's been so long since you've washed that you look quite savage!

ORESTES. Help me lie back down on my bed. When the madness subsides my body is limp and drained.

ELECTRA. There. The possession of a bed is like a friend to a sick person: a necessary pest.

ORESTES. Now lift me up again and turn me over on to my other side. Invalids are so helpless that it's hard to please them.

ELECTRA. Would you also like me to settle your feet on the ground? It's been a long while since the earth received their imprint, and everyone enjoys a change.

ORESTES. Yes, please. At least I'll be imitating health that way, and an imitation isn't too bad, even if it falls short of reality.

ELECTRA makes ORESTES sit up.

ELECTRA. Now, listen to me, brother, since at the moment the demons of destruction aren't robbing you of your wits.

ORESTES. You have some news to tell me. I welcome it if it's good, but if its outcome is likely to be painful, I already have more than my share of unhappiness.

ELECTRA. Your uncle Menelaus has arrived, and his ship is riding at anchor in Nauplia.

ORESTES. What's that? Someone has arrived to dispel the gloom of the troubles darkening my life and yours? A kinsman who is in debt to us for our father's various kindnesses to him?*

ELECTRA. Yes, he's here, and you can take my word for this too, that he's brought Helen from the walls of Troy.

ORESTES. I would congratulate him if he had been the only one to be saved, but if he's brought his wife with him, he has come with a heap of troubles.

ELECTRA. What a remarkable brood of daughters Tyndareus fathered—remarkable for the hostility they arouse, and notorious throughout Greece!*

ORESTES. Well, you had better prove yourself different from them, since it is within your power to do so; and the difference should come from your heart, not just your words.

ORESTES starts to display signs of madness.

ELECTRA. Oh, no! Brother, there is a wildness in your eye. Your madness has returned so quickly: just a moment ago you were in your right mind.

ORESTES makes as if to ward off the Eumenides.

ORESTES. Mother, I implore you, don't set them on to me! They come! They come, those women with their eyes of blood and serpent forms!* They're bounding towards me!

ELECTRA. Ah, how you suffer! Stay! Lie quietly on your bed! This is a hallucination, not as real as you think.

ORESTES. Phoebus, the hound-faced, savage-eyed, dread goddesses who slaughter victims for the dead—they're killing me!

ORESTES goes into convulsions.

ELECTRA. I won't let go of you. I'll entwine my arms in yours and check these horrid spasms.

ORESTES. Let go! You're one of the demons who are after me! You want to hurl me into Tartarus*—that's why you've got a grip on my waist!

ORESTES breaks free of her grip and jumps to his feet.

ELECTRA. Oh, this is too much for me! I need help—but from where shall I get it, when the gods are against us?

ELECTRA covers her head with a fold of her khiton in distress.

ORESTES. Pass me my horn-tipped bow! Loxias gave it to me* and told me to defend myself with it against the goddesses if I was terrified by the fits of insanity with which they plague me. A missile, released by mortal hand, will strike an immortal in a moment, if she remains within my sight! Do you hear me? (He notches an arrow on the invisible bow and shoots) Don't you see the feathered shafts of my far-shooting bow hurtling towards you? Aaah! So what are you waiting for? Scale the highest heaven with your wings! Guilt lies not with me but with Phoebus and his oracles. (He comes to himself)

Oh! What's happening? I'm so confused and short of breath. Where . .. where was I off to, leaping up from my bed? The storm is over and again I see calm waters.* Sister, why are you weeping? Why have you covered your head with your robes? I feel so ashamed for involving you in my pain and burdening a young woman with my sickness. Please don't let my troubles grieve you. It's true that you agreed to the business, but it was I who carried out our mother's murder. I blame Loxias, because it was he who prompted me to perform such an abominable deed, though his encouragement took the form of words not deeds. But suppose it had been my father I had consulted, eye to eye, about whether I should kill my mother: I think he would have taken my face in his hands and pleaded with me,* over and over again, not to drive a sword into a mother's throat, since it wouldn't bring him back to life, and I would be afflicted with these terrible torments. So uncover your head now, sister, and dry your eyes, however pitiful our situation. When you see me sunk in despair, you must reduce the terror and chaos of my mind and raise my morale; and when you are despondent, I should be by your side, telling you kindly what to do. This is the right kind of help for people who love each other to give. 3 You poor thing! Why don't you go inside the palace, lie down, let sleep close your sleepless eyes, and then find your appetite for food and bathe yourself?* I'll be lost if you let me down or get ill from sitting by my side. For you are the only person I can rely on for help; as you can see I have no one else.

ELECTRA. No. I shall stay with you whether this choice means life or death. It makes no difference to me, because if you die, what can I, as a woman, do? How shall I be safe, when I shall be all alone, without brother, father, friends? If that's what you want, though, I shall do as you suggest. {She smoothes his bed) But lie down to rest and try to resist whatever it is that startles you in terror from your bed. Rest quietly on your bed, which I've tidied up for you. After all, even if illness is imaginary rather than real, we mortals feel exhausted and helpless.

Exit ELECTRA into the palace

ORESTES lies down again on the couch.

CHORUS (sings). Ah, woe! O fast, furious, winged goddesses,
who form a joyless coven amid tears and lamentation,
you dark-featured Eumenides, who scour the high heavens
exacting the penalty due for bloodshed, the penalty due for murder,
I beg you, I beseech you, let Agamemnon's son be free
of the raving bewilderment of madness. Ah, wretched man,
overwhelmed by trouble! What a terrible deed you attempted,
to your undoing, when you accepted the oracle,
the oracle spoken by Phoebus from the tripod
on the floor said to house the recess of the navel of the world.*

O Zeus, what pitiful, murderous contest urges you on,
miserable Orestes? Some ruthless demon, haunting the house,
is piling tears on tears for you, driving you insane

in revenge for your mother's blood.
I grieve for you, mourn for you. Here on earth
great success is insecure. As if he were shaking the sail
of a swift boat, some god overwhelms great success
in the violent, deadly waves of a sea of terrible suffering.
For which house should I yet sooner revere than
that of Tantalus, descended thanks to that first union from the gods?*

Enter MENELAUS. The CHORUS stop singing and the Chorus-leader continues alone.

But here comes the king, lord Menelaus, in all his might and luxury, an obvious descendant of Tantalid blood. Prime mover of the thousand-shipped invasion of Asia,* I bid you welcome. That you are personally attended by good fortune is shown by the fact that the gods have answered your prayers.

MENELAUS. Royal palace, though I am surely pleased to have got back from Troy and to be seeing you, yet the sight of you makes me grieve, because I have never seen a house more beset on all sides by appalling troubles. For I learnt what happened to Agamemnon when I put in at Malea.* Glaucus, the prophet of Nereus, who is the sailors' seer and a soothsaying god, appeared from the waves and told me the news. He came before me and said: 'Menelaus, your brother lies dead. His wife made sure that the bath she gave him was his last.' I and my companions shed many tears at the news, and then, when I came ashore at Nauplia, with the intention of enfolding in a kinsman's arms my brother's son Orestes and his mother, on the assumption that good fortune attended them both, I heard from one of the harbour salts of the foul murder of Tyndareus' daughter. So, young women, tell me where I may find Agamemnon's son, who brought himself to commit such a terrible deed. For when I left the palace and went to Troy he was just a baby in Clytemnestra's arms, so I wouldn't recognize him if I saw him.

*ORESTES runs forward and adopts the suppliant position, clasping MENELAUS' knees.*

ORESTES. Here's the person you're asking about, Menelaus. I am Orestes. I shall not hesitate to inform against myself and tell you of my crimes, and the first act I perform as a suppliant is to clasp your knees, though the prayers I utter lack a suppliant's leafy boughs.* Save me from my troubles! You have come at just the right time.

MENELAUS. Ye gods, what am I seeing? Is this one of the dead?*
ORESTES (standing up). You're right: alive I may be, but my troubles have killed me.
MENELAUS. You poor thing! And how savage your lank hair makes you look!
ORESTES. What disfigures me is not my looks but what I've done.
MENELAUS. Your gaze is terrifying, your eyes harsh.
ORESTES. My body has gone. All I have left is my name.
MENELAUS. O hideous! Inconceivably hideous to look at!
ORESTES. Yes, that's me, the killer of my poor mother!
MENELAUS. I've already heard the news. Restrain yourself: evil does not bear repetition.
ORESTES. I am restraining myself, but fortune is generous in sending evil my way.
MENELAUS. What exactly are you suffering from? What illness is destroying you?
ORESTES. Awareness—because I know that I have done terrible things.
MENELAUS. What do you mean? Clarity, not vagueness, is a sign of knowledge.
ORESTES. What is destroying me above all is grief...
MENELAUS. Yes, Grief is a fierce spirit, but she can be allayed.

ORESTES. … and then there are fits of insanity, in retribution for my mother's murder.

MENELAUS. And when did this madness begin? On what day?

ORESTES. It was the day when I was heaping the earth over my wretched mother's tomb.

MENELAUS. And were you at home when it began, or still sitting beside the funeral pyre?

ORESTES. I was outside, waiting for the bones to be collected for burial.*

MENELAUS. Was anyone with you, to stop you falling down?

ORESTES. Yes, Pylades,* my accomplice in the bloody murder of my mother.

MENELAUS. And what kind of apparitions do you see in your times of sickness?

ORESTES. I seemed to see three maidens, as dark as night.

MENELAUS. I know whom you mean, but I would rather not name them.

ORESTES. No, for they are formidable. It was tactful of you to avoid mentioning them.

MENELAUS. They are the ones who are driving you out of your wits for murdering a member of your family.

ORESTES. Oh, they hunt me, they hound me, miserable wretch that I am!

MENELAUS. There's nothing terrible in the terrible suffering of those who have committed terrible deeds.

ORESTES. But I do have a means of settling disaster …

MENELAUS. Don't talk of dying. That's just stupid.

ORESTES. … on to Phoebus, on whose orders I carried out my mother's murder.

MENELAUS. Yes, proving himself rather ignorant of propriety and justice.

ORESTES. We are slaves to the gods, whatever the gods may be.

MENELAUS. And yet does Loxias do anything to protect you from your troubles?

ORESTES. He's biding his time, in typically divine fashion.

MENELAUS. How long is it since your mother breathed her last?

ORESTES. It was five days ago. Her funeral pyre is still warm.

MENELAUS. It didn't take long for the goddesses to come after you for your mother's murder!

ORESTES. The god may be ignorant, but he is true to his own.†*

MENELAUS. Does it help you at all that you were avenging your father?

ORESTES. Not yet—and there's no difference, in my opinion, between 'not yet' and 'not at all'.

MENELAUS. How do the citizens treat you as a result of what you've done?

ORESTES. They hate us so much that they refuse to talk to us.

MENELAUS. And haven't you even purified the blood on your hands in the customary way?*

ORESTES. No, because I am barred from people's houses wherever I go.

MENELAUS. Which of the citizens are striving to drive you from the land?

ORESTES. Oeax, who blames my father for the antagonism towards Troy.

MENELAUS. I understand: he's punishing you for the murder of Palamedes.*

ORESTES. Which was nothing to do with me. But there are three reasons for my destruction.

MENELAUS. Who else, then? Some of Aegisthus' friends, I suppose.

ORESTES. Yes, they abuse me, and they have the ears of the citizens at the moment.

MENELAUS. But don't they let you hold Agamemnon's sceptre?

ORESTES. Of course not, since they don't even let me continue my life.

MENELAUS. What are they doing? Can you tell me exactly?

ORESTES. They are going to condemn us today.

MENELAUS. And yet you aren't fleeing across the border?

ORESTES. No, because we are surrounded on all sides by fully armed men.

MENELAUS. Were these men mustered by your enemies on their own, or are they official Argive forces?

ORESTES. The entire citizen body is involved. They want to see me die. That's all there is to say.

MENELAUS. I feel for you. Your situation is as bad as it could get.

ORESTES. YOU are my hope, the safe haven from the troubles that afflict me. Success attends your arrival here, so please share your good fortune with those dear to you who are in a desperate plight. Don’t take the good and keep it for yourself, but play your part and share some of our trials too. In this way you will recompense those you should for my father’s favours to you. People are friends in no more than name if their friendship fails in times of adversity.

CHORUS. Here comes Tyndareus of Sparta, his aged legs rivalling each other for haste. He is wearing dark clothes and he has cut his hair short in mourning for his daughter.

ORESTES. Menelaus, I am lost! Look, Tyndareus is coming up to us, and there’s no one I scruple more to meet because of what I’ve done. For he brought me up when I was 3’oung and showered me with kindnesses. For instance, he used to carry ‘Agamemnon’s son’ around in his arms, and Leda did as well. They treated me with as much respect as they did Castor and Polydeuces.* And—I feel it in my wretched heart, and in my soul—I have not repaid them well. What darkness can I find to cover my face? Where is the cloud I can hide behind, to stay out of the old man’s sight?

Enter TYNDAREUS with attendants.

TYNDAREUS (to his attendants). Where is he? Where may I find Menelaus, my daughter’s husband? While I was pouring libations at Clytemnestra’s tomb,* I heard that he had arrived at Nauplia with his wife, safe after all these years. Take me to him. I want to stand by him and clasp him by the right hand. It’s been so long since I saw my dear friend.

MENELAUS. YOU are very welcome, sir, whose wife was also loved by Zeus.*

TYNDAREUS. And greetings to you too, Menelaus, my son-in-law. (He catches sight of ORESTES) But what’s this? The serpent who killed his mother is here in front of the palace, noisome lightning gleaming from his eyes. How I loathe him! Are you talking to the foul creature, Menelaus?

MENELAUS. So what if am? His father meant a lot to me.

TYNDAREUS. Could such a creature really be Agamemnon’s son?

MENELAUS. He is, and I am obliged to honour him in his misfortune.

TYNDAREUS. You’ve spent so much time among foreigners that you’ve taken up foreign ways.

MENELAUS. But it is Greek practice to honour one’s kith and kin under all circumstances.

TYNDAREUS. And also not to want to subordinate the laws to oneself.

MENELAUS. Wise men say that anything which is the result of compulsion is servile.

TYNDAREUS. YOU may have accepted that idea, but I won’t.

MENELAUS. That’s because two things are making you stupid: your anger and your old age.

TYNDAREUS. Yes, a debate on stupidity is relevant to this man’s case.| When everyone knows what is and what is not acceptable behaviour, was there ever a more stupid person than him? He gave no thought to justice, nor did he have recourse to standard Greek practice. After Agamemnon had died from the blow to the head he received from my daughter—a shocking action, which I shall never condone—he ought to have punished her for murder, while keeping religious propriety in mind: that is, he should have expelled his mother from the palace. Instead of facing disaster, he would have gained a reputation for good sense, he would have kept within the law, and he would have shown himself to be a man of religious sensibility. As things are, however, he has made himself liable to the same fate as his mother. For although he was right to regard her as bad, in killing his mother he proved himself even worse.

I’ve only one question for you, Menelaus. Suppose Orestes’ wife were to kill him: next his son will kill his mother, and then this son’s son will avenge blood with blood—how long will these horrors go on?* When will they end? Our forefathers arranged things well: they would not allow anyone tainted with blood to meet or encounter anyone else, but rather than seeing a life taken in exchange for a life, they had him purify himself with exile. Otherwise there would always be a single individual involved in bloodshed, his hands polluted by the most recent act. Speaking for myself, I loathe women who ignore religious propriety, and my daughter above all, for killing her husband. And not only will your wife Helen never meet my approval, but I shall refuse to speak to her. In fact, I don't admire you for having gone to the land of Troy for the sake of a vile woman. But I shall do my utmost to defend the law and to end this murderous savagery, which never fails to destroy a land and its communities.

(To ORESTES) For what did you feel, you wretch, when your mother bared her breast and begged you for mercy? Although I was not a witness to the horrors that happened there, tears flow from my poor old eyes. And one thing certainly confirms what I've been saying: these fits of insanity and terror show that you have incurred the hatred of the gods and are paying the penalty for your crime against your mother. I have no need to hear the truth from other witnesses when I can see the evidence myself. So just to make sure you understand, Menelaus: if you choose to help this man, you will be acting contrary to the will of the gods. Don't do it; let him be stoned to death by the citizens. My daughter's death was what she deserved, but it was wrong of him to kill her. My daughters have been the only blight on my otherwise fortunate life, the only respect in which my happiness is marred.

CHORUS. Enviable is the man who has met with good fortune in his children and has avoided notable disaster in this respect.

ORESTES. Sir, if I respond to you I am bound to upset you, and that makes me hesitate. If we can keep your old age, which is what makes me worried about speaking, from being a factor in our argument, then I shall go ahead, even though in fact I am anxiously aware of your grey hair. What should I have done? Set the pairs of factors opposite one another. On the one hand, there was my father, who planted his seed; on the other, your daughter, the field which received the seed from someone else. In killing my mother I committed an immoral act, but from another point of view you could call it moral, in that I was avenging my father. And your daughter (I shrink from calling her my mother) was carrying on an unsanctioned, licentious affair with another man. In slandering her I blacken my own reputation, but I shall speak out all the same. I killed this other man too, and slaughtered my mother, which was an immoral act, but performed to avenge my father.

The acts for which you say I deserve to be stoned actually make me the benefactor of all Greece. Here is my argument for this. If women are going to be so brazen that they murder their husbands and then find protection from their children by using their breasts to seek mercy, they'd be making little of killing their husbands for any old grievance. Although what I did was terrible, as you insist, I did put an end to this practice.

I can justify the hatred which led me to kill my mother. When her husband was abroad on armed service, commanding an army on behalf of all Greece, she betrayed him by failing to preserve the purity of her marriage-bed. Aware of her sins, she did not punish herself, but, in order to avoid retribution from her husband, she punished him, my father, instead, and put him to death. Sir, in fathering a wicked daughter, you have proved my undoing; thanks to her brazen behaviour I have lost my father and killed my mother. By the gods—even though it may be inappropriate to mention the gods who judge guilt in cases of murder—if I had tacitly approved what my mother had done, what would the murdered man have done to me? Out of hatred for me, wouldn't he be goading me into madness with his demons? Or could it be that my mother has deities on her side while he does not, even though the wrong committed against him was greater?

Let's turn now to Apollo, who resides at the central navel of the world and speaks to mortal men with supreme reliability. It was in obedience to him that I killed my mother. It is him you people should regard as immoral and put to death; the sin is his, not mine. What should I have done? Or does the god not carry enough weight for me to be cleared of pollution by referring matters to him? If not, then where else might one flee for safety, if the one who issued the order will not save me from death? You should not say, then, that the deed was wrong, but only that it has been the ruin of me, the person who did it.

CHORUS. When they involve themselves in the affairs of men, women always make things worse.

TYNDAREUS. Your brazen and unbridled words, and the deliberately upsetting nature of your response, will only kindle all the more enthusiasm in me to encompass your death. I actually came here only to arrange my daughter's tomb, but I shall consider your death an excellent bonus to this task. I shall go before the assembled Argives and, whether or not they want it, I shall set the citizens on to you and your sister, and make sure that your punishment is death by stoning.

Your sister deserves death even more than you do, because she aroused your anger against your mother by constantly filling your ears with stories designed to increase your hatred. She went on proclaiming as scandalous the business with Agamemnon and the love-affair with Aegisthus (which I pray the gods below may find appalling, just as the gods of this world found it vile), until she set the palace ablaze—though not with fire.*

(He turns to MENELAUS) Menelaus, I should warn you—and this is no idle threat—if you are taking no account of my hatred and our kinship,* not to go against the will of the gods and protect this man from death. If you do, you had better not set foot on Spartan soil. I won't say anything more about this, but you mark my words: don't side with impious men and reject the friendship of those with greater piety. But now, slaves, take me away from this palace.

Exeunt TYNDAREUS and attendants.

MENELAUS paces in distress.

ORESTES. Yes, go. I'd like my next remarks to reach Menelaus here without being interrupted and without being restricted by your old age. Menelaus, what's the matter? Why are you pacing to and fro, marking out the double path that indicates a divided mind?

MENELAUS. Leave me alone. I'm turning something over in my mind, since I don't know what to do in the present circumstances.

ORESTES. Well, don't come to any conclusions yet. First hear what I have to say, and then do your deliberating.

MENELAUS stops pacing.

MENELAUS. Go on, then. You're right: although silence is sometimes preferable to speech, the opposite may also be true.

ORESTES. Here I go, then. Long speeches are better than short ones and make their points more clearly. Menelaus, I'm not asking you to give me anything that belongs to you, but only to give me back what was not originally yours, what you gained from my father. I have done wrong, and the evil I have done requires from you some wrong in return. After all, even my father Agamemnon did wrong when he formed the Greeks into an army and went to Troy, when he had committed no crime himself, but because he wanted to remedy the crime and wrong committed by your wife. As men should in response to an appeal from those who are dear to them, he gave genuinely of himself and fought alongside you, so that you could retrieve your wife. All I'm asking, then, is that you repay me in exactly the same way as you were repaid then. Nor will it take ten years: I want you to help us out just for one day by standing firm and protecting us. You should do this single thing for us in repayment for the single thing that was done for you. As for the sacrifice of my sister at Aulis,* I shall let you have that: you don't need to kill Hermione. Given my current situation, you're bound to come off better and I'm bound to make concessions. But make my life your repayment to my poor father, because my death will leave my father's house with no means of perpetuating itself.

'Impossible,' you may say. But the point is this: it's when those dear to us are afflicted by troubles that we have to help them. When the gods grant success, what need have we of friends? The gods themselves are enough, when they're prepared to help us.

It is generally held throughout Greece that you love your wife, and I say this not out of any desire to flatter my way under your guard. But I implore you in her name. (To himself) I hate this! Look at the depths to which I have sunk! But so what? I have to abase myself. If this appeal of mine succeeds, the whole house will benefit. (He again takes up the suppliant position at MENELAUS' knees) Uncle, imagine that your brother, though dead and buried, is listening, with his soul hovering over you, and is saying what I am saying. I have said what I wanted to say; I have made my request. All I want to do is survive, and that is something everyone desires, not just I.

CHORUS. For all that I am a woman, I too implore you to help those in need. It is within your power to do so.

MENELAUS. Orestes, I respect you, and I'd like to assist you in your time of trouble. By means of such assistance we should help our kin to rid themselves of their troubles (if, thanks to the gods, we have the power) by killing or being killed by their enemies. But on the other hand I do need to get the power from the gods, because I have come here poorly equipped with military support; after all the countless trials I encountered on my wanderings, I am left with few friends and have little in the way of military might to offer. So it would be impossible for us to overcome the Pelasgian Argives* in battle, but if we could make use of soft words—this is a hopeful situation for us to find ourselves in. For when the populace of a city becomes angry and passionate, it is like trying to extinguish a furious fire. But if one gently yields and gives way while the energy is running high, while watching out for the opportune moment, it may well blow itself out. If it does die down, you can easily get everything you want. I'll go and try to persuade Tyndareus and the city to make good use of their excessive zeal. For a violently taut sheet makes even a ship go under, but it rights itself again if one slackens the sheet.† The gods hate excessive displays of enthusiasm—a hatred shared by the common people of a city. If I am to save you from superior forces—and what I say is true—I must use cunning rather than force. You might perhaps be thinking that I could use force of arms to save you, but that is not so: it's no easy matter for a single spear to win through against the troubles that are besetting you.*

Exit MENELAUS.

ORESTES sits down on his couch.

ORESTES. YOU coward! You're no help to your friends at all! All you can do is go to war for the sake of a woman! Do you turn from me and run away? Are Agamemnon's claims on you forgotten? And so it turns out, father, that you have been abandoned to your misfortune by your friends. Oh, I have been betrayed! My last hopes of finding a way to escape death at the hands of the Argives have been dashed! For he was my safe haven, my best chance of survival. But I can see my closest friend Pylades running here! He's come from Phocis.* What a sweet sight! In times of trouble a man welcomes the sight of a true friend more than sailors do calm water.

Enter PYLADES, running.

PYLADES. Here I am! I made my way with excessive haste through the city, because I heard that a general assembly was taking place (and in fact I saw it clearly with my own eyes) with a view to killing you and your sister before long.† What's going on? How are things with you? How are you, my dearest companion, friend, and relative? For you are all this to me.

ORESTES. To explain my troubles to you in a nutshell—it's all over with me.*

PYLADES. Your ruin would mean mine too, since friends share everything.

ORESTES. Menelaus has behaved in a despicable fashion towards me and my sister.

PYLADES. Of course, since bad women make their husbands bad.

ORESTES. As far as getting anything from him is concerned, he might as well not have come.

PYLADES. So he really has come here to this land?

ORESTES. He took his time getting here, but it didn't take long for the hollowness of his friendship to be exposed.

PYLADES. And did he ship that awful wife of his here too?

ORESTES. It wasn't he who brought her here, but she who brought him.

PYLADES. Where is she, this woman who single handedly destroyed so many Greeks?

ORESTES. In my palace, if you can call this palace here mine.

PYLADES. And what did you say to your uncle?

ORESTES. I asked him not to stand idly by while my sister and I were put to death by the Argives.

PYLADES. And tell me: how did he respond to that? I'd really like to know.

ORESTES. He gave the kind of circumspect reply you'd expect from a false friend. pylades. And what reason did he give for his caution? When I understand this I'll have the whole picture.

ORESTES. It was the arrival of our friend, (sarcastically) the one with such noble daughters.

PYLADES. You mean Tyndareus. I suppose he was angry with you about his daughter.

ORESTES. You've got it. And Menelaus gave more weight to his connection with him than to his connection with me.

PYLADES. And he lacked the courage to step up and take on some of the burden of your trials?

ORESTES. Yes, because he lacks martial spirit. It's only when he's surrounded by women that he displays any valour.

PYLADES. So your situation could hardly be worse. Is there no way for you to avoid death?

ORESTES. The citizens have to cast their votes about us on the charge of murder.

PYLADES. I'm frightened to ask, but what will be decided by the vote?

ORESTES. Whether we live or die. A simple answer about a complex matter.

PYLADES. So leave this place and run away with your sister.

ORESTES. Can't you see? There are guards watching us on all sides.

PYLADES. I did see armed men barricading the streets.

ORESTES. Our bodies are as beleaguered as a city by a hostile army.

PYLADES. And what about me? It's time for you to consider my situation. For it's all over with me too.

ORESTES. Thanks to whom? This would be another disaster to add to my troubles.

PYLADES. My father Strophius has turned me out of his house in anger and banished me.

ORESTES. On what grounds? Was it a private quarrel, or did he and your fellow citizens bring a public suit against you?

PYLADES. The charge was that I helped you murder your mother, which he claims is an act of impiety.

ORESTES. You poor wretch! It looks as though my troubles are going to afflict you too.

PYLADES. But I'm no Menelaus. I shall endure the burden.

ORESTES. Aren't you afraid that the Argives might want to kill you as well as me?

PYLADES. It's the Phocians' job to punish me, not theirs.

ORESTES. But the masses can be terrifying when they gain unscrupulous leaders.*

PYLADES. But with good leaders they always make good decisions.

ORESTES. Anyway, we had better share our thoughts.

PYLADES. What do we have to do?

ORESTES. Suppose I were to go before the Argives and say ...

PYLADES. … that your actions were justified?
ORESTES. Because I was avenging my father.
PYLADES. But beware: they may just welcome the opportunity to arrest you.
ORESTES. But shall I cower and die in silence?
PYLADES. That would be a cowardly option.
ORESTES. What should I do. then?
PYLADES. Is there any way for you to survive if you stay put?
ORESTES. No.
PYLADES. But if you go there's some hope of your finding a safe way out of your troubles?
ORESTES. Yes, that might perhaps happen.
PYLADES. Isn't it better than staying put?
ORESTES. So shall I go, then?
PYLADES. At any rate, if you die your death will be more honourable this way.
ORESTES. You're right. I avoid cowardice this way.
PYLADES. More so than you do by staying.
ORESTES. Yes, and my cause is just.
PYLADES. But all that's important is for you to make sure it appears just.
ORESTES. And I might make people feel sorry for me …
PYLADES. Your noble birth is an important factor.
ORESTES. … out of anger at my father's death.
PYLADES. All this depends on how they see it.
ORESTES. I had better go. An inglorious death isn't fitting for a man.
PYLADES. I approve of your decision.
ORESTES. So shall we tell my sister?
PYLADES. No, definitely not.
ORESTES. There would certainly be tears.
PYLADES. And wouldn't that be a significant omen?*
ORESTES. So it's clearly preferable not to say anything.
PYLADES. Yes, you'll be saving time.
ORESTES. The only thing stopping me is …
PYLADES. What new point are you raising now?
ORESTES. … the worry that I might be overcome by the goddesses' madness.
PYLADES. But I'll look after you.
ORESTES. It's distasteful to touch a sick man.
PYLADES. Not to me, when the sick man is you.
ORESTES. Beware of catching my insanity.
PYLADES. No, never mind about that.
ORESTES. So you won't hesitate?
PYLADES. No, because it's terrible for friends to hesitate.
ORESTES. Come, then, steer my feet …

ORESTES struggles to his feet.

PYLADES. Yes, for I hold dear the bond of friendship.
ORESTES. … and take me to my father's tomb.
PYLADES. What for?

ORESTES. So that I can beg him to save me.

PYLADES. That would be the right thing for him to do.

ORESTES. I hope I don't catch sight of my mother's tomb.

PYLADES. Quite: she was your enemy. But hurry up: you don't want to be overtaken by the Argives' vote. Let me support you, since you have been enfeebled by illness. You should know that I'll bear you through the city without the least embarrassment, and taking little notice of people. How am I to demonstrate my affection for you if I'm not there for you when your situation is disastrous?

ORESTES. That's it! Make your companions, not just your family, your friends! The friendship of a man whose character melds with yours, even if he doesn't belong to your immediate family, is worth more to a man than countless thousands of relatives.

Exeunt ORESTES and PYLADES, who is supporting his friend.

CHORUS (sings). The great prosperity and prowess that held high its head
throughout Greece and beside Simois' streams* have receded
once more away from good fortune for Atreus' line—
yes, once more receded as a result of the ancient doom of the house,
when the dispute over the golden lamb* came to the Tantalids †
with hideous, pitiful feasting and the slaughter of high-born children.
Since then woe succeeding woe achieved through blood
never abandons the twofold house of Atreus.*
It's wrong, not right, to cut parent's flesh with fire-forged steel,
and to display to sun's light the sword in its black sheath of gore.
To do a 'good' crime is nothing but the tortuous impiety
and muddled thinking of wrong-headed men.
In fear of death Tyndareus' wretched daughter screamed:
'My child, this is an impious undertaking, to kill your mother.
Beware, lest in honouring your father's kindness
you bind to yourself an undying name for infamy!'

Can there be in the world a greater sickness—
or a greater source of tears and sadness—
than tainting one's hand with matricidal blood?
For this crime the son of Agamemnon
is being goaded with fits of insanity,
hunted down by the Eumenides, his eyes rolling with fear.
How I pity him! When from his mother's robes,
threaded with gold, he saw her breast appear,
he made his mother his victim,
in exchange for his father's fate.

Enter ELECTRA. She looks for ORESTES.

ELECTRA. Women, would I be right in thinking that poor Orestes' god-given madness overwhelmed him and drove him from this place?

CHORUS. Not at all: he has gone to face the people of Argos.

ELECTRA. Oh, no! What has he done? Who persuaded him to go there?

CHORUS. Pylades. But here comes a messenger, who will presumably soon give you news of your brother and tell you what happened there.

Enter MESSENGER.

MESSENGER. My lady Electra, Agamemnon's daughter, I bring bad news. What I have to tell you is ...

ELECTRA. Ah, woe! We are finished! That's clear from what you say.

MESSENGER. ... that the Pelasgians have voted today to put you and your brother to death.

ELECTRA. Oh, no! This is what I was afraid of. The prospect that has been making me weep for a long time has now arrived! But what happened in the trial? What were the arguments used before the Argives which convicted us and condemned us to death? Tell me, old man. Am I to breathe my last as a result of being stoned to death or put to the sword? And is my fate to be the same as my brother's?

MESSENGER. It so happened that I was on my way into the city from the countryside because I wanted to find out what was going on with you and Orestes. In the past I was always loyal to your father, and I depended on your household for my daily bread; I am poor, but that doesn't stop me being a true friend. I saw a crowd hurrying up to the hill where they say Danaus was the first to muster and assemble the people, when he wanted to grant Aegyptus a legal hearing.* When I saw that the townspeople were assembling I asked one of them, 'What's new in Argos? Has a declaration of war stirred the city of the Argives?' In reply he said, 'Don't you see Orestes? There he is, approaching us over there. He's come to enter the lists in a trial for his life!'

I saw a sight I hoped never to see, and wish I never had. Pylades and your brother were walking together, the one drooping and enfeebled by illness, the other, like a brother, just as distressed as his friend, conscientiously tending his illness. With the Argives packed into their assembly-place, a town-crier stood up and said: 'Who wants to speak on the question whether Orestes should or should not be put to death for matricide?' At this Talthybius* got to his feet. Now, he was with your father at the sack of Troy, but since he is always influenced by those in power, his speech was ambivalent. On the one hand, he expressed great admiration for your father, but on the other hand, twining bad arguments into good, he criticized your brother for establishing unsound rules in respect of parents. And at the same time he was constantly giving a bright look to Aegisthus' friends. This is typical of his kind: heralds always run over to a successful man and side with whoever has political influence and authority.

Next lord Diomedes* addressed the people. He was against killing either you or your brother, but recommended banishment as the penalty that would satisfy religious sensibilities. His speech met with shouts of both approval and disapproval, and then an outspoken, arrogantly self-assured fellow stood up. He spoke in favour of stoning you and Orestes to death, but his proposals were really made by Tyndareus. Then someone else got to his feet and argued the contrary point of view. He's not an attractive man, physically, but he's brave; he rarely makes his presence felt in the city or the main square. He's a smallholder—and these men alone are the salvation of the land—but prepared to confront the issues intelligently, and with self-discipline acquired in the course of an incorruptible and blameless life. He spoke in favour of rewarding Orestes, Agamemnon's son, for having been prepared to avenge his father by killing an evil, godless woman, who would have made it impossible for a man ever to take up arms and campaign abroad, if those left behind were going to subvert his domestic situation and corrupt his marriage. These arguments struck all decent men, at any rate, as valid.

No one else spoke after that, so your brother stepped up and said: 'Gentlemen, inhabitants of the land of Inachus,* when I killed my mother I was defending you just as much as my father. For if murdering men is to be legitimate for women, your deaths will soon follow, or you must be the slaves of women.' But the assembled people failed to find his argument convincing, even though he seemed to have a point, and when it came to a show of hands the majority gave victory to the bad man I spoke of, who argued in favour of killing you and your brother. It was only with difficulty that poor Orestes persuaded them not to stone him to death. Instead he promised that he and you would commit suicide today. Pylades, with tears in his eyes, is bringing him here from the assembly, and they are accompanied by their supporters, who are weeping in sorrow. A bitter sight, a wretched spectacle, is on its way. Anyway, you had better start preparing a sword, or a noose for your neck, since you have to end your life. No advantage has come to you from your high birth, nor from Phoebus and his Pythian tripod;* in fact, it is he who has destroyed you.

Exit MESSENGER.

CHORUS (sings). O Pelasgia,* I start the lamentation, with cheeks raked
in bloody disfigurement by pale fingernail,
with head beaten, as is the due of the fair maiden goddess
Persephone, queen of the dead below the ground.*
Let the Cyclopian land* resound with the woes of the house,
as we take iron to shear our heads.
I see pity drawing nigh, pity for those about to die,
who once led Greece to war.*

For gone, lost and gone, is the entire line of Pelops' children
and the success that once crowned his blessed house.
The gods' envy has doomed it, and the bloody vote,
cast in hatred by the citizens of this place.*
O fleeting race of mortals, whose life is naught but tears and trials,
see how fate comes, confounding expectations!
As the long years pass men exchange one woe for another,
and the whole of human life is unfathomable.

ELECTRA (sings). Suspended midway between heaven and earth
on golden chains floats a rock,
a fragment torn from Olympus,*
driven along by the cosmic whirl.
Would that I could go there now
and in tears sob out to old father Tantalus,
the ancestor, the forebear of my line,
the tragedies I have seen befall his house.
First there were winged colts giving chase,
when on his four-horse-drawn chariot
Pelops rode over the open sea
and as he drove over the sea's surge
by Geraestus' surf-beaten shores
hurled Myrtilus to his death in the swell of the waves.*
Next there came to my house a much-mourned curse,
when among the flocks of horse-farming Atreus†
there arose that fatal prodigy,
the lamb with the golden fleece.
Then Strife took the Sun's winged chariot

and changed its route, fitting the one-horse car
of Dawn to the westward path of heaven,
and Zeus altered the running course
of the Pleiades with their seven tracks. *
And for that death * Strife added further death—
the banquet that bears the name of Thyestes,*
and the marriage-bed of Cretan Aerope,*
traitress in a treacherous union.
And now the final end has come
to me and my father
in the tragic doom of our house.

CHORUS. But here come your brother, now condemned to death, and that most loyal of friends, Pylades, who, brotherlike, is guiding his infirm footsteps here,† carefully keeping pace with him and sticking close to his side.

Enter ORESTES and PYLADES, who supports him as before, and seats him on his couch.

ELECTRA. Alas! Brother, the sight of you before your tomb, before the pyre of the dead, stirs me to grief. Again I cry alas! This final sight of you has scattered my wits.

ORESTES. Hush, now! No more of this womanish wailing! Try to submit to what is fated to happen. It's a hard fate, but you must try to accept it.

ELECTRA. How can I keep quiet? This is the last chance we poor wretches have to see the Sun-god's light.

ORESTES. Stop! Don't you kill me too! Isn't it enough that I've been put to death by the Argives? Don't go on about the troubles that beset us!

ELECTRA. I feel sorry for you, Orestes—so young, and doomed to untimely death! You are dead when you should be alive!

ORESTES. Please, I beg you, don't unman me! By reminding me of our troubles you'll reduce me to tears.

ELECTRA. We're going to die! It's impossible not to weep for our plight! Everyone holds life so dear that its loss is grievous.

ORESTES. This is the decisive day for us. We must either tie a rope around our necks as a noose or sharpen a sword to wield.

ELECTRA. I want you to kill me, brother. It would be an insult to Agamemnon's house were one of the Argives to do it.

ORESTES. Having my mother's blood on my hands is enough for me. I won't kill you. You must kill yourself, in a manner of your own choosing.

ELECTRA. All right. You'll find me your equal with a sword. But now I'd like to put my arms around your neck.

ORESTES. Enjoy the empty pleasure, if pleasure it is for those near death to embrace.

They embrace.

ELECTRA. My darling! There's nothing more precious and sweet to your sister than you. Our lives are one.

ORESTES {weeping). See! You've made me break down and cry. And now I'd like to hug you in return. Why should I in my wretchedness hold back any more?

ELECTRA. Oh, if it were right, how I wish that the same sword might kill us both, and that a single coffin, wrought of cedar, could receive us both!

ORESTES. Nothing would be sweeter than that! But you can see how few members of our family remain, to bury us together.

End of embrace.

ELECTRA. Didn't Menelaus make an effort in his speech to save you from death? Oh, the wicked man, the betrayer of my father!

ORESTES. He wasn't even anywhere to be seen.* With his hopes set on the throne, he was careful not to protect his family. But come now! Let's make sure we die in a noble fashion,* worthy of Agamemnon. I plan to demonstrate my high birth to the city with a sword-thrust to my vitals, and you should match the boldness of my action. Pylades, please would you oversee our suicides, and when we are dead array our bodies well, take us to our father's tomb, and bury us together. (He gets to his feet) And now farewell. As you see, I am off to do the deed.

PYLADES. Wait! Apart from anything else, I take exception to one aspect of your plans. Did you really think that I would want to live after you're dead?

ORESTES. Why is it your business to die along with me?

PYLADES. I can't believe you had to ask that question. What sense does it make for me to live without your friendship?

ORESTES. YOU didn't kill a mother, as I did, to my misfortune.

PYLADES. Yes, I did, along with you. So I ought to suffer the , same fate.

ORESTES. No, don't die with me. Go back to your father. For you have a city, while I have none, and you have your father's palace and the refuge of great wealth. As for marriage, it's true that you have lost my poor sister, whom I betrothed to you in honour of our friendship, but you can find someone else to wed and bear your children. We no longer have any relationship to bind us. And now, my dear friend, farewell—as you can and we cannot, since faring well is what we dead relinquish.

ORESTES again makes as if to leave.

PYLADES. You could hardly be further from understanding what I have in mind. May the fertile ground not receive my blood, nor the bright air my soul, if ever I treacherously abandon you while ensuring my own freedom. I shall not seek to deny that I was your accomplice in the murder you committed, and I helped you plan everything for which you are now being punished. So I too should die along with you and Electra here, whom I consider to be my wife, in so far as marrying her found favour with me. For how could I ever go to Delphi, the citadel of the Phocians,* and explain myself with honour, if I supported you as your friend before your downfall, but deserted you now that your luck has changed? Impossible. I am just as involved in this as you. But since we are to die, let's put our heads together and try to find a way to make Menelaus suffer too.

ORESTES. My dearest friend, if only I could see that before I die!*

PYLADES. Do as I say, then, and delay the cutting thrust of your sword.

ORESTES. I shall, if I am to find some measure of revenge on my enemy.

PYLADES (lowering his voice). Be quiet. I have little trust in women.

ORESTES. You needn't worry about these ones here. They're on our side.

PYLADES. Let's kill Helen.* That will cause Menelaus bitter grief.

ORESTES. How? I commend your readiness, provided the outcome is good.

PYLADES. Put her to the sword. She's hiding in your palace.

ORESTES. So she is. In fact she's putting her seal on all my property.*

PYLADES. Not any more she isn't, now that she has Hades* as her bridegroom.

ORESTES. But how do we do it? She has her foreign attendants,

PYLADES. Who are they? No Phrygian* would cause me fear.

ORESTES. They tend to things like her mirrors and perfumes.

PYLADES. So she's come here with all her Trojan luxuries?

ORESTES. Yes, Greece was always too small an abode for her.

PYLADES. Slaves stand no chance against non-slaves.

ORESTES. If I could see this through, I would not hesitate to die twice over.

PYLADES. The same goes for me too, since I'll be helping you.

ORESTES. Explain what we have to do. Finish telling me what you have in mind.

PYLADES. We'll go into the palace making out that we intend to commit suicide there.

ORESTES. That's clear, but I still don't understand how we manage all the rest.

PYLADES. We'll go up to her, complaining of our plight.

ORESTES. At this she will be all tears on the surface, but happy inside.

PYLADES. Just as we shall too; we'll be no different from her.

ORESTES. And then how shall we go about our assignment?

PYLADES. We'll have swords hidden in these clothes of ours.

ORESTES. But first how will we encompass the death of her attendants?

PYLADES. We'll lock them out in various parts of the palace.

ORESTES. Yes, and we'd better kill anyone who tries to raise the alarm.

PYLADES. After that the deed itself will make clear how we have to proceed.

ORESTES. To murder Helen. I understand your implication.

PYLADES. You're right. But now listen to the beauty of my plan. If the woman we were killing were a more upright person, there would be no glory in murdering her. But as things are, we shall be punishing her on behalf of all Greece, for the fathers she killed, the children she destroyed, the brides she robbed of husbands. There will be cries of joy, and people will burn thanks-offerings for the gods, as they pray for us to be showered with rewards, because we exacted retribution in blood from an evil woman. Once you've killed her, you won't be called 'the matricide' any longer. That will be a thing of the past, and your reputation will improve, because you'll be known as the killer of the mass-murderer Helen. It's quite unthinkable that Menelaus should prosper while you, your father, and your sister all die, and your mother ... but in common decency I refrain from mentioning her case. Anyway, it's unthinkable that Menelaus should recover his wife and occupy your palace thanks to Agamemnon's prowess. I would certainly deserve to die right now if my dark sword remains in its sheath and is not used against her. And should we fail to encompass her murder, we'll set fire to this palace here* before killing ourselves. One of these two endeavours will succeed, and we shall be applauded either for the manner of our deaths or for the way in which we saved our lives.

CHORUS. Tyndareus' daughter is a disgrace to her kind and every woman should find her hateful.

ORESTES. Oh, there's nothing better than a reliable friend—not even wealth or kingship. A true friend is worth as much as an incalculable number of people. For instance, not only did you devise the mischief we made against Aegisthus* and stand by me when danger threatened, but now you've found a way for me to be revenged on my enemies and again you remain by my side. But I'll stop singing your praises, because even that—even being praised to the skies—is somewhat oppressive. Since I am in any case on the point of death, I would like to do something to my enemies before I die, to repay those who betrayed me and to ruin the lives of those who ruined mine. I am, remember, the son of Agamemnon, who became the leader of Greece on his merits,* not as a result of autocratic authority—though he did, in fact, have a certain godlike power. I am not about to disgrace him by dying a servile death. No, I shall depart this life as a free man should, and I shall be avenged on Menelaus. There's only one thing we need for complete success: if somehow we could remain alive, unlikely though it seems, and kill without being killed—well, that's what I pray for. I'm glad even to give my mind the easy satisfaction of voicing this desire of mine in fleeting words.

ELECTRA. Brother, I think I know how to achieve exactly that—safety for all three of us, you, me, and Pylades here.

ORESTES. Your plan needs divine providence. But where will we find it? I know that intelligence is a strong component of your mind, so tell us what you mean.

ELECTRA. Listen, then, to what I have to say. And the same goes for you, Pylades pay attention to me.*

ORESTES. Go on. For what pleasure is there in the postponement of good things?

ELECTRA. You know Helen's daughter? But that's an unecessary question.

ORESTES. Yes, of course: Hermione, whom my mother brought up.

ELECTRA. She's gone to Clytemnestra's tomb …

ORESTES. What for? What prospect are you holding out?

ELECTRA. … to pour libations for her mother at the tomb.

ORESTES. And why are you telling me this? What has it to do with our safety?

ELECTRA. You must take her hostage when she returns.

ORESTES. In what respect will that remedy things for us three companions?

ELECTRA. Once Helen has been killed, if Menelaus makes an attempt against you—or indeed against Pylades and me, since we're all united in this—you must tell him you will kill Hermione. You should have your sword drawn and close to the girl's throat. Now, if he removes the threat against your life because he doesn't want Hermione to die, let the girl go into her father's keeping. But he's an irascible man, and if he loses his temper and moves to kill you, then you make as if to cut the girl's throat. I think that for all his initial bravado he'll eventually soften his resolve. After all, he's not temperamentally bold or warlike. This is the strategy I have for securing our safety. That's what I wanted to say.

ORESTES. You may be physically as womanly as any of your sex, but you have the mind of a man! Indeed, you deserve to live rather than die. Pylades, you will rue the day you lose such a woman—but if you live, you will be lucky to have her as your wife.

PYLADES. That's what I pray for—that she may come to the city of the Phocians the worthy subject of fine wedding songs.

ORESTES. But when will Hermione reach the palace? After all, the undoubted excellence of your plan depends on our success in capturing this whelp* of an unholy father.

ELECTRA. I would think she's close to home now. She's been away as long as one might expect.

ORESTES. Good. So, Electra, you had better stay in front of the palace so as to be here for the girl when she arrives, and also to keep an eye out in case anyone enters the palace too soon, before the murder has been carried out. If anyone does come, let us know within the palace, either by banging on the door or by sending word to us inside. As for us, let's go inside and equip ourselves with swords for the final ordeal.

Father, from the halls of dark Night you now inhabit, hear your son Orestes as he calls on you to come to his aid!

ELECTRA. Yes, father, come, if from within the earth you hear the cries of your children, who are dying for your sake.

PYLADES. Agamemnon, close kin of my father,* hear my prayers too: keep your children safe.

ORESTES. I killed my mother …

ELECTRA. I put my hand to the sword …

PYLADES. And I offered my encouragement and banished doubts.

ORESTES. … to proffer aid to you, father.

ELECTRA. … and never let you down.

PYLADES. Will what you're hearing not shock you into rescuing your children?

ORESTES. My tears are my libation to you.

ELECTRA. And mine are my laments.

PYLADES: Enough. Let's set about the task. For if prayers penetrate inside the earth, he can hear you. May Zeus our ancestor and Justice in all her glory grant success to this man, this woman, and me—three companions sharing one ordeal, one trial.

Exeunt ORESTES and PYLADES into the palace.

ELECTRA. Women of Mycenae,* my friends, noble women of Argos, the Pelasgian seat …

CHORUS. What orders would you give us, my lady? For you are still entitled to be addressed as such in the city of the Argives.

ELECTRA. Let some of you stand on the carriageway here, while the rest of you take up positions there on the other path. You will serve as the palace's garrison.

CHORUS. Why are you setting us this task? Tell me, dear.

ELECTRA. I don't want anyone to make our troubles worse by catching sight of my brother as he sets his hand to bloody murder.

The CHORUS divides according to ELECTRA's instructions.

SEMICHORUS A. Come on, hurry up. I shall watch over this road here, the eastward one.

SEMICHORUS B. And I this one here, which tends west.

ELECTRA. Cast your eyes to and fro.

CHORUS. From here to there and back again we keep our watch, just as you told us to.

ELECTRA. Keep those eyes moving around. Cast your glance from side to side in all directions.

SEMICHORUS A (excited). There's someone on the road. Who is it? † Who's this peasant walking by your palace?

ELECTRA. We're lost, it seems, my friends! Before long he will reveal the secret hunting of our swordsmen to our enemies.

SEMICHORUS A. Don't be alarmed, my dear: there's no one on the path as you thought.

ELECTRA. What? Can I still rely on you? Tell me truly: is the road up to the forecourt clear?

SEMICHORUS A. Yes, all's well in this direction. But keep an eye out on your side, because none of the citizens is approaching this way.

SEMICHORUS B. It's the same here as with you: there are no people to be seen here either.

ELECTRA. Wait, now, while I listen at the doors.

CHORUS. Why the hushed delay? What's keeping you people inside the palace from sprinkling the victim with her blood?

ELECTRA. They're not listening. Oh, no! As if I didn't have enough to suffer! Can it be that their swords have been blunted when faced with her beauty?

CHORUS. Soon an armed Argive will sprint up to the palace in his haste to come to her rescue.

ELECTRA. Keep a sharper eye out, please! This is not a contest of idleness. You lot look here, you lot there.

CHORUS. I patrol the path, watching in all directions.

HELEN (from within). Alas! Citizens of Pelasgian Argos, I am foully murdered!

ELECTRA. Did you hear that? The men have set about the murder! That was Helen screaming, I suppose.

CHORUS. O Zeus, O Zeus of never-failing might, come in earnest and help those dear to me!

HELEN (from within). Menelaus, I am dying! Where are you when I need you?

ELECTRA AND CHORUS (sing).
Murder her, slay her, smite her, kill her!
Strike at close range with your two two-edged swords!
Strike her who abandoned father and husband,
and caused the death of countless Greeks,
slain beside the river by hostile spears,
where thanks to weapons of iron tears fell on tears
by the eddying waters of Scamander.*

CHORUS. Quiet, quiet! I can hear the sound of someone on the path by the palace!

ELECTRA. My dearest friends, it's Hermione! She has arrived in the middle of the murder! (Lowering her voice) Let's keep our voices down. She's going to blunder into the coils of our net! If we capture her, she'll make a fine catch. Take up your posts once more with a calm look and a complexion that doesn't betray what's happened. I'll keep my eyes resentful, to pretend I have no knowledge of what has happened.

Enter HERMIONE. She carries the empty libation jugs.

So here you are, girl! Have you finished making offerings at
Clytemnestra's tomb and pouring libations for the dead?

HERMIONE. Once I secured her favour, I came straight back.

But at the moment I'm feeling somewhat afraid, because while I was still a long way off I heard a cry from inside the palace, but I don't know what it was.

ELECTRA. Well, you'd expect us to be upset, given what's happening to us.*

HERMIONE. No words of ill omen, please. But what do you mean? What new trouble has arisen?

ELECTRA. The city has condemned Orestes and me to death.

HERMIONE. Oh, no! That this should happen to members of my family!

ELECTRA. Their minds are made up; the yoke of necessity is upon us.

HERMIONE. So is this the reason for the shouting inside the palace?

ELECTRA. Yes,the cries come from a suppliant on the ground at Helen's knees.

HERMIONE. Who? Tell me. I don't want to remain in ignorance.

ELECTRA. Poor Orestes, who is begging her to save his life, and mine too.

HERMIONE. Then the house certainly has a good excuse for tears.

ELECTRA. Yes, what better reason could there be for an outcry? But since we're all members of the same family, why don't you come and join us in our supplication? Why not fall to the ground before your mother, in all her high prosperity, and beg her not to let Menelaus stand by and watch us die? Come. Remembering how my mother cradled you in her arms, take pity on us and relieve us of our troubles. Come and join us here in our endeavour; I'll show you the way. You're the only one who can guarantee us complete safety.

HERMIONE. There, I'm entering the palace as quickly as 1 can. In so far as it is up to me, you will be safe.

ELECTRA escorts HERMIONE to the door and calls inside.

ELECTRA. You swordsmen of mine there inside the palace, here is our quarry for you to seize. Hold her! Hold her! Once your swords are at her throat, calm down, so that Menelaus may know that he is up against no cowardly Phrygians, but real men, and that he's being treated exactly as cowards should be treated.

Exeunt ELECTRA and HERMIONE into the palace.

CHORUS (sings). Ah! Ah, my friends! Make a noise, a loud noise,
and raise a cry here in front of the palace,
lest the murder that has been committed
might make the Argives so fiercely afraid
that they run to offer assistance
to the royal palace before I have certain sight
of Helen's bloodied corpse lying within,
or else hear word from one of her attendants.
For though clear about some aspects of these events,
there are others of which I am less certain.
In full justice has divine wrath
come to Helen. For she filled all Greece with tears
thanks to that pernicious, baneful man from Ida,
Paris,* who brought Greece to Troy.

Enter PHRYGIAN* from palace, running and agitated.

PHRYGIAN (sings). I have fled for my life from Argive sword
in eastern slippers over the cedar-wood beams
of the colonnade and the Doric triglyphs*—
O Earth! O Earth, it's all past, past!—
running scared like the easterner I am.
Oh, woe! Where can I flee, ladies?
Would that I could fly to the bright sky
or to the sea which bull-headed Oceanus*
winds in his arms as he encircles the earth!
CHORUS. Tell me, Trojan, Helen's slave from Ida: what's the matter?
PHRYGIAN (sings). Troy, alas! Alas, Troy! O city of the Phrygians,
O fruitful soil of sacred mount Ida,
in eastern grief I raise my voice for your fall,
brought about by the beauty of that bird-born,
swan-feathered whelp of Leda,*
Helen of ill fame, ill-famed Helen,
wrath descending on the hewn towers
of Pergamum, built by Apollo.
Aaaah! The dirges, the dirges!
O Dardanus' wretched land!*
O horseman Ganymede,* bed-mate of Zeus!
CHORUS. Tell us clearly and in detail exactly what happened indoors.
PHRYGIAN (sings). Sorrow! Sorrow!

That is how with Asian voice in the east
they start the plaint—oh, woe!—when on the ground
is shed by Hades' iron swords the blood of kings.
So from me you want exact details?
Into the palace there came with matching gait
a matched pair of Greek lions.
The one named by his father the war-leader;
the other, the son of Strophius, is like Odysseus*
an evil-scheming man, devising tricks in silence,
but loyal to his friends, courageous under threat,
skilled in the arts of war, and a deadly serpent.
Damn him for his evil ways and his quiet cunning!
Inside, their eyes marred with tears,
they drew near the seat of the wife of the archer, Paris.*
They abased themselves, one on either side,
and, each clasping her from his own side,
they threw suppliant arms,
threw them around the knees of Helen.
Back they leapt at a run, the Phrygian attendants,
back they leapt, speaking one to another
in abject fear of a trick. Some thought not,
but it seemed to others that Tyndareus' daughter
was being enmeshed in a device of nets
by the matricidal serpent.

CHORUS. But where were you at this time? Or were you so afraid that you were long gone?

PHRYGIAN (sings). Following the Phrygian custom, the Phrygian way,
with rapid movement of firm, feathered fan
before her cheek I was wafting a breeze,*
a breeze past Helen's hair, Helen's locks,
while her hands wound the thread,
the thread on the distaff.
and the finished yarn fell to the floor.*
With the thread she wanted to sew
from Phrygian spoils offerings for the tomb,
purple-dyed clothing, a gift for Clytemnestra.
Said Orestes to the bride from Sparta:
'O daughter of Zeus, come away from your chair,
walk over here to the ancient hearth-seat
of my forefather Pelops, to hear my words.'
And so he took her—he took her and she followed,
with no foresight of what the future held.
Meanwhile his accomplice, the foul Phocian,
was about other business. 'Out of the way!
Begone,† you Phrygian cowards!' said he.
Each of us he shut in a different part of the palace,
some in the stables, some in the porches,

some here, some there, dividing us up,
and keeping us far from our mistress.
chords. What happened next?
Phrygian (sings). O great mother, mighty Idaean mother,
mighty goddess Antaea!* O the blood and the pain,
the foul crimes I saw there, saw in the royal palace!
Holding swords drawn from the darkness
of purple-bordered clothes, they whirled from side to side
their eyes, checking that no one was there.
As firm as mountain-dwelling boars,
they stood facing the woman and said:
'Now you are going to die, to die!
Blame your death on the coward you married,
who betrayed to death, here in Argos,
the children of his brother.' She screamed.
She screamed 'Alas! Alas for me!',
and her pale arm smote her breast and head†
with piteous blows. She was trying to run away,
trying to flee, to flee on gold-sandaled foot,
when past her in Mycenaean boots ran Orestes.
His hand shot into her hair; he bent her neck
on to his left shoulder and was poised
to plunge his dark sword into her throat.

CHORUS. And where were you Phrygian house-slaves? What were you doing to defend her?

PHRYGIAN (sings). With a shout and with crowbars
we ripped out the frames and the posts
from the doors of the buildings where we were held,
and ran to help from the various parts of the palace,
bearing stones, or hooks, or drawn sword.
But we were opposed by Pylades,
as irresistible as … as Phrygian Hector,
or as Ajax* in his three-plumed helmet,
whom once I saw, saw there in the gates of Priam's city.
Sword clashed with sword, and that was when …
yes, that was when we Phrygians made it clear
how far our martial skill and prowess fall short
of Greek weaponry. One turned and fled,
another was killed, another was wounded,
while a fourth took to begging to protect his life.
They were dying, or about to die, or already dead,
and so we fled into the shadows.
Then poor Hermione entered the palace,
to see her wretched mother, who gave her life,
sprawled on the ground at the point of death.
They ran and seized her as if they were two Bacchants,*
freed from their coven, and she a mountain cub.

Then once more they turned their attention
to the slaughter of the daughter of Zeus.
But she was nowhere to be seen in the palace!
I swear by Zeus, by Earth, by Light, by Night,
whether drugs were involved or magic craft,
or whether the gods had stolen her away,
she had vanished! I have no knowledge
of what happened next, for out of the palace
I was stealing, making good my escape.
But after enduring so much, so many trials
and ordeals, Menelaus has gained nothing, nothing,
by rescuing his wife Helen from Troy.

Enter ORESTES, running with a sword in his hand.

CHORUS. Here comes something strange, on top of the strange news we've just heard. For I can see Orestes, sword in hand, running out to the front of the palace in a high state of agitation.

ORESTES. Where's the man who fled from the palace to avoid my sword?*

The PHRYGIAN throws himself at ORESTES' feet.

PHRYGIAN. Lord, I prostrate myself before you on the ground, as is the eastern fashion.
ORESTES. This place is not in Troy, but in Argive territory.
PHRYGIAN. But the wise prefer life to death wherever they are.
ORESTES. You didn't call out for Menelaus to come and help, did you?
PHRYGIAN. For my part I would summon help for you, since you deserve it more.
ORESTES. So the death of Tyndareus' daughter was justified, then?
PHRYGIAN. Perfectly justified, even if she had three throats for striking.
ORESTES. You flatter with a coward's tongue, but you weren't of this opinion indoors.
PHRYGIAN. No? When she brought ruin to Troy as well as Greece?
ORESTES. Swear that you're not just trying to flatter me—swear it, or I'll kill you!
PHRYGIAN. I swear on my life, and I'm not likely to swear falsely on that!
ORESTES. Was it like this in Troy too? Did bare steel terrify every Phrygian there?
PHRYGIAN. Remove your sword. From close at hand it glints with grim death.
ORESTES. Are you afraid of turning into stone, as if you'd seen the Gorgon?
PHRYGIAN. No, of turning into a corpse. I am aware of no Gorgon's head here.
ORESTES. Are you afraid of Hades, though he will release your from the hardship of your slavery?
PHRYGIAN. Every man, even if he be a slave, enjoys life on earth.
ORESTES. You're right—and your intelligence saves you. Now, go inside the palace.

ORESTES removes his sword from the PHRYGIAN's neck and steps back. The PHRYGIAN gets to his feet.

PHRYGIAN. You're not going to kill me, then?
ORESTES. Your life is spared.
PHRYGIAN. That is good news indeed.
ORESTES. But I'm about to change my mind.

PHRYGIAN. That is *not* good news.

ORESTES. You're an idiot if you think that I would bring myself to slit your throat, when although you're not a woman, you're no man either.* The reason I came out of the palace was to stop you raising the alarm. For when it hears a cry, Argos is quick to respond. But I'm not worried about getting Menelaus back within range of my sword—just let him come, flaunting his yellow hair on his shoulders.*

Exeunt the PHRYGIAN to one side, and ORESTES into the palace.

CHORUS (sings). Ah! Ah, Fortune! Another conflict,
another terrible conflict faces the house,
affecting the line of Atreus. What shall we do?
Inform the city or keep it to ourselves?
In silence lies greater safety, my friends.
But look! There, in front of the palace! Look!
This smoke hastening up into the air tells us
they are lighting torches to burn Tantalus' house,*
and there is no end yet to the killing.
The end of things for mortals is in the hands
and at the whim of the gods. But mighty too
is the power of the demons of revenge.
This house has fallen, fallen through bloodshed,
because of the fall of Myrtilus from the chariot.*

The CHORUS stop singing and the Chorus-leader continues alone.

But now I can see Menelaus too approaching the palace at a run. I suppose he's heard of recent events here. Hurry! Lock and bar the doors, you members of Atreus' line inside the palace. A man at the height of success is a formidable foe to those who are doing badly, as you are now, Orestes.

Enter MENELAUS, armed, with attendants.

MENELAUS. I've come in response to news of the appalling deeds of violence committed by the two lions—I can't call them men. Someone open the house! Slaves, put your shoulders to these doors here, so that we may at least rescue my daughter from the bloodstained hands of those murderers!

ORESTES, PYLADES, and HERMIONE appear on the roof, ORESTES has his sword held close to HERMIONE's throat, and is holding a slab of masonry in his other hand, PYLADES is holding burning torches.

ORESTES. You there! Keep your hands off the doors! They're locked! I'm talking to you, Menelaus, in all your towering audacity! Do as I say, or I'll smash your head with this slabI've broken off the roof, the work of builders long dead and gone. The doors are barred: they'll stop this hurried rescue attempt of yours and keep you out of the house.

MENELAUS. Oh, what's this? I see the light of torches on the roof where they're beleaguered, and I see a sword guarding my daughter's neck.

ORESTES. Are there questions you want to put to me, or do you want to listen to what I have to say?*

MENELAUS. I don't want to do either, but it looks as though I have no choice but to listen to you.

ORESTES. You might like to know that I'm going to kill your daughter.

MENELAUS. You've already murdered Helen, and now you're committing another murder as well?

ORESTES. If only I'd managed that and hadn't been robbed of success by the gods.
MENELAUS. Are you denying that you killed her? Is this some kind of high-handed joke?
ORESTES. It hurts me to deny it. If only I had …
MENELAUS. … done what? Tell me, because you're making me afraid.
ORESTES. … sent the polluter of Greece hurtling to Hades.
MENELAUS. Give me my wife's body, so that I can bury her.
ORESTES. Ask the gods for her body, but I shall kill your child.
MENELAUS. Your mother's blood is already on your hands. Isn't that enough for you?
ORESTES. I'll never tire of killing evil women.
MENELAUS. What about you, Pylades? Are you going to help him commit this murder?
ORESTES (after looking at PYLADES). His silence is agreement.*
There's no need for him to speak as well as me.
MENELAUS. But you won't get away with it, unless you can fly away.
ORESTES. We have no intention of escaping. We'll set fire to the palace.
MENELAUS. You'll destroy this house, your family home?
ORESTES. Yes, to stop it falling into your hands. And I'll slaughter this girl over the flames.
MENELAUS. Go ahead, then: kill her—but rest assured that then I'll make you pay for what you've done.
ORESTES. Be quiet, then, and face the fact that your misery is justified.
MENELAUS. Put up your sword! Keep it away from my daughter!
ORESTES. But you're a liar.
MENELAUS. Are you really going to kill my daughter?
ORESTES. Now you're telling the truth.
MENELAUS. Oh, no! What am I to do?
ORESTES. Go to the Argives and persuade them …
MENELAUS. … to do what?
ORESTES. Ask the citizens to spare our lives.
MENELAUS. Otherwise you'll murder my child?
ORESTES. That's right.
MENELAUS. What? Do you deserve to live?
ORESTES. Yes, and to rule.
MENELAUS. Where?
ORESTES. Here, in Pelasgian Argos.
MENELAUS (sarcastically). Oh, yes, you're just the person to handle the sacred basins …
ORESTES. And why not?
MENELAUS. … and to slaughter victims before battle.
ORESTES. Would you be the right man for the job?
MENELAUS. Yes, because my hands are free from pollution.
ORESTES. Your hands, maybe, but not your heart.
MENELAUS. But who would talk to you?
ORESTES. Anyone who respects his father.
MENELAUS. And what about those who respect their mothers?
ORESTES. They are lucky.
MENELAUS. As you are not.
ORESTES. Because I have no liking for evil women.
MENELAUS. O Helen, poor Helen …
ORESTES. What about poor me?

MENELAUS. … I brought you back from Troy just to be a victim …

ORESTES. If only that were true.

MENELAUS. … after all my trials and tribulations.

ORESTES. None of which effort was spent on me.

MENELAUS. I suffered terribly.

ORESTES. Yes, when you proved to be no friend in need.

MENELAUS. I am in your power.

ORESTES. Your own villainy put you there. (He calls down inside the palace) Hey, Electra! Set fire to the palace there! (Quieter, to PYLADES) And Pylades, truest of my friends, put the roof here to the torch!*

MENELAUS. O land of the Danaans and inhabitants of horse-rearing Argos! Come on, now! Aren't you going to arm yourselves and run to help? For this man is forcing the whole of your city to let him live, when he has committed the abominable crime of matricide.

APOLLO appears above the backdrop with HELEN.*

APOLLO. Enough, Menelaus! Enough of this whetted passion! It is I, Phoebus, son of Leto, who address you from close at hand! And you, Orestes: remove the threat of your sword from the girl, so that you may hear the message I bear. First, Helen, whom you failed to kill, for all the determination your anger at Menelaus gave you: acting on Zeus' orders, I rescued her and snatched her from under your sword. As Zeus' daughter, she is to have eternal life, and she will sit enthroned with Castor and Polydeuces in heaven's hollows, a saviour to sailors.†*

That is how things stand with Helen. As for you, Orestes, you must depart beyond the borders of this land and live for a full year in a place in Parrhasia, which will be named after the fact that you passed your exile there.* From there you must go to Athens and submit to judgement by the three Eumenides for the crime of murdering your mother. The gods will supervise the trial on the Areopagus and will cast their votes in accordance with full righteousness, and you are fated to win there.

As for Hermione, against whose neck you hold your sword, Orestes, she is destined to be your wife.* Neoptolemus, who thinks he is to marry her, will never do so, because he is fated to be killed by Delphic sword when he comes to ask me for compensation for the death of his father Achilles.* You have already agreed to the marriage between Pylades and your sister, so give her to him, and the life that awaits them in the future will be happy.

As for Argos, let Orestes rule it,* Menelaus, while you go to Sparta and take up the throne there, the dowry left you by your wife. Hitherto she always caused you countless troubles, but that is over now. You must find another wife to take into your house. For Helen's beauty was merely the instrument used by the gods to bring about the encounter between Greeks and Phrygians, and to cause enough deaths to relieve the earth of the foul burden of a vast swarm of humans. And I shall put right the relations between the city and Orestes, since it was I who compelled him to murder his mother.

ORESTES. O Loxias, god of prophecy! It turns out after all that your oracles were true and contained no deceit. There were times when I was afraid, though, that when I thought I was hearing your voice I was actually hearing some vengeful demon. But all's well that ends well, and I shall do as you say. There! I release Hermione from slaughter, and I agree to marry her when I have her father's permission.

MENELAUS. Farewell, Helen, daughter of Zeus! Soon you will join the gods in their blessed palace, and I congratulate you on that. Orestes, I betroth my daughter to you, as Phoebus commands. As you are noble and from noble stock, I pray that you may do well from this marriage—and that I may too, who give this woman to you.

APOLLO. Go, then, each of you, to the places I have assigned you, and let there be no more discord between you.

MENELAUS. It shall be as you command.

ORESTES. I agree. I have no more quarrel with events, Menelaus, or with your oracles, Loxiasf.

Exeunt severally ORESTES, PYLADES, HERMIONE, and MENELAUS, along with his attendants.

APOLLO. Be on your way, then, and respect Peace, the fairest of the gods. Right across the bright starry vault of heaven I shall take Helen to Zeus' palace, where a throne alongside Hera and Hebe, Heracles' wife,* awaits her, and men will honour her as a goddess for ever with libations. Along with Castor and Polydeuces, sons of Zeus, her domain will be the safety of sailors on the waves of the sea.

Exit APOLLO.

# Thyestes

## Characters

TANTALUS' GHOST, grandfather of Atreus and Thyestes, he is punished in the underworld for having killed his son Pelops, whose body he then served to the gods

FURY, who forces Tantalus back to earth to inspire his house to further sins

ATREUS, a son of Pelops, he is king of Argos and brother of Thyestes

ATTENDANT of Atreus

THYESTES, a son of Pelops, he is the brother of Atreus who has been driven into exile

TANTALUS, son of Thyestes

PLISTHENES, son of Thyestes (mute part)

THIRD SON of Thyestes (mute part)

MESSENGER

CHORUS of Mycenaeans

SERVANTS of Atreus (mute parts)

*SCENE: A* courtyard of the palace of Mycenae in Argos.

(TANTALUS' GHOST *is revealed downstage, and also, in half-light and farther back,* FURY. *Even more dimly lit and farther upstage,* ATREUS, *the king, is seated, his chin propped in his palm and his elbow resting on a chair arm. He is meditating, either attending to* TANTALUS' GHOST *or else inventing him.*)

TANTALUS GHOST: Who calls me from the infernal regions, who
drags me back, plucks at my tortured spirit,
to grab at me as I have been grabbing at empty
air? What worse ordeals have the judges of hell
devised for Tantalus' Ghost? Hunger in plenty,
and thirst in the midst of running water are hard,
as my parched lips can testify. But I've learned,
barely, to bear these torments. Whatever new
comes to me now cannot be better! A heart
of stone would melt at the thought of anything further

heaped on the burden I already carry. The light
dazzles my dimmed eyes; I tremble with dread
to return to the world again, where my clan is swarming,
a multitude, each of whom bids fair
to make those crimes for which I suffer forever
trivial, almost innocent compared
with what they do and dare. Whatever space
is not yet filled in the land of the damned, whatever
cell is unassigned by the terrible judges,
my children and their children shall lay claim to
with the right of terrible wrongs, so long as my house,
Pelops' damnable house, stains the light
that assaults my vision.

FURY: That's it, villain. Goad
your heirs to madness! Let there be competition
among your issue to exceed one another in guilt.
Let swords be drawn on this side and that. Let passions
know neither bounds nor shame. May fury egg
all of them on to hatred, of parents for children
and children's children and the other way round. The egg
will hatch sooner or later monstrous evil,
evil on evil compounded, its reasons confounded
and altogether surpassed. A kingdom will fall
and the king will scarcely notice, his glittering eyes
fixed on the brother he hates, a slave to vengeance.
Your house will be an asylum for madmen, violent,
blustering, bragging, and then, in a moment, cringing,
crooning, and desolate—power and wretchedness changing
madly as in a lunatic's wavering fancies.
Chance, stone blind, will lead on a treacherous path
as your heirs are exiled for vile misdeeds and return
to worse crimes. But no onlooker will pity
or feel for them anything other than sheer
disgust, while in that arrogant house, in hatred
and fear, brother will mistrust brother, as father
will fear his sons, who will quail at the sight ot their father.
Born in disgrace, they will die in an earned vileness.
A wife will strike the blow to dispatch her husband,
and blood will flood the land to bring forth lusts
like vermin, corrupting every virtue. The sky,
clear and pure overhead, will here seem tainted,
the stars themselves winking and leering, as spite
and slaughter wheel and settle on Tantalus' house.
Then let them deck the votive pillar with laurel,
hang green boughs on the portals, and light the festal

torches to welcome Tantalus home and do him
reverence. Men will respect this place as a shrine,
the holy of unholies, for here the worst
and bloodiest crimes in mankind's dismal annals
will be outdone. Your grandson Atreus sits
brooding now the cloudy thoughts that will stain
the ground with blood. From the delicate pulse that throbs
in his motionless wrist temblors will come to topple
the citadel's walls. That hearth's embers some servant
will fan into blood-red flame, and its cauldron will seethe
unspeakable evils. You say you are hungry? Feast
on the gory banquet we have prepared, and drink
deep of the bloodied wine till your belly is full!

TANTALUS' GHOST: I beg you, let me go back to my pools of recoiling
waters, back to that tree that teases and shrinks
just out of reach. Should that seem insufficient,
consign me, instead, to Phlegethon's currents of fire,
and there I shall frisk like an otter, sing like a bird,
and let my fellows in suffering know they are blessed
to endure no more than the torments their sins have earned them.
Who lies beneath an unstable cairn of boulders
awaiting their crushing blow, let him rejoice!
Who faces the gaping maws of ravening lions
poised to pounce, or shudders to see the Furies
advancing toward him with fiery brands extended,
let them bid welcome to these proportionate trials,
glad not to be Tantalus, thrust back
into the land of the living.

FURY: Goad them on:
in hatred and lust, they finger the hilts of their swords,
warming their passions, savage, blind, and mad—
a terrible thing in rulers.

TANTALUS' GHOST: I have learned
to be torture's victim, not its henchman. I cannot
bear it that I have become a visitation,
a pestilence infecting my grandchildren
and then, through them, the city at large. No,
I will not do it! To the high gods I cry out
to set some limit to what mankind may suffer.
I will not hold my piece. I shall defy
the Fates and Furies, will warn them myself, speak out
to keep their hands from such an evil thing.
(*Addressing* ATREUS)

The holy altars ought not to be so defiled
by a madman's crime and the innocent blood of children.
(*To* FURY)
Do you think your scourges can frighten me? Can serpents'
writhings do worse than the knottings of my stomach
in hunger and the burning of my thirst?

THE FURY: Yes, this rage, its just what we want. Let its fire
light your house! The deep thirst you have felt,
let them feel too—for one another's blood.
The walls of the castle tremble at your approach
as if the stones themselves recoiled in horror.
Your loathsome spirit presides. As a blessèd presence
can grace a hill, a grove of trees, or a house,
you have brought disgrace to all of Argos,
but most of all to this particular dwelling.
You have done destiny's bidding. It is enough!
The earth can no longer endure your presence. Go back
to your accustomed caves in the underworld
lest the waters here also retreat and the fruits
of generous trees wither. See how the winds
harry the clouds along in an ominous sky!
The trees are nervous, and in your presence their fruit
withers. The isthmus churns, but the local rivers
choke on themselves as if their currents gasped.
The frosts on Cithaeron have fled, as if Phaëthon
had returned to parch all Argos, and Titan falters,
unwilling to launch the sun on this odious day.

(CHORUS *enters, a mixed group, some male, some female, some of them wearing togas, others dressed in modern dinner clothes as if at an opening night at the theater.*)

CHORUS: (*Speaking at first in unison*)'
If any god has ever regarded this place
with love, or affection, or even attention, if any
spirit has found some respite here in these gentle
streams, let him come back here now, for pity's sake,
to prevent a crime beyond imagination
from happening here.

FIRST CHORISTER: (*He is one of those in dinner clothes*)
Unspeakable perhaps,
but not, alas, beyond imagination.

SECOND CHORISTER: (*He is in a toga*)
I'm afraid you're right. What we dread, we can surely imagine,

as that one there imagines and even savors
its every ghastly detail.
(*He points to* ATREUS, *upon whom the light now shines more brightly*)

FIRST CHORISTER: These old Greek
stories have helped us imagine terrible deeds.

SECOND CHORISTER: Or allow us now to allude to current events
and speak, albeit in code, of the actions of people
in power here in Rome. A grandfather's crimes
taint the lives of grandsons, whose greater crimes
astonish lesser, less fastidious men.

THIRD CHORISTER: A brother betrays his brother who kills his brother.

CHORUS: (In unison again)
There ought to be limits to wickedness. Bonds of affection
that animals recognize, we, human beings,
ought to acknowledge. Tantalus' dreadful spirit
infects not only the Argive plain but the whole
earth, and all of us suffer, for humankind
knows now what depths have been plumbed and may be again.
The innocent child Pelops runs to his father,
in joy to welcome Tantalus home, and his cries
of delight become abruptly the cries of anguish,
his and ours as well, that any father can skewer
his own child.

SECOND CHORISTER: Some in the audience may
find that their thoughts wander away from the horrors
before them on stage to others they have not seen
but know about, as one knows of a dead body
malodorous, rotting somewhere nearby. Who doubts
that Nero arranged to have his adoptive brother
killed, or that he and mother Agrippina
arranged for Claudius Caesar's murder—his father
at least by adoption? To entertain such thoughts
even in silence is dangerous; to pronounce
aloud what everyone thinks would be sheer madness.

FIRST CHORISTER: It crosses our minds, nevertheless, that Nero's
childhood tutor and then confidential adviser
was Lucius Annaeus Seneca, this evening's
playwright.

THIRD CHORISTER: One cannot ignore the coincidences.

CHORUS: Tantalus' penance hardly atones for the bloody
wounds he inflicted that ooze still in the soul
of every man. Although we may dream of justice,
we cannot believe it—except as a children's story
our grandparents might have told us, who could not bear
that we should learn too soon the unpleasant truths—
prime among which is that even one's own grandparents
cannot be trusted. Minos was judging for us
when he condemned the transgressor to such baroque
and complicated atonements. We would ourselves
make such a decree, to let Tantalus scoop
from the current and bring to his thirsty villain's lips
nothing! Let him drink from a handful of dust.

(CHORUS *retires to seats at either side of the stage. There, as part of the audience, they watch while* ATREUS *raises his head and looks out to the auditorium.*)

ATREUS: O villain, O incompetent, inept,
and—worst of all for a king—O unavenged!
Of so many crimes have I been victim,
enduring a brother's treacheries, my disgrace
is vile, worse than his guilt, which is limitless.
And I do nothing, stew in useless complaint
when the whole world should resound with the clash of arms.
There should be scenes of violence and wails of grief
in desolate cityscapes the flames have made
memorably garish. Drawn swords should gleam
where they are yet unsmirched by the gouts of blood
that have not yet recompensed my offended honor.
The countryside should resound with horses' hoofbeats
and cries of the wounded and dying—their proper reward
for having sheltered my wicked brother. Wherever
he lay his hateful head, let there be heads
on pikes! These fortress walls bear down, accusing.
Let them collapse upon me, if only their fall
can bury my brother, too, whose moans will soothe
my pains like gentle music. My spirit rouses,
as that of a sick man who drags himself
from his bed to go and vomit. I must dare
something atrocious, spectacular, so bloody,
and altogether beastly that my own brother
will be driven to envy, even as he suffers
its dire effects. His proud spirit will break,
as mine will heal to see it. The gory pudding
stands on the banquet table. We must serve

each other and ourselves.

(*Atreus'* ATTENDANT *enters and makes a formal bow*)

ATTENDANT: And public opinion?
Do you count that as nothing?

ATREUS : The point of being a king
is exactly this: that whatever the people cannot
praise in your actions, they have to endure.

ATTENDANT: When fear
can compel their praise, it can also make them angry.
Your good repute must be found in their hearts as well
as upon their obedient tongues.

ATREUS: Any poor fool
can deserve sincere praise. Only the strong
can wring it from the reluctant. Let them cheer
for what they despise!

ATTENDANT: Let the king do right,
and all his people will cheer him.

ATREUS: But do I care?
Do you think I want to be king on sufferance? Let them
suffer whatever they must and, first of all, me.

ATTENDANT: Without honor and virtue, what is a throne?

ATREUS: I sit where I please, and any chair I honor
becomes a throne!

ATTENDANT: But sir, it is still wrong!
You cannot do such harm to your own brother!

ATREUS: Whatever is wrong to do to a brother, I
shall do to him, and be right to do it. The black
stain of his crimes against me leaves not even
a chink of light for mercy or grace to shine through.
He debauched my wife and then he stole my kingdom,
snatching the ram with the golden fleece, that symbol
of all our power the oracle said would keep us
secure on the throne. Sacred, alone, it grazed
in a meadow surrounded with high stone walls my brother
breached. He fouled my bed and chair and smirched

the honor of this house. I was cast out
to wander the earth in exile. What kept me alive
all that time was the dream of doing harm
to him who had done me harm. There was nothing else
I could trust, not even my own sons, who could be
his. I have brooded for years upon revenge,
and its time has come. I must put on my courage
and dare what Tantalus dared and Pelops, defying
every craven, decent instinct that stays
the clenched fists of most men. But mine will strike
to cause him the foulest hurt it can inflict.
Only say how. In what way shall I wound?

ATTENDANT: Hack with a sword so that his spirit spews?

ATREUS: You leap ahead to the result. Before that,
there is the pain itself, that will make him wish
for death to come as a merciful gift.

ATTENDANT: Disgusting!
Does piety mean nothing to you?

ATREUS: Nothing!
In our house, it has never counted for much.
Let the Furies, Erinys and Megaera,
come, brandishing torches further to heat
my frenzy. Unbearable horror is what I want!

ATTENDANT: What mad scheme are you hatching?

ATREUS: Unprecedented
woe! There is NO crime in mankinds annals
to satisfy me. This must surpass them all!

ATTENDANT: Not the sword?

ATREUS: It is not enough!

ATTENDANT: Then, fire?

ATREUS: Still, not enough.

ATTENDANT: But what weapon is left?

ATREUS: Thyestes will be the weapon.

ATTENDANT: That would make it
worse.

ATREUS: Worst! I tremble with rage and my heart
races, and what I need to soothe my spirit,
to stop the ground from shaking, to keep the sky's
lightning bolts from crashing upon our heads,
and the household gods from turning away in disgust
is that man's exquisite, unendurable pain!

ATTENDANT: What will you do?

ATREUS: Something huge and awful
I cannot yet imagine, but I can feel it
growing in my hands that tingle with it.
My lively fingers quiver. I cannot name it,
but it calls out to something in my soul
that answers, "Yes, so be it! Let Atreus do
what his brother has deserved. Let each perform
his part in the dreadful rite." In Thrace, they say,
there was once an unspeakable sacrifice and a feast
of infamy beyond man's imagination.
I speak of Philomel, Procne, and the evil
king they repaid, serving so well. Their rage
is what now fills my soul, as I will fill
Thyestes' belly full. Let the father tear
the flesh from his sons' bodies and let him drink
the blood of his blood and gnaw the bone of his bone.
This *amuse gueule* I'll prepare for him, so that he
may carry out with his own gory hands
my dire sentence. Then let him hate himself
with something like my own hot hatred.

ATTENDANT: How
do you propose to entrap him? How will you bring him
willingly into the city where you, whom he fears,
sit on the throne?

ATREUS: I could not manage it
without his help, but he is a schemer, ambitious,
deceitful, full of guile. In his own snares
I'll let him entangle himself. He will brave the heavens'
worst rages, and mine, if he sees some profit,
and particularly some dishonest profit
that may accrue.

ATTENDANT: But whom will he trust? On what
will he rely to take such risks?

ATREUS: His hopes
will be enough to persuade him. To them, he'll listen
like a credulous child. I'll give my sons the message
to carry to their uncle—that the exiled stranger
may now come home to share in the rule of Argos.
Thyestes, should he spurn my offer, will hear
his innocent children's pleadings as they repeat
their cousins' invitation. He'll be moved,
for their sake if not his own, and his thirst for power
will aggravate his sense of his own wrongs,
that he should suffer while I thrive. . . . He will yield.

ATTENDANT: He has learned by now to bear his troubles.

ATREUS: No,
his sense of having been wronged only increases,
irritating the galled place.

ATTENDANT: Must you send
your children to do this deed?

ATREUS: Why not? All children
love to play games. Let them learn to dissemble!

ATTENDANT: What kind of men will they be, having learned such lessons?
What if they were to turn one day on you
or Argos?

ATREUS: They would learn sooner or later.
The throne, itself, would teach them. In any event,
they were born evil, heirs of an evil house,
whether they're his or mine.

ATTENDANT: But will you tell them
the message they bring is a ruse, a part of a trap?

ATREUS: No, for the lessons of silence are hard to learn.
Only the ills of our lives can instruct us in them.

ATTENDANT: But they will have learned deceit from their own father,
for you are deceiving them.

ATREUS: For their own good,

that they may be free from the blame of the heinous crime
I have in mind. What is the good of spreading
the guilt to them? A part of my own soul shrinks
from what I'm about to do. If Agamemnon
and Menelaus assist me in this deed,
I shall reclaim them, for they will think themselves mine,
beyond question: doubt would open the door
to the burdens of parricide. Sooner than that,
they'll choose to believe they played a part in the murder
of an evil uncle. I shall not disclose my plan,
and neither should you, my friend.

ATTENDANT: Oh, I'll keep quiet.
Fear and loyalty both will be keeping my lips
sealed. But mostly . . .

ATREUS: Mostly?

ATTENDANT: (*After a slight pause*) Loyalty.

(ATREUS *laughs. They exit,* CHORUS *rises and walks to center stage. Members seem to confer among themselves for a few moments, nodding and gesticulating, and then they speak.*)

CHORUS: Peace, at last, between the brothers!
The long years of spite and madness
come to an end. The skies clear
in a new dawn of understanding
that riches and power don't make a throne.
True kingship has nothing to do
with Tyrian robes or jeweled tiaras.
A king is that man who knows no fear,
whose heart is free of the restless longings
ambition and envy prompt in men.
The love of the mob is fickle and therefore
worthless. Treasure is momentary,
something to count but never to count on.
In spite of the gaudy wheel of fortune's
turnings the king is never dizzied
or dazzled. Indifferent to hardships, he holds
his lands and indeed his life lightly,
serene as if immortal and glad
to meet whatever fate may come.

FIRST CHORISTER: The true nobleman earns his title
from the hard campaigns he has fought alone
in the small hours, subduing his own

baser nature. Having conquered
himself, he has nothing left to fear
from what the capricious world can do.

SECOND CHORISTER: Fear and desire make us villains,
but he has freed himself from such
tyrannous masters. He needs no horses,
armed soldiers, or show of state,
just as he fears neither traitors nor spies.
His steadied soul is a stronger fortress
than Parthian catapult can threaten
with huge rocks. Bold Sarmatian
hordes can never hope to besiege it.

FIRST CHORISTER: The only true kingdom is that
a man can bestow on himself, from which
he never can be deposed. The world
may beckon, offering pride of power,
but he knows better. The heights are steep
and the views may be fine, but down at the bottom
are mangled bodies to make us aware
of what the costs can be. I pray
only for clear judgment to see
how, in my humble station, I may
enjoy untroubled and sweet repose.

CHORUS: Men's lives have been likened to rivers.
Let mine flow in untroubled currents
that keep to the grassy banks. In the showy
rapids and towering falls of the great,
disasters lurk. Their ride is exciting
but how many come in the end to grief.
Better to paddle in quiet waters
dappled by sunlight that drifts through the leaves
of the overhanging trees and enjoy
the talk of our friends and the laughter of children.
Until in the lengthening shadows, we drift
into a doze. Happiness' secret
is easy enough for a man to grasp,
provided only he holds it lightly—
to live simply and then, full of years,
learn to let go. It is not death
we fear but the leaving of what we've loved.
The lesson is simple enough for children
who learn, each day, to go to their beds
and endure without any fear the dying

light that signals the end of a day
that wasn't given but only lent.

(CHORUS *is seated,* THYESTES *enters, accompanied by his three young sons.*)

THYESTES: How good to see the familiar dwelling places,
handsome as I remember them. An exile
dreams of this moment, yearns as a blind man would
for the vision of what he holds most dear. But dreams
are not to be trusted. I reach out with my hand to touch
the Cyclopean walls and feel their huge smoothed stones.
One sense confirms the others report as true,
and still I find it hard to believe. I'm home,
can turn to see the racecourse, empty now
and silent, but I can remember the cheering crowds.
Those were my great days, driving my father's
chariot in those races, and winning the palm.
Will they cheer now to see me again? Will they come
to crowd around me? Will Atreus, my brother,
welcome me? Or should I be content
with this one moment, turn away, and hide
in the dark woods, where outlaws live and beasts?

YOUNG TANTALUS: *(Aside)* I am afraid. My father's behaving strangely.
His step is uncertain, as if he were dazed or ill.

THYESTES: I don't believe my brother's promise. I don't
trust him. I should never have come. The hardships
I have already learned to bear may prove to be
trivial as compared with what he intends.
It's not too late. I can still turn around, turn back,
having seen the city, and save myself and my sons.

TANTALUS: Why do you hesitate, father? What can be wrong?
Is this not what youve prayed for all these years?
Now that the blessing falls from heaven, why not
hold out your hands to receive it? Instead, you defend,
as if from a blow What do you fear? Your brother?

THYESTES: I am, indeed, afraid but cannot say
what it is I fear. I should like to believe, but cannot.
Something feels wrong. I'm like a laden ship
making for port, urged on with oars and sails,
and yet there's a strong tide running, so that I slip
backward, moment by moment. I feel that tug.

TANTALUS: It's nothing that you can name? Why, then, it's nothing.
Think of the prize that waits within these gates.
Father, you can be king!

THYESTES: Long live the king!

TANTALUS: Think of the wealth and power!

THYESTES: They're nothing to me.

TANTALUS: And your sons will succeed you!

THYESTES: A throne seats only one.

TANTALUS: Who would choose to be wretched rather than happy?

THYESTES: What has a throne to do with being happy?
Men suppose that power delights in itself
and that hardship is something to fear, but I have been
up there on that giddy height, and the fear
of falling is what I remember. Down at the bottom
the footing is more secure. To lie on the ground
is safest, and not to have to eat one's bread
in fear of thieves, who prefer to invade mansions.
In golden goblets, there's often poisoned wine,
and you look to your taster, and he looks to your friends,
and on his face is the fear you try not to show.
Believe me. I have been there, and I know.
What we believe to be misfortune carries
certain compensations. No man fears me,
or covets what I have or envies me.
My own conscience is clear, for I have not
plundered the earth for more than my fair share
of what it offers mankind. I don't tax
brutish Getae off at the end of the map.
Savages aren't roaming the woods for rare
incense for my lamps or exotic plants
to grow in hothouse tubs to impress my guests.
I never sleep all day or carouse all night,
and I walk the streets without armed men's protection.
Want, as I've learned, is a boundless and peaceable kingdom.

TANTALUS: But would you refuse a throne a god bestows?
Your own brother invites you to share the kingdom!

THYESTES: Invites? That scares me. Some gift horses bite.

TANTALUS: The affection that brothers feel is like a stream
that runs underground for a time but then must surface.

THYESTES: My brother loves me? It's not what I'd expected
any more than I'd thought to see fire and water
come to terms, or life and death commingle,
or the fickle winds steady themselves to faith
and wed the restless sea. Sicilian tides
will sooner lie there motionless and bring forth
fields of ripening grain in the midnight's dazzle!

TANTALUS: But what betrayal is it you fear?

THYESTES: Betrayal
itself. His hatred is boundless as his power.

TANTALUS: What can he do to you?

THYESTES: To me? Nothing.
But I fear what he can do to you, my sons.

TANTALUS: You're already on your guard.

THYESTES: What good does that do,
once you have fallen into the pit? On guard?
Impaled on spikes, more like. But lead the way.
Ill follow, for your sake, but I won't lead.

(ATREUS *enters, sees* THYESTES *and his three* SONS, *and gloats having them in his power*)

ATREUS: My victim! Trapped in the nets I've set! The whole
brood, father and sons together. Hatred
is bitter but at moments like this can bloom
with a wonderful sweetness. Hunger pales, and love
is a wan shadow. My spirit's alive, my heart
sings. My nerves are on fire, but all in pleasure.
When the boarhound's on the leash and his muzzle is down,
he tracks the boar almost in silence, and snuffles
across the fields, but then, when the quarry is near,
bells, bays, breaks free, bounds ahead.
He's a trained animal, mind you, but he goes,
drags his laggardly master along behind him,
and he's eager for the kill. It's rage, blood lust
in the sight of blood, and it's just unbearably fine!
How lovely to gaze at that unlovely face I have longed

to see before me! How can I hide my feelings?
And yet, I must, to draw out the pleasure, to keep
the game going longer.
(*To* THYESTES)

Hail, good brother!
I rejoice to see you again. Let us embrace
as I have longed to do, all anger gone
and only the ties of love to hold us together.

THYESTES: Your goodness shames me, brother. I could contrive
excuses for my wicked deeds, but your
generous welcome undoes me. I'VE done wrong
and am heartily sorry. In the gleam of your love my sins
seem all the blacker. I have offended virtue
itself, and my tears must plead my case, for no
words will do. My extended hands beseech
that never before reached out like a beggar's to plead.
I clasp your knees, in the hope that you'll put by
your righteous anger, and pledge as tokens of faith
my guiltless boys.

ATREUS: Arise, brother. Embrace
not just my knees, but me! And your sons, as well!
Let us hug one another. Put off those vestments
of squalid exile. I hate to see them. Royal
trappings you all shall wear, as fine as my own,
for we shall share together in all things.
I reserve for myself only the glory of giving—
or better, say, of restoring to my dear brother
what is his by right. The wielding of kingly power
happens through chance; the bestowing of it, through love.

THYESTES: May the gods repay you. The crown you are kind to offer,
but I refuse it. My hand recoils from the scepter.
Let it be mine to blend m as one of the crowd.

ATREUS: The throne's big enough for two.

THYESTES: Yoy may have it all.
My share is yours.

ATREUS: You spurn the gifts of fortune?

THYESTES: I've learned never to trust them.
ATREUS: But will you deny me

the honor of giving? Of sharing?

THYESTES: That's yours already,
but mine will be in refusing what you have offered.
There's honor enough for two of us to share.

ATREUS: But I lose mine if you don't accept your part.

THYESTES: Very well, I accept the title of kingship—but you
shall keep the power, and I shall be your subject.

ATREUS: (*Putting the crown upon* THYESTES' *head*)
Wear, then, this crown I set upon your dear head,
and I shall perform the sacrifice in your honor.

(*They exit,* CHORUS *rises and confers among themselves.*)

CHORUS: Who can believe such things? The wonder
of love exceeds our fondest hopes.
The brothers are reconciled, their anger
melted like metal in fire. Strangers
may keep their hatred going, but brothers
are bound to each other forever. It does us
good to see that it can happen,
restoring our faith in human kindness.

FIRST CHORISTER: Hatred can come to eclipse the steady
light of affection's lamp, and in darkness
men will grope, flail out, afraid
to show their fear. The world turns hostile,
and enemies everywhere menace with fleets
of warships, parading cavalry squadrons,
in battle's terrible panoply.
THE thirst for blood is a dreadful thirst,
but Love can stay the brandished weapon,
disarm the combatants, take their hands
and join them once more in peace and friendship.

SECOND CHORISTER: See what the god has contrived for us here!
Throughout Mycenae, mothers were frightened
and clasped their innocent babes to their bosoms
as wives feared for their husbands in arms
and awaiting orders. The sword in the corner
that had rusted in peace was glinting bright
in the menace of imminent action. The walls
we'd long neglected, we reinforced

and we strengthened the gates with bars of iron.
Worse than war is the fear of war,
but now that cloud is gone from the sky
and a civil peace is restored to the city.

CHORUS: It happens this way, when the raging sea
and whipping wind batter the boats.
The sailors who make for a safe harbor
can hardly imagine that lee shore
they struggle to reach beyond the walls
of water that crash down on the decks.
But then, somehow delivered and moored,
they make fast and can barely remember
the salty taste of terror that burned
all that time at the backs of their throats.

FIRST CHORISTER: What emotion endures? Pain
fades, thank heaven, but also pleasure.
Time turns fortunes topsy-turvy,
and he whose head is crowned with laurel,
he whose hand is clasped on a scepter,
he will bend his knee and grovel
down in the dust before the man
he'd thought of before as beneath his notice.

SECOND CHORISTER: Let us therefore try to maintain
our balance, remembering modesty's lesson.
Success and prosperity come unbidden
and undeserved, as their opposites also
happen at random. No one should preen
in self-congratulation, and no one
ought to despair. Whom the rising sun
shines on in triumph, the setting sun
may wash in the long shadows of woe.

CHORUS: Let us all learn these difficult lessons,
keeping in mind that any power
must yield in turn to a greater power.
No man ought to enjoy the moment
without giving thanks to the gods, who in turn
acknowledge the Fates' powers. No man
ought to give in to despair either
for we remember we live like leaves
on the whim of the fickle winds that any
moment can bear us up or dash us
down from whatever height we have clung to

having persuaded ourselves it is home,
where we belong and what we have earned.
Clotho braids the skeins of our lives
weaving weal and woe together.
No man, therefore, ought to rely
on tomorrow or even this afternoon
as the swift wheel of fortune continues
its dizzying whirl.

MESSENGER: (*Enters in a great hurry*)
Good sirs, I beg your pardons.
I come to tell a fearful thing. A shame!
Evento Pelops and Tantalus' house, a scandal!
I can hardly bring myself to impose upon you
with the dreadful words!

FIRST CHORISTER: *(Patiently)* Sir, tell us your news!

MESSENGER: What kind of world is it, what kind of place
are we living in, where such vile things can happen?
Far beyond the pale of civilization,
out in the Scythian wastes, such monstrous crimes
might, I suppose take place. But this is Greece!

FIRST CHORISTER: (*Less patiently*)
Whatever this evil is, we pray you, tell us!

MESSENGER: I will, I promise. Once I've composed myself,
and have mastered my terror, I will. But still, I can see it,
a ghastly image seared on my eyes. I close them,
but still that image persists. I would rather flee
to the other end of the world than impose upon you
the scar I bear.

FIRST CHORISTER: You impose ON us, sir, with doubt!
Tell us what makes you shudder. Say who did
this dreadful deed you can barely report. Tell us!

MESSENGER: At the topmost peak of the citadel, the palace
of Pelops looks to the south. You know where I mean,
where the wall of the mountain becomes the palace wall
that looks down on the town in what seems like menace,
daring the insolent townsmen below to return
its menacing stare. Inside is the great hall there
splendid with columns painted in all those colors.
Beyond that hall, the palace extends to the north

and follows around the hill, but hidden within
those courtyards, pavilions, and colonnades, at the heart
and innermost retreat, is the ancient grove
where the old trees are safe from the pruner's knife,
a bower of yew and gloomy ilex and oak
towering high overhead. Into that quiet
shaded place, the sons of Tantalus come
in moments of grief or doubt, for calm and solace,
and here, too, they have hung their votive gifts:
war trumpets, fragments of chariots, trophies
of battle. The place, we may say, is a private shrine,
and in its silence one may imagine the cries
of warfare as well as other and worse outrages—
crimes of the tribe, for example. The coronet
in the Phrygian style of Pelops is hanging there,
along with his richly embroidered robe. In the shade,
a spring arises, bubbling water as dark
as if from the Styx itself, on which the gods
are said to take their oaths. There are also stories
of how, at night, in the darkness, there at the pool
the spring has made, you can hear moans of the dead
welling up from the source of those deep waters.
Ghosts are said to howl, and terrible creatures
that never lived make frightening visitation,
chilling the marrows of rationalists and skeptics.
Flashes of eerie light float through the air,
and the branches of trees flicker and glow, inflamed
but there's no fire. Howls that could be from dogs
resound in dissonant clamor, but no dogs there.
The rooms of the palace that overlook that grove,
nobody uses. At night the place is a horror,
but even at dawn the taint persists, continues
as if night clung to the trees that were sanctuary,
even at high noon, to the sinister spirits.
Here, the oracle speaks, announcing the Fates
in a pained moan. And here, Atreus came,
dragging his brother's sons to the decked altars. . . .
But who could describe, who could believe what happened?
He binds their hands behind their backs. They let him.
What do they know? He drapes the purple braiding
upon their foreheads. They still have no idea
that anything's odd. There's incense, wine, a knife,
and the salted meal to sprinkle over the victims.
It's all correct, an observance of ritual, only
where are the victims? The ox? The unblemished lamb?

FIRST CHORISTER: Who takes the knife in hand?

MESSENGER: He does, himself.
He serves as the priest, officiating, himself
at the nightmarish rite, that vile and bloody observance.
He chants the dirge as the grove begins to tremble,
its balefulness now surpassed by the ceremony
that now befouls it further, forever. The earth
shudders as if in revulsion from what happens,
and the skies recoil, meteors shooting their murk
in the sinister quarter. He sets them upon the altar
and pours the wine upon the burning fire,
but the wine as it spills is turning to clotted blood.
The crown on the king's head slips, falls down,
and he puts it back, but it slips again and again.
The ivory statues weep in dreadful portent,
but Atreus is not moved. He seems to be pleased,
defying the menacing gods with prayers like curses.
Only his eyes move as he stands at the altar
looking at this one and that, like a Ganges tigress
that cannot decide which ot a herd of bullocks
to pounce on first with bared and terrible fangs.
He hesitates, or perhaps just savors the moment,
delightfully pregnant, knowing it will bring forth
savage revenge.

SECOND CHORISTER: And which one does he strike?

MESSENGER: The pride of place goes to the eldest, the nephew
who bears the grandfather's name—it's Tantalus first.

FIRST CHORISTER: How did he bear this terrible death?

MESSENGER: How?
He did not plead. He knew all prayer was vain.
The king thrust in with the sword, making a wound
so deep the hand on the sword hilt touched the skin
of the young boy s neck. He pulled the blade back out,
and the corpse still stood for a moment, upright, balanced,
and wavering crazily, as if to choose which way
it wanted to fall. Then it collapsed on the uncle.
He let it fall to the ground and dragged Plisthenes
to the same altar and cut the head off* clean.
It rolled away, its mouth agape in a scream
that made not even the shadow of any sound.

FIRST CHORISTER: And after this double murder, did he not spare
the third, the youngest child? Could he show no mercy?

MESSENGER: They say a lion that falls on a herd will kill
even after its hunger is sated. The blood
acts like a drug to put the beast in a frenzy
to kill, crazy with gore and eager for more
and more. And I can believe it, having seen
how Atreus, now pure savagery, turned on the third
and, waving the bloodied sword overhead, struck,
driving clear through the body. The sword point entered
beneath the lad s sternum, and came out near the spine.
He fell on the already bloodied altar, and new
blood flowed from both wounds.

FIRST CHORISTER: Beyond belief!

MESSENGER: You're horrified? If the crime had ended there,
that would have been—in relative terms—a blessing.

FIRST CHORISTER: In relative terms? What are you saying? What worse
can we even imagine?

MESSENGER: But Atreus had imagined,
and thus far it was only the preparation.

FIRST CHORISTER: What else could he do? Throw their mangled corpses
to the scavenging beasts? Deny them the rites of the dead?

MESSENGER: O, would that he had done so! If only dogs
had gnawed their bones! What happened is so much worse
that what you consider dreadful appears to me
the dream of pity itself. Better that crows
should have pecked their flesh. The declension of horror is such
that some of the smaller outrages become
pleasant to contemplate. Their bodies thrown
in a ditch by the side of the road where their father could see them . . .
that would have been no more than a lapse of decorum
compared to this. Atreus sliced them open,
tore out their quivering vitals, the little hearts
twitching with life's last spark. Then, like a butcher,
he hacked the limbs from the trunks, cracked their bones,
and stripped off the flesh he fixed on cooking spits
and set on the fire to turn and drip. Their organs
he tossed into kettles to stew over fires that gagged
at what they were made to do. The livers sizzled,

and the logs beneath them crackled in an outraged
antiphon beyond all imagination.
The smoke that rose was black and pitchy and stung
the eyes as if to remind them what weeping was.
The sun itself shrank from what it beheld
and fled the sky, but too late not to witness
the noxious feast Atreus brought to the table.
The father carves his sons' bodies and chews
flesh of his own flesh. He wipes his lips
with a napkin and takes a sip of wine to wash down
meat that has stuck in his throat. The single mercy
for poor Thyestes, at this point, is in his total
ignorance—-and that can't possibly last.
In despair, one tries to imagine time turning back
to run the other way. The stunned sun shudders
and flees eastward, undoing what has been done.
But nothing can blot out these ghastly events.
The blow has fallen, and what awaits is the pain
of realization of how the world is sick,
mad and sick, that such vile things can happen.

There's nothing to do now but wait for the groans.
(*During this speech, the light has been fading almost to darkness*)

CHORUS: What kind of world do we live in? How
does a man bear the brutal blows
a life entails? These evils await us
like adders, sunning themselves on rocks.
The sun should flee from the sky, and sky
shrink from the foul earth beneath it
before permitting such profanation
to poison the landscape. Close your eyes,
but the terrible images still persist
as if the gates of Hades had opened
and rotting bodies strolled in the streets,
their cerements streaming foulness behind them.

FIRST CHORISTER: The Giants return to wage their war,
Tityos wrathful and Typhoeus crazed
and strong enough to throw off those mountains
that have held his huge body captive.

SECOND CHORISTER: One need not look so far to find
parallel cases. At home, in Rome,
someone has his own half-brother
poisoned at dinner. Everyone sees

but says nothing and does nothing.
Then he murders his own mother,
and nothing happens, nothing at all.
The sun continues to rise in the east
and travel its usual course across
a clear baby-blue heaven, but how?
Is there no justice? Are there no gods
to keep such foulness away from the world?

FIRST CHORISTER: A man's soul, sickened to death
from what he has seen, cries out to whatever
power he still believes in, protesting
that nature continues its usual course.
The sun and the moon are indifferent. His own
body's organs persist in the stupid
business of living, while all he wants
is that everything stop, the day, the seasons,
and his own heartbeat and bitter breath.

SECOND CHORISTER: If life must go on, let it at least
bear witness to horror. The world should provide
cataclysms, earthquakes, ruin.
The caricatures of nighttime horrors
should walk about in broad daylight.
Those dreary creatures whose unconcern
affronts the intelligence . . . let them suffer,
let them share in the general outrage
and pay in pain for the sin of indifference.
The walls of houses crack, and the people
run in the streets, crying in panic . . .
as well they should. As they ought to have done
from the very first moment when madness
seized the world.

FIRST CHORISTER: We know how it is.
Everything turns around, and evil
becomes the standard. Pain is real
and everything else is merely a moment
of respite, irrelevant. Scars are the only
parts of the body to trust. The rest
of the smooth and innocent flesh is merely
waiting to feel the fire, the steel,
and send the news of pain to the brain,
which all along was waiting to hear it.

CHORUS: Let us correct the calendar. Feasts

will be no more, but only fast days
marking the marvels of what we have borne,
what we have not given into yet,
although there were moments when each of us prayed
for release at last from the trials and torments.
The coming of spring, the heat of summer,
the time of harvest in autumn, the cold
winter weather in one or another
occasions some recollection of grief
the look of the day brings back. He holds
his hand to his jaw as if he had toothache,
or buries his head in his arms in pain.

FIRST CHORISTER: Perhaps the gods are only preparing
that dreadful cleansing they have it in mind
to visit upon us. One learns to long
for such a conclusion, when every blade
of grass is an outrage, a green affront.
One wants the satisfaction of seeing
justice done. However oppressive
the penalties are, the world deserves
more and worse. The life we hate
wants some extravagant extirpation.

CHORUS: Some crimes can be so heinous
they spread their taint beyond the one
who struck the blow. The blemish extends
out of the house and along the decorous
streets to the fields beyond the gates
of the town walls. Total strangers
are guilty of having lived and survived,
contemporaries of absolute evil.
Mixed in with our grief is guilt
of the eyes for having seen, of the ears
for having heard such abomination,
for what kind of person, receiving such news,
would not have much preferred to die?

(ATREUS *enters, exulting. He is accompanied by two* SERVANTS.)

ATREUS: I know now how the gods must feel. Their power
sings along my nerves. I thrill to their giddy
altitude, as if I peered down from heaven
to watch as the tiny figures of men scurry
on what they take to be paths of important purpose.
I have accomplished all that I prayed to the gods

to let me achieve. What I had longed for and dreamt,
I saw in the waking world, the father feasting
on the flesh of his sons. The gods granted my plea
and then, as if astonished by what they had done,
fled. No god remains, but only myself,
my pure will imposing itself on the world
in all the detail they wanted not to witness.
It doesn't matter, so long as Thyestes sees,
and, pleased as I am, my last delight remains
that perfect consummation of my scheme—
I wait now for the sun of his understanding
to rise at last in a crimson drawn from the blood
of his three sons.
(*To* SERVANTS)
Throw open the temple doors
and let my remarkable banqueting hall be shown.
(*Again, to himself*)
I still have the heads to display, to prove the truth
of words he won't believe from my mouth. Theirs,
mute now, will incontrovertibly speak.
And then will his well-fed cheeks turn ashen, pale
as the blood flees. But I have prepared him drink,
to restore his strength.
(*The doors are opened, and* THYESTES *is revealed at table*)
It is lovely to be a man,
even better to be a king, but a god,
immortal, invincible, limitless in the power
to turn thought to event, that's best of all.
To see him wretched is gratifying, but still
it is even better to watch as the wretchedness happens,
the beautiful change as, when an animal, quick
and alive, becomes, amazingly, mute meat.
His dinner done, he toys now with his wine,
blood-red, flavored with real blood, and he drinks!

THYESTES: (*He sits at the banquet table, surrounded by empty plates, and holding a goblet*)
To be home at last, safe and secure,
all my wanderings past, my woes
almost forgotten . . . I've come to rest,
free of ambition that drove me once
and quite content to enjoy the plain.
The kingdom's riches that tempted me then
seem to have shrunk. Those golden baubles
are nothing but toys. The real riches
are those of the soul, the talent to take
the small satisfactions that come to hand—

or can if it is not clenched to a fist,
or clutching a swords hilt or a scepter.
Still, I am apprehensive, the worries
that hounded me then are faithful still,
and I cannot believe in the peace of the present
moment, the respite. Chance has turned me
skittish and shy like an ill-used dog.
Even here in the palace's safety,
I'm apprehensive. I wait for a blow
to shatter the calm and its pretty illusions.
Do the flowers that wreathe my brow mock me?
Too used to bitter tears, I bridle
at what's too strange to be understood.
Will these rich robes I put on be rent
in lamentation? I do not trust them!
I've no reason to fret, no cause
to suspect that the Fates are waiting to show me
my old face in the mirror, contorted
by weeping and ranting, barely human.
Surely the Furies must show me mercy
after such long and faithful attendance.
But it doesn't work that way, the talent
one learns from a craft is what one becomes,
and what I have learned as a faithful apprentice
is how to grieve. Like a wary sailor,
I look to a fair sky and a calm
sea and see the portents of storms
coming from nowhere, walls of water
breaking over the puny ships.
I already hear the cries of the drowning
and taste the brine they swallow, salty
and bitter as tears. I trust my brother.
Why then does my hand tremble
holding the cup of wine? Why should I
fear that disaster is crouched in the corner
waiting to pounce and fasten its fangs
into my heart? I cannot help it.
Knowing better, I ought to distinguish
between what's real and what I imagine
and learn at last how to be happy.

ATREUS: (*Advancing toward* THYESTES)
Good brother! Let us keep this day for feasting
for all time and rejoice in the bond of peace
between us now that secures the throne we share.

THYESTES: I have eaten and drunk my fill of food and wine.
All that remains to perfect my content and delight
is that my sons may join in the celebration.

ATREUS: I assure you, they're here. Your sons are with you always,
safe in your bosom. They cannot be taken from you.
I promise that you and they shall never be parted.
Those boys will sustain you, nourish and fill you
with a father's pride. They'll satisfy you, I swear!
I am just now come from the children's table. They share
in the festive meal. I'll summon them here for you.
Take, meanwhile, this ancient cup, refilled.

THYESTES: I accept with pleasure your generous gifts. Let wine
be poured to the household gods and then be drunk. . . .
But what's the matter? My hand isn't right. The cup
is heavy, hard to lift. I can scarcely hold it
or carry the wine to my lips. And the wine's peculiar. . . .
It doesn't want to be drunk but sloshes and spills
as if it were something alive. And the candles gutter.
What has come over me? I'm not well. There's something
terribly wrong. The light is fading, and shadows
menace. I'm frightened. Whatever it is, I pray
it may spare MY brother. My sons, I hope, are safe.
The gods are angry with me—I've sins to atone for—
but my sons are innocent children. Let them be
brought! I want my children. Please!

ATREUS: I'll bring them,
and never shall you be parted again, I swear.

(ATREUS *exits*)

THYESTES: I tremble! I'm feeling sick. My heart is beating
fast, in terror. Are they all right? My children!
If they are well, I do not fear for myself.
Where are they?
(ATREUS *returns with a large salver*)
You said you'd bring them. Are they safe?

ATREUS: Open your arms to receive them. Here they are.
(ATREUS *removes the cover)*
You recognize your sons' adoring faces?

THYESTES: I recognize my brother! Oh, gods!
How can the earth endure so vile a crime!

Crack, and let him fall into hell. Chaos
must snatch him away, the king and kingdom with him.
The whole damned palace, let it be razed,
and all of Mycenae. You and I should be dead,
should have died long ago. This accursèd house
ought to have been exterminated like vermin,
or thrown into some abyss, some bottomless pit
where souls guilty of crimes less heinous than ours
could tread on our heads with their filthy feet. Gods!
But there are no gods! The earth lies there, like a
lump of stupid rock. And the gods have all gone away,
leaving us here abandoned, like little children
suddenly orphaned. We call out, and our voices
echo in emptiness and mock our grief.

ATREUS: But be of good cheer! I have brought the children you loved.
You see how your brother obliges. Take them. Kiss!
Nibble their little lips. Embrace all three!

THYESTES: Is this what you swore? Is this your honor? Your trust?
Is this how you put our hate behind us? My brother!
I ask you, nevertheless, a last favor,
which you may grant, hating me nonetheless.
Let me bury their bodies. Give me back
the rest of their corpses that I may see them burned
and perform their rites. You cannot refuse me that.

ATREUS: Whatever remains of them, brother, you have. What does not,
you also have.

THYESTES: What is this riddle? Where are they?
Are they prey for the wild birds now? Food for the beasts?

ATREUS: One might say. They were, just now, your dinner.

THYESTES: *(Moans)* It was this that shamed the gods. From this, they fled.
And the light fled and the candles guttered. What words
are there? What gods to hear them? I see the heads,
the remains' leavings. Their flesh seethes in my own.
I gag on my crime. Brother give me your sword
that I may cut my belly open and free them.
But a sharp sword from you would be a mercy.
Contrive some other death, then. Crush me with stones.
Do what you will, but release me from this torment.
When I descend to meet the shades, they will shudder
in fear and disgust at what goes on up here

in what they thought was the world of the light. Such crimes
the beasts don't know, nor the savages out in Asia
roaming the rocky steppes. What have I done?
Whatever there was between us, this is wrong,
disproportionate, crazy! Even a crime
ought to have some logic to it.

ATREUS: A crime
ought to have limits beforehand. I agree with you there.
But this is repayment of crime, is vengeance, is different,
and even this isn't enough. I'd have rather
poured the hot blood fresh from their wounds
down your retching throat that you could have drunk
the gore of your still-living sons. I hurried.
It was all too quick, too easy. I drove my sword
into their bodies there at the altar. They died
at once—and never knew what happened after.
They could not see me tear their bodies apart,
didn't watch as I stuck their livers on spits
and roasted them over the fire, could not hear
the sputtering sounds of cooking. And neither did you!
I should have preferred that you watch me prepare your banquet,
slicing the meat and arranging it there on the platter.
I should have delighted to see you chew and swallow,
knowing what food you were eating.

THYESTES: O great gods!
How can you not hear this? How can you stand it?
I pray you all, attend. Gods of the earth,
gods of the sky, gods of the sea, see
what has been done here, and not at all for my sake—
for I am beyond all help or comfort—but yours,
for the sake of your own honors, the sake of the world
you rule, send down to us your drastic, cleansing
anger. With fire, burn away this filth!
Set the winds to work to scour this blackness
white again. The sky should blaze with lightning
and the torrents pour to purge and purify
this blot on creation. Let the thunder clap
and show again your fury that undid Giants
and tamed the earth. And do it now! I beg.
Or, better, I defy you. I dare you! Do
to him or me the worst you can do. With flame
of your lightning bolts, strike this breast to burn
in a proper rite the bodies of my three children.
Blaze and cleanse, I say, or admit forever

there's nothing there. Nothing but black space,
in which case we must worship night and cold,
and learn to love death and adore corruption,
for either this is real and all the rest
has been a delusion, a poet's pretty conceit,
a children's story, or else the world we live in
is yours, the real world, and this an offense
unparalleled on earth.

ATREUS: Very nicely said.
It's sweet music, better than any praise
I could imagine. My labors are not in vain,
as they might have been without these complaints of yours
I delight to hear.

THYESTES: What was my children's sin?

ATREUS: That they were yours. And now are my own sons mine,
restored to me-—if you bedded my wife or not.
Your sons were surely yours, and restored to you.

THYESTES:I call on the gods who protect the innocent.

ATREUS: Gods?
Why not call on the marriage gods?

THYESTES: You punish
a crime with a worse crime.

ATREUS: You're jealous, I think,
and sorry you couldn't have done to me what I
have done to you. But you couldn't. Cook my children
to feed them to me? But what if they were yours?
That was what stayed your villain's hand.

THYESTES: To the gods
I commend you for their eternal curse.

ATREUS: To your sons'
shades I offer you up-—as I just offered
them to you. I wish a long life to you all!

(*They glare at each other for a moment. Then, blackout.*)

# Ariel

Marina Carr

## ACT ONE

*Curtain up. Lights up as* Fermoy, Frances, Ariel, Elaine, Boniface, Stephen *and* Sarah *stand around a birthday cake on the table. The cake is lit with sixteen candles. All are singing:*

All 'And so say all of us,
And so say all of us,
For she's a jolly good fella,
For she's a jolly good fella,
For she's a jolly good fella,
And so say all of us.'

Ariel *blows out the candles, claps and cheers.*

Frances Happy birthday, sweetheart. *(Kisses her)*

Boniface Sweet sixteen and never been kissed. *(Kisses her)*

Fermoy We hope, we have our doubts.

Ariel What ya don't know won't bother ya. Does this mane I get the keys a the car, Daddy?

Fermoy Mebbe ud manes ya get your own little banger.

Ariel Whah?

Fermoy Look ouh the winda.

Ariel *runs to window followed by* Elaine.

Ariel Ah, Daddy, you're mad, you're mad.

Fermoy *gives her the keys, lifts her up, sings to her, dancing around the room.*

Fermoy 'Whin first I seen the love ligh in your eye
I thought the world held nough buh jiy for me
And aven though we drifted far apart

I love ya as I loved ya,
Whin ya were sweet,
Whin ya were sweet sixteen.'

*(Puts her down)* You're noh a child anymore buh we'll hould onta ya long as we can, won't we, Frances?

FRANCES Leh go, Stephen, leh go a me dress. *(To* FERMOY*)* Yeah, a cuurse we will.

ARIEL Can I go drivin now?

FERMOY Were ya drinkin wine?

ARIEL Just a glass.

FRANCES Yeah, come an, I'll go for a spin wud ya.

*Exit* ARIEL, FRANCES, STEPHEN.

SARAH Anywan for cake?

FRANCES When we come back.

SARAH *(Exiting, muttering to herself)* Was up half the nigh makin thah. Whin I was a girl we had wan cake ah Christmas, now ud's cake all the time, cake and more cake, swear ud was Versailles yees were brough up in.

FERMOY Elaine, g'wan wud your mother, good girl.

ELAINE Sing a song to me, Daddy, sing sweet sixteen to me.

FERMOY Whin you're sweet sixteen, darlin, then I'll sing sweet sixteen to you.

ELAINE Sure thah's years away.

FERMOY Ah g'wan for a drive in Ariel's new car, good girl.

ELAINE Will ya gimme a puff a your cigar if I go?

FERMOY Whin ya come back I'll give ya a puff.

ELAINE And a swig a brandy?

FERMOY Two puffs and two swigs if ya lave me in peace for five minutes.

ELAINE Alrigh so. I'll be back shortly to hould ya to your word.

*Exit* ELAINE.

FERMOY I've no doubt ya will. God, they'd drive ya mad, kids. I spind the whole day duckin them.

BONIFACE And me thinkin ya were an adorin father.

FERMOY And I am, an adorin father who doesn't know what to do wud em. I can't waih for Mondays. Wakinds should be banned. More paple gets murdered on Sundays than any other day a the wake. Whah does thah mane?

BONIFACE I suppose ud's wan way a passin the time after the roast beef and the trifle.

FERMOY *(Pouring brandy for himself)* Ya still on the wagon?

BONIFACE Liver like a newborn. For whah, I ask meself.

FERMOY *(Pouring a coke for* BONIFACE*)* And how's things up ah the monastery?

BONIFACE The last a the Mohicans. I'm the ony wan under sixty. Spind me days changin nappies, ferryin thim to hospitals, funeral parlours, checkin they take their medication, givin em glasses a whiskey to shuh em up, breakin up fights over armchairs and toffees. They go ah wan another like three-year-aulds. Caugh Celestius goin for the back of Aquinus' head wud a hommer last wake. I swiped ud ouh a hees hand just in the nick a time. Noh today, I says to Celestius, noh today, and he gives me this avil grin and slinks off. And Aquinus manewhile is oblivious to the whole thing, he's dribblin and droolin away to hees horse. He has this horse goes everywhere wud him.

FERMOY Noh a rale horse?

BONIFACE No, no, ud's all in hees addled little head. Him and the horse does everthin together, makes room in the bed for him and all. There's a place seh for him ah the table, betwane me and Aquinus. No wan else'll sih beside the horse. Ya'd want to see Aquinus fadin him rashers. I don't enquire whah goes on in bed betwane em. I'm afraid he'd tell me. And Bonaventura is in intensive care, thanks be to the lord God.

FERMOY He's the wan calls ya Mammy?

BONIFACE Thah's him. And whin he's lucid he's worse. Wint inta see him yesterda, gev him a Padre Pio relic and he flings ud back ah me. Whah do I want wud Padre Pio's britches, says he. Well, is there anhin I can get ya, says I. There is, he says, me youh and Billie Holida. And then he goes into a swirl abouh bein cremahed, thah he's noh a Catholic anymore, thah he never belaved in the first place, and him takin chunks ouha the chalice hees whole life. And despihe all the lunacy they cry like babbies at nigh, hare em whingin in their cells. Some part of em knows ud's over and they goh ud all wrong and still they hang on.

FERMOY Well, wouldn't you?

BONIFACE Apparently I am. Are ya goin to swing ud this time?

FERMOY Ud'll be a dogfigh. ,

BONIFACE Aye, Hannafin's mug is everywhere, he's some cowbiy, had the nerve to come canvassin me ah the monastery.

FERMOY Whah had he to say for heeself?

BONIFACE Asked me to talk sinse to you. Tould me to tell ya ya don't stand a chance, that you're ony makin a fool a yourself.

FERMOY Four votes. Four. That's all was in ud last time.

BONIFACE He still has the whole machine behind him. You're on your own.

FERMOY I've God behind me and what's a little civil war coven compared to God backin ya. I'll geh in this time alrigh. Been havin powerful drames lately. Drames of a conqueror.

BONIFACE Have ya now?

FERMOY Oh, aye. Dreamt last nigh I was dirtin wud Alexander the Greah, Napoleon and Caesar, and we all had tigers' feeh under the whihe linen tablecloth. Ud was brillint. And ya know thah famous portrait a Napoleon, up on hees whihe horse, the fah legs of him diggin inta the flanks, off to destriy the world? Well, I can't stop dramin abouh thah picture, ony I'm the wan on the whihe horse insteada Napoleon.

BONIFACE Noh another wan wud a horse. You should take up wud Aquinus.

FERMOY Laugh away. Me and God's on a wan to wan.

BONIFACE Oh, excuse me. And whin did this greah event occur?
Ud wasn't in the papers.

FERMOY Ya think I'm jokin. I'm tellin ya I've direct access to him.

BONIFACE Well, you're the first I meh thah has. Tell him to scahher a few bars a gold in my pah next time yees are houldin hands.

FERMOY The last person ya should ever talk to abouh God is wan a the religious. Yees are the most cynical, rational, mathemahical shower I ever cem across whin ud comes to God.

BONIFACE a have to be mathemahical when you're dalin wud mystery.

FERMOY Well, yees have him ruined for all true belavers.

BONIFACE What do ya expect? Facts are he hasn't been seen for over two thousand year, for all we know he's left the solar system. We're goin on hearsay, gossip, the buuk. Times I wonder was he ever here.

FERMOY Well, if he wasn't none of ud makes sinse.

BONIFACE There's many belaves wasn't him med the earth ah all, thah ud was Satan and hees fallen armies, thah we were masterminded in hell, only Lucifer's pawns to geh ah God. Now I wouldn't go thah far meself, ih'd be too frightenin if thah was the case, buh for you to claim the privelege a God's ear is ouhrageous. Ud's blasphemy. Does paple belave in blasphemy anymore?

FERMOY I do.

BONIFACE Well, if ya do why're ya claimin God's talkin to ya?

FERMOY I'm claimin natin, forget the whole thing.

BONIFACE No, ya've me curious now. And whah does he say to ya?

FERMOY I'm noh tellin ya, forgeh ud, cheers. *(Raises his glass, drinks)*

BONIFACE I've offindid ya.

FERMOY I'm sick a ya talkin down to me from the heights a your canon law and the foosterins a the Pope a Rome and your cosy mehaphysics and your charihy. For all your religion ya know natin abouh the nature a God.

BONIFACE And you do?

FERMOY I know a couple a things.

BONIFACE And tell me, what's he like, this God a yours?

FERMOY Oh, he's beauhiful. When he throws hees head back hees hair gets tangled in the stars, and in hees hands are seven moons thah he juggles like worry beads. Hees eyes is shards of obsidian, hees skin is turquoise, and hees mouth is a staggerin red, whah the first red musta been before ud all started fadin. I'm noh capturin him righ, for how can ya parse whah is perfect.

BONIFACE My God is an auld fella in a tent, addicted to broccoli.

FERMOY No, God is young. He's so young. He's on fire for us, heaven reelin wud hees rage at not bein among us, the eternihy of eternihy hauntin him. Time manes natin to him. He rises from an afternoon nap and twinty centuries has passed.

BONIFACE No, no, no, he never slapes. Christianihy is based on God never slapin. You're wrong there, God does noh slape.

FERMOY My God slapes.

BONIFACE How d'ya know, did ya tuck him in? Rade him a bedtime story?

FERMOY Didn't I see him, a mountain slapin on a mountain.

BONIFACE Ah, you've had too much brandy. FERMOY Don't you try pullin rank wud me, wud your cross and your robes and your broccoli God. I entered the landscape a God before you, long before. You can't tell me anhin abouh God.

BONIFACE Ya talkin abouh Ma, a'ya?

FERMOY No, I'm noh talkin abouh Ma. Why d'ya have to brin her up every time?

BONIFACE Do I brin her up every time?

FERMOY Wudouhfail.

BONIFACE And is thah a crime? FERMOY Was thirty-five year ago, Boniface. She's gone, she's gone.

BONIFACE And whah an exih.

FERMOY She was never the suurt was goin to die in her bed.

BONIFACE She'd a died in her bed if she'd been leh ... I remember goin home to see you wan time, soon after, and Auntie Sarah was sittin ah the table wearin Ma's clothes, the hair up in wan of her slides, prancin round the kitchen like ud was hers.

FERMOY Someone had to wash the dishes.

BONIFACE Now ud's comin ouh.

FERMOY Whah?

BONIFACE Thah I didn't lave the novitiate to look after ya.

FERMOY Auntie Sarah looked after me fine, fierce good to me, a packet a biscuits and a bottle a red lemonade every nigh before I wint to bed, whah more could ya ask for?

BONIFACE A wonder ya've a tooth in your head. No, shoulda been me looked after ya, ony I was a maniac for religion ah the time. I goh the full benefih a Ma's christianihy, no douh abouh thah, a novice ah seventeen. Ya know ud never occurred to me to go agin her. At laste ya were spared thah, buh I shoulda looked after ya.

FERMOY I grew up, didn't I? Furthest thing from me mind righ now. I've an election to win. D'you think I stand a chance?

BONIFACE Hannafin has the core vohe. He's held thah seat for twinty year. Be hard budge him.

FERMOY Nearly done ud last time. This time I will.

BONIFACE Whah makes ya so sure?

FERMOY Horse sinse and God. That's all ya nade to get by in this world, horse sinse and God. That's whah goh me this far and thah's what'll take me to the moon.

BONIFACE Ya may geh past Hannafin first.

FERMOY Ah, ud's noh Hannafin's the crux ah all, ud's meself, alias meself. Hannafin's a gombeen, like the rest of em. Why do they all want to be nice? What's so greah abouh bein liked? Am I missin somethin here? Swear ud was beahification they were after and em all cut-throats in their own kitchens. All chirpin the wan tune like there's no other—aqual wages, creches in the workplace, no ceilin on the women, the pace process, a leg up for the poor, the handicapped, the refugees, the tinkers, the tachers, the candlestick makers. In Sparta they were left on the side a the hill and that's where I'll lave em when I've the reins. I swear to God I'm goin to brin in a new religion, no more guilt, no more sorrow, no more good girls and good biys, just the unstoppable blood pah a the soul.

BONIFACE Ya wont win an election on thah speech.

FERMOY Migh surprise ya to know how many agrays wud me. The earth's over, paple knows thah in their bones, ozone layer in tahhers, oceans gone to sewer, whole world wan big landfill a dirty nappies. We're goin to lave this place in ashes like the shower on Mars.

BONIFACE I don't belave in much anymore. Gardenin, if ud was puh to me and me back to the wall I'd say I belave in cornflowers. I'd like to think whahever happens us thah this ground will survive us.

FERMOY The age a cornflowers is dead and gone. Last two thousand year a complahe farce. Well, ud's nearly over. We'll pick up where we left off.

BONIFACE And where's thah?

FERMOY The mortal sins is back in fashion. Welcome back, we missed yees. Age a compassion had uds turn, never took rooh. Well, way past time to banish the dregs to heaven's dungeon. The earth is ours wance more and noh before time.

BONIFACE If thah's your manifesto I may start prayin ya don't geh in.

FERMOY Ud's mine for the takin, I know ud is, all ud nades on my part is a sacrifice.

BONIFACE Whah suurt of a sacrifice?

Fermoy A sacrifice to God.

Boniface Buh whah suurt?

Fermoy The only suurt he acknowledges. Blood.

Boniface Blood?

Fermoy This thing's been edgin me to the cliff all year. And there's more. If I don't offer up this sacrifice he demands, he's goin to take ud anyway. And me for good measure. Whichever road I take is crooked. Thah's the price a God. If I make the sacrifice, then ud's all mine. Buh the cost, the cost. Impossible. Buh if I refuse this sacrifice, I'm facin the grave meself and, worse, facin him after refusin me destiny and, worse agin, after refusin him the wan thing he asks as payment for this enchanted life.

Boniface Spakin a blood, ours is streaked, Fermoy. You know thah well as me. The auld fella.

Fermoy This is different. We're talkin a different league here. We're talkin whah I was puh on this earth for.

Boniface Nowan knows whah they're on the earth for.

Fermoy I do. I'm on this earth to rule. Was born knowin ud. Timidihy has held me back till now. Ud'U hould me back no longer. I refuse to spind any more a me life on the margins. I refuse to succumb to an early exih. I'll give him whah he wants for ud's hees in the first place anyway.

Boniface And whah is ud he wants?

Fermoy I tould ya, blood and more blood, blood till we're dry as husks, then pound us down, spread us like salt on the land, begin the experiment over, on different terms next time.

Boniface We've moved beyond the God a Job, Fermoy. Two thousand year a civilization has taken us to a different place. Now I'm noh sayin this is Utopia or anywhere near ud, buh we have advanced a few small steps along the way. And for you to call up the auld God is terrifyin. I don't care how beauhi-ful he appears. He's a wolf and ud's a wolf you'll be growlin wud if ya dredge him up. You're playin dangerous games here. God does noh do dales, ah laste the God I know doesn't. I mane whah exactly is this blood sacrifice? Is ud some suurt a pagan calf ritual or are we talkin somethin far older and more sinister here?

Fermoy Can't a man air the festerins of hees soul withouh bein convicted?

Boniface No, I don't think he can. Thah's why there's such a thing as custody a the tongue. Thah's why our thoughts is silent, so we can do away wud em before they're spoken. And ud's a mighy short journey from say in a thing to doin ud.

Fermoy Ah, forget the whole bleddy business.

Boniface Ih'd fit yourself behher to forgeh ud.

Fermoy Alrigh. Alrigh. Ud's forgotten. Gone. I'll lave ud wud the nigh where ud belongs and hope ud'll lave me. In the manetime I've an election comin and I've a problem wud the hospitals, wonderin could ya help me.

Boniface If I can.

Fermoy Ud's all the wans dyin in their beds wud their faces to the wall, nade their votes.

Boniface Ah, would ya lave em alone.

Fermoy Ya think I want to be botherin thim? There's only a spider's leg between me and Hannafin. Whah would ya say to a dyin person thah'd make em vote for ya?

Boniface Say natin ony sih and talk to em.

Fermoy I'm noh the Sisters a Mercy, talk to em abouh whah?

Boniface I'd'n know … heaven, mebbe?

FERMOY Whah? Say natin abouh votin ony soother em wud eternihy? Alrigh, I've a good workin knowledge of eternihy. I'll melt em wud pictures of uds silver avenues and uds houses a tarnished gold and the blue waher lappin offa the whihe marble pier as the brass-bodied angels grates em wud mugs a tay. If they don't serve tay in heaven there won't be an Irish person in the place.

BONIFACE And ya call yourself religious.

FERMOY Yes, I do, buh my eternihy is noh for the herd.

BONIFACE The herd's eternihy will do fine for me.

FERMOY No douh ud will, a swate little postcard heaven. Have you any idea of the vastness of heaven? Your heaven would fih on a stamp. Mine can noh be measured.

BONIFACE Then I think ud's a dangerous thing noh to have the square rooh a heaven in your mind.

FERMOY Look, I nade to wrihe a lehher to thah eegih thah runs the health buurd. Whah's this hees name is agin? The wan wud the coconuh hair?

BONIFACE Alloni.

FERMOY Thah's him, noh returnin me calls. I nade the run a the hospitals, auld folks homes, day cintres, thah suurt a thing. You should know the kind a lehher thah'll geh him. He's givin Hannafin free rein and he won't leh me in. What's hees pisin anyway?

BONIFACE Bates the wife. Mebbe he's stopped. See her goin round wudouh her sunglasses, perfect face on her.

FERMOY Anhin else?

BONIFACE He puh wan a hees kids in hospital a while back. Med em take ouh her appendix, noh a thing wrong a the girl.

FERMOY I suppose if ya run the health buurd ya can have the whole family operahed on for free.

BONIFACE Mebbe ud was a sign of affection.

FERMOY Or a birthday present. Come an down to the den and we shape this lehher. *(Upwards)* I'll geh in yet, sir, w'ud or wudout ya. *(Exiting by the cake)* Ya want a slice a cake?

BONIFACE Naw.

FERMOY Me aither. Hate cake, so does the kids.

*He smashes the cake.*

Alias wanted to do thah to a cake. Ah, Auntie Sarah, spyin agin.

SARAH Wanta be fierce bored to be perchin on your conversation. I hear Hannafin's goin to win.

FERMOY Ya won't rise me, missus.

SARAH Only tellin ya the word abroad.

FERMOY I won't be countin on your vohe so.

SARAH And the missus is votin green, heard her on the phone.

FERMOY Ah, the little protest vohe. The Granes'll comes back to me Mutually. She'll vohe for me in spihe of herself. Why does all the women in this house want to kill me?

SARAH Law a the world, don't take ud personally.

*Exit* BONIFACE *and* FERMOY *as* ARIEL *enters, talking on her mobile,* SARAH *tries to fix the cake.*

ARIEL *(On her mobile)* Yeah, a suurt of a buhherfly yella . . . brand new, I swear ... Yeah ... Whah're y'up to? . . . Yeah, I seen ud, fierce, isn't ud? . . . Ya love ud? Ah, ud's wocious, ya still belave in Noddyland, ah, Stephanie … Yeah, yeah, whah time yees matin ah? … No, they'll never leh me, never leh me anywhere, afraid somewan'd run off wud me. I wish … Did he say he'd be there? … Damn ud … Sunda nigh they'll never leh me …

FRANCES *(Entering)* You're goin nowhere in the dark, Ariel, so don't bother askin. ARIEL *(Exiting)* Ah, Ma … (To *Stephanie on the mobile)* Ya heard thah, did ya? Look, tell him I'll see him in school tomorra … Yeah, yeah. *(She's well offstage by now)*

FRANCES Whah happened the cake?

SARAH Didn't heeself puh hees fist through ud.

FRANCES *(To* STEPHEN *who stands beside her, looking at her)* I said no, Stephen, you're noh getting ud.

STEPHEN Just a Sup.

FRANCES I'm noh a lollypop.

STEPHEN *(Climbing on her knee)* Come an and don't be so manchey wud em. *(Going for her breast)*

FRANCES I said, no. *(Stops him)* No, Stephen, no. *(A struggle)*

SARAH Ah,leh him suck away. If there was wan goin I'd be suckin on ud too.

FRANCES *(Struggling with him)* No way, Stephen. Whah would your Daddy say?

STEPHEN Don't you dare tell him!

FRANCES I'll tell him righ now if ya don't stop.

STEPHEN Alrigh, alrigh, just leh me lie up agin ya. *(Lies up against her)*

FRANCES Don't fall aslape on me now, I'm warnin ya. *(To* SARAH) Here, give us a bih a cake, love cake, I'd ahe ud all down to the plahe.

SARAH *gives her a lump of cake. Enter* ELAINE.

Ya want a bih a cake, Elaine?

ELAINE No. *(Stands there watching* FRANCES)

FRANCES Damn ud, he's aslape.

ELAINE He's ony pretendin.

FRANCES Wake up, Stephen, come an wake up, love. *(To* ELAINE) What do ya want, peh?

ELAINE Natin, just lookin at ya.

FRANCES Did ya like Ariel's birthday?

ELAINE No.

FRANCES And why, migh I ask?

ELAINE Birthdays is ony interestin when they're your own.

FRANCES A'ya lookin for a scrap, are ya?

ELAINE Yeah, I am.

FRANCES Ya'd too much coke, that's what's wrong a ya.

ELAINE Daddy tould ya noh to be doin thah thing wud Stephen.

FRANCES Whah thing? I'm noh doin anhin wud him.

ELAINE You're a liar. A big liar.

FRANCES Don't you call me a liar, and stop givin me the avil eye. I'm tired, Elaine, I'm tired.

ELAINE *stands there looking at* FRANCES.

EARAH She's like her grandmother, thah wan, she'd stare the world down, biggest eyes y'ever seen. I goh the hands, she goh the eyes.

ELAINE And where is me grandmother?

SARAH Never you mind where she is.

ELAINE She's ah the bohhom a Cuura Lake where me grandaddy puh her, in a bag wud a boulder, nowan ever found her.

FRANCES If ya know why're ya askin?

ELAINE Want to hear her say ud. She's ah the bohhom a Cuura Lake where me grandaddy puh her. Love the sound a thah.

SARAH Ya do, don't ya, ya babby witch in the cauldron. Thah child knows too much.

ELAINE And where were you when ud was happenin, Auntie Sarah?

SARAH Never you mind where I was.

ELAINE Ya were warmin me grandaddy's bed, that's where ya were.

SARAH And what's ud to you if I was?

ELAINE Ud's information and information is useful.

FRANCES Thah's enough, Elaine. G'wan ouhside the duur and don't come back in till ya say sorry to Auntie Sarah.

ELAINE Well, ud's true, isn't ud, what's to be sorry for when ud's true? *(Squeezes* FRANCES*)*

FRANCES Ow, ya rip, ya!

ELAINE Thah's for the last twelve years.

FRANCES Geh ouh!

ELAINE *(Sauntering out)* Ya think ud bothers me goin ouhside the duur? Love ud ouh there. Can't waih to be ouhside your duur forever.

SARAH There's a madam. I'd like to see her whin she's twinty-wan.

FRANCES Thah child hates me, I don't know why ud is, buh thah child hates me.

SARAH Mebbe she'll grow ouh of ud.

FRANCES Ud's noh natural. From the very beginnin she wanted rid a me. Times I think she's me penance for James. Isn't thah an awful thing to think?

SARAH High time you stopped torturin yourself over James.

FRANCES Why will no wan in this house leh me talk abouh James? Fermoy goes mad if I mention him, he thinks I'm blamin him. If I wanted to I could, for James' death was as much hees fault as mine. I wanted to brin him on the honeymoon. Fermoy says no, lave him wud your aunts. And oh … when they rang and tould me … three thousand miles away and James dead from the belt of a hurl … still can't belave ud. *(Produces locket)* Look ah him. And hees father. I wasn't good to thah man. Two calves they were. Look at them.

SARAH Seen ud before, Frances, seen ud before, many, many times.

FRANCES Aye … and these tears is natin to the wans I'll shed in the future. I still have to pay for James. Every mornin I ask meself is this the day the roof's goin to fall in for whah I done to James. And if I as much as look ouh the winda a second too long or pause in the hall of an avenin, Fermoy goes inta a reel of how I loved James and the first husband more than him. Well mebbe I did. Fermoy threw the dust in me eyes. These two I loved.

SARAH *(Exiting with dishes)* The beauhiful dead, the beauhi-ful dead, everywan loves em.

ELAINE *(Head around the door)* I've a fierce destiny, Ma, and you're in ud.

SARAH *(Shoos her out)* Away wud ya and lave your mother alone.

FRANCES *sits there with* STEPHEN *asleep on her knee, looking at locket. She looks from locket to* STEPHEN *to locket. She strokes his head.*

FRANCES You've a look of him alrigh. The eyes, yees boh have my eyes. Buh ya don't have hees black curls, you've Fermoy's hair. James had the most beauhiful, beauhiful head a blue black curls. Paple'd stop us in the street to touch hees curls. I had to puh a clip in your hair to kape the curls ouha your eyes and still I wouldn't cuh em. Whin a'ya goin to cuh thah child's hair, they'd ask. Never, I'd say, never, and I never did. Five years a black curls wint inta thah grave and me wud em.

*Enter* BONIFACE.

BONIFACE I'm away, Frances. Ah, the child, the child, is there anhin lovelier than a slapin child?

FRANCES There is, aye. A dead wan. *(Closes locket)*

BONIFACE Is thah so?

FRANCES If he doesn't geh in this time there'll be war.

BONIFACE He's overdue a dressin down.

FRANCES Help him, will ya, Boniface? He's us all driven mad here, you know everywan, geh em to vohe for him. He's noh a bad man, just all wrong, behher than Hannafin.

BONIFACE Ah, Hannafin's harmless, he's the auld school, sell the whole country down the Swanee for an extension to hees bungalow and a new jape.

FRANCES Well, I'm the wan'll suffer if he doesn't geh in. I'm the wan'll be blemt.

BONIFACE I've an awful falin he's goin to swing ud. He's down there in the den rattlin on abouh blood sacrifice and destiny and vision. God help us all if he gets in, thah's whah I say. The auld fella was a tyrant too.

FRANCES I ony meh him the wance, thought he was a fine auld gintleman.

BONIFACE He'd the charm a forty divils alrigh. They alias do, buh back a the charm was the stuck-up rebellis heart of all a Lucifer's crew. Does he ever talk to ya abouh the auld lad?

FRANCES Me and thah man doesn't talk ah all. Wance ya go past hello wud Fermoy he wants to kill ya. Asier say natin.

BONIFACE Ask him abouh the auld lad and Ma sometime.

FRANCES God, no, don't want to open thah buuk a butchery. Sooner leh an ud never happened.

BONIFACE Oh, ud happened, and me man in there in the middle of ud all. Auld fella med him hould Ma down.

FRANCES He was ony a child, wasn't he, wasn't hees fault.

BONIFACE I'm noh sayin ud was. All I'm sayin is somethin like thah is bound to take uds toll on a person's view a the world. I don't like the way he's goin an.

FRANCES And why did your father do ud?

BONIFACE In cuurt he said ud was to save her the trouble a dyin laher an. Figure thah wan ouh at your leisure.

FRANCES And whah had she done? I don't mane she deserved to be puh in a bag and pegged to the bohhom of a lake, buh whah was goin an?

BONIFACE He tried to make ouh she was havin an affair. She wasn't. Thah woman was in love wud wan man and wan man only. Padre Pio of San Giovanni.

FRANCES Hard compate wud Padre Pio.

BONIFACE Her party piece was Padre Pio hearin her confession. And ah the end of ud he puh hees hand through the curtain and the stigmaha bled onta her blouse. She had the blouse folded in tissue paper wud lavender sprigs all over ud. And if ya were really good she'd take down the blouse and leh us trace our fingers over the blood. That's eternihy you're touchin, she'd say. That's eternihy, be careful wud ud. Christ, I could tell ya stories abouh thah woman, never a dull moment, and the eyelashes on her and the big dark mane of her, like a horse, like a beauhiful Egyptian horse. And the auld lad doesn't know whah to do wud her so he does away wud her.

FRANCES And Fermoy there in the middle of ud all. The size a the nigh in thah man is past measurin.

FERMOY *has entered.*

FERMOY Is ud now? ... Was he on ya agin?

FRANCES He's ony sittin on me knee.

FERMOY Know you're lyin. Can smell the milk.

FRANCES You slape better ah nigh thinkin I'm a liar.

FERMOY I certainly do. *(Takes* STEPHEN) C'mere, me little man, till we snake some gristle inta your drames.

FRANCES Whah'd ya go and mash the cake for? Ya know I love cake.

FERMOY And ya love witholdin ud. I'm married to a nun, Boniface, a born agin virgin. Ud's noh every man can say he's hitched hees cart to the reverend mother.

BONIFACE Ya may lave me ouha the sheets.

FRANCES I'll take off me wimple when you learn how to trahe a woman righ and noh before.

FERMOY And where am I supposed to learn? On a rockin horse?

FRANCES Ya know natin, Fermoy Fitzgerald.

FERMOY Then tell me, missus! G'wan, tell me! Listen to this now, Boniface, listen to wan of her dirges on love.

FRANCES Waste a breah dirgin you.

FERMOY Sure, the only rason I married ya was so I could have ud on demand. And all she does is talk abouh ud, talk abouh ud wud this lad here latched onto her. Look ah hees teeth, he's whah? Ten, and he still has hees milk teeth. They won't fall ouh till she weans him. Buh she won't wean him. Ya know why? Because then she'd have to dale wud me. I've the length a you, missus. I know whah's goin on in thah little bantam head a yours. You should be tratin me like a king steada grindin me down to bone male.

FRANCES You and your auld election. Ya never have a nice word. Ya never have a word. *(Exiting)* In and ouh like a fox. Sooner be palin a bag a spuds.

FERMOY *(Goes after her, yanks locket from her neck)* Knew ud! Just knew ud. Sure there's no talkin to ya when ya've thah yoke round your neck.

FRANCES Gimme thah back if ya value your life.

FERMOY *(Fending her off)* Look whah she wears round her neck.

FRANCES Give us ud.

BONIFACE Ah, would ya give the woman her locket.

FERMOY Look ah him! Look whah I have to puh up wud. The first husband. Pugnacious puss of him.

FRANCES Gimme thah back now, ya gone too far.

FERMOY High time ya forgoh abouh them. They're dead. Dead as stones. I'm your husband. There's your son *(Stephen).*

FRANCES *(Pointing at locket)* And there's me other son. Look ah him if ya dare. The wan ya killed.

FERMOY Oh, here we go.

FRANCES You killed him or as good as.

FERMOY How, tell me how did I kill him and I on another continent?

FRANCES Wud black thinkin and wishin him away.

FERMOY Brin him wud us, I told ya. Brin him on the bleddy honeymoon for all I care.

FRANCES Like hell ya said brin him wud us. You're greah ah re-jiggin the past, alias wud yourself as the haroh. Give him to me, ud's me favourihe picture, give him to me.

FERMOY Well now, missus, you shoulda taken the edge off of me this morning.

*Exit* FERMOY.

BONIFACE Y'alrigh?

FERMOY This is ony the warm up. This is natin.

BONIFACE Ya want me to get your locket back?

FRANCES No, thah's whah he'd like. Leh him cool hees jets. He'll be back for another round.

BONIFACE Righ, I'm away durin the calm.

FRANCES Nigh, Boniface.

FRANCES *Wakes* STEPHEN.

C'mon, peh, up to bed.

STEPHEN Whah am I doin noh on your knee.

FRANCES Your Daddy was nursin ya.

STEPHEN Ya didn't tell him, did ya? Make a holy show a me.

FRANCES No, I didn't tell him.

STEPHEN I'm givin y'up for Lint, ya may puh up wud me till then.

FRANCES Alrigh, ya mane thah now, do ya?

STEPHEN I do. Will ya come up and say goodnigh to me, I'll be fierce fast.

FRANCES Alrigh, me little man.

*She kisses him. He walks sleepily from the room as* ARIEL *stands in the doorway.*

ARIEL Ah, Ma, leh us ouh for five minutes, will ya, want to show Stephanie the car.

FRANCES Buh ud's dark, love.

ARIEL I'll be wary. Ah, Ma, ud's me birthday, I'll be righ back.

FRANCES Ya enjiy your birthday?

ARIEL Aye, never thought I'd see sixteen.

FRANCES Swear ya were ninety.

ARIEL I know ud's mad, buh I never thought I'd make me sixteenth birthday. I've this thing abouh a girl in a graveyard, don't know where ud cem from, buh just before I go to slape and me mind's blanked ouh, this sintince kapes comin. Girl in a graveyard, girl in a graveyard, I tap ud ouh on the pilla, puts me to slape like a lullaby. Mad, isn't ud?

FRANCES Ud's somethin. G'wan then to Stephanie. I'm timin ya.

ARIEL You're a great little Ma.

*She blows her a kiss and she's gone.* FRANCES *sits there eating the cake. Hold a minute. Then enter* FERMOY *with a CD. He puts it on. Stands there listening to it, looking at her. Dancing.*

FERMOY Ya wanted some romance, missus.

FRANCES Take more than Spanish eyes to romance me.

FERMOY *(Dances towards her, for her)* You're the wan, you're the wan. I'm just busy, busy, you're lookin ah the next Taoiseach. Go aisy on me a while, will ya, and then I'm yours agin.

FRANCES Where's me locket?

*FERMOY takes locket from his pocket, gives it to her, dancing all the time. She examines it.*

What's your phoho doin here?

FERMOY I left in the child's phoho. Don't be getting thick over natin agin. I don't mind ya wearin a phoho of the child but noh heeself. I'm the wan should be straddlin your heart.

FRANCES And what ya do wud Charlie's phoho?

FERMOY On me desk.

FRANCES Ud's important to remember whah has been lost.

FERMOY *(Pulling her to him)* I know. I know.

FRANCES Like hell, ya know. Ya don't remember yesterda, you're thah suurt of a man.

FERMOY *(Dancing with her)* Oh, I remember everythin, don't you ever fear, buh ud's important to forget too.

*Kisses her, a long lovely kiss. Enter HANNAFIN, stands there watching and listening.*

FRANCES We started on the wrong fooh, Fermoy, no way to puh ud righ.

FERMOY Ud was meant to be.

FRANCES I wish I could be as certain as you. Facts are me goin wud you cost me me husband's life, me son's life and forever more me peace a mind.

FERMOY Whah happened James and Charlie was strokes a destiny.

FRANCES Strokes a destiny?

FERMOY Aye, natin to do wud you or me. The man above cleared the way, is all. Ony for destiny you'd a ran back and forth between me and Charlie. Ya'd be runnin still. Ya should be grateful the chice was med for ya.

FRANCES And James?

FERMOY James was left field, I'll admih thah. James' death shook me to the core. And then I began to understand the God we're dalin wud. He was boulsterin us for things to come.

FRANCES Whah things to come?

FERMOY We mustn't be afraid, we mustn't baulk, ony dance to the music till the music's done. And when I'm Taoiseach you'll be there wud me, where ya belong. That's whah's wrong a the country, noh enough sex. I'm goin to creahe a new ministry, the ministry a sex. You'll be the minister and I'll be your assistant. We'll give em demonstrations on the national airwaves, we'll be the new Angelus.

HANNAFIN And put the whole nation off their tay.

FERMOY Hannafin … Whah do we owe this pleasure to?

HANNAFIN Look, Fitzgerald, ya wont geh me seah offa me. I've the core vohe wrapped up, whole county in me fist.

FERMOY Four votes, Hannafin. All I naded last time, four votes. Thah's never happenin agin.

HANNAFIN Ya want to play dirty. Alrigh. I'm the Baron a Dirt when ud's called for.

FERMOY I'm squaky clane, and ya know ud. Thah's why you're here whimperin like a girl.

HANNAFIN Squaky clane. Whah abouh your father and mother?

FERMOY Whah's thah got to do wud me?

HANNAFIN Everywan knows you were there.

FERMOY I was there alrigh. But you're noh criminally responsible ah seven. Ya don't know your law.

HANNAFIN I know me law and I know the pulse a the paple. The apple doesn't fall far from the tree. And here, I've the figures a the new poll. *(Produces fax)*

FERMOY That's noh ouh till the mornin.

HANNAFIN For the likes a you, mebbe. For us in the know any information can be goh. I'm miles ahead a ya. Here, look ah ud yourself.

FERMOY *(Hits it away)* Them polls, alias wrong.

HANNAFIN *smiles, lets poll sheet fall to the floor.*

HANNAFIN And how is the lady a the house?

FRANCES Very well, thank you.

HANNAFIN Was visihin the Mother's grave today, do thah every Sunda, brin the auld daffodils to lay on her bones, and I passed be your son's grave, tiny little yoke of a yoke, fierce neglected lookin, reminded me a you. Just who do yees think yees are? Yees think the wind is in yeer favour just because yees built the big house wud the Grake columns and the fountains goin full blast and the lions roarin on the gates and the money pourin in from the cement and gravel. Ud's my wind yees goh a whiff of and be careful ud doesn't blow yees away. You're messin wud my votes, Fitzgerald, the hurlers on the ditch who'd go wud me if you weren't banjaxin everythin. Back down now before ya make a hames of ud all. Sure they're ony laughin at ya. The murderers' son for this county. That'll never happen. Back down now and I'll owe ya wan.

FERMOY The county's sick a ya, Hannafin, and ya know ud. Ya do natin ony drink whiskey and lap-dance. Whin's the last time you spoke in the Dail apart from tellin them to close the winda?

HANNAFIN Alrigh, I asked ya nicely. Now we'll do ud the hard way. If you don't back down I've an interview done that'll put ya in your place. All I have to do is make a call and ud'll be all over the mornin papers.

FERMOY I know what's in ud. You're noh the ony wan can geh information. Natin ony hoh air abouh me laineage. Me mother and father, Frances' son and first husband, me brother Boniface and hees addictions, long cured, ya didn't put thah in. Thah's all ya have, thah's all there is. Pathehic. Oh, aye, there's me greah grandfather, they say he ate a child durin the famine. So did everywan's durin the famine. So did yours.

HANNAFIN Well, if he did, he didn't ate wan of hees own.

FERMOY Hunger is hunger. Laineage manes natin anymore. You're the auld generation thah'd like to kape us in our place forever. We new wans comin up judge a man for whah he is in heeself, noh where he cem from. We judge a man these days be hees own merit, as if he'd ne'er a smithy bar God heeself.

HANNAFIN The pipe drames of the self-med. You were forged in a bloodbah, Fitzgerald, and the son alias carries the father somewhere inside of him. I know thah much, he carries the Da inside of him sure as he carries hees kidneys, the family jewels, the heart. And ud's time the paple beyond this parish knew the gruesome blacksmith hommered you to earth and the symmetry can be predicted from there.

Fermoy And whah abouh your own symmetry, Hannafin, and your father dancin up the field the last three year of hees life, waltzin wud the sheep, or your mother stealin jars a coffee from every shop for miles around? Whah was ud abouh coffee thah everthin collided in her over jars a coffee? Or your grandmother walkin inta the silver river ah eighy-seven? Christ, if ya could puh up wud ud all till you're eighy-seven and thah new asbestos plant, there's noh a lake or river we can swim in anymore, thanks to you. And thah piggery, who's been fundin thah all these years? There's lots a questions to be asked concernin you if ya want to play ud thah way.

Hannafin And there's a few inquiries to be med as to how the cement and gravel empire goh off of the ground.

Fermoy The cement and gravel was grown from the air be me and Frances and ya know ud. I heard ya been snoopin round our accounts, whadlin the tax biys, and ya found natin because there's natin to find. I'm warnin you, Hannafin, you open your gob abouh my personal life and I'll take ya to the claners.

Hannafin There's somethin rotten in you, Fitzgerald. I know ud, know ud like me own hand. I just can't puh a finger on ud yeh. Bun I will before long. In the manetime thah interview goes ouh in the mornin. That'll get the ball rollin. If ya've any thoughts to the contrary ya know me number. I'll give ya an hour, no more.

*Exit* Hannafin.

Frances *(Poll sheet)* Is these polls accurahe?

Fermoy Accurahe enough.

Frances Well, I'm noh looking forward to radin abouh meself in the papers. Me aunts'll go through the roof. Peg in the towel, Fermoy, ud's obvious he's goin to win. Ring him, geh him to cancel thah interview.

Fermoy A'you goin to start layin inta me as well?

Frances Everywan says he's goin to hould hees seah. Look, we been through this before wud Hannafin.

Fermoy Ya don't same to know how important this is, missus.

Frances I know whah ud's like livin wud you after a defeat.

Fermoy I'm noh losing this time. Geh thah inta your head.

Frances You're the ony wan thinks thah.

Fermoy I suppose ya'd like me to lose agin.

Frances I'd like a bih a peace round here. I'd like a bih a help wud the cement. Ya know, mebbe too many bad things has happened, Fermoy, for you to win. Mebbe you losin agin is God tellin us our golden reprieve is over.

Fermoy Kape your auld guilt trip to yourself. Charlie and James have natin to do wud this and they've natin to do wud me.

Frances You tould Charlie abouh us. You tould Charlie abouh us though I begged ya not to.

Fermoy Somewan had to tell him. You weren't goin to.

Frances I would have. In me own time.

Fermoy Like hell ya would. Ya'd still be stringin the both of us along.

Frances You just couldn't waih to hurt somewan. You knew thah man loved me.

Fermoy And I don't?

Frances He was my husband. You were just a fling, a fling thah wint wrong.

FERMOY Then whah're ya doin wud me this seventeen year?

FRANCES You're the father a me children. That's whah I'm doin wud ya.

*Exit* FRANCES, FERMOY *sits there brooding. Hold a minute. Enter* ARIEL.

ARIEL Meh Hannafin in the lane.

FERMOY Aye, he was here.

ARIEL The car's mad.

FERMOY Is ud?

ARIEL Yeah. Thanks. *(Kisses the top of his head)*

FERMOY Whah'd Hannafin to say for heeself?

ARIEL He puts wan a hees cowbiy boots up on the bonneh, lanes in the winda, pats me on the head, 'Aren't you the fine girl, Ariel Fitzgerald, considerin who spawned ya?' Tould me to give ya this.

FERMOY *examines it.*

Whah is ud?

FERMOY Ah, ud's an auld newspaper cuttin abouh me father's trial.

ARIEL Whah was he really like?

FERMOY Whah was he really like? He was really like whah he really was, a man in a navy raincoah thah butchered me mother . . . Ya know whah he done after?

ARIEL Whah?

FERMOY Lih a cigarette, puh me up on hees shoulders, all the way up from the lake, across the fields to the Sea Dew Inn. We sah at the counter, him drinkin four Jemmies, the eyes glihherin, glancin from me to the glass to the fluur, then lanin over and whisperin Time to be turnin ourselves in'.

ARIEL And what did you say?

FERMOY Don't remember if I said anhin ... All I remember is lookin ah him, the low sounds of Sunda evenin drinkin, the barmaid puttin an lipstick and him smilin, yeah, smilin. How can ya describe thah to anywan?

ARIEL He shouldn't a said 'we'.

FERMOY Ya think noh?

ARIEL A cuursenoh.

FERMOY No, 'we' was righ. I was there too. And though I was ony seven, an excuse on this earth, I was also seven thousand and seven millin, for the soul is wan age and mine just stood and watched. I'd seen him drown a bag a kittens, blind, tiny pink tongues and fairy teeth. Really this was no different.

*A pause,* FERMOY *studies* ARIEL.

ARIEL Whah? Whah is ud, Daddy?

FERMOY Ya want to take me for a spin in your new chariot?

ARIEL Alrigh. Where do ya want to go?

FERMOY Anywhere.

ARIEL Then anywhere ud is. Will we brin Ma?

| | |
|---|---|
| FERMOY | Gone to bed. |
| ARIEL | I'll puh ouh the ligh so. |

*She looks out. Puts out the light. 'Mors et Vita' music. Blackout.*

## ACT TWO

*'Mors et Vita' music as curtain comes up. Ten years later,* FERMOY *sits centre stage. Beautifully groomed. An interview is in progress,* VERONA, *the interviewer, sits to the side. Cameraman, soundman, to the other side,* ELAINE *stands watching, in a suit, taking notes.*

| | |
|---|---|
| FERMOY | Yes, I've held three ministries over the past ten years. |
| VERONA | And of the three, Minister, do you have a favourite? |
| FERMOY | They're all very different. I enjiyed tremendously Arts and Culture though I was only there for a year. Hi was an area I knew very little abouh when I took over the brief. I used look up to artists and poets before I got to know em. Ih was a greah education to realize they're as fickle and wrongheaded as the rest of us. Thah said, ih was a huge learnin curve for me and, I'll tell ya, it's hard to beah a pride a poets and a tank a wine for good conversation. |
| VERONA | And what is it, Minister, that's just so great about their conversation? |
| FERMOY | It's noh aisy puh a finger on ud, buh I think ud's their attempts, mostly banjaxed mind you, buh an attempt anyway to throw eternihy on the table. |
| VERONA | You're a great believer in eternity, aren't you, Minister? |
| FERMOY | Yes,lam. |
| VERONA | You said it was divine providence that won you your seat ten years ago. |
| FERMOY | I said ih was divine grace. |
| VERONA | With all due respects to divine grace, Minister, didn't you rise in proportion to Hannafin's fall? |
| FERMOY | A cuurse I did, but thah doesn't diminish divine grace. If that scandal had broken a week laher, Hannafin would've kept hees seat. |
| VERONA | There were suggestions at the time, Minister, that you were instrumental in the breaking of that scandal. |
| FERMOY | Malicious gossip. |
| VERONA | And still the rumours persist, Minister. |
| FERMOY | Yeah, by them thah'd like to take me down. Facts are I was elected fair and square by the people. Why make a mountain ouh of a molehill? |
| VERONA | I wouldn't call the suicide of a highly respected politician a 'molehill', Minister. |
| FERMOY | I wasn't referrin to Hannafin's suicide as a 'molehill'. I was referrin to how I was elected. Hannafin's suicide was tragic. We weren't exactly bosom buddies but ud wint hard wud me thah he thought ud necessary to take hees own life. And ud has been devastatin for hees wife and children. |
| VERONA | No doubt it has. However, you went on to become Minister of Finance after Arts and Culture. How did you find that transition? |
| FERMOY | Well, there's more fiction written in Finance than in Arts and Culture, so the transition wasn't that difficult. |

VERONA I remember, Minister, the outrage at the time, both within your own Party and from the Opposition, when you were appointed. They said you were untried, untested, too green.

FERMOY They said a loh of other things too, not fit for public consumption.

VERONA The former Taoiseach took a big risk on you.

FERMOY Ih turned ouh to be no risk. My term in Finance was wan of the most successful in the history of the State.

VERONA And it begs the question why you haven't remained in Finance.

FERMOY I'd learned all I had to learn there.

VERONA It's on the record, Minister, that you said of Finance, and I quote, 'I'm fed up being the nation's handbag.'

FERMOY Thah was said in a private conversation, on Christmas Eve, after seven brandies. Are ya goin to crucify me for thah now?

VERONA You're also on the record as saying that your term in Finance left you feeling like Granny on pension day with the bag of gobstoppers.

FERMOY Look, I spent five-and-a-half year in Finance. I brough ud kickin and screamin inta the twenty-first century. I brough money inta the country from places yees didn't know existed and in ways ye'd never dreamt of. I done me service in Finance. Ih was time to move on.

VERONA But your refusal to remain in Finance caused a huge rift between you and the former Taoiseach.

FERMOY Yes, ud did, but don't forgeh I served him faithfully for the best part of eight year. He taught me every-thin I know.

VERONA Was it a question, Minister, of the pupil outstripping the master?

FERMOY Ih was more complicahed than thah.

VERONA Whatever it was, it led to the no-confidence motion in his leadership last year.

FERMOY Mebbe ud did.

VERONA Come on, Minister, the whole country knows you were behind that no-confidence motion. The word abroad is that the present Taoiseach, Mr Dudley, is your puppet and that very shortly he'll get the axe too.

FERMOY Well, the word is wrong. As usual. I wish I knew as much abouh meself as yees reporters know. The facts are very different.

VERONA And what are the facts, Minister?

FERMOY There's an optimum moment for everywan, few recognize ud when ud comes and fewer still recognize when the moment is gone. Never to return. The Taoiseach was jaded. The party had lost direction and the party cannoh be sacrificed to wan individual, whahever our privahe estimations of thah individual may be. And belave me when I say I held him in the highest esteem and will always. Hard decisions cost us all and I know more than most the price a those decisions. You think I enjiyed the public humiliation of a close friend. You're wrong. You're very wrong.

VERONA It's not over yet, is it, Minister?

FERMOY What d'ya mean?

VERONA Dudley's leadership has been disastrous.

FERMOY That's a mahher of opinion.

VERONA The electorate is losing patience, Minister. They'd rather you came clean.

FERMOY I've no idea what you're talkin abouh.

VERONA That you have your eye on the leadership. That it's only a matter of time before Dudley goes. The Party's in such a state right now they'll give you the reins. That you've the whole place in uproar. You control the Cabinet as it is. You are Taoiseach in everything but name.

FERMOY You overestimahe my power. I'm Minister for Education. That's my job.

VERONA Can you categorically state you will not be orchestrating a no-confidence motion in Mr Dudley's leadership in the next week or two?

FERMOY That's somethin for the Party to decide.

VERONA Could you answer the question, please, Minister? Are you or are you not interested in Leadership?

FERMOY Well, a cuurse I'm interested. I wouldn't be where I am if I wasn't. But I'm noh interested in power ah any price. I love power, yes, I love ud, buh I love ud as an artist loves ud.

VERONA You love power as an artist loves it. You're quoting Napoleon, Minister.

FERMOY I'm paraphrasin him.

VERONA Are you comparing yourself with Napoleon, Minister?

FERMOY Who can compare wud Napoleon? I can't, aven if I wanted to, because I'm born inta the wrong century, surrounded be the wrong people. If you're a Napoleon lover you'll know whah he said as he was dyin on St Helena, 'If I had sailed for Ireland instead of Egypt, where would England be now, and the world?' This country has missed ouh on everythin, overlooked be Alexander the Greah, overlooked be Caesar, overlooked be the Moors. Overlooked, overlooked, overlooked. The rest a the world gets Napoleon, we get a boatload a Vikings, a handful a Normans and the English. We get the nation a shopkeepers.

VERONA Napoleon's verdict on the British. Are you anti-British, Minister?

FERMOY No, a cuurse I'm noh. I'm talkin abouh imagination. If ya have to be colonized ya migh as well be colonized by somewan wud a bih a vision. I'm talkin abouh a way of lookin at the world. D'ya look ah ud from behind a till or d'ya look ah ud from the saddle of a horse on a battlefield? And, like ud or noh, the legacy the Brihish have left us is the till, whereas for Napoleon the world was wan big battlefield. He talked abouh hees battlefields like they were women. Which a the battlefields was more beauhiful than the other. That's the stuff we nade to learn, or rather re-learn, we knew ud wance. Aven Caesar while butcherin the Celts had to acknowledge whah a strange tribe he was dalin wud. "They measure periods a time be nights, noh be days.' That's whah he said abouh us. Wance we had a calendar, markin out time be the nigh. Them were the biys had the perspective. Look, the outsize ego a this nation is built on sand and wind, a few dramers, natin else. We nade to go back to first principles. We nade to re-imagine ourselves from scratch.

VERONA You've been much criticized by the Opposition for precisely this going back to first principles, Minister, which you've outlined in your Education Papers.

FERMOY It's the Oppositions's job to oppose so I don't take them too seriously.

VERONA They're not the only ones unhappy over some of the contents of these Papers.

FERMOY I'm noh interested in cosmehics. If you're goin to do somethin, do ud righ or don't do ud ah all. Learned thah on me mother's knee. Look, I chose to go inta Education. Lots has seen thah as a step down. Well, ud's noh. I chose Education because ud all begins and ends wud education. And my business righ now is to re-educahe a nation. Thah won't be done in a day.

VERONA Some of us think we don't need to be re-educated, Minister, not to mind your refusal to consult with the experts. A sizeable portion of the public is alarmed by the last three Papers your party has pushed through.

FERMOY There's natin to be alarmed abouh. I think we've proved over and over we have this country's interests at heart.

VERONA But your Theology Paper, Minister, has caused uproar.

FERMOY I belave in God well as the next.

VERONA Come on, Minister, your God is as far from the traditional notion of God as it is possible to be.

FERMOY Yes, he is, and I make no apology for thah.

VERONA The Church has spoken out against you on several occasions, and I quote a recent statement from the Archbishop's office. 'What the Minister proposes is the antithesis of the nature of God. What he proposes is ancient, barbaric, and will take us back to the caves.'

FERMOY What does he mane take us back to the caves? Does he think we've left em?

FRANCES *enters, coat, briefcase, stands listening.*

VERONA The statement refers to your Paper on the nature of Christ. Could you clarify what you meant by that Paper, Minister?

FERMOY I though ih was clear enough ah the time. I was talkin abouh the sullen nature a Christ, somethin thah has been hushed up for centuries. Somethin I'd long suspected and was brough home to me by a particular paintin by Piero della Francesca. His 'Resurrection'. Puts manners on them thah tries to tell us that the deah a Christ was for us. That the resurrection a Christ was for us. Let's noh mix words here. The deah a Christ was by us, noh for us, and the resurrection a Christ was for heeself. Look ah this paintin and you'll see whah I mane. It's magnificent. A big, cranky, vengeful son a God plants a leg like a tree on hees new opened tomb. He looks ouh inta the middle distance and hees eyes say wan thing and wan thing only Ye'll pay for this. Yell pay for this. No forgiveness in them eyes. The opposihe. Rage, and a staggerin sense a betrayal, as if he's sayin, I've wasted Eternihy on ye band a troglodytes thah calls yeerselves the human race. Children should be taught this along wud Barney. So I get shot down for tryin to introduce a little balance inta the education system. Well, I'm used to bein crihicized and thankfully I don't suffer from the national disase.

VERONA And what's that, Minister?

FERMOY Wantin to be liked. Ya'd swear thah was the politician's job these days. To be liked. Well, ud's noh. The politician's job is to have a vision and to push thah vision through, for wudouh a vision the people perish.

VERONA I suppose, Minister, whatever else they say about you, you're not afraid to speak your mind.

FERMOY Ud's ony slaves thah fear to speak their mind.

VERONA Perhaps. Ten years ago, Minister, you were running a cement factory and now you're tipped as the next Taoiseach. Do you ever stop for a minute and say to yourself, this is a dream?

FERMOY Well, ud's all a drame, isn't ud? Wan beauhiful heart-breakin drame, but, no, I don't ever stop, and I'll tell ya why. Fate gev me the hand, I hardly have to play ud.

VERONA And the hand fate dealt you hasn't always been so good, has it, Minister?

FERMOY No, ud hasn't.

VERONA Alongside what can only be described as your meteoric rise is a huge personal tragedy.

FERMOY Yes ... Ariel.

VERONA Your daughter. I know this is difficult, but could you tell us what happened to Ariel?

FERMOY Ariel walked ouha this house on her sixteenth birthday to show a friend her new car that we'd goh her as a present. She never cem home.

VERONA They never found her?

FERMOY They never found her, no.

VERONA Have you given up hope, Minister?

FERMOY Yes, I have.

VERONA You believe she's dead.

FERMOY I know she is.

VERONA How do you know, Minister?

FERMOY In me bones. Don't ask me how I know, buh I know and wish I didn't and wish ud was otherwise. I would give me life for her to walk through thah duur agin. Buh that's noh goin to happen.

VERONA It's an appalling thing at the centre of your lives.

FERMOY You have no idea.

VERONA Thank you, Minister.

FERMOY Thank you.

VERONA *(Stretches. To Cameraman)* You got all that? *(Cameraman nods)*

FERMOY Elaine, what do ya think?

ELAINE Three things. Ya can't admih ya love power. Thah has to go. God. Paple's fierce touchy abouh God. We may pare thah back. And three, Ariel. Ariel's your trump card. Play ud. Ya nade to go wud the emotion of ud more. Thah's whah paple wants, details of your personal life. Don't be afraid to give ud to em. Don't be afraid to give em Ariel.

VERONA No, no, the Ariel section was fine. If you want people to feel for you, you hold back a bit yourself. Your instincts are spot-on there, Minister.

ELAINE I'm noh so sure, buh I'm prepared to lave Ariel the way ud is if ya edit the lovin power bih and the God speech.

VERONA All right. I'll pull back a bit on God without losing the whole thing, but the loving power stays. I think it's refreshing to hear a politician admit they love power. Everyone knows you do. What's the big deal?

ELAINE Dudley'll be gone by Friday. We have to geh this wan righ. Daddy?

FERMOY Lave ud. Migh as well be hung for a sheep as a lamb.

VERONA Great.

ELAINE There's a bite to ate in the conservatory. *(Hands papers to* FERMOY*)* Sign these.

FERMOY Whah have we here?

ELAINE Ya can just sign. I've been over em.

FERMOY I'll jine ya in a minuhe, Verona.

*Exit* VERONA *and* ELAINE. FERMOY *gets up, throws the papers aside, stretches, turns, sees* FRANCES.

Ah, Frances.

FRANCES How do you know she's dead?

FERMOY Ten years, Frances, ten years.

FRANCES Buh ud was the way ya said ud. Ya sounded so certain.

FERMOY Nowan shows up after ten years.

FRANCES And now she's your trump card. I thought her memory would be more … sacred to ya. Today is her tenth anniversary. Have you no respect?

FERMOY I know today is her tenth anniversary. Why d'ya think I'm here?

FRANCES You're here because the press has descended like crows on the church to phohograph the big bronze lug a ya glowerin inta your daugher's empty grave. Ariel's a good phoho opporrunihy. The gravin father wud hees arms tightly around the gravin mother. Don't you touch me ah her Mass this avenin. I'm goin up to geh changed. Ud's ah six. FERMOY I know ud's ah six.

FRANCES Ya'd never think ud.

*Exit* FRANCES, FERMOY *looks after her, begins signing papers, lights a cigar, puts on a CD, dances around, smoking, drinking, signing papers.* STEPHEN *appears in the doorway, dressed in black.*

FERMOY Stephen, ya look like an undertaker.

STEPHEN Ud's the way Ma wants ud.

FERMOY Anhin strange?

STEPHEN Naw . . . Yourself?

FERMOY I'd love to walk down Grafton Streeh and just drink coffee. Sick a watchin other people live. I'd love to w[T]alk inta a shop and buy me own newspaper and then noh read ud, forgeh ud somewhere. Were ya at the match on Sunda?

STEPHEN Ya know I've no interest in Ga.

FERMOY Well, you're the first Fitzgerald thah hasn't. How's college?

STEPHEN *Shrugs.*

You're graduatin this year, aren't ya?

STEPHEN Yeah.

FERMOY Ya studyin?

STEPHEN Yeah.

FERMOY Ya never call inta see me anymore.

STEPHEN You're busy.

FERMOY Not thah busy. Drop inta me next week, we'll go for lunch.

STEPHEN There's no pint.

FERMOY Why noh?

STEPHEN Because ya'll cancel ud.

FERMOY Ah, Stephen, Stephen, Stephen, you're all grown, when did thah happen?

BONIFACE (*We hear him before we see him*) Lilies for the dead. Lilies. Lilies for sale. Lilies for the dead. Whihe lilies for all the whihe dead.

*Enter* BONIFACE.

STEPHEN How is Boniface?

BONIFACE Don't ever geh auld, Stephen, promise me thah.

STEPHEN Thah's a promise.

*And exit* STEPHEN.

FERMOY I thought you were above in Pat's dryin ouh.

BONIFACE And I could die up there before you'd come visih me. Pour us wan a your fortified, rectified, sanctified thousand-year-auld brandies there like a good lad.

FERMOY I haven't been called a good lad since the last time I seen you.

BONIFACE Well, mebbe ya should see me more. If natin else I'd remind ya of where ya cem ouh of.

*Enter* FRANCES, *dressed in black, coat, handbag.*

FRANCES Boniface. Was wonderin would ya show.

BONIFACE Haven't missed Ariel's anniversary yeh. Used to be the birth a Christ was the big wan. Gets whittled down, ud all gets whittled down. Now ud's the death a me niece is the feast a feasts.

FERMOY Ring a taxi and have him driven back to Pat's.

FRANCES Ring wan yourself.

BONIFACE *has moved to drinks cabinet, about to pour.*

FERMOY *(Stays his hand)* You've had enough, sir.

FRANCES Give him a drink. Give him a drink. Let somewan be intoxicahed round here. *(Pours for* BONIFACE*)* I drink to forgeh buh wud each glass ud all comes clearer.

BONIFACE Does ud?

FRANCES Too clear, too clear to bear.

BONIFACE For Ariel *(lilies)*. Grew em meself. Stripped the hoh house this mornin. I know her grave is empty. We do these things for ourselves.

FRANCES They're lovely, Boniface, thanks. *(Lays them on the table, straightens them)*

BONIFACE May God have mercy on your carcass, and may he have mercy on mine. Up Offaly. *(Drinks. Pours another, stands at drinks cabinet, drinking and pouring, pouring and drinking)*

FERMOY *(Watching* FRANCES *fixing the flowers)* Ya miss me ah all?

FRANCES Miss ya?

FERMOY Tell the truth for wance in your life.

FRANCES Alrigh. Yeah, I miss ya, noh you in yourself, noh you now and the riddled pelt a ya, buh the spangled idea I had a ya which is the best part a love.

FERMOY I miss you too.

FRANCES Aye, wud your cartload a virgins spread across five continents.

FERMOY You're noh exactly livin like a nun yourself.

FRANCES I bed the min whin the fancy takes me which isn't often.

FERMOY Ya tryin to make me jealous?

FRANCES I'm past your jealousy. Way past.

FERMOY They're welcome to ya, snow quane that y'are, turn any man to ice. You're noh the ony wan is beddin them down. I've more women than votes linin up for me. Beauhiful young women, bodies a bronze, minds a gold, sophisticahed, beauhiful women, teeth like delph, high-bellied, tauh as fish on a line. And ya know somethin? They like me. Ud's ony here I'm treahed like a dog. I step out this duur and I'm a king.

FRANCES *(Pushes him violently)* Then go to your high-bellied hoors. You're safer wud them and whah they don't know about ya.

*Exit* FRANCES, FERMOY *stands there looking after her.* BONIFACE *watches him from the drinks cabinet.*

BONIFACE Tell me this and tell me no more, was ud worth ud?

FERMOY Was whah worth ud?

BONIFACE And whah about me?

FERMOY Whah about ya?

BONIFACE YOU tould me, ony I didn't understand what ya were sayin, ya tould me, Fermoy, thah nigh ya were goin an abouh blood sacrifice, in this very room.

FERMOY I've no idea what you're talkin abouh.

BONIFACE No. No. Listen. Listen. Listen. I can't stop drinkin. Can't slape, can't ate, garden be moonligh, go to bed in the mornin. I'm afraid I'll tell me psychiatrist, thah it'll just spill ouha me. They don't know what's wrong a me. Me soul, I tell em, me soul ud's hurtin me fierce, like bein flayed from the inside. They think I'm some suurt a religious nuh. Burst a blood vessel in me eye, bled blood down me face for two days, they couldn't stop ud. You're the wan should be in Pat's. You're the wan should be bleedin from the eyes.

FERMOY Take ud aisy, take ud aisy, you're ouh a your mind wud drink and tranquilizers. Take ud aisy.

BONIFACE Take ud aisy! I'm facin me maker wud this on me immortal soul. Do you aven realize whah ya've done! Why didn't ya listen to me when I tried to stop ya, though I didn't know whah I was tryin to stop. Why didn't ya listen? All we have in this world is the small mercies we can extend to wan another. The rest is madness and oblivion. Haven't ya learnt thah much? Haven't ya learnt thah much on your travels?

FERMOY Oh, aye, I learnt thah much alrigh, but like every-thin worth learnin, ud's learnt too lahe. Everythin comes when you've no more use for ud, must be a law.

FRANCES *at the door in her coat.*

FRANCES We're goin to be lahe, geh an your mournin, will

FERMOY Don't you talk to me abouh mournin. *(Takes out electric shaver, mirror, shaves himself)* Most gets up offa the ground sooner or laher, dusts themselves down, rejines the land a the livin. Not you though. Everythin thah happens to Frances Fitzgerald has to be momentous, spectacular. Her jiys could never be the same as anywan else's and her grafes must be inconsolable. Live! Live! Live! That's whah we're here for. Do somethin! Anhin! YaTl have all of eternihy for pussin in the dark.

FRANCES You're noh browbatin the Opposition now.

FERMOY Amn't I? ... This funeral parlour I come home to every time.

FRANCES Ya were home wance this year. Two hours for your Christmas dinner.

*Enter* ELAINE, *dressed in black, holds out mobile.*

ELAINE Himself wants a quick word.

FERMOY *(Takes phone)* Will ya organize thah fella back to where he cem from. *(On the phone)* Boss ... No harm done ... Whah is ud?

*And exit* FERMOY.

ELAINE What ya want to do, Boniface?

BONIFACE I'll go back to Pat's after Mass.

ELAINE Alrigh, I'll drive ya, goin back tonigh meself.

FRANCES *(Sitting, muttering, drink, coat on, handbag)* Twinty-six . . . twinty-six years of age … *(Shakes her head)*

BONIFACE Whah?

FRANCES Ariel … She'd be twinty-six if she was here today … I don't think I slept a nigh straight when I was carryin her. Had meself convinced I didn't deserve her on account a James. Kept thinkin this child's goin to come ouh wrong, this child's goin to come ouh wrong. Nighmare ridin nighmare she be deformed, no face on her or wan a thim frog babbies or birdy-headed little creatures ya see phohos of, or she was goin to have no arms or die ah the last minuhe as happens oftener than paple knows. Buh ouh she cem wud everythin ya nade to look human. And for ages after I'd look ah her and whisper, thank you, God, thank you, God. For along wud the night sweats I still dared to hope I be given another chance. And for a while I thought I had. Buh the man above was ony playin wud me … ony playin wud me, is all.

ELAINE And did ya have nighmares when ya carried me?

FRANCES No, belave ud or noh, you were aisy. The trouble wud you started after ya were born. Though I had to have a jar a beetroot every nigh when I was carryin you. I'd wake up in the middle a the nigh dyin for beetroot … Kept a jar beside the bed. 'Another beetroot party, missus?' Fermoy'd guffaw from under the quilt. Buh I didn't care, I'd sih there in the dark atin beetroot and then I'd drink the vinegar. Mebbe that's why you're so bihher.

ELAINE Am I bihher, Ma?

FRANCES As a field a lemons.

ELAINE Sure ud's noh yourself you're talkin abouh and ya shrunk to a pip over your two dead children.

FRANCES You'd have me forgeh em like your father.

ELAINE I'd have ya cut your grafe accordin to your cloth.

FRANCES You'd have me grave to a timetable, throw Ariel and James aside like a pair of auld gloves or an umbrella left after the rain.

ELAINE Your empire a sorrow doesn't convince me and ya cuttin dales like a shark down ah the cement every day a the wake. Ya switch ud on, Ma, ya switch ud on when ud suits.

FRANCES And whah would you know abouh sorrow and ya dry-eyed at your sister's funeral?

ELAINE I know wan thing abouh sorrow. I learned ud watchin you. Sorrow's an addiction like no other. You won't be full till you've buried us all. Well, ya won't bury me, Ma. I'm here, thrivin, your unlovely daugher is thrivin, your unlovely daugher that ya'd swap like thah for Ariel to return. She's noh comin home, Ma. She's noh comin home. Ud's just me now, me and Stephen.

FRANCES How do you know she's noh comin home?

ELAINE Thah's none a your business.

FRANCES Do you have information you're kapin from me?

ELAINE And if I had?

FRANCES You and your father, swear ya were married to him. You tell me now what you know!

ELAINE I know natin, Ma, natin ya don't know yourself.

*Enter* SARAH.

SARAH Ah, Boniface, ya do a runner agin?

BONIFACE The savage loves hees nahive shore.

SARAH And what d'ya think a the antics a your little brother? They're goin to puh him on the throne. I used change that fella's nappy. Seen ud all now. *{Watches as* BONIFACE *pours another drink for himself)* Ya were thirsty as a child too, a bottle in each fist as ya snoozed in the coh. Your Ma used love watchin ya guzzlin. The little sounds of him, she used say, isn't he like a little bonamh?

BONIFACE You'd reminiss the future, missus, if ya though ya'd geh away wud ud.

SARAH Aye, I would and noh wan a yees would belave me.

STEPHEN *has entered.*

STEPHEN It's ten to six.

ELAINE Give him a minuhe. We'll make ud, they'll wait for us.

BONIFACE Stephen, I hear you're the new John Ford.

STEPHEN I wish.

ELAINE He won a prize and all.

BONIFACE Didn't I rade about ud in the paper.

STEPHEN That's ony because a Daddy.

BONIFACE A prize is a prize. These things is important. Never won as much as a turkey meself. Whah was the film abouh anyway?

STEPHEN Ma'll tell ya, she's fierce proud of ud.

FRANCES Ah, ud was disgustin, Stephen, no two ways abouh ud. Near fainted when I seen ud. Ya've this mother and her son and ud's the son's weddin day and then the son goes missin, and the bride is lookin all over the hotel for her new husband. And where does she find her new husband? In the bridal suihe, on the bridal bed, bein breast-fed be the mother. Now what's thah abouh, I ask ya? What's the pint in makin a film about thah?

STEPHEN Does there alias have to be a pint, Ma?

FRANCES I'll tell ya what the pint was. The pint was to geh at me.

STEPHEN You think everthin comes back to you. Ud doesn't.

FRANCES Then why did ya call the mother Frances in your film? Why was she dressed like me? Why was she drivin an auld Merc? That's whah I drive. I don't nade this, Stephen. Pack a lies, the whole thing.

STEPHEN Ud's noh a pack a lies. Ud happened.

FRANCES Didn't happen here, me bucko.

STEPHEN Buh ud happened. Read abouh ud in an Italian newspaper. Ya don't have to make anhin up.

BONIFACE Thah's for sure. Everythin ya can possibly imagine has happened already or, if ud hasn't, will shortly.

FRANCES And manetime the cement is waitin on ya.

STEPHEN I'll puh a bullet through me head first.

FERMOY *stands in the doorway. He has changed into his mourning clothes.*

FERMOY Righ, are we off?

FRANCES You come back here after Mass. Don't go scurryin away, ya hear?

FERMOY I've a seven o'clock meetin in the mornin.

FRANCES You come back here or I'll folly ya to Dublin. (To *theothers, exiting)* Come an, we're lahe, we're lahe.

*Exit* FRANCES *followed by* BONIFACE *and* STEPHEN.

ELAINE A'ya alrigh, Daddy?

FERMOY Your mother.

ELAINE Don't mind her, brazen ud ouh, we'll be gone straih after Mass, won't have to see her for another year.

FERMOY Have Bernard drive yees down. I'll walk.

ELAINE We should all arrive together.

FERMOY I nade two minutes to meself, Elaine.

ELAINE Alrigh, alrigh, I'll send Bernard back for ya.

*Exit* ELAINE. SARAH *pours a whiskeyfor herself*

FERMOY Ya noh goin down to dunk your soul?

SARAH A millin Masses wouldn't bleach ud.

FERMOY Nor mine.

SARAH Nor yours. *(Raises* FERMOY's *chin with her hand)* That's ih. Never leh em see ya wud the harness off.

*Exit* SARAH. FERMOY *stands there a moment, gets out pocket mirror, checks himself in it, teeth, hair, eyes, a long look.*

FERMOY Who are ya, sir? Who are ya and from where do ya come? Geh a hould, stranger, geh a hould. *(Clicks mirror shut. Takes a deep breath)* Righ, let's rock and roll.

*The phone rings. Note on* ARIEL's *voice: once convention of the phone has been established, let* ARIEL's *voice come from everywhere,* FERMOY *does not talk into the phone after the first couple of exchanges.*

Yes?

ARIEL Hello.

FERMOY Elaine, I'm on the way, tell her I'm on the way.

ARIEL Ud's me.

FERMOY Who's me?

ARIEL Me, Ariel.

FERMOY Ariel ... Who is this? I'm in no mood for ...

ARIEL No, ud's me, Ariel.

FERMOY Buh ud can't be ... ud can't.

ARIEL Buh ud is.

FERMOY Oh, Ariel. . . you're alive . . . you're alive.

ARIEL Come and get me, will ya? Ud's awful here, ud's awful. There's a huge pike after me, he lives in the belfry, two rows a teeth on him and teeth on hees tongue, bendin back to hees throah. He won't rest till he has me. Come and get me, will ya?

FERMOY How? Tell me how can I come and get ya?

ARIEL *(Sounds of terrible weeping)* I don't know ... I want to go home ... I just want to go home. Please, just brin me home.

FERMOY Ariel. . . Ariel ... don't. . . don't.

*He listens as sound of* ARIEL'S *weeping fades and fades to silence,* FERMOY *stands there. Let him stand there, utterly still, looking out. Then enter* FRANCES. *She stands in the doorway, in her coat, out of breath.* FERMOY *registers her after a while. They look at one another for an age.*

FERMOY Ya cem back for me. I'm comin, I'm comin.

FRANCES No more Masses.

FERMOY Well, I'm goin. Where's Bernard? Come an and we get this over wud.

FRANCES You're goin nowhere. Ud was you, wasn't ud? Ud was you.

FERMOY Y'ony realizin thah now? I thought ya knew for years.

FRANCES Knew whah for years?

FERMOY Frances ... ya didn't ... Look this is noh the time for this conversation.

FRANCES You. Alias you and me scourin the world for her. You. And me gone to ground wud grafe. You. And ony last nigh I dreamt she walked in the duur and ten year a madness just fell away. She had wan life. Wan. Are you tellin me you took ud?

FERMOY Ariel was a drame hopped among us from start to end. We had the privelege of her company a while buh she was never really ours. We brough somethin inta the world thah didn't belong here and so we gev her back.

FRANCES Gev her back? We gev her back? Gev her back where?

FERMOY Remember them wings she was born wud?

FRANCES Wings? Whah wings?

FERMOY Them wings on her shoulder blades.

FRANCES Whah are ya talkin abouh? Whah wings? On her shoulder blades? Them growths on her shoulders, is thah what you're talkin abouh?

FERMOY They were the start a wings.

FRANCES They were balls a hardened bone and gristle, thah'sall, benign, tiny, we had em removed.

FERMOY You're callin them everthin except what they were. Leh me tell you somethin, Frances. Before I ever laid eyes on you, long before thah, I had a drame, a drame so beauhiful I wanted to stay in ud till the end a time. I'm in a yella cuurtyard wud God and we're chewin the fah and then this girl wud wings appears by hees side. And I say, who owns her? And God says she's his. And I say, give us the loan of her, will ya? No, he says, she's noh earth flavour, like he's talkin abouh ice-crame. And stupidly I say, I'll take her anyway. Alrigh, he says, smilin ah me rale sly, alrigh, buh remember this is a loan. I know, I know, I says, knowin natin. And the time'll come when I'll want her returned, he says. Yeah, yeah, I say, fleein the cuurtyard wud her before he changes hees mind. Ariel. Thah was Ariel.

FRANCES Just tell me where she is.

FERMOY I'm tellin ya, thah was Ariel I fled the cuurtyard wud. And then I wake and the enchantment begins. You, Ariel, Elaine, Stephen. All the trinkets of this world showered on us. We had ten good years, hadn't we? Them were the years and we didn't know ud. He gev, he gev, he gev, and then like the tide he turned and took ud all away.

FRANCES (*A heartbroken wail, weeping like we've never seen, stands there heaving and choking and wailing)* Ariel ... Ariel ... Ariel ... How could ya? ... You loved thah child ... How could ya? *(Shakes him)*

FERMOY I had to! I had to!

FRANCES You had to!

FERMOY Yeah, I had to. Ya think I wanted to sacrifice Ariel? I had to.

FRANCES Sacrifice? Ya sacrificed her? What did you do to her?

FERMOY I tould ya I returned her to where she cem from.

FRANCES She cem from here, from you, from me.

FERMOY She rode ouha God from nowhere and to God she returned.

FRANCES You sacrificed her! Aaaagh. Why didn't ya sacrifice yourself if he wanted a sacrifice? Why didn't ya refuse?

FERMOY A cuurse I refused. I fough him till I couldn't figh him anymore.

FRANCES Thah was no God ya med your pact wud. No God demands such things.

FERMOY My God did.

FRANCES Blem God, blem the world, anywan bar yourself. Ud's all comin clear now, clear as a bell. Ya done ud for power, didn't ya, some voodoo swap in the dark for power. You laid my daughter on an altar for power. You've flourished these ten years since Ariel. You've flourished on her white throat. You swapped her to advance.

FERMOY Yes, I did. Yes, I did. I had to. Ud was the price demanded.

FRANCES And you dare to stand here tellin me fairy stories abouh her.

FERMOY Frances, I know whah I have done. I know my portion a blame, buh when I'm hauled before him I'll fling hees portion ah him, where ud belongs. I have lived my life by hees instructions. He asked the unaskable and I obeyed, and then he departs, lavin me here in ashes. And my greahest fear is he won't be there whin I go. No, I've wan greaher, thah he will.

FRANCES *(Softly)* Buh Ariel ... Fermoy ... This is Ariel you're talkin abouh.

FERMOY Don't make ud more difficult for me than ud is.

FRANCES Ya med ud difficult yourself. This was your playground well as anywan's.

FERMOY This is no playground and never was. This is where he hunts us down like deer and flays us alive for sport.

FRANCES Whah was ud I seen the day I first wint wud you?

FERMOY I'll tell ya what ya seen. Ya seen a man capable of anhin. And thah seh fire to your little bungalow life. Ya seen a man that could do away wud your children and ya ran towards him, noh away from him. That's whah drew ya the first time and that's what kapes ya swirlin round me. Tombstones, headstones, graveyard excitement and the promise of funerals to come.

FRANCES You'll say anhin for company in your carnage.

FERMOY You wanted me, missus, and ya still want me. Ud's ony your pride is stoppin ya.

FRANCES I wanted me first husband. Was through wud you before the honeymoon started. You stole me life from me, me children from me, everythin I though I was from me and I a glazed fool flung open the duurs for the plunder. Never agin.

FERMOY YOU want a divorce? Yours for the askin.

FRANCES Ya think ya'll geh off thah aisy? Where is she?

FERMOY Thah you'll never know.

| | |
|---|---|
| FRANCES | I cem from gintle people, me father used rescue spiders from the bah, mice he'd carry ouh in hees hand and leh go in the field, gintle people, Charlie, James, Ariel, gintle, gintle, gintle, no place for em in this nest a hooves. Where is she? *(Stabs him)* |
| FERMOY | *(Reels)* Frances. |
| FRANCES | *(Another stab)* Where is she? |
| FERMOY | You think you can do away wud me ... Gimme thah. |

*A struggle.* FRANCES *stabs him again.*

| | |
|---|---|
| FRANCES | And you thought I was afraid a the knife. *(Another stab)* Where is she? |
| FERMOY | *(Falls to the ground. She gets on top of him)* No ... Frances ... no ... Stop ... stop ... |
| FRANCES | And did you stop when Ariel cried ouh for mercy? Did ya? Tell me where she is. |
| FERMOY | This wasn't ... this ... Sweet God in your ... |
| FRANCES | Tell me. Where is she? |
| FERMOY | *(Whispers as he dies)* Cuura Lake. |
| FRANCES | Cuura Lake. |

*She throws down the knife. 'Mors et Vita' music, and blackout.*

## ACT THREE

*'Mors et Vita' music continues from end of Act Two. Two months later. A coffin lies centre stage,* ELAINE *lies on the floor in T-shirt and tracksuit bottoms. She's asleep. A drink beside her. Enter* STEPHEN, *suit, folders, takes in the coffin, goes to it, has a long look.*

| | |
|---|---|
| STEPHEN | Elaine ... Elaine ... *(Shakes her gently)* Ya should go up to bed. |
| ELAINE | Ah, Stephen. *(Yawns)* |
| STEPHEN | When did ud arrive? |
| ELAINE | This mornin . . . *(Stretching)* What time is ud? |
| STEPHEN | After five. |
| ELAINE | Oh, God. *(Lies down again)* |
| STEPHEN | *(Goes back to coffin)* Thought she'd be behher preserved, Cuura Lake bein a bog lake and all. |
| ELAINE | She looked behher when they took her up first. Forensics scraped her down. |
| STEPHEN | Hard to square this wud Daddy. |
| ELAINE | Ya think? |
| STEPHEN | Don't you? |
| ELAINE | I knew for a while ud was him. STEPHEN Didya? |
| ELAINE | Didn't you? |
| STEPHEN | No, a few stray thoughts. Never wahered them. How did ya know? |
| ELAINE | He tould me ... Well, I asked him abouh her wan time. Venice. Some conference. Drink on the table in a little restaurant lookin on to the Rialto. And he tould me the whole thing. Very emotional he was too. Ariel was the stroke a destiny, he said, woven into him from the beginnin. Ariel was Necessity udself, the thing thah's decided ouhside a time. And he tould me all abouh Necessity. How before ya come to this world, Necessity and her sisters weaves a carpet for ya. And ya watch as they weave so ya know how things will fare ouh below. And |

then ya turn your back and Necessity puts a twist in the weave. Thah's the wan thing ya can't foresee and thah's the wan thing will define your stay here. And then you're flung to earth wud this weave and this twist in the weave thah some calls fate.

STEPHEN Ya belave thah?

ELAINE Belaved ud thah nigh. The lights on the waher, ud's hard to be rational in Venice.

STEPHEN Ma wants to puh her in beside Daddy.

ELAINE If thah wan as much as touches a pebble of my father's grave.

STEPHEN Well, you shouldn't a puh up thah headstone, her name noh even on ud. Ma wanted to puh up hees headstone. You're like an alsatian the way ya guard hees grave.

ELAINE And you're still slurpin ah her altar after all she's done.

STEPHEN There was a pair a them in ud. She keeps askin for ya, Elaine, to go visih her. Ya wouldn't know her. She's still our mother.

ELAINE Ariel's the ony wan she cares abouh. Ariel and James, her dead children, while she bates her livin inta the dirt.

STEPHEN Thah's noh true, sick a ya givin ouh abouh her.

ELAINE And I'm sick a you makin your weekly pilgrimages to her, brinin information abouh me. I warned ya noh to tell her anhin abouh me. I'll live like a tinker in me own house if I want, me father's house. She's natin to me anymore. Natin.

STEPHEN Well, ya certainly proved thah, ravin agin her in cuurt.

ELAINE Ya know I wish I'd said more agin her.

STEPHEN A spew a lies.

ELAINE I tould ud as ud happened.

STEPHEN Like hell ya did. Anyway ud's been struck.

ELAINE I knew ud would, buh ud was still heard. You don't seem to understand whah's goin on here, Stephen. She killed our father, slashed him till blood ran down the walls. I had to bury him in pieces. I was the only mourner ah hees funeral. Me, Boniface, Auntie Sarah. You were too busy swaddlin Ma to go to your own father's funeral. Such as ud was. She wouldn't aven allow him a public funeral. Paple loved Daddy. You saw the size a the removal. She aven tried to stop thah. But she couldn't. They just kept comin.

STEPHEN They kept comin to have a gawk.

ELAINE They cem because they loved him. You never seen Daddy in hees element. You never seen him the way he seen Mmself, the way he was born to be seen, the way he could work a room, the way he held himself when he spoke, the big mellifluous vice, ya'd hear a pin drop. He was goin to run this country. He was goin to cahapult the whole nation ouha sleaze and sentimentalihy and gombeenism. I'm goin to take this country to the moon, he used say to me, and he would've, ony for her. And she's still noh happy havin done away wud him. No, now she had ud in her head to take away hees name and mine wud ud and yours, though ya don't seem to care. Draggin this yoke up ouha Cuura Lake. All to destriy what's left of hees reputation. All to make her look like a martyr.

*Enter* FRANCES *and* BONIFACE.

STEPHEN Ma, we weren't expectin ya till tonigh.

FRANCES They let me ouh early to avide the press. Hello, Elaine.

ELAINE *looks at her.*

I was hopin we could be civil for Ariel's funeral.

ELAINE Were ya?

FRANCES *goes to coffin. Looks. Leans in. Kisses* ARIEL. *Leans in for ages.*

FRANCES *(Whispers)* YaTl soon be the girl in the graveyard ya tould me abouh wance. Ya'll soon rest aisy. Who picked ouh her dress?

STEPHEN Elaine did.

FRANCES Thank you.

ELAINE Was in her wardrobe. They had to staple ud on to her. I didn't do ud for you.

BONIFACE Elaine. Elaine. Elaine.

ELAINE You're goin to geh off on insanihy, a cuurse y'are, ya can shooh a baby in the face these days and geh off on insanihy.

FRANCES Well, if I do ud'U be no thanks to you.

ELAINE Ud was murder. Cold-blooded murder, and if you geh off on insanihy I'll open me own cuurtroom here.

FRANCES You weren't aven here and ya med out ya were.

ELAINE I was here. He died in my arms. You were standin in the hall lookin at the radiahor.

FRANCES And would you have done different if he done to wan a yours whah he done to Ariel?

ELAINE Yes, I would.

FRANCES Oh, ya would, would ya?

ELAINE Yes, I would. I can tell the difference between a crime of eternihy and a low, blood-spahhered, knife-frenzied revenge. And then your coward's insanihy plea on top of ud. Whah my father done to Ariel had the grandeur a God in ud. Pure sacrifice. Ferocious, aye. Buh pure. Whah you done to him was a puckered, vengeful, self-servin thing wud noh a whiff of the immortal in ud.

FRANCES So your father spills blood and he's a haroh. I spill ud and I'm a coward. You've spint too long around the min, me girl, too long cavortin the corriduurs a power to understand the first thing abouh justice. Ya know, there's ony wan thing I regreh. Thah I didn't do ud sooner. And I won't apologize to you for thah or for pleadin insanihy. I'll plead whahever ud takes to geh my freedom back. And don't tell me you'd do different if you were in my shoes.

ELAINE I'm as different to you as the auld world is from the new, sem as my father was. Oh, to be Joan of Arc goin up in a blaze to me maker.

FRANCES Then go up in a blaze to your maker, ony lave me alone. I've wan nigh here, wan night's freedom to mourn my daugher, to puh her in the clay tomorra beside her father.

ELAINE She's noh goin in wud him. My father's grave stays the way ud is. Can't ya just lave him alone?

FRANCES She's goin in beside him and thah's the end of ud, Elaine. Ud's whah he'd have wanted. ELAINE Whah he'd have wanted?

BONIFACE Ud is, Elaine, ud's whah your father would've wanted.

ELAINE Whah my father wanted was to be above the ground, noh under ud. Above ud! You're noh shovellin her in on top of him. You stand here givin orders abouh hees grave. I organized hees burial. I picked the ploh, under the elms, near the path so he won't be too lonely. I paid for hees headstone. You weren't aven ah hees funeral.

FRANCES I wasn't fit to go, Elaine.

ELAINE But you're fit for Ariel's. You're ony here to swing the jury. Don't touch hees grave. Ud's mine. Ud's all ya've left me wud. I'm warnin ya now.

FRANCES Keep your grave. I've a new ploh arranged. Your father's moving, lock, stock and barrel as we spake. Ariel's goin in wud him. And I'll arrange the headstone this time. You think you can kick me when I'm down. I'm down, aye, righ now I'm lower than the lowest low. Buh I'll rise agin in spihe a your efforts to wipe the ground wud me. Why don't ya go and stay in the hotel tonigh, be asier for all of us. I'll be gone tomorra.

ELAINE I'm stayin here, to haunt ya.

FRANCES You? Haunt me? Oh, Elaine, you're ony the fallouh. We never goh on, I don't know why I want us to now. This skirmish betwane us is ancient. Y'ever feel thah? Seems to me we been battlin a thousand year.

ELAINE I'm goin down to hees grave and I hope for your sake there's natin disturbed.

*Exit* ELAINE.

FRANCES Where did I geh her from?

*She pours a drink.*

BONIFACE *(Looking at* ARIEL *in coffin)* The divers found the remains a seven people and they draggin the lake. Wan wud a boulder tied round the skelehon of a wrist. Most a them just an assortment a bones. Found the skelehon of a pike too, massive, musta been over two hundred pound, all the teeth intact.

FRANCES Did they find your mother?

BONIFACE We don't know yeh. They're tryin to date em all. I tould em, she's the wan wud the boulder, but they want to do their tests. *(To* ARIEL) I liked you, little girl.

FRANCES *(To* STEPHEN) Shouldn't you be down ah the cement?

STEPHEN I was, cem home early because a the day is in ud.

FRANCES I been goin through the figures. Big losses these last two months.

STEPHEN They don't listen to me.

FRANCES Make em listen. Tell em ud's comin down from me. Ud's your inheritance.

STEPHEN I'll sell ud soon as ya sign ud over.

FRANCES Ya too much of a swank wud your film degree to lower yourself to the cement and gravel.

STEPHEN I don't have me film degree yeh, thanks to certain events round here.

FRANCES Well, mebbe ya should think abouh jackin in the films and start turnin your mind to cement.

STEPHEN Thah's noh goin to happen, Ma.

FRANCES Me and your father built thah cement up from wan lorry smuggled in from England, an auld shed and the lase of a quarry. Cement built this house, cement gev ya your education, your fast car, your designer clothes, your foreign holidas. Cement finances your arty films. You think you're above the cement and gravel? Well, you're noh. You're med of ud like the rest of us. Sure ya were nearly born in wan a the lorries. Me and your father drivin through the nigh, big delivery, me follyin him along the weh roads. Elaine aslape beside me, Ariel in front wud Fermoy. Me bapin like a madwoman for Fermoy to pull over, him bapin back thinkin I'm messin, and you surgin to be born. I fling open the winda, wavin and yellin. He sees me in the mirror and pulls over. Me in a panic, geh me to the hospital, geh me to the midwives. Him laughin ah me, I'll be your midwife, missus, and the rain as balmy on him and the head of him thrown back, laughin, just laughin ... Was fierce sorry after I didn't leh him be me midwife. He'd a done ud too. Thah man was afraid a natin.

STEPHEN Ya boultin the stable now and your horse is gone.

FRANCES Doesn't everywan?

STEPHEN No, they don't, some knows when they're happy ah the time. You had your chance, Ma, now ud's mine, and I won't be buried under a ton a cement on your whim. I tould ya I'd help ouh till the trial's over. And I will. Buh then I'm gone.

FRANCES Is thah a threah?

STEPHEN Ud's a fact.

FRANCES Ya been listenin to Elaine. She's turnin ya against me.

STEPHEN Can make up me own mind, Ma. Count yourself lucky I can stand in the same room as ya.

FRANCES So that's the way ud is. I thought ya were on my side.

STEPHEN Ya though wrong. Ud's time ya stopped pullin ouh a me, livin through me.

FRANCES I don't live through ya! How dare you! I've never lived through anywan, to me own greah cost. Alias I've resisted. Alias! When ud'd be asier bow down. Whah are you sayin to me?

STEPHEN I'm sayin ...

FRANCES All month long I been dramin I'm breastfeedin a snake. I thought ud was Elaine, buh ud's you. And insteada milk comin ouh ud's blood. And ya kape suckin though I'm roarin wud the pain. Ud took me ten year to wean you. Ten year I didn't have. And now you tell me thah doesn't count.

STEPHEN Ten year pretendin I was James. Ten year I went along wud ud. I used pray to die so you'd be given back James, I loved ya thah much. When strangers'd ask me me name, I'd say, James, me name is James, I'm James of the blue black curls.

FRANCES Whah are you talkin abouh, Stephen?

STEPHEN Don't pretend ya don't remember.

FRANCES I know I'd never win Mother a the Year, buh, Christ, Stephen, I wanted you as I wanted all me children. I swear, in me heart, what's left of ud, there's a tahhered chamber for each wan a ya. And them chambers is of equal measure.

STEPHEN And if they are, then why did ya kill my father?

FRANCES You know why.

STEPHEN Tell me.

FRANCES You know why, you know, because of her. *(Coffin)*

STEPHEN Wudouh a thought for Elaine or me. Wudouh a care of how thah rippin away has shahhered us. Ya did ud for Ariel. For James. There was ony ever two chambers in your heart, Ma, two dusty chambers, me and Elaine tryin to force our way in. Our playground was a graveyard, Ma, we ran among your tombstones like they were swings, we played hop, skip and jump on the bones a your children, your real children, while we whined for ya like ghosts. Isn't thah the way ud was? *(Gestures to coffin)* Isn't ud the way of ud still?

FRANCES Stephen . . . where a'ya goin?

STEPHEN *(Exiting)* The thing is, I'm goin.

*She runs after him, tries to hold him hack.*

FRANCES Ariel's funeral, me trial ... Stephen! Don't, sweeheart, don't. Don't do this to me now. Please. Noh now. Noh now.

STEPHEN *stands there, immovable.* FRANCES *withdraws eventually. Exit* STEPHEN. FRANCES *stands there distraught, disbelief.*

*(Whispers)* He's gone ... he's gone ... my baby is gone.

BONIFACE And leh him. Whah I shoulda done forty year ago. Good man, Stephen. How did ya do thah? Mammy's off the menu for ever more. Thah's how ud's done. Like thah big fah cluckin Mammy owl I seen on National Geographic the other nigh. And this Mammy Owl is huntin like Billy-O to fade Owl junior. And she comes back to the nest this nigh, big rah in her mouh, all important like, I'm fadin the young lad, aren't I a model Ma. And Junior's gone, fled when her back was turned, no goodbyes, thah's the way to do ud. Or salmon, sure salmon has ne'er a Ma ah all, and y'ever watch them, lords a the waher, sun shin in for em. Or trees, don't get me started on trees. Seems to me everythin worth lookin ah in this world has ne'er a Ma ah all, ud's just there be udself in a flowerin gorgeousness, orphaned and free.

FRANCES Geh ouha my house, you.

BONIFACE Whah?

FRANCES You call yourself a man a God. Fermoy wud all hees divilry had more religion. Prancin around in your robes, watchin me like a hawk, cheerin on me ony son's departure.

BONIFACE Frances, I was talkin abouh meself.

FRANCES You knew all along and ya never said a word.

BONIFACE Whah could I have done? I'm payin for this too.

FRANCES Spare me your remorse. I rue the day I ever she eyes on the Fitzgeralds.

BONIFACE I think we can return the compliment.

FRANCES Just go.

BONIFACE I'm charged wud your care.

FRANCES The place is crawlin wud cops. I'm goin nowhere. Just go. I want five minutes on me own wud Ariel.

BONIFACE I'll sih in the car. If ya nade anhin, I'll be in the car.

*And exit* BONIFACE. FRANCES *goes to coffin, looks in.*

FRANCES *(Whispers)* Mother a God, ya could be anywan.

*Enter* ELAINE, *stands there watching* FRANCES.

ELAINE So ya dug him up.

FRANCES Elaine, please, no more, no more, our love affair wud the knife is over.

*And exit* FRANCES.

ELAINE *(To herself)* Alrigh. Lave her alone. Lave her alone. Say natin. Do natin. She'll be gone tomorra and ya can just dig him up agin. *(Wanders to coffin, looks in)* Mebbe I'm unnatural buh I never fell under your spell. Then the wrong things has alias moved me ... and if there's such a place as paradise, leh ud be impty, oh leh ud be impty.

SARAH *has entered, listens.*

SARAH I've an inklin of whah you're plannin.

ELAINE I never plan anhin, Auntie Sarah.

SARAH Don't ya? *(Looks into coffin)* God, she's wizened to a nun. Wud a squaze ya'd fih her in a fishbowl.

ELAINE She's after diggin him up.

SARAH So? He was her husband, noh yours, and this is her house, noh yours, and a body can do whah they like behind their own front duur.

ELAINE Whah planet were you brough up on? Behind your own front duur's the wan place ya can do natin ya like. Behind your own front duur's where ya face em all down wud your tail to the wall. And by God I'm goin to face thah wan down before long.

SARAH There's a divil the size of a whale inside you. Where in God's name is this hatred a your mother comin from?

ELAINE If I knew thah … I can't look ah her for too long or me head swims. She appals me, alias has. *(Shudders)* Her eyes, her shoulders, everythin abouh her. I look ah her and I think there's somethin missin. I don't know is ud in me or in her.

SARAH And whah is ud ya think is missin?

ELAINE I think she has no soul.

SARAH And since when have you become the decider a souls? A cuurse she has a soul, if she hadn't a soul she wouldn't be alive.

ELAINE They say there's some born wudouh em and I think she's wan a them. She tells me we been slashin wan another since time began. Well, if we have, this here is my turn, this is my opportunihy to geh a good go ah her and silence her till Judgement Day.

SARAH And on Judgement Day what'll ya tell the man above wud hees seven eyes level on ya? Ya won't face him down so aisy.

ELAINE You dare to talk to me abouh God and you the first thah coaxed the darkness in. I know you of an auld dahe. Addicted to nigh is what y'are, slobberin over ud like the cah wud the crame. But ya won't grab your own piece a nigh, no, ya covet mine from the corner. You ud was watched the first murder in this house. You watched your sister die, ya watched me grandfather tie her wud stones and ya said natin and ya done natin, ony watched in a swoon, black flowers sproutin ouha your chest. Yes, ya whispered, yes, I'll watch anhin, I'm the woman who'll watch arihin.

SARAH You don't know the first thing abouh me and me sister and your grandfather.

ELAINE I know ya married him.

SARAH Thah was the ind! Thah was the ind! I'm sick a bein judged on the ind. Whah abouh the start? Ya think I was never young? Ya think I like these auld hands, wud the veins risin on em like rivers in flood? Ya think I never burned? Ya think the world started wud you? I loved my sister. I adored thah woman.

ELAINE Aye, and ya adored her man wud your grady plain Jane heart. Oh aye, ya loved her alrigh, loved her so much ya wanted her life, her eyelashes, her children, her husband. And some goblin in me grandfather heard your prayers and answered em.

SARAH Ud was me he wint wud first. Me! Ya didn't know thah, did ya! And she took him from me wudouh a by your leave, wudouh an apology. And I took him back. Fair is fair.

ELAINE And you try to bate me over the head wud God, like you're hees favourihe, like you'll be sittin on hees knee on Judgement Day, wud me prostrahe before yees. God won't like me. I know thah. Buh he'll have more time for me than he will for you. You married your sister's husband as she turned to bog oak in Cuura Lake. Ya watched Ariel die, ya watched me father die. Is there anhin ya wouldn't watch?

SARAH To watch a thing is ony to half wish ud. And to half wish a thing is a long way off from doin ud. Buh I'll watch no longer. I'm bo win ouh here. I'm no match for ya anymore.

*Exit* SARAH.

ELAINE *(After her)* Good. Good. Good.

ELAINE *goes to coffin. Takes out skull of* ARIEL, *with a few strands of hair attached to it. She holds it up.*

*(To skull)* I drame abouh you all the time. Strange, wakin there's no animosity, we're friends, friendly as sisters can be, buh aslape we're enemies, enemies till the end a time. Whah does thah mane? Remember them black dolls we had when we were scuts and how we used torture em on Sahurday mornins, line them up on the bed and tear em limb from limb? That's what ya remind me a now, them black dolls. Did ya go aisy, Ariel? Or did ya figh him ah the end? Or did ya think ud was all a game, smokin hees cigar and swillin hees brandy as the stars leant down to watch?

FERMOY *stands in doorway, dressed as he was at end of Act Two. Covered in blood. He watches* ELAINE *dancing. She finally registers him, backs off.*

*(A whisper)* Daddy.

FERMOY *(Advancing)* Whah?

ELAINE Go way, keep away.

FERMOY Who are you?

ELAINE Ya don't know me.

FERMOY Don't I? I thought ya were familiar, walkin up the drive, the lawn, the fountain, thought I recognized this place from somewhere. Who are ya?

ELAINE Ya never give the dead your name.

FERMOY Am I dead?

ELAINE Oh, you're dead alrigh.

FERMOY Dead as thah? *(Points to skull)*

ELAINE Yeah.

FERMOY Who's thah?

ELAINE Me sister ... Ariel. . . Ya remember her?

FERMOY Who?

ELAINE Ariel.

FERMOY No, should I?

ELAINE No.

FERMOY Then why did ya ask me?

ELAINE Nevermind.

FERMOY Look, I'm tryin to find this place, ya may be able to help me.

ELAINE And whah place is ud you're tryin to find?

FERMOY I don't know the name of ud. *(Thinks)* Ud's a cuurt-yard, yella, or the ligh in ud is yella. There's some girl there I have to meeh. D'you know the place I'm talkin abouh? Is ud anywhere 'round here?

ELAINE I never heard if ud is.

FERMOY Yasure?

ELAINE Yeah.

FERMOY I have to get there ... I have to meet this girl. Nowan seems to know where ud is. I may kape goin.

*And exit* FERMOY *as* FRANCES *enters.*

FRANCES Elaine.

*Takes skull off* ELAINE, *who looks after* FERMOY

Just whah d'ya think you're doin ... maulin her like thah?

*Puts skull back in coffin.*

ELAINE I tould ya not to touch me father's grave. Tould ya ih'd disturb everythin. But ya wouldn't listen, would ya?

FRANCES Just geh ouh! Geh ouh a this house and don't come back. You're so full a your own hate ya don't nohice the hate of others. Some zebra stallion grafted you onta me. I wanted a son to make up for James. And I goh you. Now g'wan wud thah piece of information and leh ud sustain ya on your travels. G'wan, geh ouha me sigh.

ELAINE Aye, some zebra stallion grafted me onta ya alrigh, and I festered there, bidin me time. Ya say ya prayed for a son to make up for James. Well, I am James. I'm James returned. And I'm me father that ya butchered to hees eyeballs. And I'm Ariel. And I'm Elaine wud your deah on me palm, carved inta my plain a Mars like stone. Whah a relate to be finally livin ud.

*Stabs* FRANCES *in the throat.*

FRANCES *(Reels, falls)* Elaine ... no ... no ... no more ...

ELAINE *(Watching her reel, die, flounder)* After this, no more.

FRANCES No ... *{Tries to get up, holds her throat, blood spilling from her mouth)* Had to . . . had to ... puh ud off. . .

*A massive effort to get up, gets up, holds onto coffin, looks into it, a blood-curdling wail.*

No ... no ... Don't ... don't leh me ... don't leh me ... don't leh me . . . don't leh me go . . .

*Falls against* ELAINE *who lets her slide to the floor.* ELAINE *stands there. Throws down the knife. Looks out.*

*'Mors et Vita music, and blackout.*

# Electricidad

By Luis Alfaro

After awhile it comes down to a question
of life choices not a choice between you/or her
this sea town/or that bruising city
but about putting one foot in front of the other
and ending up somewhere
that looks like home.
—Cherrie Moraga, "The Last Generation"

## LA CASA DE ATREDAS

**ELECTRICIDAD (23)**, the oldest daughter, an old-school chola, in grief, cannot break the cycle.
**AGAMENÓN "EL AUGGIE" (R.I.P.)**, el rey, el hombre formerly known as Father, a veterano from way back, head of the East Side Locos.
**CLEMENCIA (40)**, the mother, total veterana, goes way back, has issues.
**IFIGENIA (20)**, the other daughter, formerly muy peligrosa, possibly born-again, looks good in black.
**ABUELA (50)**, the grandmother, a veterana, old-school chola, muy sexy this vieja.
**ORESTES (17)**, the brother, a peewee, heir to the trono, exiled to Las Vegas.
**NINO (52)**, the godfather, el atendido, the most veterano, exiled to Las Vegas.
**LAS VECINAS**, a chorus of mujeres from the hood, have seen it all, the voz of the city:
**LA CARMEN**
**LA CONNIE**
**LA CUCA**

## LUGAR

City of Los, the East Side, by the river, that house at the end of the street over by the freeway.

## SONIDO

The city, a live wire, electricity running from a transformer.

## TIEMPO

Right now, baby.

## SETTING

We see a yard in front of a casa at the end of the block. Not one of the kept-up yards, pero una yarda filled with dirt, shrubs, stones and some stuff that doesn't fit in the house.

En la yarda is an altar made of stones. Nestled between the stones are objects that live on altars: votive candles, burning incense, fragrant flowers, a Bart Simpson piggy bank from the border, old and faded pictures.

At the center of the altar lies the decomposing body of **Agamenón** "El Auggie" Atridas, the father. El former rey de la neighborhood. Eyes plucked. Tongue missing. He is wrapped in a shroud.

Sitting in the yard and draped over El Auggie is **Electricidad**, la youngest hija. She has been sitting in the yard for five days. Waiting. For what? Quien sabe. A layer of earth bakes on her. A canvas for the recent Santa Anas. But you know what? Her makeup is holding on pretty good … She wears Levi's, a black tank top and chancla flip-flops. Her hair is matted and dirty. She has not spoken for days, but her wailing, which has been heard throughout el barrio 24/7, becomes an echo when it hits the valley at Mariachi Plaza. This homegirl is a young chola with old-school ways. Always has, always been. Even at night when little cholos dream of Krispy Kremes and fresh graffiti, Electricidad sits with her father.

We can clearly see inside la casa. The walls are missing and a wood frame is revealed. We see some furniture inside. Seventies stuff. Some cosas from layaway.

Moving nervously through the house, como una bird in a cage, is **Clemencia**, la mama. She is smoking—pero always. (It helps with the nervios, you know.) The cigarette is long. A Virginia Slim. She is dressed in chola evening wear. Y with some heel, of course. Sometimes she puts on a hat. When she wants to look good. Tu sabes.

## Electricidad—A Chicano Take on the Tragedy of *Electra*

## SCENE 1

### As I Sit Here

*An East Los rooster crows. Daybreak. The sound of work begins. The sweep, sweep, sweep of brooms. Electricidad sleeps at her altar. The faint sound of chisme approaches as we see a trio of Vecinas sweep down the street. A Griego chorus in house dresses and aprons. Very mitoteras these mujeres. Their chisme is accompanied by the rhythmic sweeping of their brooms.*

**LA CARMEN**: Apoco.
**LA CONNIE**: No me digas.
**LA CUCA**: Ai …
*Beat.*
**LA CARMEN**: Did you see?
**LA CONNIE**: No, que?
**LA CUCA**: She's still there.
**LA CARMEN**: There at her altar.
**LA CONNIE**: Ai, don't stare, vecina!
**LA CUCA**: I can't help it.
**LA CARMEN**: It's so sad.
**LA CONNIE**: Such a tragedy.
**LA CUCA**: A story like this.
**LA CARMEN**: Makes you wonder.
**LA CONNIE**: Where you can live these days.
**LA CUCA**: Esta asi all over.
**LA CARMEN**: Every part of the city.
**LA CONNIE**: No one can escapar.
**LA CUCA**: Must be fate.
**LA CARMEN**: Must be luck.
**LA CONNIE**: Must be the city.
**LA CUCA**: Especially over here.
**LA CARMEN**: Split by the freeway.
**LA CONNIE**: Border the river.
**LA CUCA**: In the shadow of skyscrapers.
**LA CARMEN**: But still.
**LA CONNIE**: It's not right.
**LA CUCA**: We should say something.
**LA CARMEN**: I ask you …
**LA CONNIE**: How many neighbors …
**LA CUCA**: Keep a body in their front yard?
**LA CARMEN**: As if he was a car.
**LA CONNIE**: Without wheels.
**LA CUCA**: On cinder blocks.
**LA CARMEN**: She's all confused.
**LA CONNIE**: But a body, mujer?
**LA CUCA**: It can't be good for barrio pride.
**LA CARMEN**: She can't help it.
**LA CONNIE**: Let her grieve.
**LA CUCA**: Let her weep.
*Beat.*
**LA CARMEN**: Apoco.
**LA CONNIE**: No me digas.
**LA CUCA**: Ai …
*Beat.*
**LA CARMEN**: How long can it go on?

**LA CONNIE**: As long as it takes to forgive.
**LA CUCA**: Ai, but what if she's a grudgeholder?
**LA CARMEN**: We'll never get any sleep.
**LA CONNIE**: We'll never get this barrio clean.
**LA CUCA**: We'll never get back to una vida normal.
**LA CARMEN**: And all of this for what?
**LA CONNIE**: She wants revenge.
**LA CUCA**: Who doesn't these days?
**LA CARMEN**: But, ah que sad.
**LA CONNIE**: What a tristesa.
**LA CUCA**: To lose someone.
**LA CARMEN**: A father.
**LA CONNIE**: El rey.
**LA CUCA**: Yes, the king.
**LA CARMEN**: Even if he was a cholo.
**LA CONNIE**: A warrior.
**LA CUCA**: A parolee.
**LA CARMEN**: Protected his family.
**LA CONNIE**: Protected his territory.
**LA CUCA**: And all of us.
**LA CARMEN**: But from what?
**LA CONNIE**: The elements, mujer.
**LA CUCA**: The city.
**LA CARMEN**: The other gangs.
**LA CONNIE**: The thieves.
**LA CUCA**: La policia.
**LA CARMEN**: And the politicians.
**LA CONNIE**: Thank dios for cholo protection.
**LA CUCA**: And lo-jack!
**LA CARMEN**: But still.
**LA CONNIE**: It's not right.
**LA CUCA**: And why do we let them?
**LA CARMEN**: It wasn't always this way.
**LA CONNIE**: It was different.
**LA CUCA**: Another way of life.
**LA CARMEN**: Do we remember, vecinas?
**LA CONNIE**: Remember our story?
**LA CUCA**: How can you forget a history?
**LA CARMEN**: Then let us tell it.
**LA CONNIE**: To our comunidad.
**LA CUCA**: So that they will know.
*Beat.*
**LA CARMEN**: In the beginning.
**LA CONNIE**: Before Mayor Bradley.
**LA CUCA**: And Gloria Molina.
**LA CARMEN**: Before the great wars of the seventies and eighties.

**LA CONNIE**: Before the Chicano moratorium.
**LA CUCA**: And the death of Ruben Salazar.
**LA CARMEN**: There was the cholo.
**LA CONNIE**: And the cholo was no myth.
**LA CUCA**: He wasn't even a god.
**LA CARMEN**: No, he was made by man.
**LA CONNIE**: The product of racismo.
**LA CUCA**: And neglectful mamas.
**LA CARMEN**: The cholo was just a homeboy.
**LA CONNIE**: With his zoot suit.
**LA CUCA**: And his switchblade.
**LA CARMEN**: Pushed out by la cultura.
**LA CONNIE**: Chased out of the neighborhood.
**LA CUCA**: Kicked out of the Chicano tribe.
**LA CARMEN**: Like a coyote he hid in the shadows.
**LA CONNIE**: In the coolness of midnights.
**LA CUCA**: His silhouette seen in the doorway of a cantina.
**LA CARMEN**: But they were "us."
**LA CONNIE**: Our otro yo.
**LA CUCA**: The dark side of us.
**LA CARMEN**: We can't live with them.
**LA CONNIE**: But we tolerate them.
**LA CUCA**: And use them.
**LA CARMEN**: To protect us.
**LA CONNIE**: And watch our neighborhoods.
**LA CUCA**: We don't dial the 911 no more.
**LA CARMEN**: No place for la policia in these barrios now.
**LA CONNIE**: We handle our own now.
**LA CUCA**: Or we call Father Greg.
*Beat.*
**LA CARMEN**: Apoco.
**LA CONNIE**: No me digas.
**LA CUCA**: Ai …
*Beat.*
**LA CARMEN**: What is to be done, vecinas?
**LA CONNIE**: Yo no se.
**LA CUCA**: What is to be done?
**LA CARMEN**: She killed him.
**LA CONNIE**: Who?
**LA CUCA**: The mother.
**LA CARMEN**: La Clemencia.
**LA CONNIE**: What kind of name is that?
**LA CUCA**: Texas, I bet.
**LA CARMEN**: She did it with bare hands.
**LA CONNIE**: But she's a mujer.
**LA CUCA**: How is that possible?

**LA CARMEN**: She waited after a fiesta.
**LA CONNIE**: With too many tequilas.
**LA CUCA**: And Budweiser chasers.
**LA CARMEN**: He staggered home.
**LA CONNIE**: Slept and snored.
**LA CUCA**: She didn't even break a nail.
**LA CARMEN**: But he beat her.
**LA CONNIE**: And ignored her.
**LA CUCA**: And that makes it right?
**LA CARMEN**: No, of course not.
**LA CONNIE**: She wanted algo.
**LA CUCA**: Something no woman in this barrio can get.
**LA CARMEN**: Power.
**LA CONNIE**: Her own business.
**LA CUCA**: Her own territory.
**LA CARMEN**: Wants to own the block.
**LA CONNIE**: Wants to own the casa.
**LA CUCA**: Wants to own the carro.
**LA CARMEN**: Be a queen.
**LA CONNIE**: Be an entrepreneur.
**LA CUCA**: Como la Oprah.
**LA CARMEN**: She can't see.
**LA CONNIE**: The price you pay.
**LA CUCA**: For your ambition.
**LA CARMEN**: And all para que?
**LA CONNIE**: A piece of the accion.
**LA CUCA**: Her own bank account.
**LA CARMEN**: He should have known.
**LA CONNIE**: Isn't it obvious?
**LA CUCA**: She was trouble from the start.
**LA CARMEN**: Never marry a woman.
**LA CONNIE**: From someplace way up high.
**LA CUCA**: Like the hills of Pico Rivera.
*Beat.*
**LA CARMEN**: Apoco.
**LA CONNIE**: Nome digas.
**LA CUCA**: Ai …
*Beat.*
**LA CARMEN**: Look at the daughter.
**LA CONNIE**: Our little Electricidad.
**LA CUCA**: We practically raised her for that mother.
**LA CARMEN**: She won't talk to us.
**LA CONNIE**: She's in silence.
**LA CUCA**: Like el papa.
**LA CARMEN**: Agamenón.
**LA CONNIE**: El Auggie.

**LA CUCA**: Another weird name.
**LA CARMEN**: And who told you all of this?
**LA CONNIE**: Same person who told you.
**LA CUCA**: Don't look at me!
**LA CARMEN**: Oh, you know those chismosas.
**LA CONNIE**: Gossiping.
**LA CUCA**: *Not like us …*
**LA CARMEN**: And the sister.
**LA CONNIE**: What happened to the sister?
**LA CUCA**: Ifigenia.
**LA CARMEN**: La Ifi.
**LA CONNIE**: Ran off.
**LA CUCA**: No?
**LA CARMEN**: How can a chola run off?
**LA CONNIE**: That's like a coyote in the city.
**LA CUCA**: Spiritual death for sure.
**LA CARMEN**: And she used to be the meanest of them all.
**LA CONNIE**: Didn't like the boys too much.
**LA CUCA**: Cut them up for no razon.
**LA CARMEN**: Danced with girls.
**LA CONNIE**: You mean she was …
**LA CUCA**: Yes … a Catholic schoolgirl.
*Beat.*
**LA CARMEN**: Apoco.
**LA CONNIE**: Nomedigas.
**LA CUCA**: Ai …
*Beat.*
**LA CARMEN**: And the son …
**LA CONNIE**: El Orestes, the son.
**LA CUCA**: Who should've taken his father's place.
**LA CARMEN**: She killed him.
**LA CONNIE**: Tambien?
**LA CUCA**: How?
**LA CARMEN**: En Las Vegas.
**LA CONNIE**: Murdered.
**LA CUCA**: Like el Tupac.
**LA CARMEN**: She ordered a hit.
**LA CONNIE**: Like she orders a pizza.
**LA CUCA**: This is like a whole issue of
*Alarma.*
**LA CARMEN**: Poor Orestes.
**LA CONNIE**: What is it with this family and their names?
**LA CUCA**: Must have been raised by alleluias.
**LA CARMEN**: Will Electricidad ever recover?
**LA CONNIE**: She too is also muerta.
**LA CUCA**: A living dead.

**LA CARMEN**: And the mama?
**LA CONNIE**: Smoking her cigaros.
**LA CUCA**: Laughing on her telefono.
**LA CARMEN**: Watching the *Price Is Right.*
**LA CONNIE**: Planning her takeover.
**LA CUCA**: Plotting against the children for the house.
**LA CARMEN**: She wants power.
**LA CONNIE**: She wants money.
**LA CUCA**: She wants to be single again.
**LA CARMEN**: But she'll get hers.
**LA CONNIE**: Don't they know.
**LA CUCA**: That everything is a circle.
**LA CARMEN**: What goes around comes around.
**LA CONNIE**: Everybody pays for their MTA ride.
**LA CUCA**: The ying and the yang, comadre.
**LA CARMEN**: That woman.
**LA CONNIE**: That wife.
**LA CUCA**: That mother.
**LA CARMEN**: Mala!
**LA CONNIE**: Floja!
**LA CUCA**: Cabrona!
**LA CARMEN**: Doesn't clean her casa.
**LA CONNIE**: Doesn't clean her yarda.
**LA CUCA**: Doesn't clean la calle.
**LA CARMEN**: Thank you Jesus.
**LA CONNIE**: That we
**LA CUCA**: Are not.
**ALL**: Like them!
*Beat.*
**LA CARMEN**: Apoco.
**LA CONNIE**: No me digas.
**LA CUCA**: Ai …
*The pack of Vecinas start to sweep their way down the street. You can hear the chisme and the sound of their brooms slowly fade away.*

## SCENE 2

### Keeper of Dreams

*Morning. The sound of two freeways meeting each other. Electricidad stands in the front yarda. She looks up at the sky, as if it might be following her.*

**ELECTRICIDAD**: Papa?
Why do I keep looking up to see heaven, but I only get as far as the sky?
Why is it the only light that shines on me is the happy face of the helicopter?

I wonder if you could be born again and really come back?
I am waiting for a cloud to pass by and spit in my mouth.
But the Santa Anas keep pushing them away.
To Vegas, I guess …
But I can wait.
When I finally get god to spit down on me, I am going to say that it is a blessing and I am going to use my spit to gritar my sorrow, and my rage, and my anger and all the other injusticias.
I don't care how I sound.
I don't care what they think.
I will free you, Papa.
From your death.
I will do that.
I don't know how yet, but I will do it.
*Electricidad turns to look at the house.*

## SCENE 3

### Confessin' a Feeling

*In the distance we hear a vieja coughing. A hack that only an older woman raised on menthols-in-the-box can make. Finally, she spits out a loogie. Electricidad hears it and looks up. We see a woman, la Abuela, too young to be old, too old to be young. Still trying to make it happen with the Mamie Van Doren. Pointy bra from Woolworths. Maybe a shortened version of a beehive. Can't quite let go of her period, can she? She is accompanied by Ifigenia, la Ifi, la hermana. Ifigenia is dressed like a sister in a religious order—simple skirt, shoes and blouse with a cross. Only problem is, her gang tattoos betray her as they sneak out from her neck.*

**IFIGENIA**: How long she been sitting out there?
**ABUELA:** Five days. Foo-chie!
**IFIGENIA**: Hijole, she's a stubborn chola.
**ABUELA**: Always been. She sits there forever looking up at the sky, like she's waiting for a UFO or something. And then she has these conversations with herself out loud.
**IFIGENIA**: Has she talked to Mama?
**ABUELA**: Don't talk to me about tu mama! She got the Sanitation Department to come out and scoop poor Electricidad up. But la loca Electricidad attacked the poor gabacho trashman. Pinned him like a pit bull. Threatened to drive-by him. Y se fue running, el pobre.
**IFIGENIA**: What's that next to her?
**ABUELA**: The body, mujer!
**IFIGENIA**: El cuerpo! Of my dad?
**ABUELA**: My son.
**IFIGENIA**: My god …
**ABUELA**: La loca has his body there in the front yarda, on display, like some Rose Parade float.
**IFIGENIA**: Somebody's gonna steal it.
**ABUELA**: No chansa. When she brought the body here, she stayed with it. She hasn't left, not even for a momento. She even pee-pees in the yarda. She's acting like she's at Yosemite or something. I tell you, she's a cacahuate.

**IFIGENIA**: And how does she survive?

**ABUELA**: Like all cholas do—on the grandmother … I leave her comida everyday. You know, tortillas and stuff. Some Top Ramen. I even bake pinche cupcakes for the loca.

**IFIGENIA**: Why do you do that? You don't even like us.

**ABUELA**: That's true. But let's face it, I do her a favor and maybe later she does me a favor. You know the vida. You watch your grandmother's back, and your granny watches yours.

**IFIGENIA**: I got your back, Abuela.

**ABUELA**: It's so hard, ni lo puedes imaginar. A poor vieja like me … In my twilight and back to feeding another mouth. A senior citizen como yo, making her los Rice Krispies, con el food coloring, y todo. On my pobre widow's pension …

**IFIGENIA**: Don't worry, vieja, I'll make sure Mama gives you some dinero.

**ABUELA**: Ai, gracias … And now, even worse, la loca stopped talking to las vecinas. She's got them all aguitadas. They think she is going to attack them. When she sleeps, they leave flowers and incense for her. Pues, more for the smell of the body … They hired me to hablar with her.

**IFIGENIA**: You charge them?

**ABUELA**: Well, I'm like a translation servicio.

**IFIGENIA**: My poor sister.

*Abuela looks at Ifigenia, kind of surprised.*

**ABUELA**: When did you become so nice, hard chola?

**IFIGENIA**: When I realized that someone died on a cross for me.

**ABUELA**: Oh really, who was that?

**IFIGENIA**: Don't be disrespectful, old lady.

**ABUELA**: Why you come back here, hard chola? You been gone so long we thought you gave up the vida.

**IFIGENIA**: Came back to make amends. I'm kinda like on a pilgrimage. To save the familia.

**ABUELA**: Good luck, chola. You got an hermano and a papa both dead. You don't got that many people to pilgrim with.

**IFIGENIA**: What does she do all day?

**ABUELA**: She sleeps. She's on the coyote cycle. At night, she talks to herself, or to him, like a loca. Laughing and crying. Re-living herself and her vida. Como una rerun. She's planning something, I know it.

**IFIGENIA**: And how do you know?

**ABUELA**: I stay up and watch her.

**IFIGENIA**: Oye, mujer, you should let her grieve in solitude.

**ABUELA**: But I'm a retiree! This is what we do. Besides, what kind of loca grieves in their own front yarda for everyone to see?

**IFIGENIA**: She just doesn't want to forget … How did she get the body?

**ABUELA**: She stole it from Forest Lawn the night of the velorio.

**IFIGENIA**: Y vieja, how do you know?

**ABUELA**: Mujer, I drove the hearse!

**IFIGENIA**: Shit, Abuela …

**ABUELA**: She told me she would kick my nalgas if I didn't. So, I broke into the funeral car while she went into the little Chapel of the Inocentes and took the body. Like a flan, he slid off the stretcher and into the hearse. And then she made me drive him aqui. And I don't even have a license! You know what? She's got like a rabies, I think. You need to hablar with her. She's your sister, tu sabes?

**IFIGENIA**: My hermana … we never acted like we were sisters.

**ABUELA**: But, I'm warning you, cuidado. She strikes when you least expect it.

**IFIGENIA**: She wouldn't come at me.

**ABUELA**: She thinks you were in on the viejo's murder.
**IFIGENIA**: Esta loca!
**ABUELA**: Pues, that's what I said, pero who listens to the viejas anymore?
**IFIGENIA**: Jesus does ...
**ABUELA**: Ai, don't start with that alleluia stuff, man. If there was a god, I wouldn't be making government cheese quesadillas.
**IFIGENIA**: Okay, scram old lady. I want to hablar con mi sister.
**ABUELA**: Ai, you girls got no manners, man.
**IFIGEN1A**: We learned it from you, cabrona.
**ABUELA**: No, that comes from your mama, the outsider.
**IFIGENIA**: Oh, now she's an outsider?
**ABUELA**: Well, look at her. She's not from here. Whittier Boulevard runs a long way, baby. I told my hijo, "Don't take a girl with something, 'cause soon they want everything. Take a girl with nothing and give her something, and it feels like a lot"
**IFIGENIA**: You really are the chola most high.
**ABUELA**: I don't know nothing, but what I know about nothing is a lot. And I know I hate that puta. No Vegas buffet can satisfy a mujer that hungry for power. And she doesn't even know how to dress!
**IFIGENIA**: No seas mala.
**ABUELA**: I tell you, the only Mexican I got any respect for these days is the Virgin de Guadalupe.
**IFIGENIA**: Vete,vieja.
*Abuela begins to walk away.*
**IFIGENIA**: Hey. HEY!
*Abuela stops, surprised at the threat. Ifigenia musters, with as much conviction and honesty as she can come up with:*
**IFIGENIA**: Que god bless you.
**ABUELA**: Ai, gracias ... *(Abuela keeps walking and mutters under her breath)* Religiosa cabrona ...
*Abuela exits. Ifigenia looks at the front yard.*

## SCENE 4

### Daddy's Home

*Momentos later. Electricidad in the front yard with Papa.*

**ELECTRICIDAD**: Oh, you should have seen it, Papa.
They had you lying there in that mortuary.
On display.
Like a dummy in a store window.
I couldn't have it, Papa.
Laying there all night by yourself.
Why do they do that?
Why do they leave someone alone on their
first night of dying?
It isn't right, Papa.
You are not dead to me.

You are the rey of this neighborhood.
Everybody waits for you to give your orders.
No one stopped me from bringing you here.
Thought that I had gone crazy.
They don't know what I am capable of when it comes to my love and loyalty to you, mi rey.
You are the old ways, Papa.
You are the history and the reason we know how to live.
I want to live the old cholo ways, Papa.
Simple and to the point.
You mess with me, I mess with you back.
You want to party, party in your own backyard.
You shoot, I shoot back.
It's simple.
Why can't we live the old ways?
She says I act like a man.
Good.
I'm not a girl.
I'm a chola!
DE LOS EAST SIDE LOCOS!

## SCENE 5

### Always and Forever

*A forever night in Las Vegas. The sound of a needle buzzing loudly. It grows more dim and realistic, as the lights reveal Orestes and Nino. They are both shirtless and glistening with sweat. Orestes sits facing out, looking at nothing, while Nino, with the tattoo gun, sits on a stool, pricking Orestes' chest. A trickle of blood runs from his breast down to his stomach. Suddenly, Nino hits a nerve. Orestes winces and pushes Nino's hand away. They glare at each other.*

**NINO**: You want me to stop?
*Orestes looks at Nino for a moment, nods "continue," and looks away.*
**NINO**: Good cholo. Good.
*Nino continues to work on Orestes' chest while the lights fade and the sound of the buzzing grows.*

## SCENE 6

### It's Just a Family Affair

*Still this manana. Electricidad in the yarda.*

**ELECTRICIDAD**: I scare her.
I know I do.
That's why she took my ...

Oh, Papa …
My Orestes. My brother.
My sensitive hermano, with the poet's corazon.
She's killed him too.
You should hear her, Papa.
Me espera.
She wants me to come back inside.
And pretend.
Yo no!
I will not go back inside con ella.
As long as I have this memory of you,
I will make mi casa, la tierra.
Yes, Papa, my house is now this front yard …
She laughs at us, mocks us.
Drives off en el Monte Carlo with her cigaros
and her cancer cough that she thinks is so sexy.
She doesn't sound like la J-Lo.
Esa cabrona sounds like el John Wayne!
*(Laughs a bitter laugh to herself)* She tries so hard, but everyone knows she's not from the barrio. She never learned our ways.
*(Screaming toward the house)* SHE'S ALL MUY-MUY, AIN'T SHE, PAPA?
*Clemencia looks out of the window.*
**CLEMENCIA**: Callate la boca.
**ELECTRICIDAD**: You shut up.
**CLEMENCIA**: Talking to yourself like some loca.
**ELECTRICIDAD**: Yeah, y que?
**CLEMENCIA**: Todos los neighbors think you've gone crazy.
**ELECTRICIDAD**: Maybe I have.
**CLEMENCIA**: Bah, muy dramatica. Save that little Berkeley protest out there for when I sell the house.
**ELECTRICIDAD**: This is my father's house.
**CLEMENCIA**: I got Century 21 on speed dial! But they won't sell it until you take him back to his bed at the cemetery.
**ELECTRICIDAD**: Dejame, pendeja.
**CLEMENCIA**: You look as filthy as tu papa, lying there in the dirt. I am going to call the loco house to come and take you away.
**ELECTRICIDAD**: They won't know who to take, you old witch.
**CLEMENCIA**: Don't call me "old"!
*She takes a long toke on her cigaro.*
**CLEMENCIA**: Ai, come on, no seas asi. Come inside. I'll call Yang Chow and order your favorite Chino food, and we can look at old pictures of your father.
*Electricidad throws a stone.*
**CLEMENCIA**: Ai, malcriada! While you are throwing those stones, clean the yard, you puerca. And take that cuerpo back before Forest Lawn comes and hands me a take-away bill. *(Walks away from the window)*
**ELECTRICIDAD**: Did you hear her, Papa?
**CLEMENCIA** *(From inside the house)*: Stop talking to yourself, I said!
*Electricidad spits toward the house.*

**ELECTRICIDAD**: See? She doesn't mourn you. La noche of your funeral, she put on the K-Earth 101 and served tamales and wine coolers. I didn't even know she could cook!

*Beat.*

**ELECTRICIDAD** *(Looks at him and realizes)*: Ai, Papa, I'm sorry. All this talking makes you tired. You are a man of so few words … But I must tell the stories you told me. About who we are and where we came from. Or I will forget.

We were Aztecas, huh, Papa?

And the mujer god of human sacrifices, Coatlicue, made the first cholo.

And she gave the first cholo the switchblade, so that he could leave the barrio and defend himself.

And then she gave the cholo the baggy pants, so that he could store the comida he shoplifted from the 7-Eleven.

And then she gave him Art Laboe and the oldies and taught him how to dance. *"Earth Angel" by the Penguins begins to play in her head. She dances slow, cbolo-style, in the yarda.*

**ELECTRICIDAD**: And then she gave the cholos house parties and Schlitz, to make them happy.

And she gave them the lowrider and car club, so that they could show off to one another. And finally she gave them the boulevard, so that they could cruise and see how beautiful they were … *(Stops dancing)*

But then, one of her four hundred daughters, Coyokauqui, stood up to her and was like, "Why you get all the power, vieja? Why you get to decide everything for us?"

And that's when Coatlicue cut her up in four, carniceria style, and made the four corners cholo world.

First corner—North Side Locos, control Aldephia cable.

Second corner—South Side Locos, control Vernon slaughterhouses.

Third corner—West Side Locos, got all the bail bonds.

And fourth corner—us, the East Side Locos, control neighborhood pride and "pharmacy" traffic.

And then she cut her daughter's head off and did a fly ball into the sky, and her head became the moon.

And that's the one I'm trying to see every night, Papa.

But she won't show me her expressions.

She's a stone-cold chola, that daughter.

And since the beginning of cholo time, this is how it was and always will be.

But someone wants to change that.

Oh, you know who I'm talking about.

She says it's progress. She thought that if she killed you, all the ways of the cholo would end. But she was wrong, because all she did was offend the Council of Old Cholos. Who never forget.

That's why I must say your name, Papa.

Or it will lose its power.

I must yell your name out loud or I will forget it, Papa.

*(She yells out to the barrio as if she is calling him back from the dead:)*

AGAMENÓN ATRIDAS …

VETERANO …

DE LOS EAST SIDE LOCOS …

**CLEMENCIA** *(From inside the house)*: Callate, cabrona!

**ELECTRICIDAD**: Everyday I will scream your name.

And they will get tired of hearing it and of hearing me.

*(Yells to the house)* PERO A MI NO ME IMPORTA!

*(Leans into his body as if to tell him a secret)* Papa, I am going to avenge your death.

Y la muerte of our sweetest and gentlest Orestes.

I will turn Ifigenia, my so-called sister, against her.
I will turn the vecinas against her, tambien.
Oh, Papa, it is only in the thought of her suffering that I get my energia.
Thinking of her lifeless body thrown at the doorway of El Gato Negro bar. *(Laughs at the joy of seeing such an image)* The drunks stepping on her as they reach for their cervezas.
Yes, I have a razon to live!
*(Yells)* AGAMENÓN ATRIDAS …
VETERANO …
DELOS EAST SIDE LOCOS …
**CLEMENCIA**: Ai, shut up …
**ELECTRICIDAD**: Oh yes, I would do anything to trade your death with my breath.
Sell my soul to the diablo, if only there was one.
*(She thinks about it)* There is … *(It's a confirmation and a game plan)* Y ella, Clemencia Atridas, will have to pay …
*Electricidad starts to laugh. Clemencia looks out the window and shakes her head in disgust. The sound of the current of electricity rises and sweeps away the laughter, as the lights at the altar fade.*

## SCENE 7

### I'm Your Puppet

*Vegas darkness. The sound of breathing and punching. On one side of the stage appears Orestes and Nino. Orestes is plowing away into a punching bag furiously. Nino sits on a stool drinking a Corona. Orestes is driven and unstoppable, while Nino takes a long slow gulp, gulp, gulp of his cervecita.*

**NINO**: Good cholo. Good.

*The lights fade as Orestes punches away and Nino downs his beer.*

## SCENE 8

### Earth Angel

*Mid morning and all the little mocosos are in class dozing. La Ifi enters. Electricidad sees her and takes her place for battle. She stands with one foot on each side of her father's body. La Ifi sizes her up and comes closer as if to see the cuerpo of her papa. Electricidad spits in her direction and gets ready for a* Braveheart *rush. They are staring each other down. La Ifi comes closer.*

**IFIGENIA**: Hey. They cut out your tongue too?
**ELECTRICIDAD**: Don't touch him!
**IFIGENIA**: He was my papa, too.
**ELECTRICIDAD**: Is that why you deserted him?
**IFIGENIA**: What did you say, pendeja?
**ELECTRICIDAD**: You heard.

**IFIGENIA**: Listen, I didn't even know he was dead. One of the sisters said, "The king of your barrio esta muerto!" So, I came to see if it was true and pay my respeto.

And pray for you, big sister.

**ELECTRICIDAD**: Pray for me? Pray that I don't kick your ass, deserter.

**IFIGENIA**: When I got off the Greyhound, I could hear the cherry bombs screaming a dead man's salute. I could see the lowriders putt, putt, putt on the boulevard. The old-school cholas passed by me and give me the "what's up" ... *(Nods her head in acknowledgement)* And the "so-sorrys." *(Bows her head like you're supposed to)* They were saying adios and giving me condolence. Knew it must be a cholo goodbye. The sisters didn't lie. Mi papa is dead.

*They look at each other, sizing each other up. La Ifi takes the risk, kneels and bows to her papa, el rey. Electricidad knows she is back.*

**ELECTRICIDAD**: Where were you?

**IFIGENIA**: You mean you noticed me gone?

**ELECTRICIDAD**: Yeah ...

**IFIGENIA**: Serving time.

**ELECTRIC1DAD**: Liar.

**IFIGENIA**: Why you say that?

**ELECTRICIDAD**: Every time you're gone, you're in jail. This time nobody could find you. I gave your chine. *(Does Ifi's chifle)* But only Helen Keller answered back. I thought you were a victim, so I looked for you at the bottom of the river, on the railroad tracks, under the freeways. Then I thought maybe you had walked away from your loyalty.

**IFIGENIA**: I was doing a different kind of time. Mostly paying back my past.

**ELECTRICIDAD**: Man, You're always doing time.

**IFIGENIA**: Well, I'm a woman ... But this time I wasn't doing it in jail.

**ELECTRICIDAD**: What are you talking about?

**IFIGENIA**: You better not laugh or I'll kick your ass.

**ELECTRICIDAD**: Dimelo.

**IFIGENIA**: I joined a convent ...

**ELECTRICIDAD**: Fucking liar.

**IFIGENIA**: Fuck you, I did. Why do you think I look like this?

**ELECTRICIDAD**: And the convent took you in?

**IFIGENIA**: Y porque no? *(Beat)*

I'm sorry about Papa. I know you were his favorite.

**ELECTRICIDAD**: You have to take a side.

**IFIGENIA**: For what?

**ELECTRICIDAD**: To avenge your father's death. From the monster inside la casa.

**IFIGENIA**: I see you've learned a lot of forgiveness out here by yourself.

**ELECTRICIDAD**: I'm not by myself.

**IFIGENIA**: Y aveo.

**ELECTRICIDAD**: I'm just doing lo que he tells me to do.

**IFIGENIA**: Y que es eso?

**ELECTRICIDAD**: Planning. Our father's revenge.

**IFIGENIA**: Don't forget what he was. Yes, rey of our barrio, but also a mean-ass cholo.

**ELECTRICIDAD**: How do you think he got to be cholo, down on his knees asking Jesus to make him leader?

**IFIGENIA**: Hermana, he gave us these tattoos. But these tattoos are also scars.

**ELECTRICIDAD**: Yo puedo ver que she poisons your mind.

**IFIGENIA**: "Forgiveness is a virtue."
**ELECTRICIDAD**: What are you talking about, macha?
**IFIGENIA**: I just learned that one. I don't know what the hell it means.
*Beat.*
**ELECTRICIDAD**: You like your convent?
**IFIGENIA**: It's just like jail, but with better food. And silence …
Listen, hermana, your loyalty to Papa has always been deep and kind of creepy. You demand so much of cholo-hood and its ways. I kind of get your religious loyalty now. But it's time to call a truce and let the House of Atridas mourn and move on.
**ELECTRICIDAD**: I would rather die on a cross than forgive her.
**IFIGENIA**: Man, tu eres what they call an obstacle to holiness.
**ELECTRICIDAD**: You really an alleluia now?
**IFIGENIA**: Don't know yet …
**ELECTRICIDAD**: It's like cholo-hood, either you are or you aren't.
**IFIGENIA**: It's different. It takes time. It's like standing in line at Food 4 Less, you just have to go with it … Is it all true about Orestes?
**ELECTRICIDAD**: That his own mother killed him?
**IFIGENIA**: Not even she would do that.
**ELECTRICIDAD**: She eats her young.
**IFIGENIA**: Didn't even get a chance to grow into a young cholo. We should bury him with Papa. At Evergreen.
**ELECTRICIDAD**: They shot him in Las Vegas. They threw his body into a volcano.
**IFIGENIA**: A volcano? In Las Vegas? Oh yeah …
**ELECTRICIDAD**: I know how she works. Once she got rid of Papa, she knew the Council of Old Cholos would follow the old ways and make Orestes el new Rey del Barrio. It's his birth-derecho. But she sees the men and how they hold on to their power. Oh, she can taste it. It's like she walked into a Target for the first time—she wants it all.
And now … *(She starts to cry)* She killed him.
Lo mato.
*Ifigenia goes to comfort her.*
**IFIGENIA**: My sister …
**ELECTRICIDAD**: Get away from me! She took my joy, my Orestes. And she took my love, mi papa. But when she took, she also gave.
**IFIGENIA**: Gave you what, loca?
**ELECTRICIDAD**: Gave me this pain.
**IFIGENIA**: Don't let her.
**ELECTRICIDAD**: I am going to use it against her, and give honor back to La Casa de Atridas.
*Ifigenia tries to move toward her again.*
**IFIGENIA**: Come on, man …
*Electricidad slaps her hard across the face.*
**ELECTRICIDAD**: Don't, puta! You left me here alone. I didn't have any backup. She knows it and she's already taken more than she deserves. You broke the cholo code. You walked away.
**IFIGENIA**: Forgive me …
*An awkward silence and look between them. Too much so. They turn to face Papa. La Ifi starts to cry,*
**ELECTRICIDAD**: Don't.
**IFIGENIA**: Shut up.
**ELECTRICIDAD**: What do you got to cry about?

**IFIGENIA**: He was a cabron. Look at what he left us. Our own jails.
**ELECTRICIDAD**: Yo no.
**IFIGENIA**: Oh yeah, you. Mama. Me. All trapped.
Even in his muerte, he still won't let us go.
*In her grief she tries to go to him.*
**IFIGENIA**: Papa? Por favor, let us go.
**ELECTRICIDAD**: Leave him alone!
*La Ifi reaches out to touch him.*
**ELECTRICIDAD**: No, I said!
*Ifigenia leans in and Electricidad jumps on her. They fall to the ground and do an old after-school fight. They both have each other by the hair. Neither wants to let go. Finally Ifigenia, maybe feeling overpowered, pulls away. Oh man, this might be the first time she lost a fight to her hermana.*
**IFIGENIA**: You crazy bitch!
**ELECTRICIDAD**: No one touches him!
**IFIGENIA**: You're lucky I know about that "turn-the-other-cheek" shit.
**ELECTRICIDAD**: I am making plans, Ifi. I am going to take her last breath without raising a finger. Just watch me. I am not going to walk away from this body until her stillborn heart rests in my hands.
Until I hear the final little song that a last breath makes. Until I look up and the gods smile at my loyalty.
Help me destroy her, my hard chola sister, who always lent a fist in loyalty to the Casa de Atridas.
**IFIGENIA**: I am out of my jail. But I see that you have just entered yours. Your solitude has made you loca, hermana. Your grief ain't sopa, babosa. Don't let it boil.
**ELECTRICIDAD**: My grief is the match that fuels the fire of my revenge.
**IFIGENIA**: That's poetic … but stupid. The sisters gave me a gift, idiot. It's called "forgiveness." You should try it. Otherwise, you are going to destroy yourself …
**ELECTRICIDAD**: Not me, her.
**IFIGENIA**: The sisters at Immaculate Conception say …
**ELECTRICIDAD**: You mean the dykes?
*Ifigenia looks at her, gets up and dusts off.*
**IFIGENIA**: Llamame when you are ready to talk some sense.
**ELECTRICIDAD**: At your funeral, deserter.
**IFIGENIA**: Get over yourself you stupid bitch—Jesus loves you!
*The lights begin to fade as we hear the sweeping of the brooms.*

## SCENE 9

### Reasons

*Ai, you can almost feel the morning frio leaving your cuerpo. The faint sound of chisme makes its way through the neighborhood again. The chatter grows louder as we see las Vecinas sweep their way down the street.*

**LA CARMEN**: Apoco!
**LA CONNIE**: No me digas!
**LA CUCA**: Ai …
*Beat.*
**LA CARMEN**: Did you hear La Electricidad?

**LA CONNIE**: She's going to do something.
**LA CUCA**: To la mama.
**LA CARMEN**: But what?
**LA CONNIE**: I couldn't hear good enough.
**LA CUCA**: She got all soft and dramatic.
**LA CARMEN**: They always scream at each other down the street.
**LA CONNIE**: And right when they got something good to say.
**LA CUCA**: We can't hear them!
**LA CARMEN**: It can't be good.
**LA CONNIE**: Not for us.
**LA CUCA**: Not for this barrio.
**LA CARMEN**: The daughter planning.
**LA CONNIE**: The mother scheming.
**LA CUCA**: Ai, even the sister praying is scary.
**LA CARMEN**: Vecinas, it isn't safe.
**LA CONNIE**: Not like it was.
**LA CUCA**: It never was.
**LA CARMEN**: No, it used to be.
**LA CONNIE**: I never locked the door.
**LA CUCA**: Porque eres mensa.
**LA CARMEN**: We're trapped.
**LA CONNIE**: We don't say anything.
**LA CUCA**: Dame un break.
**LA CARMEN**: We just live with it.
**LA CONNIE**: Lo aceptamos.
**LA CUCA**: Like a way de vivir.
**LA CARMEN**: I knew a time.
**LA CONNIE**: A time mas calmado.
**LA CUCA**: More simple.
**LA CARMEN**: Call me old-fashioned.
**LA CONNIE**: Call me old-school.
**LA CUCA**: Call me old ways.
**LA CARMEN**: La casa.
**LA CONNIE**: El porch.
**LA CUCA**: El barrio.
**LA CARMEN**: Cleaning.
**LA CONNIE**: Cooking.
**LA CUCA**: Sweeping.
**LA CARMEN**: La familia.
**LA CONNIE**: The vecinos.
**LA CUCA**: Los kids.
**LA CARMEN**: It wasn't always like this.
**LA CONNIE**: It was different.
**LA CUCA**: It was?
*Beat.*
**LA CARMEN**: Apoco!

**LA CONNIE**: No me digas!

**LA CUCA**: Ai . . .

*Beat.*

**LA CARMEN**: Why don't we start a barrio watch?

**LA CONNIE**: Whose children are these?

**LA CUCA**: Where are the mothers?

**LA CARMEN**: Are all the fathers dead?

**LA CONNIE**: Cuando is it enough?

**LA CUCA**: Who will stand up and be counted?

**LA CARMEN**: Who wants to be the primero to complain?

**LA CONNIE**: Whose barrio is this?

**LA CUCA**: Who paid for their house?

**LA CARMEN**: When did we give away our neighborhood?

**LA CONNIE**: When is too much, enough?

**LA CUCA**: Why don't we own anything?

**LA CARMEN**: Why are we all asking questions?

**LA CONNIE**: Because, vecinas . . .

**LA CUCA**: We're afraid to give the answers.

*Beat.*

**LA CARMEN:** Apoco.

**LA CONNIE:** No me digas.

**LA CUCA:** Ai . . .

*Beat.*

**LA CARMEN**: Look at this city.

**LA CONNIE**: City of the future.

**LA CUCA**: Ciudad with the most of everything.

**LA CARMEN**: Chinos, Japones, Coreanos.

**LA CONNIE**: Salvadorenos, Cubanos, Armenios.

**LA CUCA**: Rusos, Suecos, Polacos.

**LA CARMEN**: This city with no center.

**LA CONNIE**: No heart.

**LA CUCA**: All border towns.

**LA CARMEN**: Ai dios mio, vecinas!

**LA CONNIE**: It just hit me!

**LA CUCA**: This the wild, wild oeste . . .

*Beat.*

**LA CARMEN:** Apoco.

**LA CONNIE**: No me digas.

**LA CUCA:** Ai . . .

*Beat.*

**LA CARMEN**: Lock your doors.

**LA CONNIE**: Say goodbye to the noche.

**LA CUCA**: La luna no more.

**LA CARMEN**: The moon drips blood.

**LA CONNIE**: For them.

**LA CUCA**: Los cholos.

**LA CARMEN**: Con sus ways.
**LA CONNIE**: Con sus gangs.
**LA CUCA**: Con su violence.
**LA CARMEN**: So different.
**LA CONNIE**: But yet …
**LA CUCA**: They look just like us …
*Beat.*
**LA CARMEN**: Apoco!
**LA CONNIE**: No me digas!
**LA CUCA: Ai …**
*The pack of Vecinas start to sweep their way down the street. You can hear the chisme and the sound of their brooms slowly fade away.*

## SCENE 10

### You're Still a Young Man

*Vegas night. The sound of a punch and a grunt. On one side of the stage appear Nino and Orestes. They are both shirtless. They stand facing each other as Orestes tightens up and gives Nino a nod, indicating the silent "okay". Nino punches him in the stomach.*
**NINO**: Eighteen …
*(Orestes tightens up and gives him the nod again. Nino punches his pansa)*
Nineteen …
*(Orestes is winded, but tightens up and gives Nino another nod. Nino punches him again)* Twenty.
*(Oh man, that hurt)*
How you feeling?
*(Orestes tries to catch his breath. Nino hugs him)*
Good cholo. Good …
*(Nino lets go of him)*
Didn't mean to do so many, young homeboy, but I was bored. Just trying to kill some time.
*(Orestes is doubled over)*
The sooner you get the skills of the warrior, the faster we leave Vegas and go back home. *Orestes comes up.*
**ORESTES**: When Nino?
**NINO**: Soon, young homeboy. Your papa will be calling us back any dia. And you have to be listo.
**ORESTES**: Yes, mi maestro.
**NINO**: He's going to be so cholo happy when he sees that his attendant turned the little lion king into the poderoso heir to La Casa de Atridas. You know what, mijo? I like it when I got purpose …
**ORESTES**: I know he must be thinking about us right now. Six months is enough, right, old viejo? Cholos can't live in exile, it's against our nature. That's why they call us "homeboys," right?
**NINO**: Exile? Que's eso?
**ORESTES**: Exile. Es como, kicked out. Banished.
**NINO**: Ah, I thought you said "X-Filed" at first. You kinda freaked me out.
**ORESTES**: Remember, Nino, when we first got here? How lonely we were? Every night at the Cheetah's Strip Club?
**NINO**: Oh. You stopped going?

**ORESTES**: I wish we were in our tierra. I can't sleep here with all these lights. I miss our one-bulb barrio too much.
**NINO**: Your papa sent you away to protect you.
**ORESTES**: Remember that light in our bathroom, Nino? The one that had that string that you pulled on to give it life? Man, how I would sit on that toilet and stare at that bulb for hours. So small, but so full of light. I used to think it held my dreams ... How I would cry at night when Mama pulled the string and killed it.
**NINO**: Yeah man, Vegas ain't our lady. Cholos are all about darkness and midnights.
**ORESTES**: I miss mi hermana. My Electricidad, my Trici. I wish she could see this. A million light bulbs. A million dreams. My corazon is empty without my sister. That's why I'm painting her on my heart, old man. So that I don't forget her.
**NINO**: To each his own ...
**ORESTES**: I have to go back. If only to bring my sister here and show her what her very name has inspired.
**NINO**: Then you have to be listo. *(Comes up from behind, easily grabs Orestes by the neck and takes him down)* Oh man, we're going to be here forever ... *(Helps Orestes up)* Toughen up, puto. I'm running out of nickels!
*They walk away as the sky does a big turn from noche to dia in a casino minute.*

## SCENE 11

### We Are Family

*The yard. Medio dia. That quiet time between morning and* All My Children. *Clemencia enters la yarda, a bit nerviosa and smoking, of course. Electricidad sits up, ready to strike.*

**CLEMENCIA**: Don't worry. I won't touch him. Lo toque enough when he was alive.
**ELECTRICIDAD**: It won't do you no good to come beg his forgiveness.
**CLEMENCIA**: Oh, you're funny. We need to talk.
**ELECTRICIDAD**: I have nada to say to you, murderer.
**CLEMENCIA**: I am not charging you renta in this yarda. The least you can do is talk conmigo, "tenant." Listen, I'm sorry I called the sanitation on you. But I'm a homeowner now. "Property values," mija.
**ELECTRICIDAD**: I know what you did.
**CLEMENCIA**: Oh really? Raise you so that you could turn on me like this? You're just like him.
**ELECTRICIDAD**: Que bueno.
**CLEMENCIA**: Stubborn. Unforgiving. If I did anything wrong, it was that I let him give you too much of his filosofia. I let him try to shape you to his hardness. I let him show you the destructive ways.
**ELECTRICIDAD**: He taught us the cholo way.
**CLEMENCIA**: Yeah, but how? Everyone forgets what a bully he was. He made us think that we couldn't grow and change and make something better than what we are. He beat me and made me scared of the world. Scared of crossing over these bridges. It was the only way he could control us. Like the petty thief that he was, he took our dreams.
**ELECTRICIDAD**: And you murdered them. *(Looks at Clemencia with an absolute lack of fear)* You took his eyes and tongue because, even though you have no soul, you've been here long enough to know that you should be afraid of the gods. Then you told everybody that someone broke in. You blamed it on one of the locos from the four directions. Nobody broke in. Only you. Into this house. Twenty-three years ago. Te estoy viendo, cabrona. You're like an X ray. His sangre-stains are all over you.

**CLEMENCIA**: You got some way of looking at the world, my daughter. Don't forget that I was the one that convinced the Repo man to give us another chance on the Monte Carlo.
**ELECTRICIDAD**: You let the pit bulls attack him.
**CLEMENCIA**: Yeah, well, he gave us another chance, didn't he? I made sure the mortgage never died. I made sure you kids always had your cholo-wear. I even scared the vecinas into buying all that Avon, so we wouldn't starve when your papa got lost in some City Terrace thighs.
Oh, don't look at me that way. You think it's easy being a woman in this hombre world? Those hombres are ruthless conmigo. And they will be with you, too. They want one thing from us. And they always take it. But when we want a cut. A place in their world. Our fair share. Well ... vas a ver.
**ELECTRICIDAD**: You're the queen of excuses, Clemencia. I can't wait to see what you'll say when the hands wrap around your neck. I'll be here waiting.
**CLEMENCIA**: You think you can sit there forever? You think he isn't going to leave you at some point? They always leave you, these men. And then what? Who will watch your back then? Everyone smells the oportunidad that an empty throne brings. Without backup, little nina, you're like a wounded coyote out there.
*Ai, hold on, cigaro.*
**CLEMENCIA**: Let me protect you.
**ELECTRICIDAD**: Desperate.
*Un puff importante.*
**CLEMENCIA**: You know how I met your sweet papa? On the boulevard. I was thirteen. He smelled good, like VO5, and I flirted. What's wrong with that, huh? I was an innocent. But he took my girlhood from me. In the back of a car. And he brought me here.
My father looked at me and called me a tramp .My mother hid in a back room to save herself a black eye. And he sold me to him. Because he thought I was dirty. This is what they do.
Did I get to escojer? No my stubborn daughter, I didn't get to choose. And neither will you. History just keeps repeating itself. Cholos don't move forward. They just keep going farther into the past. Oldies, oldies, oldies ... And I want to change it. I want to take back every bruise your father gave me and turn it into a dollar. I want the memory of every one of his punches to be a kiss that could make me believe in myself. I am going to make a business. In his name, if you want. I could give you a cut. Then you could have a piece of him that's worth something. The piece that makes dinero.
*Electricidad glares at her.*
**CLEMENCIA**: You and I are cut from the same cloth, Electricidad. Imagine us working together.
**ELECTRICIDAD**: Together, ha!
**CLEMENCIA**: These hombres wouldn't know how to deal with the both of us. They wouldn't be able to ignore us, I'll tell you eso. Think about it. Then you could honor his nombre, if that's what you want to do. We could even make a statue and put it out here where his stinky body sits. Come on. Come back inside the casa.
**ELECTRICIDAD**: Not into that living coffin.
**CLEMENCIA**: A mother sacrifices. I never did. I admit that. Just like you, I like the "running around" too much. I was never good with the "domestic." But then again, I never meant to be a mother.
But now we have to start pensando about our futuro. You and I are survivors.
**ELECTRICIDAD**: No tengo nada in common with you, monster.
**CLEMENCIA**: You hate me porque me ves inside of you. We are more alike than you can ever imagine.
**ELECTRICIDAD**: Lies.
**CLEMENCIA**: No seas mensa. This could all be yours. Yes, even the house.
**ELECTRICIDAD**: Why would I want this house?
**CLEMENCIA**: Oh, you love this house mas que yo. You can't wait to live out the last of your days in the past. Looking out this window at a world that would never have us.

Not me. I am going to forget all this, sell this house and buy a condo. In Pasa-fucken-dena!
*Clemencia takes a deep drag of the cigarette. She smiles at Electricidad.*
**CLEMENCIA**: I would have even given him to you.
**ELECTRICIDAD** *(Caught off guard)*: Callate!
**CLEMENCIA**: Oh, I know you wanted him.
**ELECTRICIDAD**: Stop it.
**CLEMENCIA**: You did, didn't you? Hard chola with no friends to call her own. Your sister always in jail, and your little brother too soft for his own good. Little chola whose only friend was your hard papa. He took the soft skin from you and made you a warrior.
And you are stupid enough to thank him for it. But why wouldn't you? You were in love with him.
**ELECTRICIDAD**: I hate you …
**CLEMENCIA**: That ain't a new sentimiento. I hate me too sometimes.
Listen to me. I am offering you things. Attention. Partnership. Motherhood even, if that is lo que quieres. All of the things that no one ever gave me, I am offering to you. But you must pay me for it.
**ELECTRICIDAD**: I will pay for your casket.
**CLEMENCIA**: Pay me for being your mama! I never wanted it. They took being a girl from me and they gave me "mother." I didn't ask for it. No, my daughter, I'm not old enough to be old.
It's all yours, Electricidad. Make a choice. There's nothing to stand in your way now. You could change the destiny of La Casa de Atridas.
MIRA MENSA, TAKE SOMETHING FROM ME!
**ELECTRICIDAD**: It's your last breath que quiero.
*Beat. Clemencia composes herself.*
**CLEMENCIA**: Okay I am going to start a neighborhood association. And you are going to be the first item on the agenda, cabrona.
Last chansa. Are you going to come inside or not?
**ELECTRICIDAD**: I'll come to your funeral, old lady.
**CLEMENCIA**: I'm going to go back inside and use up my "anytime minutes."
*She flicks her cigarette butt on Auggie's corpse. Electricidad frantically runs over to him and tries to pick it off him.*
*Clemencia walks into the house. Electricidad turns to watch her leave.*

## SCENE 12

### Que Viva Las Vegas

*The night time glow of Vegas neon. The distant sonido of the ker-ching, ker-ching of a slot machine on a winning play. Orestes and Nino are backstage, working at a buffet. Nino sits on a white bucket sipping a malt 40, while Orestes struggles with a tray full of dirty dishes.*

**NINO**: Young cholo, come sit.
**ORESTES**: We're on a shift, old man!
**NINO**: Don't worry about it. I just paid a mojado to do our work. We got cholo matters to attend to.
*Orestes comes and sits with Nino.*
**ORESTES**: Okay, lazy viejo, dime.
**NINO**: A few days ago, someone tried to take you out.

**ORESTES**: What? Are you messing with me?
**NINO**: Someone showed up to stop your corazon.
*Orestes looks like a little mocoso all of a sudden.*
**ORESTES**: Should I be worried, old man?
**NINO**: Relax, nervous cholo. I took care of it. No one will hurt the next king while the old viejo's around.
**ORESTES**: Was it one of the Locos from the Four Directions?
**NINO**: Don't know. He came knocking to your doorstep. Said he was from the IRS. What a pendejo! Everybody knows cholos don't pay taxes ... I put on my Chiclets face. *(Does his pobre Chiclets card)* And he lowered his guard. He came in and looked around. Said he would wait. I offered him a malt 40, and I held it out for him to grab. When he reached for it, his sleeve raised and I could see he had a tattoo from back home. He looked down and realized his mistake, but it was too late. The bottle was already on the way to his head. I tried to get something out of him. I cut off a couple of fingers, hoping he would talk, but he was a "professional."
You have to admire a man's loyalty. I injected him with bleach, because there's no point in making a man suffer.
**ORESTES**: I know they're gonna get me. I don't think like you. I don't have the "cholo instinct."
**NINO**: Listen, young cholo. Word's coming through the cholo satellite that things are not good back home. In el mundo del cholo the Four Directions are at war. The North Side Locos are moving into the hills. The East Side Locos don't got no way to grow. We're trapped between three freeways and a Polio Loco. La Casa de Atridas is vulnerable.
But never underestimate the great cholo leader of the East Side. He knew to send you away. Your job, little homeboy, is to reemplazar a tu papa, when his time comes to go to the barrio in the sky. You need to be ready when the Council of Old Cholos calls on a new leader. I will be there as your sergeant, a tu lado.
**ORESTES**: Thank you, old viejo. For saving my life.
**NINO**: We have to step up your training.
**ORESTES**: Yes, viejo. But what if they're setting us up?
**NINO**: That's the life. It's surprise destiny, mijo. That is why we will come back in the middle of a midnight. Just in caso.
**ORESTES**: You're not setting me up, are you Nino?
**NINO**: Good cholo. Trust no one. Not even your Nino. *(Looks away)* But you hurt my feelings, son.
**ORESTES**: Oh, Nino, I'm sorry ...
**NINO**: I'm just testing you. Toughen up, puto. Now we will see what you are made of.
**ORESTES**: But, what if I'm not ready?
**NINO**: You have to be.
**ORESTES**: Why?
**NINO**: Because it's been like this since the beginning of cholo time. I didn't make the rules. I just follow them.
*As they turn to leave, the sun comes up over the state line.*

## SCENE 13

### Smoke Gets in Your Eyes

*Afternoon. El sol is out getting a tan, ese. The altar. We see Abuela. She is carrying a plastic bag for the mandado. She approaches the altar slowly. Electricidad sits staring at the sky.*

**ABUELA**: Mija, you want to comer something?

**ELECTRICIDAD**: No, Abuela. Not today.
**ABUELA**: Te estas killing yourself. You're starting to look like una lizard out here.
**ELECTRICIDAD**: Dejame, mujer!
**ABUELA**: Is that what El Auggie would have wanted for you?
**ELECTRICIDAD**: What do you care about mi papa?
**ABUELA**: Ai, he was my son.
**ELECTRICIDAD**: Well then, why didn't I see you shed a lagrima at his funeral?
**ABUELA**: I don't cry no more, it messes with my makeup. Why don't you go inside now, mija?
**ELECTRICIDAD**: How much did they pay you?
**ABUELA**: Que me dices?
**ELECTRIC1DAD**: How much did they pay you, cabrona? To come out here and make me go inside. *(Stares at Abuela,. burning a hole through her)*
**ABUELA**: Ai, forty dollars, okay?
**ELECTRICIDAD**: I knew it.
**ABUELA**: A vieja has to make money somehow. Besides, las vecinas are "concerned." Can you blame them? They clean and clean, and now they got a body in a yarda.
**ELECTRICIDAD**: Que se vayan al Diablo! I hear those old cabronas sweeping and "concerning" about us all day. And you. Drop the act.
**ABUELA**: What act?
**ELECTRICIDAD**: If you want to talk, drop the senora bit.
**ABUELA**: Que me dices, nina?
**ELECTRICIDAD**: Have it your way ...
*Electricidad runs up to Abuela and spits a loogie in her face. Ooh, she may be up there, but Abuela's going to go all Stallone on her granddaughter. She starts chasing her.*
**ABUELA**: Ai, desgraciada! You piece of trash de la calle! I'm not too old to kick some barrio ass, you little peewee.
**ELECTRICIDAD**: Ah, there you go, that's the Abuela that I know.
*Abuela wipes the loogie off her face and Electricidad begins to laugh. Abuela sees her laughing; its been so long. Ai, its not that bad. She's laughing, the pobre loca.*
**ABUELA**: Ai, mija. You remind me so much of me when I was young. I used to go up to people all the time and spit in their face. Especially guys I liked.
*Abuela looks down the street. She hikes up her falda and pulls out a pack of cigarettes tucked into her stockings. Winstons. She pulls a lighter from deep inside her cleavage and lights up.*
**ELECTRICIDAD**: Abuela, you must tell las vecinas to keep their distance. This is my grief and my anger and it might last my lifetime.
**ABUELA**: Lifetime ... Okay. They already paid me, what do I care.
*Clemencia sticks her head out of the window.*
**CLEMENC1A**: You, what are you doing here?
**ABUELA**: Visitando con mi granddaughter.
**CLEMENCIA**: Look at you, showing your varicose. You're polluting my yard, old lady. Visiting hours are over. Go home, vieja.
*Electricidad throws a stone towards the house.*
**CLEMENCIA**: Ai, stop it. Vete, vieja. I feel old just looking at you.
*She goes back inside.*
**ABUELA**: Your father always settled for so little ...
*Electricidad stares at Abuela hard. The silence and the stare make Abuela uncomfortable.*

**ELECTRICIDAD**: Abuela, te tengo que ask you something.

**ABUELA**: Ai, those forty dollars were for my cigaros …

**ELECTRICIDAD**: Not that.

**ABUELA**: Pues?

**ELECTRICIDAD**: Listen, if you tell anyone, and I mean it, vieja, I'll go down to your little casita and break all your Princess Diana plates.

**ABUELA**: Ai, que mean!

*Beat.*

**ELECTRICIDAD**: I'm going to kill her.

**ABUELA**: Ha, take it from a chola who's been there. If you think this is going to help you sleep at night, it doesn't. It makes you a victim of the noche. Little girl, the way of the chola is to keep those thoughts inside.

**ELECTRICIDAD**: But what if I left the way of the chola?

**ABUELA**: If only. You can't. What are you going to do, go off to a convent like your
sister? No, you have the soul of an old cholo. This is your life. Learn to live with it. Look at your papa. Still hanging out on a front yard. A true homeboy!

**ELECTRICIDAD**: But if I killed her …

**ABUELA**: Ooh, if it was so easy, we probably all would be doing it. Even cholos have standards. No one kills the mother.
It has to stop. All these guns, all these drogas, that's not who we are. Murdering our own, and for what?

**ELECTRICIDAD**: Don't you ever think about it, Abuela? About getting out?

**ABUELA**: What for? I'm already dead. See my crosses? *(Pulls down her blouse and on her breast there are three tattoo crosses)* They killed a mi husband and my two children. I am one of the living dead. A chola in limbo.

**ELECTRICIDAD**: Then why do you stay?

**ABUELA**: The same reason we all do, young chola. Where do cholos go in a world that
won't have us? This is the mundo we know. Good or bad. Es lo que es.

**ELECTRICIDAD**: But, if I could stop this pain …

**ABUELA**: Ai, this is getting too pesado. Let's smoke a joint.

*Abuela leans back and pulls a joint out of her cleavage. Electricidad looks on admiringly. Abuela lights the joint, takes a toke and passes it to Electricidad.*

**ELECTRICIDAD**: How long you been a chola, Abuela?

**ABUELA**: Oh, since I was an infant. I used to shoplift from my baby carriage.

*They laugh.*

**ELECTRICIDAD**: Cabrona.

**ABUELA**: I got jumped into my first gang when I was nine.

**ELECTRICIDAD**: Wow.

**ABUELA**: Yeah, I been a chola so long, they should have a beer named after me. But the mundo de la chola was so differente back then.

*Ai, una memoria. Maybe it's funny, maybe it's deep. Definitely means something to remember it.*

**ABUELA**: I used to work in a nightclub. The Del Rio. Not a lot of good dinero, but what an education! We didn't have chola teachers like you have now. We were las originals! The first Cleopatra eyeliner was laid down by me! I used to have a big ole beehive, I did! I used to have to use three cans of Aqua Net to make it stay up there. I kept everything in my hair. Knives, joints, food stamps …
And the hombres … Ai, the men. They traced themselves on your tattoos with their tongues.

**ELECTRICIDAD**: Puta.

**ABUELA**: No pendeja—"liberated." Pero, it's all different now. The mundo of the chola is muerte y sadness. What your mama did, changes todo.
Listen, young chola, if you are going to follow the way of the chola, you must accept la muerte as a fact of our life. I know I did. Otherwise, you become the ghost to all of your memories.
*Una orden.*
**ABUELA**: You've got to walk away from him now.
**ELECTRICIDAD**: Mi papa?
**ABUELA**: Yeah. You've got to walk away from this body. This cuerpo wants you to go with him. Into the lonely after-vida. But you are still alive, young chola,
**ELECTRICIDAD**: If she took his eyes and his tongue, she will need his heart to keep him in silencio forever. I am going to wait here until it all disappears.
**ABUELA**: Mensa, you will wait forever.
**ELECTRICIDAD**: My choice!
**ABUELA**: You will suffer a fate worse than your papa.
**ELECTRICIDAD**: What could be worse?
**ABUELA**: He lies here in eternal sleep. Free from his worries now. Free from all of his responsibilities as rey del barrio. But you? You're a stubborn chola. Nothing satisfies you.
**ELECTRICIDAD**: You don't know shit, old lady.
**ABUELA**: You're an open book, young chola. That's the difference between our generations. You don't know how to make the mask.
**ELECTRICIDAD**: For what?
**ABUELA**: Your feelings. Tu mama sees them. So do the vecinas. You give yourself away, peewee.
**ELECTRICIDAD**: Okay, get lost. I have to talk with my father.
*Abuela stands and puts on her rebozo. She puts out the joint. She flicks the roach onto the altar. Electricidad looks at Abuela con respeto. Abuela begins to walk away.*
**ABUELA**: Later, gator.
**ELECTRICIDAD**: After a while, crocodile.
**ABUELA**: Y, mija—cuidate. It's hard to keep your bALANCe on the edge of a knife.
*She leaves.*

## SCENE 14

### I Only Have Eyes for You

*Afternoon. The house. Clemencia stands at the window. She is dipping cotton balls in nail polish remover and doing her nails. Ifigenia stands next to her, holding a large ceramic of the Virgen under her arm. She places it on top of the T.V. Clemencia looks at it for a moment, then grabs it and puts it on the floor.*

**CLEMENCIA**: She's been sitting out there for a week.
**IFIGENIA**: I know. It's called reflection and patience, Mama. She's finding out about herself.
**CLEMENCIA**: Yeah, what did she find out? Did she tell you she knew something, or is she just doing the crazy whispering-to-her-papa act with you too?
**IFIGENIA**: Try loving her, Mama.
**CLEMENCIA**: Don't start with me, Ifi. I have tried giving her my love. I have none left.
**IFIGENIA**: No, Mama. You have enough love to last a chola lifetime.

**CLEMENCIA**: Good, 'cause that chola out there really sucks it out of you.
*Get a good look, chola.*
**IFIGENIA**: Mama, did you hurt Orestes?
**CLEMENCIA**: No! No. Tu papa sent him away. Things are going down. He did it for his safety, for his own good.
**IFIGENIA**: Where is he?
**CLEMENCIA**: I don't know, Catholic school, I guess ... Have you seen him? ...
*Ifigenia doesn't believe her.*
**IFIGENIA**: I never got a chance to say goodbye.
**CLEMENCIA**: Were you gone again?
**IFIGENIA**: A year, Mama!
**CLEMENCIA**: A year. Really? I thought you were living in the garage. Estabas en la jail, mija?
**IFIGENIA**: An order.
**CLEMENCIA**: An order?
**IFIGENIA**: An order. In Fresno. Like with nuns.
**CLEMENCIA**: You're a born-again chola? Oh, that's a good one.
**IFIGENIA**: I am buscando. Looking for answers.
**CLEMENCIA**: Me too.
**IFIGENIA**: Well then, let me help you, Mama.
**CLEMENCIA**: She blames me for everything. Why do they always blame the mother? Tell me, why do they do that?
**IFIGENIA**: They teach you a lot at the convent, Mama. About turning the other cheek, and things like that.
**CLEMENCIA**: That's not what I asked you.
**IFIGENIA**: And you learn about forgiveness.
**CLEMENCIA**: Yeah, so? What have they taught you that I didn't teach you?
*Beat. Beat.*
**IFIGENIA**: "Unconditional love."
**CLEMENCIA**: What does that mean?
**IFIGENIA**: It means love, like ... beyond the barrio.
**CLEMENCIA**: Look, I'm going to go out there and finally stop this.
**IFIGENIA**: Be nice, Mama. Just go calmada, wanting to do good.
**CLEMENCIA**: Listen, do me a favor.
**IFIGENIA**: What?
**CLEMENCIA**: If she goes off ...
**IFIGENIA**: I'll call the police.
**CLEMENCIA**: Oh no, no, we never call the police. They always take away the mother.
**IFIGENIA**: It says in the Bible ...
**CLEMENCIA**: Just get a stick.
**IFIGENIA**: A stick is not the answer. Love is.
**CLEMENCIA**: If she comes after me, you get her.
**IFIGENIA**: No way man, I won't fight her!
**CLEMENCIA**: Ai, you Christians are such a pain in the ass. Okay, okay. I'm going to go out there all peaceful and stuff. I'm going to show her my "unconditional love." But if that cabrona doesn't take my "unconditional love," I have to do something, right? Jesus did.
**IFIGENIA**: Maybe we should pray?
*Beat. Clemencia looks at* ***Ifigenia*** *intently.*
**CLEMENCIA**: You love me, Ifi, right?

**IFIGENIA**: … Okay.
**CLEMENCIA**: Well, then, if your god says it—you should say it.
*Oh, boy. This is an act of kindness for Ifigenia.*
**IFIGENIA**: … I love you.
**CLEMENCIA**: I love you … Mother.
*Ai, Jesus give me the patience.*
**IFIGENIA**: I love you … Mother.
*Clemencia smiles. It's the little victories.*
**CLEMENCIA**: They all blame me for Electricidad. That I didn't give her guidance. But it wasn't me. It was her papa. He gave her this barrio.
**IFIGENIA**: Refuge.
**CLEMENCIA**: You love me, Ifi, right?
**IFIGENIA**: I just said I did!
**CLEMENCIA**: Say it again, Jesus.
**IFIGENIA**: Damn, I love you, okay?
**CLEMENCIA**: I love you … Mother.
Okay, Jesus, I am going to kick her ass.
**IFIGENIA**: Mother … I love you.
**CLEMENCIA**: Hm … no one ever says that to me.
**IFIGENIA**: I love you. Really. Yeah, okay. I love you.
*Clemencia finally takes real notice of Ifigenia's sincerity. Or struggles with it. She doesn't like what she sees.*
**CLEMENCIA**: Go find me a stick!

## SCENE 15

### Sincerely

*Dusk, that time when day starts to clock out and night is showing up for his shift. Ifigenia exits the house quietly and slowly crosses the yard. She is carrying her statue of la Virgen. She is trying to escape without being noticed. Electricidad notices her and yells across the yarda.*

**ELECTRICIDAD**: Hey, where you going? Heaven?
**IFIGENIA**: Shut up, stupid! I'm running away again. I can't do it. She's testing my patience. It's like being tempted by the devil. The sisters want me back. I know they do.
**ELECTRICIDAD**: You going away far?
**IFIGENIA**: Fresno far.
*Beat.*
**ELECTRICIDAD**: Too bad.
**IFIGENIA**: Wow, you sad I'm going?
*So many feelings. What to do with them.*
**ELECTRICIDAD**: No …
**IFIGENIA**: It's okay, Electricidad. You can tell me. Please. It's just me. Tu hermana.
*Electricidad starts to cry. But why? **Ifigenia** holds out her hand. Close enough to offer but not be bitten. Electricidad doesn't know whether she can touch it or not.*

**IFIGENIA**: Don't bite it, bitch.

*Electricidad reaches out and grabs her hand. She brings it to her cheek. Has it been so long since she has held the living? She surprises* ***Ifigenia****, and herself by kissing it. The action is so honest and real, that they become awkward, all of a sudden. They both pull away.*

**ELECTRICIDAD**: Have you really found a god?

**IFIGENIA**: I don't know … I'm doing a lot of waiting for him.

**ELECTRICIDAD**: Me too.

**IFIGENIA**: I sit in this thing they call a grotto. It's just kind of like a clean backyard. And you think about him and ask him if he'll come.

**ELECTRICIDAD**: Yeah?

**IFIGENIA**: Yeah, And if he can't come, can he fill you with stuff. Goodness and shit. Sounds stupid, huh? It kinda works.

**ELECTRICIDAD**: Really?

**IFIGENIA**: The sisters leave me out there by myself all day. They buy me cigarettes. They're afraid of me.. .They make good cake.

*Beat.*

**IFIGENIA**: Does he ever talk back?

*Silence.*

**IFIGENIA**: That's what it's like at the convent.

**ELECTRICIDAD**: Do you remember how I was?

**IFIGENIA**: What do you mean? Like a little girl or something?

**ELECTRICIDAD**: No, the way I used to be, before she gave me the darkness.

**IFIGENIA**: She didn't give you the darkness, Electricidad. You found that on your own. You have a chansa, my sister. To make a choice. I did, and I left.

*Beat.*

**ELECTRICIDAD**: I have a confession.

**IFIGENIA**: I'm not a priest.

**ELECTRICIDAD**: That's okay. I'm going to kill her.

**IFIGENIA**: Okay. I can't stop you.

**ELECTRICIDAD**: That's not very god-like, letting us all kill each other.

**IFIGENIA**: I think god will forgive me if I marry him.

You know what? I want to live with the silent nuns. The silent nuns who don't talk anywhere as much as you and Mama. The silent nuns who give me cigarettes and leave me alone. The silent nuns who don't hear all the noise in this barrio.

**ELECTRICIDAD**: Do you really believe it?

**IFIGENIA**: I want to. So bad.

**ELECTRICIDAD**: Maybe … you should stay?

**IFIGENIA**: You don't want me to stay. You just don't want to be alone. Big difference.

*Electricidad looks away.*

**IFIGENIA**: Don't hurt her. You'll be hurting yourself.

*Ifigenia picks up her statue. A shout from Clemencia can be heard from inside the house.*

**CLEMENCIA**: IFI? …

**IFIGENIA**: I have to go. Now. *(Stands to leave)*

**ELECTRICIDAD**: We could have been friends.

*Ifigenia stops and wonders if maybe this could be her calling.*

**IFIGENIA**: We can be sisters!

**CLEMENCIA**: IFI?

So *many choices. Trying to imagine them all so quickly. Make one, make one, make one ...*

**ELECTRICIDAD**: Vete. Go, cabrona!

*They look at each other. They give the chola nod to one another. Ifigenia begins to run as if she is running for her life.*

**CLEMENCIA**: Ifi? ...

*A transformer begins to sizzle.*

## SCENE 16

### This I Swear

*The sun is tipping his hat in a final adios. Las Vecinas enter la yarda. They sweep at twice the pace. They gossip quickly and nervously.*

**LA CARMEN**: Vecinas, I got a feeling in my bones.
**LA CONNIE**: Me too, my knees started hurting.
**LA CUCA**: Oh good, I thought it was my artritis.
**LA CARMEN**: The sun is shutting its eyes.
**LA CONNIE**: He's closing early.
**LA CUCA**: Up there he can see what is going down.
**LA CARMEN**: Something is not right.
**LA CONNIE**: The chisme is traveling fast.
**LA CUCA**: The tiendas roll down their metal doors.
**LA CARMEN**: The bus took a detour.
**LA CONNIE**: The perros are beginning to howl.
**LA CUCA**: And they ran out of tamales at la marqueta!
**LA CARMEN**: The aire is thick.
**LA CONNIE**: The noche belongs to them.
**LA CUCA**: Tonight they are going to use it.
**LA CARMEN**: Lock your doors.
**LA CONNIE**: Close your ventanas.
**LA CUCA**: Pray a rosary.
**LA CARMEN**: Light a candle.
**LA CONNIE**: Ask the Virgen.
**LA CUCA**: Burn the incense.
**LA CARMEN**: Offer up an orange.
**LA CONNIE**: Sleep on the floor.
**LA CUCA**: Don't get near the window.
**LA CARMEN**: Trapped in our casas.
**LA CONNIE**: Trapped in our yardas.
**LA CUCA**: Trapped in our barrios.
**LA CARMEN**: Say goodbye to the noche.
**LA CONNIE**: La luna no more.
**LA CUCA**: Que destiny guide her.

**LA CARMEN**: Oh, I know this feeling.
**LA CONNIE**: I know it too, vecina.
**LA CUCA**: Oh, this feeling …
*Las Vecinas march off. We hear the sound of four doors slamming and four locks locking.*

## SCENE 17

### In the Still of the Night

*A Vegas night, otra vez. The sound of the needle buzzing. It grows dimmer and more realistic as the lights reveal Orestes and Nino. They are, once again, shirtless and glistening with sweat. Orestes sits, facing front, looking out at nothing with the stone cold cholo stare. Nino pricks his chest with the tattoo gun. We see the trickle of blood running down Orestes' chest, but this time we don't see Orestes react to the pain. Suddenly the sound of the gun stops. Nino wipes and pulls away to reveal the face of Electricidad on Orestes' breast.*

**NINO**: Listo.
*Orestes looks down at his chest intently. He looks up at Nino and smiles.*
**ORESTES**: It's good, old cholo.
**NINO**: Better than the Sears family portraits!
**ORESTES**: Which one should we do next?
**NINO**: The next tattoo you will have to earn.
**ORESTES**: But I have. With my loneliness.
**NINO**: That lonely tattoo you already got.
Right there.
*Nino points to clean skin on Orestes.*
**ORESTES**: It's clean. There's nothing there, Stevie Wonder.
**NINO**: Those spaces get filled in with experience.
**ORESTES**: Yeah right.
**NINO**: Look at this. *(Pulls up his shirt to reveal a canvas of tatoos over his stomach and chest)* Everybody thinks that when you go to the big house, we just sit around tattooing to kill time. It's just the opposite. We work as fast as we can to show everyone our history.
**ORESTES**: Give me my history, viejo cabron.
**NINO**: I have, little one. You have worked every muscle. You have sharpened every shank. You even know a little Bruce Lee. But do you know why you throw the punch, young cholo?
**ORESTES**: For the kingdom.
**NINO**: That's right. For the kingdom, ese.
**ORESTES**: It's time to go back, my loyal atendido.
**NINO**: Yes, mi rey. When the sun starts to wave goodbye over the pyramid, we will get on El Greyhound. We'll arrive in the darkness of midnight. To be safe, we will split up. I'll check out "last call" and you can say hello to your familia.
**ORESTES**: Finally I get to see mi papa. And my beloved sister. To our lives, Nino!
**NINO**: Or to our deaths, baboso. Barrios never stay the same. You're gone a week, and they take down the mural. Are you listo? *(Throws a surprise punch at Orestes, who stops it in midair)* Good cholo.
Good …
*Nino hugs Orestes.*

## SCENE 18

### Baby, I'm for Real

*Darkness sets in as cena is being served and the Hollenbeck police eat their burritos. Electricidad sleeps next to papa. Clemencia enters, tiptoeing quietly into the yarda. She carries a bottle of her nail polish remover and a lighter! She opens the bottle and begins to pour it all over El Auggie. She stands and looks at him. Electricidad smells the alcohol and wakes up.*

**ELECTRICIDAD**: What are you doing here, loca! Que estas haciendo, cabrona! What are you doing?
*Clemencia clicks the lighter and turns on a flame.*
**ELECTRICIDAD**: No! Stop. Please.
*Clemencia holds the lighter like a gun. Electricidad is paralyzed with fear.*
**ELECTRICIDAD**: I beg of you. Por favor. Please.
**CLEMENCIA**: He isn't worth it, mi hija.
**ELECTRICIDAD**: If you have a heart ...
**CLEMENCIA**: I have a heart. I have a heart! That's why I took these hands to him. For years he took his hands to me, why couldn't I? It's only right, isn't it? The old cholo rules.I took his last breath, in hopes that he would breathe new life into us. You and me. Our future. So that we could finally make something of ourselves. I did it for you, Electricidad. But your problem is that you feel too much. For him. So did I. *(She begins to weep)* So did I ...
**ELECTRICIDAD**: Then stop, please ... **CLEMENCIA**: It's too late for that. Do you remember when he was king? He had all of this. Todo. But he couldn't share. Have you ever seen your suenos go up in flames? I have. He was my dream.
**ELECTRICIDAD**: Don't. Please don't.
**CLEMENCIA**: I gave you a chance, cabrona. And you turned it away.
*She leans in to light the body.*
**ELECTRICIDAD**: You are going to pay for this. For eternity.
**CLEMENCIA**: I already am. *(Kneels to light the altar)* Electricidad. Your very name means light. I gave it to you. And now, mi hija. I am going to turn you off.
*She lights the fire. Electricidad begins to scream. A scream of rage and grief through el barrio. The electricity crackles as it meshes with the crackling of the fire. Clemencia is destroyed. She stands looking at the flame. She tries to light a cigarette, but her hands shake uncontrollably. Electricidad lays in a corner in the fetal position, weeping. The crackling of the fire can be heard loud, louder, loudest.*

## SCENE 19

### War What Is It Good For

*The noche washes over the barrio like a good detergent. Las Vecinas enter la yarda.*

**LA CARMEN**: Vecinas, did you see it?
**LA CONNIE**: I saw it.
**LA CUCA**: I even turned off la novela.
**LA CARMEN**: Oh, they have done things.
**LA CONNIE**: Cosas to one another.

**LA CUCA**: That offend all the gods.
**LA CARMEN**: She lit up the noche.
**LA CONNIE**: With his body.
**LA CUCA**: Like burning trash in the back-yarda.
**LA CARMEN**: Set him on fire.
**LA CONNIE**: Like in India!
**LA CUCA**: We don't do that here.
**LA CARMEN**: His body …
**LA CONNIE**: Slowly roasting …
**LA CUCA**: Like a Polio Loco.
**LA CARMEN**: Oh, they don't realize.
**LA CONNIE**: What they have done.
**LA CUCA**: Called on the dark spirits.
**LA CARMEN**: The flames.
**LA CONNIE**: So high.
**LA CUCA**: Like the riots.
**LA CARMEN**: But it's one family …
**LA CONNIE**: That destroys …
**LA CUCA**: This barrio.
**LA CARMEN**: The smoke.
**LA CONNIE**: So thick and black.
**LA CUCA**: You could see the devil inhaling.
**LA CARMEN**: And her screams.
**LA CONNIE**: Screams of injusticia.
**LA CUCA**: So mournful.
**LA CARMEN**: So heavy.
**LA CONNIE**: So sad.
**LA CUCA**: So lonely.
**LA CARMEN**: I could weep.
**LA CONNIE**: I could grieve.
**LA CUCA**: I could pray.
*They nod their heads for the lack of palabras. Las Vecinas march off. We hear the squeak of four doors closing on a world.*

## SCENE 20

### Woman to Woman

*Oh, it's dark.* The Eyewitness News *is over and midnight is peeking his head around the comer. Abuela enters la yarda. She got the 411 on the chisme line. She sees Electricidad laying over the ash remains of the altar. She is dark and dirty.*

**ABUELA**: Ai, dios! Mija? Mija? Que paso? *(Looks at the house and realizes what has happened)* Oh my dios. Esa cabrona did it. All the devils in hell are cantando her praises.
*Abuela turns to face la casa. Clemencia paces in the house. She is nervous and frantic. This is worse than when she took out Auggie. Abuela comes to the front of the house and screams for Clemencia.*

**ABUELA**: DONDE ESTAS, DAUGHTER OF EL DIABLO?

*Clemencia comes out front.*

**CLEMENCIA**: Don't even think about coming in old lady. There's nothing here for you to pickpocket.

**ABUELA**: What have you done?

**CLEMENCIA**: Cleaned up your messes. I took care of the hombre you couldn't control. You should thank me. THANK ME!

**ABUELA**: Never.

**CLEMENCIA**: This is for you tambien.

For the generations of undisciplined men that have wasted our lives. For the years that I had to sit there and watch him bully you y everyone else. For the drinks I poured. For the dinners I made. For the parties I threw. For the money he wasted. For the love without love that I had to make. For the ninos that I had to raise. For the sacrifices we make …

**ABUELA**: Not like this.

**CLEMENCIA**: You too, vieja. Show me the sacrifices on your heart. I know you made them.

**ABUELA**: Not for this.

**CLEMENCIA**: Don't act like Mother Teresa, you bitch. I cleaned up a mess. Your mess. The mess you made. The mess your mother made.

**ABUELA**: Sin consciencia.

**CLEMENCIA**: Oh, I have a conscience. If not I would have taken care of you too. For letting him become the monster that he was.

**ABUELA**: Now you think you are a god.

**CLEMENCIA**: Listen to me, cabrona. I am going to do something that none of you ever did. I am going to change this neighborhood. I am going to bring the Four Directions together and we are going to make it right. I am going to run La Casa de Atridas. Oh yes, I am. And I am going to make it better than he ever did. And you know why? Because I am the mother!

*Abuela runs away from the house.*

**CLEMENCIA**: THE MOTHER!!

*Clemencia tries to light a cigarette, but it just ain't going to happen. She buries her face in her hands.*

## SCENE 21

### You'll Lose a Good Thing

*Abuela goes into la yarda and tries to help Electricidad up.*

**ABUELA**: We have to go. Vamonos, hija.

*(But Electricidad does not get up)*

Vamonos before she comes back and sets you on fire.

*(Electricidad violently resists)*

Vamonos, chola. Por favor. Let's go. Make a choice. Towards the living. Your grief is going to kill you. Find a way!

*(Electricidad pushes Abuela away)*

I am going to help you. Enough ya! Let us leave the house of Atridas.

**ELECTRICIDAD**: Only her death will set me free.

**ABUELA**: Babosa.

*Abuela tries to grab Electricidad to drag her. Electricidad turns and gives Abuela a big fat Rocky Balboa across the jaw. Abuela instinctually reaches over and grabs Electricidad by the hair and slaps her hard across the face in an old school chola kind of way. Electricidad can't believe it. Who knew the old vieja was Yoda tambien.*

**ABUELA**: ENOUGH!! You're a baby chola. No honor. No respect. You say you're old school, but you haven't earned our ways. You don't know what it means to be chola.

*Electricidad is stunned. She looks at Abuela for the longest time unable to speak. Abuela begins to walk away. Finally, in her desperation, Electricidad breaks down.*

**ELECTRICIDAD**: Abuela. Don't go. Ayudame. I can't. I can't anymore.

*Abuela goes to Electricidad.*

**ELECTRICIDAD**: Help me.

**ABUELA**: Si, young chola. Si. Gracias. The old veterana will help you.

*Abuela runs to la esquina. She screams to the end of the block:*

**ABUELA**: Vecinas! Vecinas! I know it's late. But esta coming out of the darkness! Ayudenme.

*Abuela looks up, as if to see the electricity raging through the power lines.*

## SCENE 22

### What You Won't Do for Love

*Ai, its midnight, why's everybody up? The Vecinas run into the yarda all ready for a little accion, Abuela joins them.*

**ABUELA**: Okay, mujeres. We don't have a lot of tiempo. We're going to do a limpia, but more car wash style. She wants to walk away. Right, mija? You are going to walk away, right?

**ELECTRICIDAD**: Si, Abuela.

**ABUELA**: Go for it, vecinas.

*The Vecinas grab her like a stray dog. They wash her with Handi Wipes and un spray que tiene algo that smells like clean toilets at King Taco. As they clean her they are barking orders at one another until Electricidad speaks to them and they stop what they are doing.*

**ELECTRICIDAD**: Why do you do this for me?

**LA CARMEN**: To ayudar.

**LA CONNIE**: To remember.

**LA CUCA**: To preserve.

**LA CARMEN**: A custom.

**LA CONNIE**: Our way.

**LA CUCA**: Our gente.

*The Vecinas go at her, pulling her hair back with a rubber band, cleaning her face and hands, etc. All of this is done very quickly, as if they could feel Clemencia's breath over their backs. When they finish, they stand back to reveal Electricidad. She looks strangely angelic.*

**LA CARMEN**: Mijita.

**LA CONNIE**: It's time.

**LA CUCA**: To let him journey.

*They all look at the altar.*

**LA CARMEN**: Say goodbye.

**LA CONNIE**: Say goodbye.

**LA CUCA**: Say goodbye.
*Beat, beat, beat, like a corazon. Electricidad looks at the altar.*
**ELECTRICIDAD**: Goodbye …
*Beat.*
**LA CARMEN**: Wow, it worked!
**LA CONNIE**: Que bueno.
**LA CUCA**: Vamanos, vecinas. I'm tired.
*Las Vecinas leave. Abuela goes to Electricidad.*
**ABUELA**: Ai, what a noche. I'm too old for all of this. What do you want to do? Do you want me to sneak you into the senior projects?
**ELECTRICIDAD**: No, Abuela. I'm going to stay under the freeway tonight. You go. I want to pick up his ashes.
**ABUELA**: Well, give a chifle in the morning, and I'll make you a waffle.
**ELECTRICIDAD**: Gracias, Abuela.
**ABUELA**: Welcome back to the living, young chola. Ai, these Payless chanclas are killing me …
*Abuela leaves. Electricidad looks up at Coyolxauqui, the moon face.*

## SCENE 23

### Reunited and It Feels So Good

*The second hour of morning. Orestes can be seen in the distance. He does a chifle down the block that belongs only to his Trici. She freezes when she hears it.*

**ORESTES**: Electricidad, my sister. You look like a statue. The most beautiful statue in Caesar's. *(Whistles again while he runs into the yard)* Electricidad, mi hermana!
*Electricidad screams in horror. She runs to a corner and crouches in fear.*
**ORESTES**: Trici, que paso? My sweet sister, it's me.
**ELECTRICIDAD**: Go away!
**ORESTES**: What's up, esa? My little lightbulb, I'm back. I have returned in the middle of a midnight like all smart cholos do.
**ELECTRICIDAD**: Go away, young ghost.
**ORESTES**: A ghost? No, I am an hombre now. You don't recognize me porque I have changed.
**ELECTRICIDAD**: Please don't haunt me.
**ORESTES**: Que esta pasando? I have dreamt of this moment for months. If you don't welcome me I will die more than a spiritual death. You're freaking me out, man.
**ELECTRICIDAD**: Just tell me if you are a ghost.
**ORESTES**: Only of the past. Here I am, flesh and blood, mi hermana.
**ELECTRICIDAD**: Orestes …
*She goes to him and touches his face. If he's not Casper, could it really be him? She holds him.*
**ELECTRICIDAD**: You look like … a man.
**ORESTES**: Yes, my sister. I been doing my pull-ups and stuff. I know my creases and my cuffs. I know the hand signals and territories. I even know how to read the map of our tattoos. Oh man, Trici, I did so many pull-ups, I sleep like this. *(Puts his hands over his chest, pull-up style)* Nino even taught me "the look." *(Gives her a stone-cold scary cholo look)* Cool, huh?
*She smiles. He giggles, out of embarrassment.*

**ELECTRICIDAD**: Where were you?
**ORESTES**: In the desert. Wandering in exile. Sent away by mi papa, for the good of our barrio.
**ELECTRICIDAD**: She didn't kill you?
**ORESTES**: Who?
**ELECTRICIDAD**: Clemencia.
**ORESTES**: What are you talking about?
**ELECTRICIDAD**: They said she had killed you. She put a hit out on you.
**ORESTES**: A hit? It was mi mama? Oh my god. I can't believe it.
**ELECTRICIDAD**: So much has changed, Orestes. Since you've been gone, darkness has set on this side of the river.
**ORESTES**: But I'm her favorite.
**ELECTRICIDAD**: Oh, Orestes … There's so much you don't know.
**ORESTES**: Tell me before my heart explodes.
**ELECTRICIDAD**: She killed Papa.
*Esto is too much para el joven.*
**ORESTES**: Mi papa's dead?
**ELECTRICIDAD**: Clemencia killed him.
**ORESTES**: She couldn't have. She knows the rules.
**ELECTRICIDAD**: There are no more rules, Orestes. In the time you left, el mundo of the cholo has changed.
**ORESTES**: My papa …
*Orestes starts to cry. He holds Electricidad. Suddenly they seem way smaller and younger than they are.*
**ELECTRICIDAD**: She says he was ruining us. But it's una mentira. And just to prove her disrespect for el mundo of the cholo, she set him on fire, so that he could not visit us in the after-vida.
**ORESTES**: Electricidad, I'm scared. Who is going to protect us?
**ELECTRICIDAD**: You are, young cholo.
**ORESTES**: Me? I came back to stand at my father's side. To be his right-hand mano. I can't lead. The East Side Locos will eat me up.
**ELECTRICIDAD**: Orestes, you don't understand. I was going to walk away, homeboy. I was going to forgive her. How could I have doubted myself? Doubted you, the nuevo king?
**ORESTES**: But I'm not. Not yet.
**ELECTRICIDAD**: Time moves differently for us now, my brother.
Orestes, for the good of el barrio, for the East Side Locos, your family—you must say adios to the little homie inside of you. This is a special night. Like when you first got jumped in.
**ORESTES**: What do you mean?
**ELECTRICIDAD**: Before you hear the first drop of el newspaper, before you can smell the pan dulce rising, before el sol says buenos dias—you will become a man.
**ORESTES**: I don't understand. What's going on around here?
**ELECTRICIDAD**: Tonight you will bring the barrio back together again. Do you know how?

## SCENE 24

### Oh, What a Night

*At the same momento, in another part of the barrio. Nino stands on un lado de la calle and sees Abuela walking home.*

**NINO**: Oye, viejita, I haven't seen a pair of legs that juicy since they stopped serving carnitas at El Tepeyac.
**ABUELA**: Ai, low class viejo, cabron. Mind your manners, puto.
**NINO**: Con una boca like that, you definitely have to be an East Side Loca.
**ABUELA**: Who is there that knows my past?
**NINO**: The man they used to call La Lengua …
**ABUELA**: Nino! What are you doing here, sexy old viejo?
NINO: Just back from ex-file.
**ABUELA**: What is that?
**NINO**: Como una vacation. But forced.
**ABUELA**: So, you were doing time?
**NINO**: Yeah, doing time, so to speak.
**ABUELA**: Cuanto tiempo you've been gone
old man?
**NINO**: Six months.
**ABUELA**: Hijole, a lot has happened in the barrio.
**NINO**: Did they take away the mural!
**ABUELA**: No, worse. A lot worse. Ai, viejo, if you get through your twenties, you think you can live in the life por vida, but I never thought I would be one of the viejas asking: what happened to the good old days? What happened to rock around the clock?
**NINO**: Y el Pachuco Hop.
**ABUELA**: Beehives.
**NINO**: Lowriders.
**ABUELA**: Wine coolers.
**NINO**: Mota.
**ABUELA**: Oh, the good old days. Nothing's good anymore. This is not why we became cholos. They're all killing each other now. They don't live by the rules of the mundo,
now.
**NINO**: Man, when I hear this, it gives me pena to have these tattoos.
**ABUELA**: They had a barbecue tonight.
**NINO**: Sounds good.
**ABUELA**: You can't imagine what she cooked … Listen, viejo, there is a lot to hablar about. But right now I just want to forget.
**NINO**: Yeah, me too. I'm old, I just want to hang out with a cervecita and listen to some oldies.
**ABUELA**: Why don't you come over? I just got into senior housing. We could put on an 8-track and catch up …
**NINO**: Show me the way, sexy senior …

## SCENE 25

### Angel Baby

*Back in la yarda.*

**ELECTRICIDAD**: This is bigger than you and me. This whole barrio is calling on you. She killed him with her bare hands, Orestes. And that is how she must die. An eye for an eye. And you must do it.

**ORESTES**: But, she's my mama. And besides ... I've never killed anyone. I haven't even kicked anyone's ass.
**ELECTRICIDAD**: She isn't your mother anymore. She is the murderer of your father.
**ORESTES**: Why don't we start with the house and just take it away from her? Kick her ass and throw her out into la calle.
**ELECTRICIDAD**: What are you talking about? Things have changed, Orestes. It's what Papa would have wanted.
**ORESTES**: He wouldn't have wanted this.
**ELECTRICIDAD**: You have to do it. It's your job.
**ORESTES**: But what if I don't want it?
**ELECTRICIDAD**: What are you talking about! You are the next king. We can't be doing everything for you.
**ORESTES**: But, but ... you, you're the one that's all eager to get rid of her ...
**ELECTRICIDAD**: I can't, Orestes. Don't you understand? I want nothing more than to take these hands to her neck. But it isn't our way ... I give her to you. With a smile ...
**ORESTES**: But, I ... can't.
**ELECTRICIDAD**: Where is your loyalty? Everyone is circling La Casa de Atridas. They all want a chance to take the throne. To take our way of life. Your return is a sign, my brother. That all will be made right in el barrio once again.
**ORESTES**: But I thought. I thought maybe, maybe, we could go. I could show you the city of your name.
**ELECTRICIDAD**: We can't leave here! This is your territory. This is where you will rule.
**ORESTES**: Maybe we don't need this? Maybe we could make other rules.
**ELECTRICIDAD**: Like she did?
**ORESTES**: We can run out of here. If we really wanted, we could. Just you and I, mi hermana.
**ELECTRICIDAD**: Orestes, you are breaking my corazon. What will it take to reclaim your father's legacy?
**ORESTES**: His legacy. Not ours.
**ELECTRICIDAD**: Stop playing around! It is your duty. All the East Side Locos will respect and accept you. When they see that you have returned and that you have made things right again.
**ORESTES**: Who cares about this barrio!
**ELECTRICIDAD**: This neighborhood has been waiting. They expect it. You will gain your honor. This is your kingdom, Orestes. Take it!
**ORESTES**: I can't ...
*She slaps him hard on the face.*
**ELECTRICIDAD**: Don't disgrace your father! Show them that you can be the leader. Kings don't get crowns. They take them!
*Orestes starts to cry. She holds him while she speaks.*
**ELECTRICIDAD**: Sssh.. .Calmado, young home-boy. Orestes, remember when Papa showed us the animal instinct?
**ORESTES**: Please ... Don't ...
**ELECTRICIDAD**: When he brought that vato home from the North Side Locos and he told us that we were going to kill him. That he was going to give us the animal instinct. Remember he had him all tied up and he threw him on the floor in front of us?
**ORESTES**: We were watching cartoons.
**ELECTRICIDAD**: Oh yeah ... I remember. And Papa made us kick him and kick him and kick him until he cried.
**ORESTES**: I wanted to cry.
**ELECTRICIDAD**: But you didn't, young warrior. You didn't.
**ORESTES**: I looked at you, instead of him.

**ELECTRICIDAD**: Right, you looked at me ... Papa gave us a dollar and told us to go out and play. No big deal, right? Look at me. Look at me now. Find your courage. Find your rage. Find your darkness.
**ORESTES**: I am so scared.
**ELECTRICIDAD**: You have been born again, Orestes. You were dead once and now you have come back. Not even your father, the king, got this chance.
**ORESTES**: But I'm just ... a homeboy.
**ELECTRICIDAD**: No, you're not. You're a cholo. Call on the god of human sacrifices, Coatlicue, and moon face, her daughter, to give you enough light in la casa. Do it. And be the king. It's okay. Look at me.
*They both turn and look toward la casa. He slowly sneaks into the house.*

## SCENE 26

### Natural High

*Its three A.M. The barmaids are slipping their tips under pillows while the panaderos are getting up to roll their pan dulces. Electricidad turns around and looks up at moonface. She starts laughing.*

**ELECTRICIDAD**: I call on the darkness insidethe Four Directions.
Find the courage.
Find the rage.
Find the darkness.
Find the courage.
Find the rage.
Find the darkness.
Finally, a chance for la familia, to be together again.
Without her.
Find the courage.
Find the rage.
Find the darkness.
Let the gates of hell open.
Now!
*A helicopter roars by on a freeway chase.*

## SCENE 27

### Dedicated to the One I Love

*The rooster stands by the time clock, restless to announce la manana. Orestes can be seen as a shadow in the house. Electricidad is in la yarda. Clemencia can be seen in the house, illuminated by the television and smoking a cigarette. She laughs with the tele. Orestes enters her room. Clemencia is surprised.*

**CLEMENCIA**: Orestes?

*(Clemencia stands and paces. She doesn't know what to say or how to act. She waits to see what Orestes will do. They stand awkwardly facing one another. As if in a standoff. Finally Orestes moves towards his mother. She stiffens. He grabs Clemencia and hugs her)*

Orestes, mi hijo! You surprised me, homeboy. You've come back ... Where were you?

*(He holds onto her)*

You are still mi hijo, right? Mi hijo? My little baby, my little boy?

*(He nods. Oh, maybe he can't do this)*

You love me, Orestes? Say, "I love you, Mother."

*(He doesn't respond)*

Okay, it's okay. My most sensitive one. My razon para vivir.

*(While in her arms, he starts to cry. She relaxes a bit. Maybe the cabron can't do it)*

Ai, mijo. You missed tu mama. Pero how good that you came home. Now, we can be a family ... I was never good at making one. I didn't know how. Pero, now you and I, y Electricidad, if she wants. We can be a family.

*(He pulls back and looks at her. He has a glazed looked on his face. It scares her. She must not let him know)*

You know it wasn't me, right? Tu sabes que tu papa. He was a bully. Made him do crazy things. He wanted to beat the cholo into you. I couldn't let him do that, my sensitive one. Tu sabes, don't you? I know you do.

*He moves toward her and goes for her neck awkwardly. Electricidad starts to whisper her incantation from the yard:*

**ELECTRICIDAD**: Find the courage.

Find the rage.

Find the darkness.

**CLEMENCIA**: No! Mi hijo! No ... *(Pushes him away violently)* Stop it. You don't know what you're doing.

*(He loses his grip as she pulls away. He starts crying. Electricidad's incantation grows louder and more forceful with the scene)*

It was me, Orestes. It was me that tried to save you. From this vida. This vida that surely would have killed you. I saved you. I did it.

This is not your life.

*(He moves toward her)*

Que te dijo? She lies. She lies, Orestes. Esta loca. She's gone mad.

*(He grabs her and won 't let go)*

Don't try it, cabron. Don't!

*(She pulls away and grabs a switchblade from under a cushion on the couch. He grabs it away from her and reaches for her neck)*

No sabes. You don't know what I did for you. I saved you ...

*(He is crying. He holds her down, but he cannot do it)*

Por favor, no. You don't know. How hard it is. I'm just like you. Nobody showed me shit. Nobody gave me ... nothing ... All I wanted was to make it better. To get us out of here. Forgive me. I gave you. Mijo. I gave you my ... Unconditional ...

**ELECTRICIDAD** *(Screams from the yard)*: Orestes! DO IT!

*And with that, he cuts his mother's throat.*

## SCENE 28

### Feelings

*The East Los rooster crows. Daybreak is peeking its head around the corner. There is a quiet and a calm. Electricidad lays on her fathers ashes. Abuela and Nino run into the yarda.*

**ABUELA**: Mija, why didn't you leave? Donde esta Orestes? Have you seen Orestes?
*Electricidad looks at Abuela and smiles.*
**ABUELA**: Something has happened! What have you done? Dime, what have you done?
*(To Nino)* A la casa, viejo. Por favor. Hurry!
*Nino runs into the house; he sees what has happened and screams for the boy:*
**NINO**: Orestes!
*Abuela puts her hands to her mouth, stifling her cry. She weeps as she looks at Electricidad. Nino screams from inside the house:*
**NINO**: Mi Orestes! Alguien! Ayudenme!
**ELECTRICIDAD**: Orestes?
*Abuela goes into the house, sees the tragedia and runs out screaming:*
**ABUELA**: Eres un demonio! Is this what you wanted?
**ELECTRICSDAD**: Orestes?
*Nino runs for help and Abuela runs after him. Orestes walks out of the house. He is covered in blood. He is laughing. He has gone mad. So many dreams gone. Electricidad is terrified. She is afraid to get near him. He goes to her.*
**ELECTRICIDAD**: Orestes?
*Orestes falls to his knees over Papas ashes. Electricidad kneels to him cradles him in her arms.*
**ELECTRICIDAD**: Orestes? Orestes, please …
*Electricidad and Orestes hold each other en la yarda, while the morning comes into the neighborhood.*

## SCENE 29

### Together

*A nuevo dia. The sound of work begins. The sweep, sweep, sweep of brooms. Electricidad and Orestes kneel at the altar.*

**LA CARMEN**: Apoco.
**LA CONNIE**: No me digas.
**LA CUCA**: Ai …
*Beat.*
**LA CARMEN**: Did you see?
**LA CONNIE**: Oh yes.
**LA CUCA**: Victory.
**LA CARMEN**: Electricidad got what she wanted.
**LA CONNIE**: The gods answered her prayers.
**LA CUCA**: All is good?

**LA CARMEN**: Peace at last.
**LA CONNIE**: Now we can go back to our lives.
**LA CUCA**: To the way we live.
**LA CARMEN**: The family.
**LA CONNIE**: Together again.
**LA CUCA**: Que bueno.
**LA CARMEN**: Let's close the doors.
**LA CONNIE**: On this mito.
**LA CUCA**: En La Casa de Atridas.
*Beat.*
**LA CARMEN**: What is to be done, vecinas?
**LA CONNIE**: What can be done?
**LA CUCA**: We never learn.
*Beat.*
**LA CARMEN**: Apoco.
**LA CONNIE**: No me digas.
**LA CUCA**: Ai ...
*Beat.*

## END OF OBRA